Minerva Series

MINERVA SERIES OF STUDENTS' HANDBOOKS

No. 23

General Editor

BRIAN CHAPMAN
Professor of Government
University of Manchester

CONSTITUTIONAL
BUREAUCRACY

By the same author

GOVERNMENT AND THE RAILWAYS
IN NINETEENTH-CENTURY BRITAIN
(Routledge)

CONSTITUTIONAL BUREAUCRACY

THE DEVELOPMENT OF
BRITISH CENTRAL ADMINISTRATION
SINCE THE EIGHTEENTH CENTURY

by *Walter*

HENRY PARRIS

University of Durham

REPRINTS OF ECONOMIC CLASSICS

AUGUSTUS M. KELLEY · PUBLISHERS
NEW YORK 1969

Published in the U. S. A. by

AUGUSTUS M. KELLEY, PUBLISHERS

New York, New York

PRINTED IN GREAT BRITAIN
in 10 *on* 11 *pt Times Roman*
BY WESTERN PRINTING SERVICES LTD
BRISTOL

To my father and mother

'Amongst the writers on government whose works my limited opportunities of study have enabled me to examine, I have not met with any who have treated systematically of *administrative* government as it ought to be exercised in a free state. Authors in abundance, from Aristotle to Hobbes, have written out theories of civil society;... And whilst the structure of communities and the nature of political powers and institutions were thus extensively investigated, the art of *exercising* political functions, which might seem to be no unimportant part of political science, has occupied hardly any place in the speculations of its professors.'

Sir Henry Taylor, 1836

CONTENTS

11

CONTENTS

ACKNOWLEDGEMENTS

I have to acknowledge my gratitude to the custodians of the un-published documents used in this book, namely:

H.M. the Queen (Melbourne Papers)
The University of Durham (Grey Papers)
The Trustees of the British Museum (Peel, Aberdeen and Glad-stone Papers)
Public Record Office (departmental records and Russell Papers)
The National Trust (Disraeli Papers)
The National Register of Archives (Palmerston Papers).

Most of the research on which this book is based was done while I held a Hallsworth Fellowship in the University of Manchester, and I am most grateful to the trustees of that fund for giving me the opportunity.

Parts of the text have already appeared, in slightly different form, in the *Historical Journal*, *Public Law*, and *Public Administration*. I wish to thank the editors of those periodicals for permission to re-publish.

A great many friends and colleagues have helped by discussing various sections of the book with me, and by reading critically successive drafts. I hope they will accept this collective word of thanks and forgive me for mentioning only one name, that of Professor W. J. M. Mackenzie. I started work on the project in his department during the period 1958–61. He has maintained a close interest in the book throughout its long gestation. When I began, he told me it would take 10 years. Although I have never disbelieved him on any other occasion, I am glad I did so then. He was absolutely right, but, had I known that, I should never have had the heart to go on.

January 24, 1969   H.P.

INTRODUCTION

'The attitude of the British citizen to the government official is a curious paradox. On the one hand, he takes it as a law of nature that the British civil service is the best in the world, though he usually knows little about it at first hand, for it is of the nature of civil servants that they are not in the public eye. On the other hand, he hates a bureaucrat as Sir Andrew Aguecheek hated a Puritan. He is "proud of the civil service", but he always has an eye for vacant lamp-posts. Exactly at what point a distinguished civil servant becomes a bureaucrat he is not quite certain; he does know, however, that the thing must not happen or else he is no longer a free Briton.'[1] The citizen fears that he is, or soon may be, ruled by people who have been appointed to sit in offices instead of by those whom he has elected to sit in parliament. He thinks such hidden rulers are to be feared because they would be secure in their posts for life and beyond the reach of dismissal at the next election. Politicians, on this view, are only nominally in control of the activities over which they preside. In reality, some people suspect they are puppets in the hands of those who are styled servants—'ruling servants', as they have been called.[2]

Such fears may or may not be well founded. What is clear is that they rest on two assumptions that are true only in a few areas on the earth's surface and have been true in only a few epochs of its history. These are: firstly, that policy is one sphere, and administration another, and that it is possible to draw a clear and firm line between them; and secondly, that politicians should be temporary, liable to be sent packing at the people's will, whereas administrators should be permanent, secure in their posts during good behaviour. Only on these assumptions does it make sense to talk of administrators usurping the role of politicians. In Britain, as these words are written, there is a fair degree of correspondence between these assumptions and the observed facts of government. Are they an ideal towards which society is steadily developing? Or a survival from a past age, soon to be supplanted?

The argument of this book is that a better knowledge of the recent

[1] C. K. Allen, *Law and Orders* (1945), 173.
[2] Cf. E. Strauss, *The Ruling Servants* (1961).

history of British central administration can contribute to an understanding of such questions. To some, such an enterprise may seem superfluous. The British civil service is said to be riddled with tradition, to be hampered with the fetters of its own past. The difficulty might seem to be an excess, rather than a deficiency, of history. This is not so, however. Excellent work has been done on some earlier periods of administrative history. But the modern period has been little studied, and least of all by civil servants themselves. As one of them wrote a few years ago, 'the author remained for forty years in the civil service in complete ignorance of his predecessors, apart from a few uncomplimentary legends. Precedent-ridden though it is, no profession is more careless of its past.'[3] Moreover, a better knowledge of tradition does not necessarily mean enslavement to it. Indeed, the opposite may be true. The most daring innovators are often those most thoroughly steeped in tradition. At the present time, innovation is in the air and there is a greater receptiveness to change than for many decades. Paradoxically, a fresh look at the past may be of special value at such a moment. 'A great statesman is he who knows when to depart from traditions, as well as when to adhere to them. But it is a great mistake to suppose that he will do this better for being ignorant of the traditions. No one who does not thoroughly know the modes of action which common experience has sanctioned is capable of judging the circumstances which require a departure from those ordinary modes of action.'[4]

There is general agreement among historians that a profound change took place in British central government in the middle decades of the nineteenth century. Keir, for example, holds that 'the expansion of the administrative services' was 'the most significant feature of the period 1832–67. The growth of industry, of banking, of joint-stock enterprise, of maritime transport, of inland communications, especially railways, of town-life and the consequent need for police, sanitation, water-supply, education, and poor-relief created problems which, whatever the theoretical merits of *laissez-faire*, could not be disregarded. In response to these demands a vast system of administration, central and local, had to be improvised.'[5]

Description of the phenomenon has made considerable progress, but interpretation has been slower. Keir's interjection—'whatever

[3] Sir John Craig, *A History of Red Tape* (1955), v.
[4] J. S. Mill, *Representative Government*, Chapter V.
[5] Sir D. L. Keir, *Constitutional History of Modern Britain, 1485–1951* (5 e., 1953), 419–20.

the theoretical merit of *laissez-faire*'—sounds like an allusion to the most considerable attempt made so far, namely, Dicey's *Law and Opinion*. Dicey divided the century into three periods: (i) Legislative Quiescence, 1800–30; (ii) Period of Benthamism or Individualism, 1825–70; (iii) Period of Collectivism, 1865–1900.[6] If it was so, conditions were unfavourable to government growth during the first two-thirds of the century. 'Confidence in the beneficent effects of state control . . . is utterly foreign to the liberalism of 1832'.[7] Then things changed, and under the impulse of collectivism, the activities of the state steadily increased.

Anyone who knows anything of British history in the nineteenth century can think of things that do not fit Dicey's interpretation. The work of the Poor Law Commissioners is perhaps the best known.[8] Government support for elementary education[9] was even more important, however, as was the assumption by the state of responsibility for public health.[10] In a different field, state regulation of railways was a significant departure.[11] These examples are taken at random and the list could be extended to a considerable length.

Such developments were too numerous to be regarded as merely exceptions to Dicey's rule. What is needed is a new interpretation in which government growth is recognized as a leading trend from 1830 onwards. This book seeks to provide such an analysis. It does not challenge Dicey's characterization of the period before 1830 as one of 'legislative quiescence'. Few permanent Acts of parliament of any general importance were carried in those years. In particular, there was very little delegation of power to the Crown. Parliament regarded administration as the affair of the Crown and did not seek to control it in detail. But it was averse to any growth of the powers of the executive. There were two reasons for this, one direct and one indirect. In the first place, it was felt that the balance of the constitution would be changed. In the second, it was feared that additional patronage in government hands would increase its power to

---

[6] A. V. Dicey, *Lectures on the Relation between Law and Public Opinion during the Nineteenth Century* (2 e., 1914), 62–4. All page references here are to the paperback reprint of 1962.

[7] Dicey (1962), 39.

[8] See e.g. S. E. Finer, *Life and Times of Sir Edwin Chadwick* (1952).

[9] See e.g. N. Ball, *Her Majesty's Inspectorate, 1839–1849* (1963).

[10] See e.g. R. A. Lewis, *Edwin Chadwick and the Public Health Movement, 1832–1854* (1952) and R. Lambert, *Sir John Simon, 1816–1904, and English Social Administration* (1963).

[11] See e.g. H. Parris, *Government and the Railways in Nineteenth-century Britain* (1965).

influence elections and to win support in parliament. Hence the scale of central government remained small, and there was little provision for the enforcement of the law, except through the machinery of the courts. But all this did not mean that the legislative system was idle. Private Bill legislation was more important than ever before or since. The powers which parliament begrudged to central government it freely bestowed on other agencies, such as Turnpike Trusts and Improvement Commissioners.

The general election of 1830 made possible a new relationship between parliament and the executive. Although the old slogans about 'the influence of the Crown' continued to be heard for a generation, it had in fact been demonstrated that government could no longer secure, by the traditional methods, the election of a House of Commons favourable to its policy. Hence the old system of recruiting the public service by patronage began to decline and the ground was cleared for a new system of recruitment by open competitive examination. The reformed parliament was no longer satisfied to have ministers responsible to them for matters of general policy only. There was now a desire to extend parliamentary control over administration also. This led to the supersession of the old style of administration by boards and the establishment of the ministerial department as the standard unit of central government. Eventually, a new concept of ministerial responsibility emerged, the other side of which was the new concept of the anonymity of the civil servant. Once parliament felt confident in its control of the executive, it showed itself ready to delegate powers to ministers—the origin of the modern system of administrative law.

What, then, remains of Dicey's model? Was he wrong in asserting that Benthamite opinion dominated the middle decades of the century? Or was he wrong in identifying Benthamism with hostility to government growth? Such questions should not be lost sight of. But it will be more profitable to discuss them in detail towards the end of the book. In any case, they do not affect the balance which emerged by the end of the century. A line had been drawn between policy and administration, and the belief was prevalent that civil servants were accountable, through ministers and parliament, to society. That balance has been maintained until now. In recent years, however, it has been questioned more seriously than ever before. Civil service reform is a question of the hour. In the last chapter, contemporary issues, and especially the Fulton Report, will be set in their historical context.

An enquiry of this kind could range very wide indeed, and it has been necessary to omit many topics that clamoured for inclusion. Ireland has been entirely left out: a course of action less reprehensible than it might seem, since it is possible to refer the reader to an excellent recent book on Irish administration during the nineteenth and early twentieth centuries.[12] The development of the colonial and diplomatic services is not discussed—the latter is passed over with considerable regret, because it provides some support for the thesis urged in Chapter I. Here, too, a good account has recently been published.[13] Much more might have been said about the armed services than is said here. The functions of London departments with defence and overseas responsibilities are dealt with. But the main emphasis is on departments whose impact was felt at home rather than abroad.

How far back should this enquiry go? The basic question is, when did the permanent civil service emerge? Oddly enough, it has never been answered. The book begins by attempting to do so.

[12] R. B. McDowell, *The Irish Administration, 1801–1914* (1964).
[13] D. B. Horn, *The British Diplomatic Service, 1689–1789* (1961).

CHAPTER I

THE ORIGINS OF THE PERMANENT CIVIL SERVICE, 1780-1830

'All the political part of the English constitution is fully understood, and distinctly stated, in Blackstone and many other books, but the ministerial part, the work of conducting the executive government, has rested so much on practice, on usage, on understanding, that there is no publication to which reference can be made for the explanation and description of it.'

Lord Melbourne to Queen Victoria, 1841

When did the permanent civil service come into being? The language of historians implies that it has always existed. Ward, among others, talks of 'civil servants' in the eighteenth century.[1] Trevelyan held that 'in the Treasury of the first twenty years after the Revolution [of 1688] we see the emergence of the best modern traditions of the permanent civil service.'[2] Aylmer carries the term back to the period before the Civil War.[3] Elton traces 'the change from a civil service recruited from the King's personal servants to one staffed by professional careerists outside the household to the reforms of Henry VIII's reign.'[4] McKisack sees no incongruity in speaking of 'a permanent civil service' in the fourteenth century.[5] In fact, the term can be found in contexts going back to the early middle ages. So long as this is understood to be a convenient shorthand way of saying 'those servants of the Crown who performed functions roughly analogous, so far as any comparison is possible, to those performed by the civil servant in twentieth-century Britain', no harm is done. Without some such reservation, the use of the term in relation to periods earlier than the half-century 1780-1830 is an

---

[1] W. R. Ward, 'Some Eighteenth-century Civil Servants', *English Historical Review*, lxx (1955), 25–54.

[2] G. M. Trevelyan, *England Under Queen Anne* (1930–4), ii, 163.

[3] G. R. Aylmer, *The King's Servants: the civil service of Charles I, 1625–1642* (1961).

[4] G. R. Elton, *The Tudor Revolution in Government* (Cambridge, 1959, e.), 423.

[5] M. McKisack, *The Fourteenth Century* (Oxford, 1959), 19.

obstacle to understanding. The 'permanent civil service' prior to that time differed from its modern counterpart in three significant ways. It was not permanent, it was not civil, and it was not a service.

THE EIGHTEENTH-CENTURY 'CIVIL SERVICE' NOT A SERVICE

The expression 'a service' implies a body of full-time, salaried officers, systematically recruited, with clear lines of authority, and uniform rules on such questions as superannuation. These conditions did not exist in the eighteenth century.

Take revenue collection, for example, since this is generally allowed to be, with defence and the maintenance of internal order, the most fundamental function of government. Yet assessment to the Land Tax, one of the main props of the fiscal system, was the responsibility of unpaid amateurs of the J.P. class, acting for the various counties. They also appointed and supervised the collectors, who were paid by poundage, with the result that the central Tax Office did not know how many collectors there were and could not estimate more closely than between 20,000 and 30,000.[6] Also at the local level were the Receivers. Since they were salaried, they were to some extent under the control of the central office; but only imperfectly so, since the appointments were on principle given to local men of substance, who were held to be more trustworthy than men who depended on salaries only. Hence Receivers, having means of their own and sufficient local standing to invoke the aid of patrons, could go a long way in defying the central authority. Their handling of the cash balances entrusted to them illustrates the point. The Tax Office wished to get such balances in as quickly as possible. The Receivers wished to hang on to the money as long as they could, since custom permitted them to retain the interest earned while cash was in their keeping. The perennial difficulty experienced by officials at the centre in getting the money in demonstrates the degree of independence enjoyed by the Receivers. Land Tax administration was carried on by a blend of professionals and amateurs, full-time and part-time officials. Of those who were paid, some received salaries and some commission. With so little uniformity, hierarchy and discipline, it is impossible to talk of those who administered the tax as constituting a service.

In other branches of the administration, e.g. the Customs, many officials were appointed by patent directly from the Crown, and they could only be dismissed after a judgment in the courts. They did

6 W. R. Ward, *The English Land Tax in the Eighteenth Century* (1953), 140.

not normally act in person, but appointed deputies, who received part of the income but did all the work. The control of the Board of Customs over both patentees and deputies was imperfect. Against the former, they could not invoke the ultimate sanction of dismissal at all. In regard to the latter, they asserted some degree of authority, but it was always limited by the fact that the deputy was the servant of two masters—his principal and the Board. Against such a background, anomalies proliferated. When a patentee died, his deputy had no legal standing until (and unless) reappointed by the new principal. The business of the ports would have been frequently held up had not the Board, acting illegally but with common sense, ordered deputies to carry on as usual in such cases. When, on the other hand, a deputy died, delay often ensued because the patentee, who alone could legally appoint a successor, might live at a distance from the port concerned, or even out of the country altogether. Here, too, the Board departed from the letter of the law, making illegal appointments to prevent a breakdown in the administration.[7] These three elements in Customs administration—the Board, the patent officers and the deputies—were so disparate, and their interests so divergent, that they cannot be said to have constituted a service.

In the offices of the Secretaries of State, the officials were not even servants of the Crown, but were employed by the head of the office and remunerated by fees. In the Post Office, although packet captains were Crown servants, they were also in many cases owners or part-owners of their boats and were paid for hiring them out to carry the mail.[8] Even where professionalism was strongest, as among the officials of the Salt Board,[9] transfer from one branch of administration to another was almost unknown. The result was at best a departmental service, not one department within a unified public service.

THE EIGHTEENTH-CENTURY 'CIVIL SERVICE' NOT CIVIL

Had all administrators under the Crown in the eighteenth century been united into a service, it would not have been a civil service. That epithet implies a distinction between two branches of the executive government—the civil service as distinct from the political,

[7] E. E. Hoon, *The Organization of the English Customs System, 1696–1786* (New York, 1938), 12–24 and 118.
[8] K. L. Ellis, *The Post Office in the Eighteenth Century* (1958), 35.
[9] E. Hughes, *Studies in Administration and Finance, 1558–1825* (1934).

or parliamentary, service of the Crown. There was no such clear distinction. It is true that the administrative duties of the Lord Privy Seal, for example, were negligible, while the duties of the latest admitted junior clerk were wholly non-political. But between those extremes lay a spectrum in which differing proportions of political and administrative duties blended into one another. Some of the Lord Privy Seal's colleagues spent much of their time on detailed administrative business which their twentieth-century successors delegate to civil servants. The author of the standard account of eighteenth-century customs administration writes: 'In studying the relations between the Secretaries of State and the Customs Department one is impressed on the one hand by the triviality of the customs business laid before the Secretaries, and on the other hand by their attention to detail.'[10] This pattern of personal administration by ministers continued well into the nineteenth century. 'The most striking feature of British administration in the first quarter of the nineteenth century was the extent to which the work of government departments was performed by the ministers themselves.'[11] In the Regency period, the political heads of the Home Office 'kept a close touch with all its work, personally interviewing magistrates, Members of Parliament, and even spies and prisoners, with information from the localities, and being not merely nominally but actually responsible for even minor departmental acts.'[12]

At the lower end of the scale, quite humble officials had political tasks to perform. A Land Tax surveyor is found supplying Harley with detailed reports on the electoral situation in his locality.[13] When Tory fortunes were at their height in Queen Anne's reign, a Northamptonshire exciseman was 'a zealous man for the present Ministry, and has sense, and makes use of it, to satisfy the people in his Ride of the condition we were in, and what an excellent parliament this is.'[14] One of the county members, having secured for his son a post as Commissioner of the Leather Duty, wrote to him: 'Pray put as many as you can in the Leather Office.'[15] But it was not to last. The Commissionership was taken away following the Whig victory in 1714.[16] In 1723, the Treasury recognized that political services must sometimes be accepted as an excuse for defective

[10] Hoon, 84.
[11] D. M. Young, *The Colonial Office in the Early Nineteenth Century* (1961), 1.
[12] F. O. Darvall, *Popular Disturbances and Public Order in Regency England* (1934), 228.   [13] Ward (1953), 55.
[14] E. G. Forrester, *Northamptonshire County Elections and Electioneering* (1941), 34.   [15] ibid.   [16] ibid., 39.

administration. 'Officers who themselves or whose kinsmen or political friends were canvassing votes for parliamentary elections were hardly likely to be conspicuous in prosecuting defaulting maltsters and inn-keepers.'[17] At Harwich, the customs officers kept the seats in parliament safe for Treasury nominees.[18] Since the government was the King's government, it was no more than a patriotic duty to work for the return to parliament of men who would be good friends to the King when they got there. It might not be easy for ignorant men in provincial backwaters to know who the King's friends were. So if the Commissioners took the trouble to indicate to their underlings whom they should support, simple prudence would second patriotic duty in urging them to obey.

Thomas Lamb, Tally Cutter in the Exchequer, was a sinecurist so far as his nominal duties were concerned, but rendered valuable services as election manager for Rye. Edward Milward, Surveyor of the Riding Officers for Kent, performed a similar function at Hastings.[19] Sometimes such activities, though illegal, were connived at by heads of departments. Thus, in the Post Office, 'the staff were forbidden to meddle in parliamentary elections under the Act of 1711. They could vote, but neither sit nor influence. Occasionally, however, in the first half of the century, the Act was broken at Harwich under the clandestine direction of the [Postmasters General].'[20] At Harwich, the staff of the mail packets made up one-sixth of the small electorate, and the Earl of Leicester as Postmaster General tried—unsuccessfully—to establish an interest there independent of the Treasury.[21] In supporting his endeavour, the postal officials were serving a personal patron rather than the Crown—two loyalties which often became confused in the minds of eighteenth-century administrators. Henry Potts, for example, was a client of the Duke of Newcastle, having been appointed by him Secretary of the Post Office in 1759. From April, 1762, on the eve of Newcastle's resignation, Potts took personal charge of his patron's letters to ensure that they were not opened in the office. When Bute succeeded Newcastle in the following month, Potts wrote: 'Your Grace may depend upon my promise that it shall not be in the power of anybody to inspect or look into any letter of Your Grace's that I shall be entrusted with.' Later, when Newcastle was out of office, Potts

---

[17] Hughes (1934), 310.

[18] Sir Lewis Namier, *Structure of Politics at the Succession of George III* (2 e., 1957), 358–89.

[19] Sir Lewis Namier, *England in the Age of the American Revolution* (1930), 476–80.　　　[20] Ellis, 23.　　　[21] ibid., 18.

wrote again: 'Should any attempt ever be made on any pretence whatever to meddle with anything that came from your Grace, I would immediately inform your Grace of it.'[22]

THE EIGHTEENTH-CENTURY 'CIVIL SERVICE' NOT PERMANENT

Even if, for convenience, the term 'civil service' is used in an eighteenth-century context, it was still not a permanent civil service. In relation to British central administration, the term 'permanence' has a technical meaning, more precise than that of common speech. Prior to 1780, the conditions which give meaning to this concept did not exist. This is not, of course, to deny that some administrators did hang on to their jobs for extraordinarily long periods—far longer, indeed, than would be possible today. Thomas Pratt, for example, entered the Treasury as a boy of seventeen in 1724 and was still drawing his salary eighty years later. Many, perhaps most, of those who served the Crown in an administrative capacity did so for a long time, or even for the whole of their working lives. This was the case, for example, in the Post Office, even down to the crews of the mail packets.[23] It is also true that it was sometimes extremely difficult to get rid of administrators, even when guilty of flagrant neglect of duty. Patent officers had much more security of tenure than twentieth-century civil servants, and much more than most people would think desirable.

Nor was there a lack of awareness of the advantages of continuity. As early as 1684, when Edmund Woodroff, clerk to a Teller of the Exchequer, was turned out on the death of his chief, the Treasury was urged to compel the new Teller to reinstate him. 'If it come to be a practice to put by the old clerk on admitting a new Teller, it will tempt such an old clerk, who hath soe many opportunities, to provide for himself by sinister ways in the Teller's lifetime.'[24] Officials with secure tenure, it was supposed, were more trustworthy than temporary ones. They also became more expert, even to the point of being indispensable. In 1742, the Duke of Bedford took it for granted that Walpole's Secretary of the Treasury, John Scrope, would be dismissed, 'through whose hands such sums of money have passed, and who refused to give any answer to the Secret Committee about those dark transactions'. But he was told 'What your Grace mentions is absolutely impracticable. Mr Scrope is the only man I know, that thoroughly understands the business of the

[22] ibid., 84.   [23] ibid., 22 and 36.   [24] Hughes (1934), 268.

Treasury, and is versed in drawing money bills. On this foundation he stands secure, and is as immovable as a rock.'[25]

But it was not only administrators who held on to their jobs for long periods. Many whose posts would today be regarded as political appointments did likewise. For example, Lord Barrington M.P. held one post or another continuously from 1746 until 1778 and was Secretary at War for nineteen years under Newcastle, Devonshire, Rockingham, Chatham, Grafton and North. He should not be dismissed out of hand as nothing more than a political Vicar of Bray. Conscious first of all of his duty to the Crown, such a man thought himself justified in staying in office so long as he retained the King's confidence. The resignation from time to time of a colleague holding the office of First Lord of the Treasury was a difficulty, no doubt, but need not be an occasion for others to do likewise. Indeed to do so might increase the King's difficulties and so be positively disloyal.

By modern standards, Barrington's long tenure of office was remarkable. But in the period before 1830, it was by no means unique. The Earl of Leicester was Postmaster General from 1733 until 1759. Pitt the Younger held office for more than twenty years of his short life, including eighteen years continuously as Prime Minister. Liverpool held a succession of posts continuously, with one brief intermission during the Ministry of All the Talents, from 1793 until 1827, culminating in fifteen years at the head of the government. Bathurst was Secretary of State and Melville First Lord of the Admiralty from 1812 until 1827. Indeed, until the 1820s, most office-holders hoped to retain their posts permanently, irrespective of whether the duties were mainly administrative or mainly political in character. It was only later that something like the modern view began to emerge.

'PERMANENCE' AND CHANGES OF GOVERNMENT

But permanence in a civil servant means something more than security of tenure or the mere retention of a job for a long time. It means the retention of that job during a change of government. Hence the concept of permanence cannot be older than the concept of a change of government. Before 1780, government was the King's. Any talk of an alternative government smacked of Jacobitism or of speculation about the King's death and the succession of the heir apparent. Ministers came and went, and such arrivals and departures sometimes had great political significance; for example,

[25] Sir Lewis Namier, *Personalities and Powers* (1955), 23.

the withdrawal of Walpole in 1742 or the advent of Bute in 1760. But Walpole's colleagues did not feel obliged to follow him into the wilderness; 'the malcontents had ousted a minister, but not a ministry.'[26] Indeed, feeling ran the other way. It would have seemed wanting in loyalty to add to the difficulties of the Crown by piling resignations one upon another. 'Quitting of places is no crime,' wrote a pamphleteer, 'but if several cabal to throw up, when the government has most occasion for their service, in order to force it to comply with their unreasonable demands, this is a very criminal conspiracy.'[27] The comings and goings of individuals were normally changes within government, which was always that of the King and continuous from his accession until his death. Even when there were collective resignations, those who took part in them were liable to remorse. 'I have promised the King,' Henry Pelham wrote to Newcastle, 'and I will keep my word, that I would never enter into any cabal again, to prevent his Majesty from either removing or bringing into his service any person he had either a prejudice to, or a predilection for.'[28] Consequently they were hard to organize, and apt to misfire. When Newcastle attempted such a manoeuvre in 1762, only nine of thirty-three responded to his call, and five of those did so against their own desire.[29]

The ministerial changes of 1782–83 were different in kind, and precursors of the modern pattern. Whole teams went out, to be replaced by alternative teams. 'Walpole had resigned under pressure from his colleagues, but they remained in office . . . The opposition of 1782 had attacked, not one overgrown minister, but the whole ministry and its policies. . . . North told the King that the "present cabinet, except the Chancellor, must all be removed" as a preliminary to the formation of a new government. . . . The final procedure of demission, therefore, was in broad outline much closer to that which prevailed in the mid-nineteenth century than to the resignation of Walpole.'[30] Those who went out stayed together in a nascent opposition. The nineteenth-century party system began to emerge. In this pattern, it became essential to distinguish those offices which were permanent from those which were not. It soon became an established rule that the vast majority of offices, including all the minor ones, were permanent.

[26] A. S. Foord, *His Majesty's Opposition, 1714–1830* (1964), 216.
[27] q. ibid., 106.
[28] W. Coxe, *Memoirs of the Administration of the Rt. Hon. Henry Pelham* (1829), ii, 389.
[29] Foord, 311 and n.   [30] ibid., 364.

WHY NO SPOILS SYSTEM?

There was nothing inevitable about this solution. One possible result would have been the growth of a spoils system, as in the United States. That system was not inherent in the country's republican institutions. For almost forty years after the adoption of the Constitution, the federal government was run, under the President and his ministers, by a class of permanent administrators. Jefferson dismissed a number of them and gave their posts to his followers as a reward for party services. But with that exception, the system endured until the election of Andrew Jackson in 1828. After that, however, and the final establishment of a two-party regime, what had been the exception became the rule. Permanent officials were dismissed wholesale and their jobs distributed among the faithful. Thereafter, similar changes ensued whenever a Presidential election brought a new party to power.[31]

One half of a spoils system—the practice of filling official vacancies with an eye to political advantage—already existed. Even those who sought to diminish the influence of the Crown did not wish to abolish it altogether. 'It was impossible,' declared Fox, 'for the government of a great kingdom to go on, unless it had certain lucrative and honourable situations to bestow on its officers.'[32] There were never enough vacancies, however, to satisfy all the needs of the political managers. A natural development would have been for politicians newly come to power to create openings by dismissing those appointed by their predecessors.

Such things had happened. Trevelyan argued that it was a risk inherent in the Revolution Settlement. 'There was a danger in the new state of things. Since parliamentary government would mean party government, the security of tenure even of the lower grades of Crown servants was imperilled at every political change in the cabinet; "the spoils for the victors" threatened to become the law of English politics. Such indeed [was] the claim and design of the High Tories in 1702.'[33] Their opponents thought in similar terms. In 1714 'the Whigs and their allies accompanied savage charges of treason and sedition against "the late Queen's servants" with the wholesale removal of opponents from numerous minor offices which

[31] For a comparison between the administrative history of Great Britain and the U.S. in the period, see S. E. Finer, 'Patronage and the Public Service', *Public Administration*, xxx (1952), 329–60.
[32] *Parliamentary History*, xxiii, 1065.
[33] Trevelyan, ii, 163.

commanded considerable influence in elections.'[34] There were always obstacles to a thorough-going spoils system, but its effects in particular branches of government were considerable.

In the Land Tax administration, for example, many were dismissed 'after the swings of party fortune in 1706, 1711–12, and 1715–16. The wider purge on each occasion reflects the increasing severity of party conflict. By 1714 this sector of the administration was subject to a thorough-going spoils system. Receivers who had been dropped were in several cases reappointed after a change in party fortune . . . These purges illuminate . . . the depth and scope of the party battles under Queen Anne.' At this time 'a major object of faction was to use public patronage to mortify opponents and confer favours upon friends. In 1711 the young men of the "loyal country club" greatly disturbed Harley by declaring that "they design to have every Whig turn'd out" and their opponents in 1714 were no better.' Similarly in 1710 'surveyors of house duties were turned out by the dozen . . . Like other minor revenue offices, these posts were drawn into the political fray.'[35]

With the decline of party feeling under the Hanoverians, the chances of an administrator losing his place in a purge declined also. But an event in the 1760s showed that purges could still happen. This was 'the massacre of the Pelhamite innocents' which followed the resignation of the Duke of Newcastle in 1762. Horace Walpole asserted that 'a more severe political persecution never raged. Whoever, holding a place, had voted against the preliminaries, was instantly dismissed. The friends and dependants of the Duke of Newcastle were particularly cashiered; and this cruelty was extended so far, that old servants, who had retired and been preferred to very small places, were rigorously hunted out and deprived of their livelihood.'[36] This exaggerates both the scope and the vindictiveness of the operation, but at least sixteen men lost their positions in Sussex, Newcastle's own county. In all, some hundreds of his followers were dismissed from administrative posts, which were then given to others. Following further ministerial changes, some of the incomers were ejected in 1765–66, and 'innocents' reinstated. Such changes took place, for instance, in the Customs, the Post Office, the Tax Office, and among the members of revenue boards.[37]

If nothing was known of the aftermath of these events, they might

[34] Foord, 49.
[35] Quotations in this paragraph are from Ward (1953), 51–5.
[36] H. Walpole, *Memoirs of the Reign of King George III* (1845), i, 233–4.
[37] Ellis, 84; Ward (1953), 105; Ward (1955), 48.

be interpreted in two flatly contradictory ways. The dismissals might have been the first sparks of a fire that would spread throughout the forest. Or they might have been the last fire-up of dying embers. In fact, the second of these interpretations is correct. The 'massacre' was far less drastic than the purges of the first two decades of the eighteenth century. The victims suffered, not for party loyalties, but for their personal loyalty to the Duke of Newcastle. 'To whom did these men, appointed by Newcastle as First Lord of the Treasury, owe allegiance—to him, or to the office which he held no longer?'[38] If they were, as Newcastle claimed, 'most zealous and active friends to the government' they must be, as one of them put it, 'determined to support the interest of His Majesty and his Ministry against all opponents whatsoever', including the Duke himself. In that case, they were allowed to keep their places, but at the price of renouncing their former patron, who regarded them as ungrateful wretches. But if they adhered to him, and continued working for his political interests, was it reasonable to expect the government to leave them where they were? If those dismissed were 'innocents', it was in the sense that they were lacking in knowledge of the world, rather than in the sense of being guiltless.

In the Land Tax there were changes which were 'strongly redolent of politics'. Yet they were far fewer than might have been expected and 'the whole episode marked the change in English politics since the days of Queen Anne. . . . Very soon the brief, and by comparison with past days, not very turbulent, storm was over.'[39] Similarly, 'so far as the revenue commissioners were concerned, . . . [it] was a very kid-gloved revolution.'[40] The average Crown servant in the eighteenth century had a good chance, purges notwithstanding, of keeping his place for life, or until he wished to resign it. But the events of the 1760s showed that posts in government service were not yet permanent in the modern sense.

Why did a spoils system not take root in Britain? One reason was that, prior to the nineteenth century, office was regarded as something closely akin to freehold property. In some cases, it could be sold, though the practice was never so prevalent as it was on the Continent.[41] To deprive a man of his place seemed, therefore, only less shocking than to deprive him of goods or land. As early as 1694, a man who had been turned off the Salt Commission sued his detractor for damages sustained in the loss of his office. It is significant that

[38] Namier (1930), 412, from which all quotations in this paragraph are taken.
[39] Ward (1953), 105 and 120.   [40] Ward (1955), 48.
[41] K. W. Swart, *Sale of Offices in the Sixteenth Century* (1949), 45–67.

the court was willing to entertain such an action.[42] In any case, most officials were not directly under ministers, but worked for semi-independent boards, such as those of Customs and Excise. The members of these boards succeeded in some cases in withstanding Treasury pressure over patronage, in regard to posts that fell vacant by natural causes. Had incoming ministers sought to create vacancies by discharging large numbers of employees of the boards, they would most probably have run into opposition from the Commissioners. Indeed, this had happened in the early years of the century.[43] The Commissioners stood to suffer the inconvenience resulting from wholesale changes of staff; while the political advantage would accrue to the ministers. Moreover, if the Commissioners failed to defend the pittances of their myrmidons, how long would their own fat salaries be safe? Last but not least, wholesale proscriptions would have alienated large numbers in any eighteenth-century parliament. One constant group there consisted of the office-holders, who had a personal interest in the principle of permanence.

So for that matter had the Crown itself. Queen Anne was one of the main opponents of the 'spoils' principle which was so widely held in her reign.[44] George III's attitude was similar. 'There was a natural affinity between the official and the Crown, the one seeking permanence, the other efficiency and fidelity. A succession of amateur administrators taught George III to appreciate the services of the well-informed, hard-working official, who behind the façade of brilliant oratory from the front benches, carried on the real work of government; . . . In point of fact, as time went on, the King came to trust them more and more . . . He interceded for them in his negotiations at every change of administration, and occasionally took care of them individually when ministers tried to get rid of them.'[45] Moreover, there were always some among the ministers themselves who could see the importance of preserving continuity among the administrators. One such was Godolphin in the time of William III and Anne. 'I cannot think it for your service,' he told the King in 1694, 'to make changes in the management of your revenue to gratify party and animosity.'[46]

Just as there were features of British government, favourable to permanence, which were absent in the United States, so there were provisions of American government, favourable to a spoils system,

[42] Hughes (1934), 268.   [43] ibid., 271–7.
[44] Trevelyan, i, 206–7: ii, 164: iii, 262.
[45] N. S. Jucker (ed.), *The Jenkinson Papers, 1760–1766* (1949), xiv.
[46] *Calendar of State Papers Domestic, 1694–5*, 185.

which did not apply in Britain. 'There was not in England, as in many of the United States, a reasoned principle of rotation. In the United States the fear of the entrenched and arbitrary authority of permanent office holders, inherited from the colonial days, had led a number of states to make express provision for short official terms and rotation.'[47] Even under the spoils system, the American administrator could reasonably count on a fixed tenure of office, though a short one. Under a British spoils system, there would have been no certainty whatever. 'The party in power in England must always be ready to resign on an adverse vote in the House of Commons. . . . With a tenure of at least four years, and probably at least four more, the United States could survive rotation. . . . But no English cabinet could maintain itself in office a single year supported at Whitehall by an untrained rabble without certain tenure and opposed in parliament at every turn by an embittered and rapacious minority. . . . Who would care to enter the civil service with so hazardous a tenure? Who would want to be a government clerk for six months, or even an under-secretary?'[48]

SEPARATION OF ADMINISTRATION FROM POLITICS

For all these reasons, the spoils system did not take root in Britain. What happened instead was the evolution of the permanent civil service, in response to the novel problem posed by a change of government: who was to go and who was to stay. It involved the separation of the administrative sphere from the political sphere—for which there was, in any case, a good deal of pressure from the political side. Two factors were at work; the drive to reduce 'the influence of the Crown' and the growing demands of political life itself, which made it increasingly difficult for men to combine political with administrative roles.

'The influence of the Crown', read Dunning's famous resolution of 1780, 'has increased, is increasing and ought to be diminished.' The motives of those who sought to limit it were similar to those which led the founding fathers of the United States to write the doctrine of separation of powers into their constitution. On both sides of the Atlantic, many felt that the executive—that is, the King —had unduly influenced the legislature with harmful effects. Such influence was exercised in two ways:

    (a) by putting administrators into the House of Commons,
    (b) by rewarding M.P.s with offices—or 'places', to employ the

[47] R. Moses, *The Civil Service of Great Britain* (1914), 25.   [48] ibid., 25–6.

term preferred in the eighteenth century—for themselves and their dependants.

For centuries the Crown had sent its servants into the House to expound its policies and secure support for them. Which servants in particular were to perform this function varied from time to time. In the reign of William III, for example, an experiment was made by introducing some Commissioners of Customs and Excise into the Commons to answer for their departments. 'There is one thing necessary for carrying on your service', wrote Somers to the King, 'which was extremely wanting in these two commissions; that there should be somebody of them, who might upon all occasions give a satisfactory account in the House of Commons of what related to their proper business, which I hope Sir Walter Young and Mr Clarke will be very well qualified to do.'[49] Young and Clarke in due course became M.P.s. About 1760, the official group in the House included a number of officials whose duties designate them as forerunners of the Permanent—not the Parliamentary—Secretaries of the twentieth century. Seven such men were returned at the election of 1761, including the two Secretaries to the Treasury, the Secretary and Assistant Secretary to the Admiralty, and two Under-Secretaries of State. M.P.s in general were prepared to accept such colleagues, so long as they did not become too numerous. In 1733, when two Treasury clerks, Henry Kelsall and Christopher Tilson, were Members, the House was warned: 'they deserve it, they are gentlemen, and men of figure and fortune in their country . . . [but] we may in a little time see all the little under-clerks of the Treasury, and other offices, members of this House; we may see them trudging down to this House in the morning, in order to give their votes for imposing taxes upon their fellow-subjects; and in the afternoon attending behind the chair of a Chancellor of the Exchequer.'[50]

In far greater numbers, men were put into administrative posts on political grounds. The plum jobs were kept for the M.P.s themselves. 'On the higher and more profitable posts or sinecures in the civil service, if compatible with a seat in Parliament, its members had first lien. Newcastle's remark about the office of Keeper of the Records in the Tower is characteristic: "All the earth could not make the King give this place out of the Commons." '[51] Offices not compatible with membership of parliament were also sometimes sufficiently interesting to M.P.s to induce them to give up their seats. The government had three main motives in such transactions: to

[49] *Calendar of State Papers Domestic, 1694–5*, 180.
[50] *Parliamentary History*, viii, 1326. [51] Namier (1957), 20.

secure a vacancy in the House, to buy political support, and to provide 'for members of the political nation who were alleged to be in need'.[52] Thirty-six M.P.s were appointed to boards, membership of which was incompatible with a seat in parliament, in the period 1754–98.[53] Similar considerations prevailed right down the line, with the result that 'the men who did most of the work in parliament and in the administration can best be described as "the official class" ... In the lower ranks, they were largely drawn from voters in parliamentary boroughs and their relatives, and various dependants of influential men. In parliament and administration, and at elections, they were the labour army of the Court ... The class extended from ambitious politicians at Westminster to tide-waiters or surveyors of window-lights in some distant county.'[54]

To diminish the influence of the Crown, implied two things:
a) a reduction in the number of places compatible with a seat in parliament; possibly even to zero.
b) a limitation on the political activities of minor office-holders.

At the beginning of the eighteenth century a start was made with the first of these policies. The short experiment of having Commissioners of Customs and Excise in the House came to an end in 1700 when they were excluded. Under the Act of Settlement, 1701, all holders of an office of profit under the Crown were to be ineligible to sit in parliament, though the provision was not to come into effect until the reigning monarch died. Before that event took place, the prospective ban was relaxed and a distinction drawn between old and new offices of profit. New offices (i.e. those created after 25 October, 1705) were to be incompatible. M.P.s could be appointed to old offices, provided they vacated their seats and offered themselves for re-election. If their constituents felt that their Member had been 'bought' they could reject him. This arrangement continued in force until as recently as 1926.

The last stage of the process began in 1782 with the programme of Economical Reform. Its motives were political rather than administrative. 'The process by which the central executive was subjected to investigation and reform by parliament was begun ... not in order to increase administrative efficiency, but to diminish the royal influence based on patronage which threatened to impair the balance of the constitution and the independence of the legislature.'[55] The leaders of the movement admitted their motives at the time. 'When Fox and Burke reformed administration ... they did so (as they

[52] Ward (1955), 27.   [53] ibid., 35.
[54] Namier (1930), 181–2.   [55] Keir, 373.

were careful to point out) without any desire to increase efficiency or to save money, but solely to reduce the political influence of the Crown.'[56]

Nevertheless, such measures as the abolition of sinecures and patent offices, and the disfranchisement of revenue officers, had important consequences on the administration. They created conditions for greater efficiency and a non-political service. As the officials became non-political, so they became more permanent. The reformers recognized that permanence was a shield against Crown influence. The 'sort of influence the least dangerous of any that could possibly exist,' declared Fox, was 'to put a man into such a situation . . . that it should be out of the power of the Crown to be hurtful to him. . . . He knew of no way of doing this more effectually than by giving a man an independent situation for life.'[57] The dilemma of the Duke of Newcastle's friends in 1762–63 became ever less and less imaginable. Because vacancies continued to be filled by patronage, the trend took a long time fully to work itself out. But gradually it ceased to be possible for an official to lose his place on political grounds, and this state of affairs has endured until the present day, when the concept of 'security risk' has introduced a new element into the picture. The original object was to reduce the influence of the Crown on political life. The consequences in the political field are well known.[58] An important, though unforeseen, result was the rise of a class of non-party officials capable of serving any government which the tides of electoral fortune might return to power.

THE PRESSURE OF POLITICS ON MINISTERS

As indicated above, eighteenth-century ministers dealt personally with much business that today falls to senior civil servants.[59] This was possible, not only because of the nature of administration, but also because of the nature of politics. Parliament made fewer calls on the time of ministers before 1780 than became normal after. Opposition, though sometimes violent, was sporadic rather than continuous—opposition, but not yet His Majesty's Opposition. Divisions were fewer and majorities normally secure. In the case of ministers in the Commons, the demands of a constituency could be

[56] R. Pares, *George III and the Politicians* (Oxford, 1953), 130.
[57] *Parliamentary History*, xxiii, 1065.
[58] A. S. Foord, 'The Waning of "the influence of the Crown" ', EHR, lxii (1947).
[59] See above, p. 24.

kept low. 'The constitutional compromise of 1707, which allowed a Member of the House of Commons to accept a place under the Crown but forced him to vacate his seat and stand for re-election, obliged a ministerial politician, who meant to climb the ladder of preferment, to choose a quiet, reliable, and inexpensive constituency.'[60] This was the consideration in the mind of James West, after a contested election at St. Albans (with over 500 votes), when he remarked to Newcastle in 1761 that 'a Secretary of the Treasury should not stand hereafter for a populous borough within twenty miles of London.'[61] There were many such seats in rotten and pocket boroughs. When Palmerston entered the House in 1807, his patron made only one condition—that he should never set foot in his constituency![62]

The management of the press took little time, since there were few newspapers, and those few unimportant. Far from occupying themselves with public opinion, ministers, like other parliamentarians, 'were very jealous of any pressure from the general public, even from constituents.' Public meetings were rare; 'a meeting held . . . in order to petition parliament for the redress of grievances, was the one clearly unexceptionable form of public political assembly. Even so, there were people who did not feel quite happy unless the meeting was called by the High Sheriff of the county.' Such petitions were few partly because 'the right to petition was limited, in the interest of public order, by the Act of 1694 against tumultuous petitioning.'[63] Interest groups did exist, and some, like the East India Company, were powerful and well organized. But few were strong enough to make effective claims on ministers' time. As for 'cause' groups, parliamentarians 'looked . . . jealously on any unofficial political organization which could claim to represent the public . . . [e.g.] the county associations for parliamentary reform, which sprang up in 1780.'[64]

Nevertheless, those associations were a portent. During the decades that followed there was a quickening of national political life which had the effect of leaving ministers less time for detailed administrative work. The campaign against the slave trade showed the force of public opinion—a force of which the development of the press was part cause and part effect. The technical restrictions on the reporting of parliamentary debates became increasingly difficult to enforce. Ministers had to meet a steadily mounting demand from

[60] Pares, 8. [61] q. Namier (1957), 82.
[62] Sir H. L. Bulwer, *Life of . . . Viscount Palmerston* (3 e., 1871), i, 23.
[63] Pares, 50–2. [64] ibid., 50–2.

Members for more information, to which the stately ranks of Parliamentary Papers are the monument. They had also to watch, in addition to business on the floor of the House itself, the proceedings of an increasing number of Select Committees. These last, in addition to the other committees of the House (e.g. those on private Bills) produced appalling congestion. 'During the present session,' Members were told in 1825, 'the Members' waiting rooms, the long gallery, the House of Commons itself, and even the Court of Exchequer, have been occupied by committees. 276 sittings have been held of public committees. Four of the public committees, thirty committees on private business, have met on a single day, *nineteen of the latter having been fixed to meet in one room.*'[65]

Ministers, of course, bore the brunt of all this. Windham complained in 1809 of being 'called upon to read and write, to consider and decide, when . . . exhausted and worn down with . . . duty in parliament.'[66] They did not get much sympathy from the Whips, who were apt to ask how they could be expected to persuade country gentlemen to attend if ministers failed to set a good example.[67] In any case, the institutionalisation of opposition called for constant attendance on the Treasury Bench. 'During the first few years of Pitt's administration . . . important ministerial measures were subjected to searching criticism clause by clause. Fox spun out the procedural stages for the passage of Bills. . . . Sheridan once took nineteen successive divisions to block a government resolution. Petitions, questions, calls for papers, motions for investigation were moved so frequently that ministers complained of being teased and harassed by wanton attacks.'[68] In the session of 1821, 'Joseph Hume and a small body of Radicals made a system of this kind of opposition, and "divided on every item of every estimate". This pertinacity earned Hume great notoriety and enthusiastic approval in the country. "Until last session," said Mr Favell at a special meeting of the London Common Council in Hume's honour, "the debates on the army and navy estimates seldom took up two or three nights in all. Mr Hume, by his statements and exposures for three months, rendered the country fully aware of the useless." At the county meetings early in 1822, Members were judged according to the extent that they had aided Hume. At the Norfolk meeting, Lord Suffield told the freeholders how he had "sometimes divided with Mr

---

[65] q. W. Wickens, *An Argument for More of the Division of Labour etc.* (1829), 5.   [66] Young, 13.
[67] A. Aspinall (ed.), *Correspondence of Charles Arbuthnot* (Camden Third Series, lxv, 1941), 15–16.   [68] Foord, 413.

Hume upon them [the estimates] ten or twelve times in a night." At the Hertfordshire meeting ... the county Members were criticized for not appearing more often in Hume's divisions.'[69] Ministers more than anyone else were affected by these developments. 'Awareness of the public, together with the harder work, longer sessions, better-attended divisions, made the career of a British politician on the eve of 1830 very unlike what it had been in 1760.'[70] One of the differences was that it had become much harder to double the administrative and the political roles.

ADMINISTRATION BECOMES AUTONOMOUS

The development of administration as an autonomous sphere, distinct from politics, in the period 1780–1830 had three important aspects. First, the non-military servants of the Crown began to develop into a service. This part of the story is relatively well known[71] and calls for least discussion here, especially since it has little bearing on the argument of this book. Typical of the steps taken were the abolition of patent offices, payment by salaries (under Treasury control) instead of fees, and the introduction of superannuation (again under Treasury control).

Secondly, members of this nascent service came to be known as civil—i.e. non-political—servants of the Crown. The term 'civil servant' was first used in India in contrast to the military servants of the East India Company. When first used in Britain it had a similar sense; for example, in Palmerston's memorandum on relations between the Secretary at War and the Commander in Chief, dated 1811, where he speaks of the former as 'a civil servant of the Crown'. As if to make it clear that no distinction was then to be drawn between civil and political service, he also refers to the Secretary's 'civil character as a political servant of Crown'.[72] Although this usage never really took root, it was a long time dying. As late as 1847, it was possible to inscribe on a memorial plaque to Lt-Col. Sir George Gipps R.E. a reference to his 'honourable and useful career ... in the military and civil service of his country' although he had never held a civil service appointment in the modern sense. What appears to be the earliest document to embody the modern

[69] P. Fraser, 'The Conduct of Public Business in the House of Commons, 1812–1827' (Ph.D. thesis, London University, 1957), 145–6.
[70] Pares, 204.
[71] See e.g. E. Cohen, *Growth of the British Civil Service* (1941).
[72] Bulwer, i, 385, 392, 410, 414 and 415.

distinction is a Treasury circular, probably dating from 1816, which speaks of 'servants in the Civil Service of the country'[73] and so eligible for superannuation as distinct from political servants, who were not.

Thirdly, and most importantly, the emergent civil service had become permanent. The concept of a change of government implied either a spoils system or a more precisely defined security of tenure. 'The only alternative to party purges seemed to be permanent tenure'[74] and the latter had triumphed. The only question remaining was at what level should the break come? How far up the hierarchy was permanence to go? There were administrative advantages in allowing the rank and file to keep their posts during ministerial changes. But did the same arguments apply to posts immediately below the highest level? Edward Sedgwick, who held one of them in 1765, recognized that they could not. He wrote to a retired colleague, Edward Weston, in reference to a current political upheaval: 'No Under-Secretaries are yet declared, nor I believe, fix'd on. . . . But I understand they will all be new ones. . . . It is thought improper and disagreeable to give the entire confidence which Under-Secretaries must enjoy to men who are known to be strongly attach'd or greatly obliged to other great personages.'[75]

'MEN OF BUSINESS' IN EIGHTEENTH-CENTURY GOVERNMENT

The Under-Secretaries were an important group in eighteenth-century government. Under that name they were to be found in the offices of the Secretaries of State—as, of course, they still are. The Secretaries of the Treasury and Admiralty, and such officers as the members of the Board of Ordnance held posts of similar rank. Through most ministerial crises of the eighteenth century, such men provided an element of continuity. In parliament they were an important element in 'the Court and Administration party . . . [ready] to support any minister of the King's choice. . . . They professed direct political allegiance to the Crown . . . on a timeless civil-service basis . . . Minor ministers of an administrative type, or hard-working officials . . . [they] tried through a direct nexus with the Crown to secure permanency of employment: wherein they were, by and large, successful.'[76] In 1766, those members of the group who were in parliament described themselves as 'those who have always hitherto acted upon the sole principle of attachment to

[73] Young, 163.
[75] H.M.C., 10th Report, Weston MSS, 391.
[74] Ward (1953), 176.
[76] Namier (1955), 22.

the Crown. This is probably the most numerous body and would on trial be found sufficient to carry on the public business themselves if there was any person to accept of a ministerial office at the head of them, and this is all they want.'[77] Lord Chesterfield made the same point more pithily in 1792: 'We cannot go on well unless we have some acres added to our abilities.'[78] This indicates two main types of which an eighteenth-century government was made up. Just as there was a recognized distinction between offices with light departmental duties and 'efficient' offices, so were there two kind of public men capable of filling them. Those of the first type—'acres'—owed their places to their social standing, their electoral strength, and their influence at court or in parliament, and took little or no part in the day-to-day drudgery of administration. The Marquis of Rockingham and the Duke of Portland were ministers of this sort. There were also men—'abilities'—who might be of comparatively low social origin, own no boroughs, have little influence at Court, and take little part in the work of parliament beyond what concerned their own departments. Charles Jenkinson, who was one of them, called this group the 'sub-ministers.' Horace Walpole, a close observer, thought in terms of ministers 'of the second or third class'. Elsewhere he called them the 'Treasury Jesuits'.[79] They did the donkey work in the departments and made themselves indispensable. These 'men of business'—to use another contemporary label—performed the functions of both the junior ministers and the permanent secretaries in British government today.

As shown above, pressure to separate administration from politics came first of all from politicians, anxious to reduce the influence of the Crown. But there was also an awareness of administrative arguments for such a change. Internal pressures would probably have caused the eighteenth-century pattern to disintegrate anyway. The break came when the 'men of business' separated into the two groups still familiar today, the junior ministers and the permanent secretaries. Such a division was recommended as early as 1786 by the Commissioners appointed to enquire into the public offices. In the Treasury one Secretary, and in the office of each Secretary of State one Under-Secretary, should be made 'stationary'. This was 'for the obvious reason of preventing the confusion and serious consequences that may arise in business of such high importance from frequent changes. . . . But as we conceive that the private and

[77] Jucker, 405–6.
[78] O. Browning (ed.), *Political Memoranda of Francis, Duke of Leeds* (Camden Society, 1884), 199.   [79] Jucker, xiv.

confidential business of a principal Secretary of State may require the assistance of another person, it may be expedient that the principal Secretary of State for the time being should, on his coming into office, have the nomination of an assistant Under-Secretary for the management of business of this description'.[80] The process was more or less complete by 1830. The administrative factors involved were, firstly, the increasing bulk of departmental business and, secondly, its increasing complexity.

THE ORIGIN OF THE PERMANENT SECRETARIES

These developments did not much affect the grandees in politics. Accustomed as they were to delegate administrative chores, they were largely above such changes. Nor did they much affect the lower ranks in the offices. At that level, the machine could be made to cope by taking on more hands. It was the middle level—the sub-ministers, the under-secretaries—who bore the brunt. As it became increasingly difficult for a man with a seat in the Commons to deal adequately with a heavy burden of office work also, some went one way, some the other. The position of one stream steadily approximated to that of the ministers, so that on a change of government, they were the lowest office-holders to go. The position of the remainder, on the other hand, drew gradually closer to that of the officials, so that on a change of government, they were the most senior to keep their places. They were administrators of a new kind, as permanent as the clerks, yet competent to handle business at ministerial level. This development, though common to all departments, took a varied course in each.

Probably the War Office was the first department to have an official corresponding in function with the modern permanent secretary. There 'from 1755 the deputy Secretary at War did not resign with his chief but took his place as one of the developing group of *sous-ministres*. With Matthew Lewis, who was promoted from First Clerk to deputy in 1755 and who retained his post under seven successive Secretaries at War until he retired in 1803, the development of the post into that of permanent administrative head seems clear.'[81] The Post Office was not far behind. The dismissal of Henry Potts from the post of Secretary, his replacement by Anthony Todd, and reinstatement soon afterwards, showed that in the 1760s the

[80] P.P. 1731–1800, xl, 1st Report, 8–9.
[81] O. Gee, 'The British War Office in the later years of the American War of Independence', *Journal of Modern History*, xxvi (1954), 125.

office was still liable to change on political grounds. But from Todd's second tenure of the post (1768–98), it became permanent. The Board of Control had a permanent Assistant Secretary from its foundation in 1784. But the business there, both in the office and in parliament, was comparatively light, and the ministerial heads seem to have dealt with most of it. In consequence, the development of the Assistant Secretaryship appears to have been slow. Until 1853, it was always filled by promotion of a clerk who had spent his life in the office. The appointment of Sir Nicholas Redington in that year marked a new departure and a higher status for the post.

In the offices of the three Secretaries of State, there were six Under-Secretaries. As late as 1806, they were liable to change on a change of government, though those in the rank immediately below (the chief clerks) were by that time held to be permanent officers. Windham, the incoming Colonial Secretary, considered the status accorded to one of his underlings as 'extra chief clerk' no more than a pretext to make his position in the office more secure: 'He has been made to stand in the way of a second Under-Secretary which the state in the office required, and yet to keep the name of a clerk, so as to deprive the person coming to the head of the office, if this contrivance were yielded to, of his rights of nomination.'[82] On the formation of the 'Ministry of All the Talents' in that year, *The Times* published lists of the new government and the old. All six Under-Secretaryships were included in each list.[83] John Beckett, one of the men then appointed to the Home Office, remained until 1817 and should be reckoned the first of its permanent heads. At the Foreign Office, one of the 'old' Under-Secretaries, George Hammond, had considered himself permanent, but found to his chagrin that he was not. He was, however, reinstated the following year,[84] and from that time on, there has been a continuous sequence of permanent Under-Secretaries for Foreign Affairs. The case of the Colonial Office, which remained without a permanent head until 1825, will be considered below. One peculiarity of the offices of the Secretaries of State should be noted here. A *non-permanent* Under-Secretary was not, until well on in the nineteenth century, necessarily a *Parliamentary* Under-Secretary. Canning, indeed, thought it undesirable that they should be. In offering the post to an M.P., he wrote: 'the labour is very great, and it is daily and constant. It requires entire

[82] Young, 15.   [83] *The Times*, February 13, 1806.
[84] For George Hammond, see M. A. Anderson's study of his son: 'Edmund Hammond, Permanent Under-Secretary for Foreign Affairs, 1854–1873' (Ph.D. thesis, London University, 1956).

devotion to it. I think parliament is wholly incompatible with the due discharge of the duty.'[85] As late as 1847–48, the Home Office had a non-permanent, non-Parliamentary Under-Secretary, Sir Denis Le Marchant.

The situation at the Admiralty remained uncertain as late as 1830. The posts of Secretary and Assistant Secretary had long been held by men with expert technical knowledge, and though they often sat in parliament, in the eighteenth century not one went out on a change of ministers. Croker's career was typical. He first gained a seat in parliament in 1807 and obtained the Secretaryship in 1809; he retained both till 1830, serving under five Prime Ministers. The upheaval attendant on the formation of Canning's ministry in 1827, and of Wellington's in the following year, are rightly regarded as important stages in political development. Croker survived them. According to his own account, 'the Secretary was not looked upon as a political officer, did not change with ministries, and took no part in political debate'. When at last he did resign, he made it clear that he did not consider himself bound to do so by the change of government but was going of his own accord. To the new First Lord he wrote: 'As there never has been an instance of the Secretary of the Admiralty being removed on a change of Ministry, it cannot be improper, though it may be superfluous, to acquaint you . . . that it is my intention to resign that office.' He expressed himself more candidly to a friend: 'I suppose the new people would not have kept me, but I did not wait to know.'[86]

So Croker went while his colleague, Barrow, stayed. The latter recorded that the new First Sea Lord 'called on me at the Admiralty, at the particular request . . . of Lord Grey, to say that his Lordship earnestly hoped I had no intention of leaving my present situation'. Barrow replied: 'I have not the least desire to lead an inactive life . . . a Whig board or a Tory board . . . will be pretty much the same to me.' The new First Lord, Graham, came the next day. 'You will readily guess the purpose of this early visit,' he began. 'It is the anxiety I am under to prevail on you to remain in your present official situation; and the fear I have that your long attachment to a different party from that to which I belong may induce you to take leave with the rest of your colleagues.' Barrow answered: 'I am neither rich nor reckless enough to become a party-man. . . . I will remain.'[87]

To use anachronistic terms, Croker decided to behave as Parlia-

[85] J. Bagot, *George Canning and his Friends* (1909), i, 242.
[86] L. J. Jennings (ed.), *The Croker Papers* (1884), i, 81: ii, 74–5 and 79.
[87] Sir J. Barrow, *An Auto-Biographical Memoir* (1847), 406, 7 and 8.

mentary Secretary, while Barrow saw his role as Permanent Secretary. It is true that the former sat in the Commons while the latter did not. But this did not mean that one was a politician and the other a civil servant. The young Disraeli regarded them as politicians of the same stamp.[88] The idea of having two such functionaries in each department, one subject to change whenever government changes, the other likely to continue until retiring age, was only just taking shape in 1830. Croker had held his office for twenty-one years under a succession of governments. Barrow, on the other hand, had had the unpleasant experience of being evicted from his post in 1806, when the 'Ministry of All the Talents' came in.

THE CASE OF THE TREASURY

The Treasury got its first permanent secretary—the absence of capitals is deliberate—in 1805. The appointment illustrates two of the main factors in administrative development—the increasing bulk of business and the growing pressure of political life. Until the last decades of the eighteenth century, the amount of work transacted in public offices was so small that virtually no decisions needed to be taken below the rank of Under-Secretary. The responsibilities of those below that rank were restricted to clerical work of a mechanical kind—bookkeeping, copying, producing papers and filing them away again. Thereafter, the amount of business rose until it reached the point where this concentration of decision-making was no longer possible. The expansion of population and wealth, industrialization, the wars with America and France, the political and social unrest— all brought more work in their train.

Throughout the eighteenth century, the Secretaries to the Treasury had exercised the usual combination of political and administrative functions. At some periods, and in some holders of the office, the parliamentary character predominated; in other cases, the permanent aspect was more noticeable. After the Restoration, the Secretary 'was regularly a Member of the House of Commons, where he was expected to assist in the transaction of financial and general government business. Between 1660 and 1695 the Secretary had to attain to a degree of political importance before his appointment. In 1695, however, under very unusual circumstances, an administrative figure [William Lowndes] was made Secretary and a safe seat was found for him. The one appointment does not invalidate

[88] W. F. Moneypenny and G. E. Buckle, *Life of Benjamin Disraeli* (1929 e.), i, 76.

the general rule that a Secretary's political duties were considered at least as important as his administrative ones. Until . . . 1679 this meant that each Secretary was dismissed on the appointment of a new Treasurer. After 1679 the Secretary was retained in most cases—1689 was an exception—and he began to keep his place for life. The shift made for much great continuity in the office. Thus between 1660 and 1679 there were four Secretaries. Four other Secretaries, however, span the period between 1679 and 1752.' From 1711, when it became normal to have two Secretaries, until 1758, one was permanent while the other resigned with his patron the First Lord. Between 1758 and 1782, although there was no clear convention, 'there was an increasing tendency for both Secretaries to resign when there was a change in the cabinet.'[89] The tendency became a settled rule after 1782.

The reason for the change lay in the increased importance of the parliamentary duties of the office. John Scrope, in the first half of the eighteenth century, was a politician behind the scenes but had the reputation in the House of one who 'seldom or never spoke but to facts, and when he was clear on his point.'[90] As late as 1827, J. C. Herries professed to regard the office in a similarly non-political light: 'I am pursuing my own laborious vocation,' he wrote, 'I am not in the following of any party. My business is with the public interests and my duty, to promote the King's service wherever I am employed.'[91] Such an attitude was anachronistic by that date, for the office had become deeply involved in party warfare. John Robinson, who held it from 1770 to 1782, had been mainly responsible for developing its parliamentary role in three important respects: the distribution of patronage, the management of elections and the discipline of government supporters in the Commons. In 1804 the duties were permanently divided into financial and non-financial, with one Secretary in charge of each. The two posts came to be known as the Financial and Parliamentary Secretaryships respectively. Holders of the latter, continuing the work of Robinson, were obviously politicians rather than administrators. The revival of party politics made the Financial Secretaries primarily politicians also, as it rendered every petty estimate liable to attack in the Commons, and hence in need of defence there.

[89] S. B. Baxter, *Development of the Treasury, 1660–1702* (1957), 173–4. D. M. Clark, 'The Office of Secretary to the Treasury in the Eighteenth Century', *American Historical Review*, xlii (1936–7), 30.   [90] ibid., 38.

[91] A. Aspinall (ed.), *Letters of King George IV, 1812–1830* (Cambridge, 1938), iii, 200.

To take some of the work off the Secretaries, the new office of Assistant (i.e. Permanent) Secretary was created in 1805. The Minute appointing its first holder, George Harrison, specifically cited the bulk of business as the reason for the new post. Papers registered—less than 1,000 a year in 1767—had increased from 3,683 in 1795 to 6,186 in 1804. Comparing the period, 1 January–10 August 1805, with the corresponding period in the previous year, there had been a further increase of 779—4,164 as against 3,335.[92] In form the old mode of conducting business, through a board whose members sat in parliament, persisted. But behind the façade there soon arose a new pattern in which the Assistant Secretary held the key position. For example, when Palmerston pleaded 'inexperience in the details of matters of finance' as a reason for not taking the Chancellorship of the Exchequer in 1809, Spencer Perceval replied that 'in the office Harrison and his own secretary would be able to afford me great assistance'.[93] By 1815 the number of registered papers had further risen to 19,761 a year. A Treasury Minute of that date, authorizing a special grant to Harrison, 'upon whom . . . so much of the detail of the conduct of the business was devolved', stated that he had been employed 'in a variety of business, arising out of the arduous contest in which this country has been engaged, of a most important and confidential nature, and which could not without great inconvenience have been placed in the hands of any other person than *a permanent officer* in constant attendance, as it required the greatest readiness and despatch, and frequently the most immediate execution.'[94] By 1827, a member of the Treasury Board could write: 'The great mass of Treasury business is now in the hands of its clerks. Over these the Lords have a nominal control.'[95]

THE BOARD OF TRADE AND THE COLONIAL OFFICE

Increasing complexity of business as a factor in administrative development may be illustrated from the Board of Trade. The Board was, of course, a committee of the Privy Council, the clerks of which had formally acted for the Board *ex officio*. But patronage gave the clerkships to two well-born incompetents who found the Board of Trade beyond them, with the result that Thomas Lack, a clerk who had worked in the office since boyhood, 'was made Assistant Secretary and did the work'. This answered well enough

---

[92] Copy in Disraeli Papers, B VII/7a. [93] Bulwer, i, 91.
[94] Disraeli Papers, B VII/7a. My italics.
[95] C. R. Fay, *Huskisson and his Age* (1951), 71.

until Huskisson became President, with large ideas for liberalizing trade. He found Lack inadequate to the new work and relied instead on James Deacon Hume, who was then in the Customs. Huskisson and Hume 'made the business a science. . . . It is [Hume] who advises, directs, legislates. . . . He is one of the ablest practical men who has ever served, more like an American statesman than an English official'. One of Huskisson's successors, Vesey Fitzgerald, regularized the position by making Hume joint permanent secretary with Lack. Fitzgerald told Greville that it 'was absolutely necessary as nobody in the office knew anything of its business'. Greville could easily believe this and went on: 'Hume is a very clever man, and probably knows more of the principles of trade and commerce than anybody, but so it is in every department of government—great ignorance on the part of the chiefs, and a few obscure men of industry and ability who do the business and supply the knowledge requisite.'[96]

The administrative development of the Colonial Office in the 1820s brings out the role of all three factors discussed: increasing bulk of business; its increasing complexity; and the growing pressure of political life. Henry Goulburn was Under-Secretary until 1821. He handled all the administrative work above the clerical level besides representing the department in the Commons. (His chief, Bathurst, was in the Lords.) Growing pressure in parliament, coupled with increasing departmental business, was making it difficult for him to maintain the balance, and might have made it impossible had he stayed longer. Certainly his successor, Sir Robert Wilmot Horton, lacking his experience, could not hope to emulate him. The business of the office was even more forbidding in its complexity than in its bulk. 'There was no limit to the variety of issues on which the Secretary of State made decisions. He was consulted on the building and administration of jails, schools, churches, universities, hospitals, roads, canals, botanical gardens, defence works and barracks. He was responsible for regulations governing health, marriage, missionaries, race relations, slavery, land alienation, land use, newspapers, ship-building and shipping. He encouraged exploration and assessed the significance of geographical discoveries; he watched over currency and banking. He had to keep in mind the interests and susceptibilities of Christians, Moslems, Jews and animists. Law codes derived from British, Italian, Greek, French, Spanish, Portuguese and Dutch systems, and in many cases influenced by indigenous customary law, had to be

[96] L. Strachey and R. Fulford (eds.), *The Greville Memoirs, 1814–1860* (1938), i, 306 and n., 350: ii, 48 and 84.

amended. Moreover, general policy applicable to a number of colonies had to be fitted into the context of each individual social and legal system.'[97] Faced with this situation, Wilmot Horton concentrated on his duties in the House of Commons—the one thing he could not delegate—while devolving more responsibility on to the clerks, and drawing them into the policy-making process. The legal adviser, James Stephen, became a full-time member of the staff and came to play an important part in the general, as well as in the legal, work. Finally, in 1825, came the appointment of the first permanent Under-Secretary, R. W. Hay.

CONSTITUTIONAL BUREAUCRACY

To his own question, 'What are the basic elements of constitutional monarchy?' Namier replied that one of the essentials is 'an unpolitical civil service whose primary connexion is with the Crown, and which, while subordinated to party governments, is unaffected by their changes: the two permanent elements, the Crown and the civil service, which not by chance together left the political arena, supply the framework for the free play of parliamentary politics and governments'.[98] The departure of the Crown and the civil service from the political arena began about 1780. If the process was not complete by 1830, it had gone so far as to have become irreversible. The civil service had become a distinct entity, at the service of each successive cabinet. Ministers found themselves obliged by the bulk and complexity of departmental business, and by parliamentary pressure, to devolve much of their administrative responsibility. They also renounced any serious hope of long periods of office for themselves, accepting the idea of a political career as one in which spells of office would alternate with spells of opposition. The continuity which ministers no longer provided was supplied by a new group of senior officials, the permanent secretaries. They were at the head of an administrative machine manned by officers who can be styled, without anachronism, permanent civil servants. They were civil servants as distinct from political servants of the Crown—a distinction not yet drawn in 1780. In withdrawing from politics they became permanent; not liable to have their careers interrupted by ministerial or parliamentary crises. As the monarchy rose above party, so the civil service settled below party. Constitutional bureaucracy was the counterpart of constitutional monarchy.

[97] Young, 260.   [98] Namier (1955), 14.

CHAPTER II

THE DECLINE OF PATRONAGE

*'I suppose Prince you have not got a job going at this palace for
my friend asked the earl you see I am rubbing him up in socierty
ways and he fancies court life as a professhion.*

Oh dose he said the prince blinking his eyes well I might see.

*I suggested if there was a vacency going he might try cantering
after the royal barouche said the earl.*

*So he might said the prince I will speak to the prime Minister
about it and let you know.'*

Daisy Ashford

The establishment of permanence might seem to imply the end of
patronage. If a civil servant was to keep his job when a new party
came to power, he must be non-partisan. Yet how could his new
minister trust him to be so, if he was known to have been the choice
of a minister of another party? Yet patronage did survive, and the
question is, why? 1830 showed that it could no longer bring a
government victory in a general election. 'Patronage did not prevent
the Whig electoral strength from crumbling after 1832; the absence
of it did not keep the Conservatives from the triumph of 1841.'[1] But
the decline of the old system was long and slow.

> They thought it dying when it slept
> And sleeping when it died.

The exact moment of its death is not important, since there was
clearly an overlap with the rise of patronage in the modern sense.[2]
What is important is that neither the Northcote-Trevelyan report,
nor the setting-up of the Civil Service Commission (1855), nor the
introduction of Open Competition (1870) killed it.

On the eve of open competition, Gladstone's Treasury henchman,
G. C. Glyn, put up a plea for the old order. 'My position in the
Treasury as "Patronage Secretary" is gone and . . . I lose, without
notice and at once, the great advantage of the daily correspondence

[1] N. Gash, *Politics in the Age of Peel* (1953), 372.
[2] P. G. Richards, *Patronage in British Government* (1963).

and communication with members of the party which the ordinary dispensing of the Treasury patronage gave me, to say nothing of the power which it placed in my hands.' He had heard that although open competition was to be introduced into the Treasury and its dependencies at once, it was not to be enforced generally on all departments. He realized that it was too late to reverse the policy, but he did 'venture to ask that the scheme may be made general before the Treasury patronage goes. I submit that the Treasury patronage is the continuous stream, diminished though it is by the necessary reduction in establishments, and it alone is organized and distributed *upon a system* . . . is it too much to hope that you will save "my fall" by requiring the new system to be *generally* and not *partially* agreed to before its operation is tried upon the Treasury?' Of course, the new system was bound to lower the status of the office Glyn held, and it is easy to understand his reaction. What is significant is that he did not contend that the decline of patronage would weaken the party. 'The advantage or otherwise to the party' was 'very debatable ground' and he did not wish to enter into it.[3]

Glyn was slow to reconcile himself to the new situation. In the following year he complained that 'having nothing to give makes my task very hard—in [the] old days the men voted, and the men stayed, and looked for their reward—now it must be all done when there is not strong pressure from the constituencies by personal entreaty and work'.[4] Glyn exaggerated: the Treasury still had a good deal to give, and the Conservatives, on their return to office in 1874, set themselves to exploit it to the full. In 1877 Disraeli personally appointed a new Assistant Director of Kew Gardens, in order to show the officials in the Treasury that he was still the First Lord. At the same time he sent round an instruction that he must for the future be consulted about filling any vacancy in his gift. In 1878, Disraeli's patronage secretary strengthened his hand by directing that all proposals by departments other than the Treasury for the abolition, reduction or reorganization of an office should be sent to him before receiving Treasury sanction so that he could keep abreast of new developments. Disraeli regarded posts to which there was no recognized ladder of promotion as political prizes which might be bestowed on his followers. The effect may be seen by taking a sample of twenty important offices and comparing the number of political appointees

---

[3] E. Hughes, 'Postscript to the Civil Service Reforms of 1855', *Public Administration*, xxxiii (1955), 306.

[4] q. H. J. Hanham, 'Political Patronage at the Treasury, 1870–1912', *Historical Journal*, iii (1960), on which the following paragraphs are based.

among those who held them in 1869 with the proportion nominated during the two succeeding decades. In 1869 there were eleven political nominees among the twenty; seven former M.P.s and four protégés of former ministers. Of seventeen appointments during the '70s, Gladstone was responsible for five, including only one of a political character. Of Disraeli's twelve appointments, on the other hand, only two went to serving officials as against ten for political services.

In the next decade, however, promotions of administrators predominated over political appointments, irrespective of which party was in power. Of the twenty appointments made during the '80s, only five had anything of a political character. As an off-set against this trend, the Receiverships in Bankruptcy established by Joseph Chamberlain from 1882 onwards were given by him to active politicians, and came to be regarded as political prizes. Vacancies in the Factory Inspectorate were often filled after consultation with party managers, and party stalwarts might become Registrars of Births, Marriages and Deaths. In 1885, there still remained more than 20,000 posts in the gift of the Patronage Secretary, the great majority of them lowly paid sub-postmasterships, but also posts in the Customs, the National Galleries, the Revenue Boards and the Treasury itself.

An interesting demonstration of the way in which politics might enter into the choice of a local postmaster occurred in 1877. A vacancy occurred at Winslow, Buckinghamshire, within the sphere of the three county members, two of them Conservative, one Liberal. The Conservative Patronage Secretary offered the nomination to one of the Conservatives, the Hon. T. F. Fremantle, who lived near Winslow. A well-qualified Liberal candidate was already available in the person of the assistant postmaster, but as there had been complaints about the quality of the service at the post office his claims were by no means overwhelming. Fremantle therefore looked round for a Conservative candidate more likely to give a dependable service. When this became known the Liberal assistant postmaster wrote to Fremantle offering to vote Conservative in future if he were appointed. Fremantle, however, selected another candidate, and then wrote to the assistant postmaster saying that the man of his choice had proved his dependability by voting Conservative in the past.[5]

In 1887, the Irish Post Office patronage was transferred from the Treasury to the Postmaster General, and the English and Scottish

[5] ibid., 82.

followed in 1895. Until 1907, however, the Postmaster General was in the habit of receiving 'recommendations' from Members. The practice was finally brought to an end by Sydney Buxton as a result of the enormous increase in the number of nominations sent in by Liberal M.P.s following the general election of 1906—from sixty or seventy a month to three or four hundred.

Finally, in 1912, following a condemnation of recruitment by patronage from a committee which had been investigating Customs administration, the Patronage Secretary announced that he had transferred his remaining patronage to the departments. 'Members who are inundated with applications for these appointments will be glad to know that, with the approval of the Prime Minister, I am taking steps to waive, in the public interest, the patronage attached to my office, and to transfer the work to suitable permanent officials directly in touch with the requirements of the service.'[6] The proposed transfer was complete by the end of the year.

But long before patronage came to an end, great changes had taken place within the institution. Ministers had evolved higher standards, which were largely observed. Even Northcote and Trevelyan had conceded that civil servants were 'much better than we have any right to expect from the system under which they are appointed.'[7] In order to appreciate the significance of this evolution, some indication must be given of the spirit in which the old system functioned.

LOOKING AFTER KINSMEN

First of all, patronage exercised in favour of kinsfolk. Every minister had to count on finding at frequent intervals in his postbag letters like the following.

Mrs Cecilia Blackwood to Lord John Russell

3 Albert Terrace,
Regent's Park.
October 24 1849

If I had not been seriously indisposed I should sooner have written to thank you most warmly for having so kindly granted me an interview last month. On going over that interview in my mind, every word of which was of so much importance to me, I recollect

---

[6] ibid., 83.

[7] Northcote-Trevelyan report. Conveniently reprinted by the Fulton Committee: Cmnd. 3638. *The Civil Service.* v. 1 *Report of the Committee, 1966–8.* The quotation is at p. 109.

that you said 'I suppose the Audit Office would not do for him?' in a manner as if, had I been willing, you could have promised something in that quarter, and I mentioned my wish first to consult Mr Blackwood. Now that I am recovered, I write to say that, grateful as I am for your kindness . . . I am reluctant to accept an office of so low a grade because experience teaches that when once a petitioner is given the smallest mite he is dismissed from the mind of the benefactor as being off his hands. On the other hand, I am loth to refuse it as I know many of as good family as my son are content therewith, but I am more inclined to fix my faith on your kind and repeated assurance of "I will not forget him". You may ask now, as you might have asked when I had the pleasure of seeing you, what right have I to expect anything at your hands? None except that of distant relationship. A drowning man catches at a straw but I look upon it as a very substantial straw, you being not only the greatest man in England but the most powerful man in the world (for I look upon one who wields the destinies of this vast empire as such) and when I reflect that your mother and my father were first cousins, I hope to come within the warmth of your rays. We now propose sending my son to Cambridge—an expense we are ill able to meet and hoped to have been spared by entering him at once into his profession for life, but he will be able to perfect his education and in the meantime I shall live in the hope that he may at sometime, if not immediately, be placed by you in some suitable situation.'[8]

On assuming office in 1830, Grey was at once bombarded with claims based on kinship. Lord Carlisle wrote to ask for a seat at one of the Revenue Boards for his brother, who was in the House of Commons, and for preferment for another brother, who was a clergyman. He added: 'You will be glad that I have no more brothers to mention.'[9] Haddington suggested Hamilton to succeed Barrow as Second (i.e. Permanent) Secretary of the Admiralty when Barrow retired in 1845. But he seems to have been slightly ashamed to admit that Hamilton was related to him, since he only mentioned the fact in the third letter he wrote to Peel on the subject. Moreover, he somewhat ingenuously referred Peel to Aberdeen for a second opinion, to which Peel rather acidly replied: 'As Captain Hamilton married the step-daughter of Aberdeen, and as Aberdeen is hardly qualified to form a judgment on the question whether a civilian or naval officer be, in principle, best suited for the permanent secretary-ship of the Admiralty, I do not think there . . . there would be much

[8] PRO 30/22/8.
[9] Grey Papers: 2nd Earl. Carlisle to Grey, November 30, 1830.

advantage in a reference to Aberdeen.'[10] Sometimes an element of horse-trading was involved. In 1848, Earl Grey, as Secretary of State for the Colonies and War, wanted to help his nephew, but sought to do so in a roundabout way. He wrote to Russell, as First Lord of the Treasury: 'My sister, Lady Caroline Barrington, has applied to you for a clerkship in the Treasury for her son, who is just taking his degree at Cambridge . . . There is now a clerkship vacant in this office which would do quite as well . . . but I do not like to give it to him because I am introducing here the War Office rule that clerks are to be appointed at first only on trial and not to be confirmed until there is a regular written report from the senior under whom they are put and also from the Permanent Under-Secretary of State that they have shown such intelligence and industry as are likely to make them fit for the higher employment of senior clerks when they rise to that rank in the office. It would, I think, be very disagreeable to all parties that one of the first reports of this kind which were made to me should be about a person so nearly related to me."[11] He suggested, therefore, that Russell should put Charles Barrington in the Treasury, while he (Grey) would take Russell's nominee for the first vacancy in the Colonial Office.

Some applications provide support for Trevelyan's assertion that 'it is at present a common practice to place young men in public offices because they are intellectually or corporally unfit for other professions.'[12] For example, Bessborough wrote to Russell: 'Will you forgive me for troubling you about my brother, Gerald? He has been now two years and a half with Clarendon and I could not wish him better placed if I was not obliged to look to the possibility of a change of government, in which case he would be without any profession whatever. He is now near twenty-one and I do not think it right not to endeavour to get him into some public office *which is the only profession open to him.*'[13]

When a seat at the Excise Board fell vacant in 1858, Disraeli proposed that his brother, James, should fill it. (Six years earlier he had got him a post as County Court Treasurer.) Derby evidently felt some misgivings. 'I . . . appeal to you confidently, but also most confidentially, for your candid opinion whether your brother is fully equal to the duties of such an office. Should you answer in the affirmative, I will with pleasure submit his name to the Queen.'

[10] For the correspondence on this, see B.M. Add. MSS. 40557–8.
[11] PRO 30/22/7/4. Grey to Russell, January 25, 1848.
[12] Disraeli Papers. B/IV/C/13C. Trevelyan to Disraeli, December 2, 1852.
[13] PRO 30/22/8. Bessborough to Russell, January 2, 1850. (My italics.)

Disraeli read between the lines what he was presumably intended to read. 'I have no doubt,' he replied, 'that the individual in question is thoroughly competent, and that his appointment would ultimately reflect credit on your choice; but I nevertheless think at his moment the appointment would be injudicious. . . . I am sorry for the individual immediately concerned, . . . but if we succeed in our great enterprise you will, I doubt not, have opportunities of . . . not altogether forgetting [his] sacrifice.'[14] A few months later, Disraeli tried again. He put forward his brother to succeed Charles Greville, the celebrated diarist, as Clerk of the Privy Council. Lord Salisbury, as Lord President of the Council, regretted that he could not do as Disraeli wished: 'I must consider a little my own concerns. This is the only place which I am likely to have to give. I certainly have looked on the possibility of my son, Robert,[15] making some figure in the political world but our reform will . . . deprive him of his seat at Stamford and I fear that he is not sufficiently distinguished to render it likely that he would be chosen as the representative of a more popular constituency. Under these circumstances, I must look to the possibility of retaining him in a position of independence. Had he been fortunate enough to have been in office and thus had become known, I think his abilities would have justified him in persisting in seeking political distinction, but his chance would be lost with his seat and I should, if the opportunity occurs fairly and in the normal course of things, wish to put him in Greville's place.'[16]

A further aspect of family and patronage was that relatives of public men were the target for similar pressures. No sooner had Disraeli taken office for the first time, than his sister was writing: 'I had to grant perpetual audiences yesterday to people who want something. First came my little postman to ask me to put him on the town district; he did not ask me for my interest, but requested me at once to transfer him. I noticed he spoke with a very tremulous voice, which impressed me strongly with a sense of my extraordinary powers. Then came . . . a letter from a lady who wants a place for her husband.'[17]

DEPENDANTS BEYOND THE FAMILY

Patronage was also sought on behalf of dependants outside the

14 Moneypenny and Buckle, i, 1582–3.
15 Later 3rd Marquis of Salisbury and Prime Minister.
16 Disraeli Papers MC: Salisbury to Disraeli, December 23, 1858.
17 Moneypenny and Buckle, i, 1163.

family circle. This, of course, was a venerable tradition. In 1762, a correspondent wished Bute 'to bestow some little employment of fifty or sixty pounds a year upon Bowley, who has served me upwards of thirty years, with great integrity.' The reason was stated quite bluntly: 'My own situation does not afford me the means of making any provision for this old servant.'[18] In a similar spirit, Melbourne asked Grey for the post of Keeper of the Records in the Augmentation Office for his private secretary, Tom Young. In this, he was unsuccessful, but renewed the attack two years later: 'I am very anxious that something of a permanent and advantageous nature should be done for my private secretary, Mr Young.'[19] Following Lord Auckland's death in 1849, members of his family tried to get his personal servant a billet as a messenger.[20] The Duchess of Buccleuch wanted a clerkship for her maid's cousin, adding: 'I am anxious to oblige my maid, as she has been with me nearly twenty-three years.'[21]

Disraeli's success in placing an old servant of his father's deserves to be told at greater length. The protégé was a Venetian named Giovanni Battista Falcieri. In his youth he had been Byron's gondolier, became his devoted personal servant and was with him at Missolonghi when he died. He figures in *Don Juan*:

> Battista, though (a name call'd shortly Tita)
> Was lost by getting at some aqua-vita

and in a letter of Shelley's: 'Tita, the Venetian, is here, and operates as my valet—a fine fellow with a prodigious black beard who has stabbed two or three people, and is the most good-natured looking fellow I ever saw.' Disraeli's friend, James Clay, picked up Tita in Malta in 1830. The Venetian went with them on their subsequent Middle Eastern tour. When they returned to England, Disraeli introduced Tita into his father's service, where he remained until the latter's death in 1848. What was to become of him, Disraeli then asked himself. 'It was dreadful to think that a man who had been in Byron's service, and soothed his last moments, who had been the faithful attendant and almost the companion and friend of my father, for so many years, who had actually died in his arms, should end his days in the usual refuge for domestic servants, by keeping a public-house, or a greengrocer's shop.' Through Hobhouse, Disraeli got

---

[18] Jucker, 41.   [19] Grey Papers: 2nd Earl. 41/2/70 and 130.
[20] PRO 30/22/7. Members of the Eden family to Russell, January 8 and 23, 1849.
[21] PRO 30/22/8. Duchess of Buccleuch to Russell, November 18, 1850.

Tita a place as a messenger in the Board of Control. The link was, of course, Byron, not politics: Disraeli was in opposition while Hobhouse was a member of the Whig government. 'Another crisis occurred when the Board of Control was abolished, and Tita was liable to be dismissed, on a small pension; but fortunately we were then in power, and Stanley was head of the India Office ... The result was that Tita was appointed chief messenger at the new India Office ... without the liability of having to carry messages.'[22]

SONS OF SERVING OFFICIALS

Existing civil servants were a special class of dependants whose claims politicians recognized. Spring Rice, in asking Melbourne for church preferment for the son of a Treasury official said: 'I need not point out to you the very great importance of giving every fair encouragement to those excellent officers who are at the head of great departments and upon whose zeal ... so much depends.'[23] A former permanent secretary to the Treasury, Spearman, was 'very anxious to get his son into the Treasury'. The Chancellor of the Exchequer for the time being reported to the Prime Minister: 'I told him that as you had out of two appointments given one to a Treasury official, it was unreasonable to ask you to appoint his son now.' But how about putting him into the Audit Office? 'You know his [Spearman's] merits as well as I do and he has been working very hard on the customs commission. So I should be glad if you can do this for him.'[24] As it turned out, Spearman junior did eventually get into the Treasury. His father wrote to thank Russell; his gratitude was all the greater as 'I have no personal claim whatever upon you, and no claim indeed of any kind, beyond that which you have been good enough to allow to long and faithful service.'[25] This kind of claim was of great importance to civil servants. At least one admitted that it was the main reason why he accepted the offer of a post himself. 'The principal inducement that weighs in my mind is the *connexion* which public offers, and may be a means of pushing out five boys (and perhaps more hereafter).'[26]

[22] Moneypenny and Buckle, i, 388.
[23] Melbourne Papers: 13. Spring-Rice to Melbourne, October 4, 1839.
[24] PRO 30/22/8. Wood to Russell, January 6, 1850.
[25] PRO 30/22/9. Spearman to Russell, February 26, 1851.
[26] Day to Chadwick, November 22, 1835: q. R. A. Lewis, 'William Day and the Poor Law Commissioners', *University of Birmingham Historical Journal*, ix (1964), 166.

POLITICAL PATRONAGE

From the present point of view, however, patronage for political purposes is more important than that which was bestowed for reasons of family or because of an acknowledged client–patron relationship. The following letter, addressed by Albany de Fonblanque, the Liberal journalist, to Lord John Russell will serve as an example of the kind of claim party leaders had to expect from their followers. Fonblanque already had a post, but he was far from satisfied, either on his own behalf or on that of his son. 'When I accepted the office I now hold in the Statistical Department of the Board of Trade, it was upon the assurance that your kind intentions on my behalf would not be fulfilled by placing me in an office of such small emolument and distasteful duties. Notwithstanding many changes, however, here I remain, apparently forgotten.

'A colonial appointment in a good climate would be the thing most desirable for me in my state of health, and, unless I am deceived, Lord Grey is aware of my wish, and at one time I had reason to think that his dispositions were favourable, but as yet I have been disappointed in that quarter.

'About three years ago, I mentioned to Mr Tufnell, then Secretary of the Treasury, that my son was shortly to leave the Charterhouse, and that it was my wish to obtain for him a clerkship in a government office. Mr Tufnell desired me to make a formal application (which I did) and promised to lay it before you. I have heard nothing more about the matter. Last spring I reminded him of what had passed, and he recommended me to communicate with Mr Hayter. I did so, and understood that he would mention the matter to you. Two clerkships have, since my application, been given to sons of literary men, but mine has not been so fortunate.

'It is not my intention to trouble you with solicitation, but I think it incumbent on me to bring these circumstances under your notice, that you may judge whether or not the treatment I have had is the treatment I have merited from the party of which you are the head.'[27]

Different considerations governed the exercise of patronage at the two levels indicated by Fonblanque. A post such as that he was seeking for his son had to be filled from outside the service. A senior position, on the other hand, might either be filled by promotion or else bestowed on an outsider. Even a junior vacancy might attract a flock of petitioners. For example, 'There is a prospect of a vacancy

[27] PRO 30/22/10/3. Fonblanque to Russell, January 15, 1852.

for a clerk in the Audit Office and Sir A. Spearman, Mr Standish, Fonblanque, Lord de Freyne and Lord Portman are all in the excitement of anticipation. Lord Fitzhardinge I have persuaded to wait till 1851.'[28]

Electioneering considerations were often urged. For example, a would-be Foreign Office messenger wrote to Palmerston: 'I would not have presumed to ask your Lordship this favour had not my friends and connexions always strongly supported the Liberal interest.' His request was supported in similar terms: 'His father, brothers and connexions are respectable and well-known liberals, having been always found among the foremost to support Lord John Russell and every other liberal candidate. My friend is well known to Capt. Buller and Mr Divett, with both of whom he has often canvassed. Should your Lordship be pleased to grant this request you will greatly oblige your sincere well-wisher and ardent supporter.' This application came from Devonshire, where Palmerston's constituency, Tiverton, was situated. But as a landowner in Hampshire and former M.P. for the southern division of that county, he was also expected to do something for Liberals there. A rumour that there would soon be a vacancy for a postmaster at Fordingbridge brought a request on behalf of a man 'who is a staunch supporter of the government and who took upon himself the chief labour in the registration of the last year for that district.' The writer realized that the post was not within Palmerston's gift but assumed that the Postmaster-General would 'undoubtedly attend to your recommendation.' Palmerston evidently thought it worth trying, for he endorsed the letter: 'Wrote to Lord Lichfield accordingly'.[29]

LOCAL PATRONS

It was not only the applicants for jobs who had to be considered. There were also party stalwarts in the constituencies whose dignity might be affronted if they were not consulted. When a post as Distributor of Stamps in Derbyshire fell vacant in 1858, Derby had a candidate in mind: Samuel Lucas, a Conservative journalist with some claims on the party. But, as he put it to Disraeli, 'we ought

[28] PRO 30/22/8. Tufnell to Russell, January 9, 1850.

[29] These three letters from the Palmerston Papers were found by taking correspondents with the initial 'C' in the year 1836 under the general heading patronage. There are many hundreds of a similar character in this collection alone. Lord Lichfield was Postmaster-General at the time.

hardly to make an appointment there without some communication with Lord Chesterfield, who contested the division for us at the last election. He is one of our steadiest supporters and has never asked for anything. . . . I will write today to Lord Chesterfield; and if he has no particular person to recommend I will give [it to] Lucas'.[30] In this case, the procedure was clear; when the local sub-patrons fell out, things became more difficult. This is what happened in Gloucestershire in 1846. 'Henry and Grantley Berkeley,' Clanricarde reported to Russell, 'have written to me desiring to have all the Post Office patronage in the county and town they represent; and saying that Fitzhardinge will not spend any money upon their elections in future, but intimating that they can, and will, return themselves. This seems an absurd idea. The Berkeley interest is a great family influence, which it is a pity should be lost to the Whigs, but I really am quite at a loss with whom to side if these brethren quarrel among themselves. I suppose the chief, a peer, is the one to adhere to, but then Henry and Grantley will be angry, and I should like to know what you think ought to be done.'[31] Fitzhardinge had already put his own view forward: 'Grantley has done very wrong in applying for any government patronage . . . without . . . consulting me. Nothing can be more . . . ruinous to an interest in this county than this acting at *cross purposes* and as the *whole* expense of my brothers' elections, registration, revision and etc. falls on *me alone* it is absolutely necessary that the distribution of such appointments as may come from the government should be made by my sanction.'[32]

As might be expected, the higher the post, the wider the interest whenever it fell vacant. It was desirable, but not always possible, to avoid publicity until the succession had been settled. Laurence Sulivan, Deputy Secretary at War, resigned in 1851. His chief wrote: 'Sulivan tells me that his departure is a matter of notoriety. I am vexed at this as I only received his resignation a few days since in direct terms, and I fear you may be exposed to solicitations on the subject.'[33] Solicitation could become so pressing as almost to amount to blackmail. Carlisle declined to serve on a commission to which Russell wished to appoint him but offered to 'do anything you wish' if a protégé got the job he wanted.[34] A remark in the annual report

[30] Disraeli Papers, MC. Derby to Disraeli, December 21 and 25, 1858.
[31] PRO 30/22/5C. Clanricarde to Russell, September 8, 1846.
[32] ibid. Fitzhardinge to Clanricarde, September 6, 1846.
[33] PRO 30/22/9. Fox Maule to Russell, August 8, 1851.
[34] PRO 30/22/8. Carlisle to Russell, August 24, 1850.

of Leonard Horner, the Factory Inspector, that it would probably be his last gave 'rise to an immense number of applications for his office'.[35] When Helps thought of resigning in 1865, his chief (he wrote) 'begged me to keep this wish of mine secret, knowing no doubt that he would only be pestered with applications for the place'.[36]

PATRONAGE AND PROMOTION

Politicians were not only expected to get jobs for their dependants in the first place, but to help them up the ladder of promotion also. Thus a Hampshire Customs officer wrote to Palmerston in 1836 to seek his aid in getting a higher post, being 'fully assured that when a dissolution of Parliament takes place, my friends at Lymington, Southampton and its environs will feel themselves greatly delighted in having the opportunity of returning your Lordhip's kindness.'[37] The writer did not seem to realize that Palmerston had transferred to another constituency—Tiverton—in 1835, which he continued to represent until his death! Palmerston could ignore such an applicant. But it would have been more difficult for Disraeli, in office for the first time, to take no notice when Spencer Walpole approached him in 1852: 'I hear that Mr Ireson, the Controller of the Legacy Duty Office, is a candidate for Mr Porter's place in the Board of Trade. A better person could not possibly be chosen, and if he should be chosen my brother wishes me to bring under your consideration his claims to promotion . . . he is Chief Clerk under Mr Ireson now.'[38] 'One of my sons, who is in the office of the Registrar General,' wrote Leigh Hunt to Russell, 'came to me yesterday and asked me if I had any objection to speak a word to your Lordship respecting a vacancy which has occurred among the senior clerkships of that office. He has been thirteen years on the establishment, has been promoted from the junior to the second class, and has a wife and four children to maintain on his £150 a year.

'My son ventured to suggest at the same time, like a proper brother (though not perhaps if he had a less kindly wisdom than your Lordship's to deal with, like a wise petitioner) that I might . . . [ask] a *double favour* by mentioning for the *junior* vacancy my youngest son, Vincent, who is still living at home, unemployed except by

[35] Palmerston Papers. Lewis to Palmerston, October 9, 1859.
[36] ibid. Helps to Palmerston, October 6, 1865.
[37] Palmerston Papers, Patronage/3. Cole to Palmerston, June 23, 1836.
[38] Disraeli Papers, MC. Walpole to Disraeli, September 8, 1852.

myself, and who is nearly twenty-seven years of age, and very anxious on all our accounts for some occupation more profitable. . . .

'I had indeed often thought that I was hardly doing my duty in abstaining from troubling your Lordship with the latter request, whatever delicacy it might become me to feel after your kindness to myself . . . But . . . having heard of some vacancies in the Mint, I had scarcely written to Mr Shiel to make a request of the like two-fold nature . . . when the appearance of my son with his request forced me thus hastily into the direction which I was trying to avoid.

P.S. Although I have one anti-Whig among my sons . . . the opinions of none of my other children have taken the same direction.'[39]

Long after the political importance of patronage had begun to decline, people continued to speak of it as if it were still powerful. 'The government patronage is habitually employed,' wrote Trevelyan, 'in influencing, or according to a stricter morality, corrupting representatives and electors at the expense both of their independence and of the public interests.'[40] Hence, any proposed reform was liable to attack if it involved increases in establishment. The proposal that the Registrar General should appoint local officers under the Registration Act, 1836, was attacked on the grounds that it would distribute 'through the Unions a strong battalion of Whig attorneys to act as party agents at the public expense'.[41] Graham was worried about the 'possibly corrupting effect' of transferring the Indian patronage to the Crown, when it was proposed that the East India Company should be wound up in 1858. 'This difficulty respecting patronage has stood in the way of the transfer for the last half century,' he wrote.[42] This was the standard reaction. Disraeli's voice was very untypical when he said in 1847—perhaps with his tongue in his cheek—'I have always believed that the power of the Crown has diminished, is diminishing, and ought to be increased; and, therefore, any increase in the patronage of the Crown is a proposition I would never oppose'.[43] The value of patronage had to be weighed ✓ against plans for economy and efficiency. Many would have agreed with Palmerston's proposition: 'I do not think that a desire to retain patronage *ought* to stand in the way of an administrative reform

[39] PRO 30/22/8/30. Leigh Hunt to Russell, April 22, 1850.
[40] E. Hughes, 'Sir Charles Trevelyan and Civil Service Reform, 1853–5', *English Historical Review*, lxiv (1949), 68.
[41] Ellenborough to Chadwick, October 27, 1841. q. Finer, 126.
[42] Parker (1907), ii, 356.
[43] Moneypenny and Buckle, i, 834.

which would save any sum worth having.'[44] But realists understood that it was not always possible to live up to such lofty principles. After arguing that the Commissioners of Customs were unnecessary, an anonymous correspondent of Disraeli's went on to recognize that 'it may [be] and no doubt often is beneficial to the public interests that a government should have the means of conferring appointments on faithful political friends, [and] it [may] be deemed expedient therefore on political grounds to retain the Board'.[45]

PATRONAGE AND PARTY LOYALTY

After patronage had ceased to be of much use in influencing the electorate at large, the champions of the old system still argued that party claims should be heard in order to maintain party loyalty. In 1850, Russell was on the point of filling a vacant joint permanent secretaryship at the Board of Trade. 'I should not be in a hurry', Ellice advised him, 'in giving Le Marchant's place . . . to [Booth] . . . He may be a fit person—but you have also those . . . who are equally fit; and you should recollect that this is one of the few offices for life at your disposal; and a great opportunity of providing, with . . . justice to the public, and care for the due performance of the public service, for some of your attached and faithful followers. I do not want you . . . to job—but men . . . who serve us well and faithfully should feel that we have their welfare equally at heart.'[46] Party leaders ignored this feeling at their peril, and had to gratify it from time to time. There was nothing uniquely Whiggish in this view. A few years later Disraeli was writing to Pakington: 'There is a great error on the part of some of my colleagues on the subject of patronage. They are too apt to deem the preferment at their disposal to be merely a personal privilege. In my opinion, it partakes of a corporate character. No doubt the head of a department should exercise a chief and general control over the distribution of its patronage; but there should be habitual communication on this head with his colleagues; and especially those who are charged with the management of the House of Commons, never a light task, doubly difficult when the administration is carried on in the teeth of a majority. The spirit of the party in the country depends greatly on the distribution of patronage: none can be more aware of this than

[44] BM Add. MS. 48581. Palmerston to Gladstone, December 19, 1859. (My italics.)

[45] Disraeli Papers. B/IX/B/19.

[46] PRO 30/22/8. Ellice to Russell, September 3, 1850.

Lord Derby and myself. The whole patronage of the Treasury is devoted to public purposes—one of its chief Secretaries is known by the title of the Patronage Secretary—but . . . [it] is not enough for the government to rest upon, and subsidiary aid is required from the other chief departments. There is nothing more ruinous to political connexion than the fear of justly rewarding your friends, and the promotion of ordinary men of opposite opinions in preference to qualified adherents. It is not becoming in any minister to decry party who has risen by party. We should always remember that, if we were not partisans, we should not be ministers.'[47]

EFFECTS ON CIVIL SERVICE MORALE

But the price to pay for keeping up the morale of the party was a fall in that of the civil service. 'The public will not be served as it ought to be, until, as your Lordship remarks, the permanent servants are brought under the stimulating influence of administrative rewards. This might, I think, be accomplished without difficulty and without any additional expense, but it would be a further interference with patronage. The revenue boards, the Audit Board and other permanent situations of that class would afford ample means of rewarding those who distinguish themselves by zeal and ability, if instead of being almost systematically bestowed from personal or political motives, these offices were conferred on the most highly qualified persons selected for the purpose from the whole public service. The work would be better done, and new life would be given to the whole body of public servants.'[48] An Admiralty official wrote in a similar vein: 'Your ablest permanent civil servants feel keenly the prizes of the service being given to merchants, barristers and others, who have no connection with the civil service.'[49]

When an outsider was brought in near the top of the ladder, resentment was not confined to the man in the office who would have been most likely to succeed to the post. It might extend right down to the base of the hierarchy. In 1849, George Butler expected to succeed Richard Byham as Secretary to the Board of Ordance. 'This expectation was justified by what I believe to have been the immemorial practice in the Ordnance Department, as exemplified at least in the cases of Mr Byham and his two predecessors, Mr Crew

[47] Disraeli to Pakington, December 19, 1858. q. Moneypenny and Buckle, i, 1657–8.
[48] PRO 30/22/8. Trevelyan to Russell, August 13, 1849.
[49] Disraeli Papers: GC. Bromley to Disraeli, June 16, 1855.

and Mr Griffin, whom the Master-General at the time, on the recommendation of the Board, immediately appointed to the situation of Secretary from that of Chief Clerk as the vacancy occurred ... It was not on my own account alone, but also as an encouragement to the fair and legitimate hope of promotion to which the other gentlemen of the Office naturally look in the event of my elevation —an elevation which I covet far more for the honourable distinction it would bring with it than for any accompanying pecuniary advantage.'[50]

PARTY AFFILIATIONS OF CIVIL SERVANTS

A further consequence of patronage was to retard the development of a non-partisan civil service. If ministers could not count on permanent civil servants to be neutral between parties, the next best thing would be to ensure that their own party was well represented among the officials. Howick put this point of view to Melbourne in 1835: 'Now I am sure you will agree with me in thinking that nothing can so much contribute to the influence of our opinions upon the future policy of the country, as the introduction into the more important offices which are usually held independently of change of administration, of persons whose views coincide with our own. You know how great a disadvantage it has been to the Liberal governments of the last five years their finding all the situations to which I allude filled by their opponents, and I think you ought *now* to take care that even a very short return of that party to power is not made the means of perpetuating that disadvantage'.[51] It was alleged that civil servants might fix their dates of retirement so as to favour the party which they supported. R. W. Hay, Permanent Under-Secretary at the Colonial Office, held 'from Sir Robert Peel's ministry the grant of a pension on which he may retire at will; and on which, I presume, he will retire whenever he can surrender his place to his own friends'.[52]

Years later the writer of those words expressed a very different view on the neutrality of civil servants.[53] 'All who have had experience of the manner in which the business of our great public departments is transacted, would, I am sure, concur with me in bearing witness, that it is a point of honour among the permanent members of these

[50] PRO 30/22/8. Butler to Anglesey, October 18, 1849.
[51] Melbourne Papers. Howick to Melbourne, December 22, 1835.
[52] Grey Papers: 3rd Earl. Stephen to Grey, January 7, 1836.
[53] On his father's death in 1845, Howick became the 3rd Earl Grey.

departments, not to allow any party feelings to interfere with the zealous and faithful discharge of their official duties; to give their assistance, within the sphere of those duties, as cordially and honestly to a ministry from which they differ in political opinions, as to one composed of their own friends; and to abstain carefully from taking part in active opposition to their official superiors for the time being, however much they may be opposed to them in feeling.'[54] The reversal of opinion reflects the hardening of the convention of neutrality during the middle decades of the century.

That convention did not, however, prevent officials avowing their party affiliations to politicians. MacGregor, Joint Permanent Secretary of the Board of Trade, stood as a Whig candidate in the election of 1847. He concluded a letter to Russell, in which he had discussed his election prospects in detail, with the words: 'By Thursday next, I will be able, I think, to ascertain with some degree of certainty my prospect of success, and will then, accordingly, forward my resignation to your Lordship.'[55] But Russell was at least on the same side, and MacGregor claimed to have been equally candid to his Conservative masters. 'During Sir Robert Peel's ministry, I made it to be distinctly understood both by him and several Presidents of the Board of Trade that they must not consider me in any more favourable light then as a firm adherent of your Lordship.'[56] In 1864, Helps confessed to Palmerston 'my sincere attachment to your government, and, if I may say so, to yourself'.[57] But he was not less frank when the opposite party came to power. 'I am, as you know, a Whig,' he wrote to Disraeli. 'I owe my present appointment to Lord Granville, and I shall always go as far as I can with my party.' He went on to add, however: 'I care for government more than for any party.'[58] Hamilton, who had been a Conservative junior minister before becoming Permanent Secretary to the Treasury, was said to be 'rather hurt at not being made a Privy Councillor by his own party before their resignation'.[59]

Civil servants were sometimes also party journalists. At the Board of Trade, for example, Fonblanque wrote for the Whigs and Emerson Tennent for the Conservatives.[60] Tennent maintained other links with his friends in opposition.

[54] Earl Grey, *Parliamentary Government* (1858), 191.
[55] PRO 30/22/6. MacGregor to Russell, July 17, 1847.
[56] PRO 30/22/9. MacGregor to Russell, December 25, 1851.
[57] Palmerston Papers. Helps to Palmerston, March 6, 1864.
[58] Disraeli Papers: GC. Helps to Disraeli, August 7, 1868.
[59] BM Add. MS. 44301. f. 126.
[60] Moneypenny and Buckle, i, 1309.

He passed on to Disraeli in 1854 the information that the *Morning Chronicle* was for sale cheap, if the Conservatives wanted it.[61] Tennent might have pleaded in his defence that he had not come by this information in the course of his official duties. He could, presumably, not have said the same eleven years later when he told the Conservative leadership that the government had 'not resigned, but agreed at the Cabinet to go on'.[62]

A natural consequence of all this was that ministers sometimes felt they could not trust their civil servants. The issue of Free Trade divided the officials of the Board of Trade from the Conservative ministers in 1852. 'In case anything is to be done,' wrote Disraeli to Malmesbury in reference to commercial negotations with France, 'it should be done with as little knowledge of the Board of Trade as practicable. That office is filled with our enemies. Lord Cowley, therefore, should conduct the business entirely; or we should send some confidential circumspect agent of our own.'[63]

Even if a minister wished to promote a civil servant to a responsible position, it was not always possible to find the right man inside the service. Sir Henry Taylor, author of *The Statesman*, and himself a clerk in the Colonial Office, explained why. Intake was always at the bottom. 'The system of the offices being that men should rise by seniority, the vacancy was always that of a junior clerk.' Such appointments 'were made without due reference to qualifications, ... for the propriety of requiring any other qualifications than that of writing a legible hand, seems never, up to this day, to have been recognized. ... The business of a junior clerk is to copy, and the qualification for a copyist is a good handwriting, whence the inference seems to have been that any person possessed of this requisite was good enough to be put into the vacancy of a junior clerk.' Something might have been made of these young men, had the work been such as to engage their interest. In fact, the reverse was often the case. Young men of good social standing—or, in Taylor's words, 'boys ... taken at haphazard from the idlest classes of society'—'were expected to apply themselves to the mechanical drudgery of copying. With this they were naturally disgusted—it was contrary to all their manner of living, and had nothing in it which, by stimulating ambition or emulation, or awakening intellectual interest, might have induced an activity to which they had been unaccustomed'. When promotion at length came and 'gave

---

[61] Disraeli Papers, GC. Tennent to Disraeli, June 25, 1854.
[62] ibid. Derby to Disraeli, n.d. [1866.]
[63] Moneypenny and Buckle, i, 1201.

them an opportunity of exercising their intellectual faculties, if any such faculties belonged to them, the power of exertion was gone and the habits of life were inveterate'.[64]

A CASE STUDY

The story of 'Mr Porter's place in the Board of Trade' and how it was bestowed shows how the system worked. Porter was born in 1792. After failing in business as a sugar-broker, he was recommended to Lord Auckland (then President of the Board of Trade) as a statistician, and became first head of the Board's Statistical Department in 1833. From 1840 until 1845, he was also involved in the railway responsibilities of the Board, and became Joint Secretary in 1847. He died in 1852. Shortly after his death, Disraeli must have suggested to his chief, Derby, that the post might be offered to Sir James Emerson Tennent, M.P. for Lisburn and a junior minister. Derby replied: 'The Emerson Tennent arrangement is a very good idea; and having your approval, and a note from himself, I have acted upon it at once and have obtained this morning the Queen's approval of the appointment.' There was an ulterior motive—Derby wanted Tennent's seat for the Lord Advocate, who was not in Parliament. 'I have given him a hint to ascertain whether our Lord Advocate would go down at Lisburn: and I have written by this post to Lord Hertford, announcing to him the vacancy of which it is right that he should be so early apprised, and throwing out the same suggestion to him. I do not think it off the cards that a North of Ireland Presbyterian constituency may accept a Scotch lawyer of eminence, and of high office.' It was only at this stage that Derby thought of consulting his President of the Board of Trade, J. W. Henley. Henley did not like it at all: 'I regret that any successor has been appointed to Mr Porter. I think so far as I can judge two secretaries are not needed and that the work would be far better done with one secretary, and a chief clerk in each department . . . and I do not think it is possible to justify in parliament the retention of so large a staff in this office—at least, I could not do it.' Tennent wrote to tell Disraeli how delighted he was, adding that he knew that Derby was writing to Hertford 'whose influence is supreme at Lisburn to apprise him of the vacancy . . . [in] my opinion, as to the

[64] Grey Papers: 3rd Earl. Box 143. Taylor to Hyde Villiers, April 2, 1832. This letter has been printed: see H. Parris, ' "On the Best Mode of Constituting Public Offices": an unpublished document by Sir Henry Taylor', *Political Studies*, ix (1961), 179–87.

probable return of the Lord Advocate ... there would be no difficulty'. On learning Henley's view that the post should be abolished, he wrote again to Derby 'to entreat him that no personal consideration affecting me individually might be allowed to obstruct any fresh arrangement which the letter of Mr Henley might induce him to adopt and in such case that he would act as freely, as if his letter to me, and my own in reply, had not been written'. Meanwhile, Derby had heard from Henley, to whom he had 'returned a very mild and apologetic letter, at the same time saying that I thought the Whigs could not attack an appointment, on a scale of establishment which they had thought necessary. ... I wish you would see what can be done'. Disraeli took up the buck which had been passed to him. He found Henley standing pat on his former position: 'With the amount of business a second secretary is not only not needed but by dividing the responsibility prevents unity in the conduct of the business of the department, and so would be rather a hindrance.' Nevertheless, Henley accepted that 'it is in these matters for the Treasury ... to decide'. The Treasury, in the person of Disraeli as Chancellor of the Exchequer, did decide, and Tennent kept the job.[65]

PATRONAGE IN THE POLITICAL SYSTEM

The value of patronage to the politician depended on the proportion of supply and demand. Even in the days of the unreformed parliament, when the total electorate was small, and when the electorate in many constituencies was very small indeed, the amount of patronage was never equal to the demands made on it. But it was at any rate large enough to be useful. In 1827, for example, Palmerston took it for granted that patronage would reconcile the right-wing extremists to Canning's ministry. 'As to the Tories,' he wrote, 'who would hardly vote for our measures before, we must not look for any cordial support from them now. Not but that, by degrees and one by one, they will all by instinct come round to the oat-sieve.' There remained the question whether government *should* be carried on by such means: Palmerston thought not. 'I know, however, that Canning means to deal out that sieve very sparingly, and to found his government upon public opinion rather than borough interests, *in which I think he is as right as possible.*'[66] The increase in the size of the

[65] Disraeli Papers. Derby to Disraeli, September 12, 1852 and September 18, 1852 (enclosing Henley to Derby, September 14, 1852). Tennent to Disraeli, September 17, 1852. Henley to Disraeli, September 21 and 25, 1852.
[66] Bulwer, i, 190.

electorate by the first Reform Act, modest though it was by any absolute standards, destroyed the old balance once and for all. In particular, the abolition of many small constituencies, where the judicious distribution of posts could have a decisive effect, led to a situation in which patronage was a liability rather than an asset. Politicians continued to go through the ritual for another generation. But even they came to see that, from the practical standpoint of political advantage, it had become meaningless. The supply of patronage after 1832 fell so far short of the demand that, for every friend gained by the award of a post, the patron had to reckon one or more enemies made by the refusal of their requests. The situation was soon reached in which a patron could write, as Derby did to Disraeli: 'This Commissionership of Excise is really a considerable embarrassment. I enclose you the list of candidates among whom there is hardly a good name, while there are several who will think themselves very ill used at being passed over. . . . I shall be very glad if you can assist me in this matter, for I really know not where to turn.'[67] There was, as in the Tennent case discussed above, an electoral angle. 'If it were offered to F. Scott, we should get the seat for Berkshire for our Lord Advocate, and though he is not anything remarkable, he might do.'[68] But elections were tricky. 'Would Newdegate take it? And if so, could we keep his seat? . . . You would I suppose prefer keeping Lord Robert Cecil in the House—besides which . . . it would hardly be fair to make another vacancy for Stamford.'[69] On the eve of his resignation in 1859, Derby found himself with four valuable posts to fill. But he was far from pleased with the prospect, and did not welcome it as a chance to help four of his party henchmen. He sought rather respectable excuses for handing over to his successor as many of the troublesome babies as possible. The Poor Law Board, which needed a new Secretary, was the greatest difficulty. There was an Assistant Secretary, Henry Fleming, who could be promoted, and 'if we do not appoint Fleming (which I do not desire to have the credit of doing) we go counter to the advice of all the late Presidents, including March'. March was Derby's own President of the Poor Law Board and, in spite of having at some time recommended Fleming, he was 'also anxious to get the vacant place for his cousin, Fitzroy. On the other hand, if we do, we shall equally disappoint him, if we do not give Fitzroy the place'. On balance, the best plan seemed to be to leave the patronage for the

[67] Disraeli Papers, MC. Derby to Disraeli, August 15, 1858.
[68] ibid.
[69] ibid.

71

incoming Prime Minister to dispose of, even though Derby did 'not know whether I shall have made one *ingrat*, but I know I shall have made three *mécontents*'.[70] After the change of government, Fleming got the job. Fitzroy was then pressed on March's successor, but to no effect. 'I am very sorry that it will not be in my power to give effect to your wishes in respect of Mr Fitzroy, as the appointment vacated by Fleming's promotion will be filled up by a person in the office if it should be found necessary to keep up the appointment.'[71]

LIMITED COMPETITION

The system of limited competition introduced in 1855 was a compromise between the older pattern of influence, and the newer concept of efficiency. Heads of departments still had something to bestow, in the form of nominations, which were required before the candidates could sit the examinations. On the other hand, there could be only one victor, who was presumed to be the most efficient. Palmerston explained the system in telling a correspondent that he would put her grandson's name down for a Treasury clerkship: 'When a vacancy happens I appoint three candidates for competitive examination, and the one who is recommended as the best by the examiners receives the appointment.'[72] The snag was that the least bad of the candidates might not be up to the job. Indeed, the story went round that Hayter, Parliamentary Secretary to the Treasury, had a recipe to ensure the success of any favoured aspirant. He was said to have two young men—the 'Treasury Idiots'—who could be counted upon to do less well than *any* third candidate. But there's many a slip—the day came when one of the 'Idiots' slipped into a clerkship! Whether the legend is true or false, it was the case that the scheme was tightened up by the addition of a qualifying examination, as a preliminary hurdle to the limited competition.

The new system made it easy for patrons to fob off clients with the minimum of offence. 'I am sorry . . . I cannot do what you wish about young Puller as I named ten days ago three candidates to compete for the vacant clerkship in the Treasury.'[73] If a client complained that his protégé had failed to get in, the new system enabled the patron to shrug off responsibility on to the Civil Service

[70] Disraeli Papers, MC. Derby to Disraeli, June 12 and 13, 1859.

[71] BM Add. MS. 48581. Palmerston to Euston, July 6, 1959.

[72] ibid. Palmerston to Hon. Mrs. Herbert, October 18, 1859.

[73] Palmerston Papers. Letterbook: Palmerston to Hankey, February 21, 1865.

Commissioners. For example, a Shropshire clergyman wrote in August, 1866, to Disraeli to seek help in getting his nephew, Arthur P. da Costa Wellings, into the Civil Service. The lad was godson of an old friend of Disraeli's, Mrs Brydges Willyams. She had left him £3,000 and had asked Disraeli to look after him—although Disraeli wrote: 'I never saw him, nor wish to see him . . . [but] I don't want the boy to be unnecessarily plucked, and therefore I would wish you to write to his uncle, and inquire whether he is prepared to pass the preliminary examination.' The assurances must have been satisfactory for soon the uncle was writing to ask the date of the examination and where he could get copies of old examination papers. Then he wrote again to beg a few weeks' grace so that the nephew might 'get up' his book-keeping. This request seems to have been granted, but in spite of that, the candidate failed. In May, 1867, the uncle solicited another chance. This time, young Arthur got through the qualifying examination but failed to beat his rivals at the competitive stage.[74]

THE STANDARD RISES

'I believe that the times are in your favour,' wrote Henry Taylor to the third Earl Grey in 1847. 'Ministers can make appointments and create offices now without much reference to parliamentary influence in the choice of public servants.'[75] He did not mean that parliament took no interest in appointments, but that ministers need not think parliamentary support was only to be had in exchange for patronage. On the contrary, the best way of securing the good-will of Members as a whole was to choose men on their merits. Long before the age of open competition, some politicians had learnt this lesson. Even when Grey was trying to get his own nephew into the Treasury, and promising a post in his own department in return, he stipulated: 'Of course, both appointments ought to be made subject to the condition of the persons to whom they are given turning out fit for them.'[76] Palmerston expressed the new spirit: 'I always consider the right which my office gives me to appoint to certain offices of essential importance to be a trust imposed upon me for the public advantage and not a power given me for the gratification of personal feelings. I have, therefore, always endeavoured to find out the best man for a vacant office. It is a great satisfaction to me when I think that I have succeeded in doing so.' If he had gone on to say

[74] Disraeli Papers, C/II/C/4. Moneypenny and Buckle, ii, 215.
[75] Grey Papers, 3rd Earl. Box 124. Taylor to Grey, October 17, 1847.
[76] PRO 30/22/7. Grey to Russell, January 25, 1848. See p. 55.

no, he might be suspected of coating his refusal in principle in order to sweeten the pill. In fact he had already said yes, and may be supposed to have spoken with sincerity. 'But it is a double pleasure when I find that in choosing the best man I have also lighted upon the relative of an old and valued friend and that double pleasure I have fully derived from the choice I made of your son on this late occasion.'[77]

The manner in which Herman Merivale succeeded Sir James Stephen as Permanent Under-Secretary of the Colonial Office is an extreme case of appointment by merit alone. (Whether the merit in question was relevant to the task to be performed is another thing.) Stephen announced to Grey (the third Earl) his decision to retire, on grounds of ill health, in October, 1847. He mentioned that the reaction of Hawes, his parliamentary colleague, had been to broach 'the difficulty of finding a successor to an office making such peculiar demands on the holder of it; on which I pointed out to him the name of a gentleman who he and I both thought eminently qualified for it, and quite sure to accept it if offered. There is, I am convinced, in this respect no insuperable difficulty'.[78] A few days later, he wrote again: 'As you invite me to suggest the name of my successor, I mention that of Mr Herman Merivale, the lecturer on colonisation. *I know him, however, only by reputation.*'[79] A week later, Grey wrote to Merivale, virtually offering him the job, without even interviewing him. 'I beg leave to offer for your acceptance the situation of Assistant Under-Secretary of State and Counsel to the Department. This was the position occupied by Mr Stephen previously to the retirement of Mr Hay and what I propose to you is that you should hold the same position at the same salary, namely, £1,500 a year. In making this offer I think it right to inform you that I have been principally guided by the advice of Mr Stephen, who judging I believe from your reputation, has expressed to me his opinion that if you can be prevailed upon to undertake the duty it could not be committed to better hands. If Mr Stephen should not on his return from abroad be able to resume his duties (and of this I fear there is very slender chance) you might naturally expect to succeed him, and in all probability you would do so.'[80] Not surprisingly, Merivale accepted. Stephen's sick-leave merged into retirement, and Merivale took over his post a few months later.

[77] BM Add. MS. 48580. Palmerston to Sir T. D. Acland Bart. n.d.
[78] Grey Papers: 3rd Earl. Box 123. Stephen to Grey, October 12, 1847.
[79] ibid. Stephen to Grey, October 16, 1847. (My italics.)
[80] Grey Papers: 3rd Earl. Box 112. Grey to Merivale, October 23, 1847.

PERMANENCE AND PATRONAGE

The concept of permanence itself put a premium on good appointments, at least at the highest level, since any suspicion of a job might afford a pretext for a government of the opposite party to turn out the incumbent. Peel expressed this point apropos of the appointment of Baillie Hamilton to succeed Barrow at the Admiralty. 'It is of great importance, I presume, that the office ... should be permanently held. But in order to ensure its being so ... there must be a conviction that the appointment was made after full consideration of the functions and duties of the office and that the person selected for it combined the qualifications entitling him to the confidence of successive administrations of opposite parties.' Haddington agreed that there was, in principle, a danger but argued that it was negligible in this instance. 'I ... do not see why my successor, being one of the hostile camp, should be more desirous of getting rid of a man because he had been my [private] secretary than he would be of shaking off any man of known Conservative opinions appointed by me. No man can have held the cup more even, and dealt with more impartiality than Hamilton has done in his official capacity and I doubt very much if any newly appointed First Lord would assume the perfectly gratuitous responsibility of turning out an official who was doing his duty well merely because he had been connected with his predecessor.'[81] It could be argued that the bestowal of a sinecure called for even more care than the filling of a working post. 'Strange to say, in these days it requires as good a man in a sinecure as a working situation, or nearly so ... [since] the character of the holder may maintain the place, which might be put into jeopardy with an inferior man to fill it.'[82]

Ministers were dependent on their senior officials and so had a direct incentive to choose good men. Such was not the case with junior appointments. 'That junior clerks usually grow into senior clerks is a fact that never seems to have attracted any notice, because under the system of rising by length of service, the prospect was too remote to make the head of the Department, by whom the patronage was exercised, foresee that he had any interest in it, and neither could it often happen, in point of fact, that it concerned him even in the days of durable governments.'[83] When a senior post was to be

[81] BM Add. MS. 40457. Peel to Haddington, December 29 [1844]. Haddington to Peel, January 7, 1845.
[82] PRO 30/22/9. Sir Charles Wood to Lord John Russell, May 24, 1851.
[83] Taylor, April 2, 1832.

filled, whether by promotion or from outside, the situation was quite different, since 'the duties . . . nearly concern the heads of the office, as affecting their own convenience and the reputation of their Departments'.[84] This was clearly the thought in Labouchere's mind, anxious lest Melbourne should appoint someone to a vacancy in the Mint over the head of his own protégé. 'The Queen's Clerk acts a secretary to the Mint Board, and it is absolutely necessary that he should be a person in whose character and fitness the Master of the Mint should be able to place confidence.'[85] Peel recognized the principle when his First Lord wished to make his kinsman, Baillie Hamilton, Permanent Secretary of the Admiralty. After serious consideration, Peel acknowledged that Haddington had an interest in a good appointment that must outweigh nepotism. 'As it appears to be the general opinion of all . . . *the parties most interested in a good selection*, . . . that none better could be made than that of Capt Hamilton', Peel would not stand in the way.[86] Lewis begged Palmerston not to come to a hasty decision in appointing a new Chairman of the Board of Inland Revenue: 'It is extremely important to the Chancellor of the Exchequer . . . that the Chairman . . . should be efficient, judicious and trustworthy.'[87]

PATRONAGE UNDER A SPOTLIGHT

Ministers had a second direct interest in good appointments. As the century wore on, it became more and more necessary for appointments to be defensible before parliament, the press and the public. Naturally, it fell to the minister at the head of the department to defend all appointments within it. On these grounds, Molesworth claimed the right to exercise in practice the patronage of the Office of Works, part of which was vested by law in the Treasury. 'The head of any department ought when vacancies occur to nominate the officers for whose conduct he is responsible to parliament.'[88] G. C. Lewis early in his career lost a chance on the grounds that his appointment would be hard to defend. Nassau Senior recommended him for a post under the Poor Law Commission. He had taken part in two government enquiries. 'These circumstances, and his being the author of a very clever book, would I think perfectly save you

[84] ibid.
[85] Melbourne Papers, 28/2. Labouchere to Melbourne, March 1, 1840.
[86] BM Add. MS. 40458. Peel to Haddington, January 9, 1845. (My italics.)
[87] Palmerston Papers. Lewis to Palmerston. October 12 [1856?].
[88] BM Add. MS. 43200. Molesworth to Aberdeen, August 11, 1853.

from the imputation of a job.'[89] Melbourne agreed that, personally, it would be a good appointment. 'But upon the whole, considering the jealousy and hostility, with which every proceeding of the Commissioners is viewed and scrutinized, I should be disposed to recommend it as the more prudent course, that he should not be appointed an Assistant Commissioner.'[90]

After Sir James Stephen retired from his post as Under-Secretary at the Colonial Office, there came into being an open conspiracy to find him another berth. (He eventually wound up as Regius Professor of History at Cambridge.) One of the possibilities was a post at Chelsea Hospital, which eventually went to a Col. Alderson. Granville commented: 'Although Stephen's appointment would have been defensible, I cannot help thinking that Alderson's appointment will save you some leading articles, and a question in the House of Commons.'[91] Later, Grey wished to make Stephen a paid member of the Board of Trade, so as to retain his services as an adviser on colonial policy. Labouchere, as President of the Board, objected, 'because I find it difficult to defend the establishment of my department as it now exists. Several useless offices have of late been added to it. I have abolished one of them, and whenever a vacancy occurs either in the place of Secretary or that of Head of the Statistical Department to which Northcote could be raised, I hope to be able to abolish another. In the meantime, I am unwilling to invite attacks'.[92] A year later, Russell was warned, apropos of Booth's appointment to the Board of Trade: 'You should be on the look out for some arrangement for Sir E. Ryan. The House will not think both lawyers necessary at the Board of Trade.'[93] Disraeli summed it up when he said: 'The interests of the party can never require an improper appointment: an improper appointment is a job, and nothing injures a party more than a job.'[94]

The changes were little appreciated by the world at large. In the late '50s it was still possible to write as if nothing had happened for decades. 'The patronage of government situations is vested in the ministers of the Crown, and is by them distributed amongst those Members of Parliament who support the ministry by their votes. Unless a person, therefore, is acquainted with some Member of

[89] Melbourne Papers: 67. Senior to Nicholls, May 11, 1835.
[90] ibid. Melbourne to Nicholls and Shaw Lefevre, June 16, 1835.
[91] PRO 30/22/7. Granville to Russell, December 18, 1848.
[92] PRO 30/22/8. Labouchere to Russell, December 11, 1849.
[93] ibid. Ellice to Russell, October 19, 1850.
[94] Moneypenny and Buckle, i, 1658. Disraeli to Pakington, December 19, 1858.

Parliament on the ministerial side, it is in vain for him to hope to succeed in obtaining a government situation; nor does the bare knowledge of such a person, or the mere application to him ensure a favourable issue. On the contrary, a Member of Parliament is so beset with these applications, and is bound as it were to return a encouraging answer to all, when, in many instances, he well knows that it will be utterly impossible for him to grant the request that is being made. It is not sufficient, therefore, to simply make the request and there let the matter rest, but it is absolutely necessary that from time to time, and at frequent intervals, the Member should be constantly reminded of his promise, until at length (perhaps with a view of escaping further importunity) the favour is granted.' Limited competition left the writer quite unmoved. 'With regard to patronage, a new order of things has recently been established, by which certain government appointments are supposed to be bestowed by public competition. This, however, is only a nominal concession producing no result, and the patronage is in reality administered under precisely the same system that it ever was.'[95]

Those on the inside saw things differently. Even the reformers were prepared to admit that the evils of patronage were much less than they had been. The report on the Colonial Office, for example, which was part of the preparatory work for the Northcote-Trevelyan report itself, concluded that 'the appointment of proper persons to fill the higher stations ... must be left to the conscience and the judgment of the Secretary of State; and it is so extremely important ... to the Secretary of State himself, that these offices should be effectively executed, that the best selection is likely always to be made of which circumstances admit.'[96] Graham—always a purist in these matters—thought the worst was past a decade before open competition came in. 'Publicity is a check, and I am disposed to think, having closed my career of patronage, that, on the whole, public character is so valuable to public men, that much abuse of patronage, in the days in which we live, is not to be apprehended.'[97]

The conditions under which patronage had been useful to politicians had passed away long before the old system itself came to an end. Even during Peel's lifetime 'patronage ... was little more than a time-honoured and conventional function ... a dying and ineffective system, from which much of the political value had been extracted. ... For a system of influence to survive in politics, two

[95] q. P. Keene (ed.), *Never Nonplussed* (1967). I owe this reference to my brother, Leslie Parris.
[96] P.P. 1854, xxvii, 81. [97] P.P. 1861, v, 154.

constituent elements were necessary. In the first place the means of influencing persons had to be present; in the second place opinion at large had to sanction or at least tolerate the employment of those means.' Public opinion had ceased to do so, and had become very alert to the scent of jobbery. 'Party leaders were therefore peculiarly anxious to prevent such charges being levelled at their own ministries; and, to do them jusice, honestly concerned to avoid not only the imputation but the fact of using patronage for improper purposes. Both parties reflected this change in public opinion.' Politicians continued to go through the motions. But 'what degree of positive power either politicians or parties derived from the exercise of patronage is a doubtful question. ... To the individual politician, or to the party managers engrossed in immediate concerns, patronage must have often seemed an inescapable but burdensome duty with little more than marginal value attaching to it'.[98]

[98] Gash, xx, 323, 344 and 371–2.

CHAPTER III

MINISTERIAL RESPONSIBILITY:
THE NINETEENTH-CENTURY REFORMULATION

'It is no arbitrary rule, which requires that all holders of permanent offices must be subordinate to some minister responsible to parliament, since it is obvious that, without it, the first principles of our system of government—the control of all branches of the administration by parliament—would be abandoned.'

Earl Grey, 1858

Responsibility can be followed by one, or both, of two prepositions. There is responsibility to, and responsibility for. A person is responsible to someone for something. Ministerial responsibility is an ancient feature of English government and this sometimes obscures the fact that neither the someone nor the something have remained constant. Basically ministers are responsible for the advice they give to the Crown. 'The maxim that "the king can do no wrong" . . . we may translate thus: "English law does not provide any means whereby the king can be punished or compelled to make redress". . . . [But] though the king cannot be prosecuted or sued, his ministers can be both prosecuted and sued, even for what they do by the king's express command. . . . Royal immunity is coupled with ministerial responsibility.'[1] But to whom were ministers responsible, beyond the Crown itself? Medieval demands that the king should dismiss his evil counsellors implies a claim that they were, in some sense, responsible to the political nation. This claim became explicit from 1376 onwards in the procedure of impeachment which 'is a presentment by the most solemn grand inquest of the whole kingdom'[2]— that is, the House of Commons—and is heard by the House of Lords, sitting as a court. From Tudor times, ministers were also responsible to the ordinary courts. 'The law courts will not recognize any document as expressing the royal will unless it bears the great seal or at least the privy seal. This insures that some minister will

---

[1] F. W. Maitland, *Constitutional History of England* (Cambridge, 1908), 482 and 484.
[2] Sir Matthew Hale, *Historia Placitorum Coronae* (1736), ii, *150.

have committed himself to that expression of the royal will. The ministers themselves are much concerned in the maintenance of this routine; they fear being called in question for the king's acts and having no proof that they are the king's acts. The chancellor fears to affix the great seal unless he has some document under the privy seal that he can produce as his warrant; the keeper of the privy seal is anxious to have the king's own handwriting attested by the king's secretary. ... In this doctrine of the royal seals we can see the foundation for our modern doctrine of ministerial responsibility—that for every exercise of the royal power some minister is answerable.'[3]

But ministerial responsibility in this sense—'the legal responsibility of every minister for every act of the Crown in which he takes part'[4] —is no more than a special application of a more general rule. 'The action of every servant of the Crown, ... is brought under the supremacy of the law of the land. ... The acts of ministers no less than the acts of subordinate officials are made subject to the rule of law.'[5] The expression is normally used in a sense which distinguishes ministers from other servants of the Crown. 'It means in ordinary parlance the responsibility of ministers to parliament, or, the liability of ministers to lose their offices if they cannot retain the confidence of the House of Commons.'[6] This meaning is of comparatively recent origin. As it evolved, several questions had to be answered. How could ministers take responsibility for administration unless every branch of administration were placed under a specific minister? How could ministers be responsible to parliament without taking responsibility for the acts of members of their departments? How could they take responsibility for the acts of their underlings without abrogating the personal responsibility of the latter as servants of the Crown? It took many years 'for the House to be finally convinced that the device which offered the best means of ensuring that administration was carried out in accordance with its wishes was ... the individual responsibility of ministers. Once this idea had been accepted in practice ... it soon became one of the features by which the British system of government is most widely characterized. ... The latter Victorian era was the golden age of ministerial administration'.[7]

[3] Maitland, 203.
[4] A. V. Dicey, *Law of the Constitution* (4 ed., 1893), 303.
[5] ibid., 305.   [6] ibid., 303.
[7] F. M. G. Willson, 'Ministries and Boards: some aspects of Administrative Development since 1832', *Public Administration*, xxxiii (1955), 48 and 49.

A ministerial department, such as became the norm of British government in the period between the first Reform Bill and the Crimean War, may be defined as 'a department of state whose powers are vested, either by law or by convention, in a single person who sits in one or other House of Parliament and is responsible to Parliament for every act performed by that department'.[8] It has been held that the ministerial department was one of the 'three major inventions' in British governmental machinery in the nineteenth century. (The other two were the civil service and local authorities.)[9] One of the main strands in its evolution is the process by which it superseded almost all other types of administrative organ, of which boards were the most important.

THE BOARD SYSTEM

Administration by boards of public officials was common prior to the nineteenth century throughout Europe as well as in Britain. 'Parliament . . . was seldom slow to interfere by remonstrance, by insisting on the removal and punishment of favourites and bad advisers . . . but, except on such occasions, it meddled little with the conduct of the executive government.'[10] Hence the Crown could foster the board pattern in preference to the ministerial type, and had certain motives for so doing. Ministers were risky. Some broke in the king's hand, others grew into over-mighty subjects. Boards tended to avoid both extremes. Hence some of the most ancient offices were put into commission. Pares called this 'the practice of breaking down great offices into what one may call small change—the substitution, for example, of five Lords of the Treasury and five Lords of the Admiralty for a single overmighty Lord Treasurer and Lord High Admiral'.[11] 'The career of Southampton proved that a weak Treasurer could cripple the government. The career of Danby proved that a strong Treasurer could reach the same end, though by a different road. Treasury commissions avoided this dilemma, and in the period between 1660 and 1702 it became normal to have the Treasury in commission. A commission could be efficient and businesslike without causing jealousy. It had the great advantage of increasing the representation of the Court in the House of Commons. . . . The need for such representation became much greater after the

[8] ibid., 44.
[9] B. B. Schaffer, 'The Idea of the Ministerial Department: Bentham, Mill and Bagehot', *Australian Journal of Politics and History*, iii (1957–8), 60.
[10] Grey, 6.   [11] Pares, 27.

removal of the Customs and Excise commissioners from the Commons in 1700.'[12] A board, moreover, was a means of securing continuity. Like a college, a cathedral chapter, or a corporate borough, it never died. It was thought, too, that a board tended to be less wasteful of the king's money than a minister, because each member would act under the eyes of the others. There would be 'a check upon any extravagant act. . . . The proceedings of a board . . . afford security in certain transactions which may not, to the same extent, be found when the whole business is entrusted to a single officer.'[13] Another factor in favour of boards, from the point of view of the Crown, is that they increased the amount of patronage available.[14] All these factors applied irrespective of the location of the board. But, where it was desired to decentralize functions of central government, a board had special advantages. Hence, in Scottish and Irish administration 'the use of boards was favoured because of the difficulties of communication between Dublin and Edinburgh and London, and the consequent need to have a high degree of administrative independence in the two smaller capitals. It seems to have been felt that the concentration of all Scottish and Irish administrative powers in single ministers was undesirable when those ministers spent at least half their time at Westminster'.[15]

The system worked well so long as boards were responsible in fact as well as in name to the King. But once the executive became primarily responsible to parliament, the system came under strain. The result was a decline in the board pattern of administration and its supersession to a large degree by a ministerial pattern. The trend was not peculiar to Britain but made itself felt throughout Europe. Only in Sweden, thanks to the institution of the *justitieombudsman*, has it survived into the twentieth century.

In Britain the turning point was the first Reform Act. At that period, central government was carried on by twelve ministries and sixteen boards. But although 'the ministerial department as the normal form of organization for central government was a creation of the nineteenth century', its general adoption was slow. 'Until the 1850s . . . non-ministerial organization was still freely employed and added to.'[16] In the years 1832–55, three new ministries came into

[12] Baxter, 261.   [13] P.P. 1833, xiv, 356 and 359.
[14] F. M. G. Willson, 'A Consideration of Administrative Commissions represented in Parliament by Non-ministerial Commissioners &c' (D.Phil. thesis, Oxford University, 1953), 27–8.
[15] ibid., 16–17.
[16] B. B. Schaffer, 'A Consideration of . . . Non-ministerial Organization in . . . Central Government, etc.' (Ph.D. thesis, London University, 1956), 13.

being (all of which had formerly been boards) while fifteen new boards were created (two of which were transformed into ministries during the period). Why? First, tradition. Everyone was used to the idea that a new task meant a new board. In particular, temporary commissions were an immemorial tool of government, and governments could often meet ideological objections to state intervention with an assurance that the life of a new board would be limited. For example, the Poor Law Commissioners of 1834 were first appointed for five years only. Secondly, the new functions of government during this period were rarely important enough to require a new minister, and the existing departments 'were small and ill-equipped to undertake new duties'[17]—none had so large a staff as the Board of Customs. Lastly, the House of Commons did not like increasing the number of 'official Members'.[18] Hence, 'such appointments would have been highly suspect to a House of Commons which had for over half a century been largely occupied in attempts to rid itself of place-men'.[19]

BOARDS IN DECLINE

Nevertheless, throughout those years the arguments in favour of boards were continually losing their weight. Kings had something to fear from over-mighty subjects. Early Victorian parliaments had not. The permanent civil service had proved its ability to provide continuity as well as, if not better than, a board system. 'I think [continuity] absolutely necessary; but then the question . . . is whether the continuity is best obtained by keeping two commissioners permanently in office, or by keeping the secretaries and professional advisers permanently in the office. My experience inclines to the latter arrangement.'[20] Then again, a board might provide some check on extravagance. But was not the combination of Treasury control and a House of Commons containing such men as Cobden and Joseph Hume an even better check? As for the argument that boards increased the amount of patronage at the disposal of the Crown, the great majority of M.P.s wanted to reduce it. The improvement of communication by steamship, railway and telegraph made distinctive patterns of administration for Ireland and Scotland less necessary.

The most general complaint against the boards was that they were too large. 'Where there are several co-ordinate heads of a department,

---

[17] Willson (1955), 49. [18] Sir Charles Wood, 3 *Hansard*, cxviii, 179–80.
[19] Willson (1955), 49. [20] P.P. 1860, ix, 563.

there are generally one or two who are fond of work and of the degree of distinction and influence which attend it, while the rest prefer to take their ease. This constitution of public departments therefore allows of a considerable number of the highest-paid class of officers giving much less than the proper proportion of their time to the public.'[21] But the waste of money was the least defect of the system. More serious was a kind of Gresham's law by which the bad members tended to drive out the good. 'The number of the boards being unnecessarily large, less attendance is obtained from those whose services are really useful; for each member will generally claim an equal proportion of absence, which . . . will be greater in proportion to the number of commissioners beyond the number whose attendance is required.' Hence, 'a board is made efficient not in proportion to its numbers, but by its members being competent and attentive to the business. An inefficient member is of no practical utility to any board . . . In fact, his attendance sometimes embarrasses the business. A small number of efficient Commissioners giving full attendance will transact the business much more expeditiously and with more satisfaction to the public and the government, and with more advantage to the revenue, than a larger number of Commissioners of whom a considerable proportion are not men of business.' Small boards were, therefore, preferable to large since 'the members would be obliged to give more attendance and consequently understand their business better, and take more interest in it from that cause, and also from their increased responsibility'.[22]

Responsibility was the crux of the problem. 'Public officers acting together in boards have not the same keen sense of responsibility as those who act in an individual capacity. A single member of a commission is lost in the crowd, and he can neither expect to be rewarded for his exertions nor to suffer for his neglect as an individual would who was in the sole or principal charge of a department.'[23] To some extent, the difficulty could be met by giving each member of the board some individual responsibility. T. F. Kennedy, a newly appointed member of the Board of Woods, suggested as much to Lord John Russell: there ought to be 'some division of duties, which should create *individual action* and *responsibility*'.[24] 'With divided *responsibility*, I have no fear, and feel confident that I could discharge my share of the duties . . . but upon the division of

[21] PRO 30/22/7. Memo by C. E. Trevelyan, April 26, 1848.
[22] Grey Papers: 2nd Earl. Finance, 14/8/17.
[23] PRO 30/22/7. Memo by C. E. Trevelyan, April 26, 1848.
[24] PRO 30/22/8. T. F. Kennedy to Lord John Russell, October 8, 1850.

the duties everything depends.'[25] In a projected reorganization of the Education Department in 1867, a Board was proposed, but it was 'not intended to make the whole Board perform the work of each person. Each member is to do the duty of his separate Department.'[26]

It was sometimes suggested that, if boards functioned as boards, all would be well. Sir Charles Wood told Russell in 1849 that 'compelling the Ordnance to act more as a board, so that the Clerk, who is the financial officer, should be cognizant of all that goes on, is the first step' towards better administration in that department.[27] But even when a board was of the correct size, composed of reasonably able and conscientious men, and acting as a board, it might still be at fault through insufficient delegation of power. This seems to have been the case with the Customs in the 'sixties. 'Almost every operation is based on some order or regulation for which the Board alone is responsible. Every officer is now an automaton or a machine which must move in a given direction.' Not only was the 'effect of this the creation of an incredible amount of useless correspondence, which is very vexatious and inconvenient to the public, troublesome and laborious to the officials, and expensive to the state'. It did not even achieve its intended end. Each officer 'knows the value of the maxim, *quieta non movere*, and he carefully adheres to it ... at present a Collector cannot incur an expense exceeding £2 for any piece of work [e.g. repair of office furniture] without having obtained the previous sanction of the Board ... Now this is practically no check at all; for if a carpenter, for example, has three jobs, one £5, one 5s. and the other 2s. 6d. the thing can be so managed ... that no one of the accounts will appear to exceed the stipulated sum'.[28]

There were other defects of boards as such, even when efficient. 'As every member ... is anxious to enforce his own opinion, much time is lost in useless discussion, and the decision come to is generally of the nature of a compromise. When the maintenance of the discipline and activity of large departments is concerned, this evil is felt in increased degree. Every person has his advocate at the board, and it often becomes impossible to promote a deserving, or pass over an undeserving, officer.'[29]

It is not surprising, then, that the board system declined. Trevelyan held that 'however well adapted boards of public officers may be

[25] PRO 30/22/9. the same to the same, May 19, 1851.
[26] Disraeli Papers, B IX/B/1.
[27] PRO 30/22/8. Sir Charles Wood to Lord John Russell, September 1, 1849.
[28] Disraeli Papers, B IX/B.
[29] PRO 30/22/7. Memorandum by C. E. Trevelyan, April 26, 1848.

for the performance of certain descriptions of duty—for enquiring into and reporting upon particular subjects, for instance—they lack, as a general rule, in the promptness, vigour and unity of action required for the successful performance of executive junctions'.[30] Bromley of the Admiralty reported to Disraeli: 'Sir Charles Napier has been with me today. He is *trying* to work up a case against the Board of Admiralty as a *board*. He told me he saw Lord Palmerston yesterday, who stated to him that he was opposed to all boards.'[31] The pattern preferred was that of the ministerial department. Trevelyan again was quite firm on the point: 'If the administration of each of our great departments depended upon a single individual, with one or more superior officers to advise with him, and to take his place during his absence, it would be impossible to appoint incapable persons to these situations, and each successive government would, for its own sake, look out for the ablest persons who could be found, to be appointed to its vacancies ... the same remarks apply in a greater or less degree to all the executive Departments which are administered by Commissioners, and I would suggest that these Commissions should be reorganized on the same principle.'[32] Lord Morpeth, as First Commissioner of Woods and Forests, reported— and supported—Joseph Hume's view that 'he had no objection to my having all power—but that it ought to be in one hand—that I might have as many secretaries as I like, but that the Board is a faulty and bad-working system.'[33]

All the criticisms so far considered apply to boards in general. There were in addition difficulties peculiar to a board of a particular type. Boards containing nominated honorary members might face the difficulty of the quorum. Such was the case of the Metropolitan Commission of Sewers. 'Our numbers are so small that in making up the quorum requisite for transacting any business of any kind ... we find the greatest difficulty ... the number having been unfortunately maintained by your government ... in spite of the remonstrances of myself and others engaged in practically working the law. ... Some of [the members] are already rather tired of the waste of time and trouble occasioned by the absurd provision above mentioned and other technicalities of the Act.'[34] At the same time, some quorum rule was desirable, if a board was not to become only

[30] ibid.
[31] Disraeli Papers, R. Bromley to Disraeli, January 25, 1856.
[32] PRO 30/22/7. Memorandum by C. E. Trevelyan, April 26, 1848.
[33] ibid. Morpeth to Lord John Russell, July 7, 1848.
[34] ibid. Ebrington to Lord John Russell, November 14, 1850.

a name, as (for example) the Board of Trade had. Boards containing honorary members had in any case come under a new strain once political life became polarized around the government and the opposition. This was one of Morpeth's two objections to a proposal from the Prince Consort for the reform of the Board of Woods. 'I was aware', he wrote, 'of the Prince's feeling in favour of a sort of unofficial Council; I cannot think that it would be likely to answer. It seems to me that it would have most of the faults, and less of the efficiency, of the present system. The desirable object is to deepen and concentrate responsibility; this would rather tend to weaken and diffuse it. I do not think it would be acceptable either to the class of persons who have of late been appointed Chief Commissioners, or to the independent councillors themselves who ... must still as long as the income of the Crown Lands form part of the annual revenue, have their decisions submitted to the control of the Treasury, with whom such members may be more or less in party conflict.'[35]

It was sometimes suggested that boards consisting largely of honorary members might be stiffened by the appointment of one or more paid members. This was what Grey proposed as part of his scheme to revive the colonial functions of the Board of Trade.[36] Overwhelmed with the weight of individual responsibility, he hankered after the shelter of a board. 'I am more and more painfully conscious,' he wrote, 'that the business of the Colonial Office is more than I can manage as it ought to be managed, and that what is wanted is not more assistance within it but some authority without its walls to which certain subjects could be referred in such a way that the responsibility for the decision might be shared by those who advised it.'[37] The Board of Trade was a committee of the Privy Council and Sir James Stephen (who had lately resigned from his post as Permanent Under-Secretary at the Colonial Office) was a Privy Councillor. Grey's plan, therefore, was to give Stephen a salary in order to ensure that the work he wished to transfer, such as the preparation of colonial constitutions, would be effectively performed. But Labouchere pointed out that if Stephen 'was made a paid Commissioner it would detract from the usefulness of the Board. Its decisions would be attributed to him more exclusively than they ought to be or could really be ... For the House of Commons

[35] PRO 30/22/7. Morpeth to Lord John Russell, September 26 [1848].

[36] Cf. J. M. Ward, 'The Retirement of a Titan', *Journal of Modern History*, xxxi (1959).

[37] PRO 30/22/7. Grey to Russell, February 24, 1848.

is impressed with the notion that a paid Commissioner always does the whole work'.[38]

If politicians and civil servants sat together, the result was often the worst of both worlds. 'When two permanent Commissioners and one changing Commissioner met together they often differed in opinion . . . and the result generally was that the opinion of neither . . . prevailed but that there was a compromise.'[39] Any member could carry obstruction further, as Morpeth pointed out, drawing no doubt on his own experience of the Board of Woods and the General Board of Health. 'I have known instances in which one Commissioner did not feel inclined to concur with his colleagues and therefore withheld his signature.'[40] In an extreme case, a majority of a board might outvote its political head. Derby foresaw that the proposed Secretary of State for India might be placed in this situation unless an uncautious concession made by Disraeli were withdrawn. 'Whereas our main principle was that the Secretary of State . . . should exercise an absolute authority, his council being only advisers, your amendment alters the whole form of the arrangement, and subjects him to the acquiescence, certified by signature, of three members of the council. Lord Ellenborough plainly declares that, under conditions, neither he, nor any man who knows anything of the affairs of India, would hold office for a moment.'[41]

BOARDS AND PARLIAMENT

The point at issue here was the most fundamental of all. How was a board to be made responsible to parliament? By making each member eligible to sit there? This was tolerated in the case of the Board of Ordnance, because of its venerable antiquity, right down to its end during the Crimean War. The rule was not without its defenders even in its last days. When Russell proposed in 1849 to make some, at least, of the members permanent and therefore non-parliamentary, Sir Charles Wood disagreed. 'It is true that neither the Storekeeper nor Surveyor of the Ordnance are now in parliament, but I am not disposed to diminish the number of parliamentary officers. . . . Suppose a change in the Clerkship and that your new Clerk failed in his election you would have nobody to move the Ordnance estimates. . . . To constitute a good board you really want two or three parliamentary officers, and therefore I think that your

[38] ibid. Labouchere to Russell, December 11, 1849.
[39] P.P. 1860, ix, 562–3.   [40] q. Schaffer (1956), 30.
[41] Moneypenny and Buckle, i, 1539. q. Derby to Disraeli, April 30, 1858.

plan of reducing the higher officers to permanent persons out of parliament is in the wrong direction.'[42] But whatever might be said about a particular case, it would have been out of the question to make all seats on all boards compatible with membership of the Commons, because it would have evoked the 'influence of the Crown' cry.

At the other extreme, the fate of the Poor Law Commissioners of 1834 showed what happened to a board none of whose members could sit in parliament. 'The first administration of the new Poor Law was by "Commissioners"—the three kings of Somerset House, as they were called. . . . But the House of Commons would not let the Commission alone. For a long time it was defended because the Whigs had made the Commission, and felt bound as a party to protect it. . . . But afterwards the Commissioners were left to their intrinsic weakness. . . . The Commission had to be dissolved.'[43]

Public men were slow to learn the lesson of the Poor Law Board. In the '40s, when its main victim, Chadwick, was pressing for a central department to handle questions of public health, it is significant that he did not suggest a ministry. The experiment was tried of letting one member of a board represent it in parliament. This was done in the case of the Board of Woods, Forests and Land Revenues, and the example was followed in the General Board of Health, set up in 1848, with the First Commissioner of Woods and Forests as *ex officio* President. But the President was 'in no sense a ministerial head, since he shouldered no more responsibility for policy than any other member of the Board'.[44] The first head of the General Board, Morpeth, worked closely with Chadwick so that the defects in the structure only became fully apparent under his successor, Seymour. He did not bother to attend the meetings; neither did he try to carry out the Board's decisions, nor indeed to conceal his disagreement with many of them. Conflicts with his colleagues naturally ensued, revealing the ambiguous nature of the President's status. 'Was he simply the first among his equals, or did he sit at the Board as a departmental chief with his subordinate advisers? By the Public Health Act he was on the same footing as the other three members of the Board; yet, as a minister of the Crown, his shoulders carried more responsibility and his opinion more weight. . . . The question had another aspect. While the critics objected that the Board were independent and uncontrolled,

[42] PRO 30/22/8. Wood to Russell, September 1, 1849.
[43] W. Bagehot, *English Constitution* (2 e., 1872), Chapter VI.
[44] Lewis, 145.

Chadwick complained on the other hand that no minister gave his full attention to the subject of public health.'[45] At last there came a day when Seymour could not even find a seconder for a crucial motion he wished to put before the Board![46]

Both the Woods and Forests and the Board of Health were converted into ministries, whilst retaining the title of boards, in 1851 and 1854 respectively. 'These ... changes were partly due to the realization that a board which was represented in parliament by one of its members was not thereby made fully responsible to Parliament. The First Commissioner of Woods could be outvoted at both the Office of Woods and at the General Board of Health of which he was *ex officio* President, and those boards were, therefore, no more amenable to parliamentary control than the Poor Law Commission had been. What was needed was not merely direct representation, but representation by a person who was also exclusively responsible and who could be dismissed by parliament if he failed to use his powers as parliament wished. Morpeth saw this plainly enough when he wrote to the Prime Minister welcoming an enquiry into the Office of Woods because 'it must issue into a recommendation to put more unity of authority and responsibility in the Chief Commissioner.'[47] Once it had been accepted that boards must be represented in parliament and that the representative (or the most senior of them, if there was more than one) should take responsibility for its acts, it was natural to wonder whether the rest had any function left to perform at all.

With certain exceptions such as the Charity Commissioners, the solution eventually found was either to make an individual minister responsible for each board or to turn the board into a ministry. The former alternative is illustrated by the situation of the revenue boards under the Treasury. It permitted a board to continue functioning as such. The latter need not involve a disuse of the term board, and no departments were *called* ministries in the nineteenth century. Trevelyan was prepared to contemplate such a transformation for the revenue boards themselves, the chairmanships being 'made parliamentary offices like the Chairmanship of the Poor Law Board, which I think is the true system'.[48]

A necessary condition for the transformation of a board into a ministry—irrespective of terminology—was that at least one of its members should sit in parliament. The sufficient condition was that its principal, or sole, parliamentary spokesman should enjoy a

[45] ibid., 267.   [46] Finer (1952), 402.   [47] Willson (1955), 52.
[48] PRO 30/22/8. Trevelyan to Russell, August 13, 1849.

position vis-à-vis his colleagues like that in the (presumably apocryphal) story about Abraham Lincoln's cabinet. 'Ayes, one; noes, seven: the Ayes have it.' This was the situation, for example, in the short-lived Railway Board of 1844–5. It was presided over by Lord Dalhousie, as Vice-President and later President of the Board of Trade; the four other members were all permanent officials. At the height of the 'Railway Mania', Dalhousie's position was precarious. The Board weakened his position rather than strengthening it. His enemies could represent him as the mere spokesman of 'a few clerks in a subordinate government office.'[49] To a former President of the Board of Trade, the experiment seemed 'a cumbrous and inconvenient mode of proceeding [which] raised subordinate members of the Board of Trade to a parity with the President.'[50] Reports from the Railway Board bore the signatures of the members, which implied that Dalhousie was no more than *primus inter pares*. At the opening of the parliamentary session of 1845, rumours were going round about dissensions in the Board. An M.P. asked whether it was to be inferred from the five signatures that the reports were unanimous. On the answer to that question, their weight could depend. Another Member referred to a speculation that one of the members had abstained from voting on a particular report. Ministers declined any statement about the opinions of individual members of the Board.[51] But the discussion left embarrassing implications behind. If decisions in the Railway Board were made by the vote of the majority, why should members stop at abstaining? Could not the minister find himself outvoted by his own permanent officials?

In fact, no votes were taken at the Board. Nor would Dalhousie have considered himself bound by such a vote. He stated the position clearly to his colleagues on the Board: 'If in preparing a report to be laid before parliament, a difference should arise between the member of the Privy Council ... presiding and the Inspector General, the Secretary, or any other member of the Board, the institution of this new form of the Railway Department would require ... that the dissentient members should nevertheless sign the report, if called upon to do so by the presiding member ... If any concurrence of circumstances should make it the duty of the presiding member to insist on the signature of the dissentient member, then it would be for that gentleman to consider whether he should affix his name to the report, or whether he would prefer to resign his office.'[52]

---

[49] *Railways and the Board of Trade* (3 e., 1845), 10 and 12.
[50] 3 *Hansard*, lxxxvii, 541.　　　　　[51] 3 *Hansard*, lxxxvii, 530–41.
[52] Parris (1965), 70–1.

In Dalhousie's case, the contrast between the appearance of a board and the reality of a ministry did harm. But soon the terminology became a matter of indifference. Even when a new board was proposed, it was recognized that a ministerial pattern of administration was intended. When a plan to set up an Education Board was under discussion in 1867, it was laid down that, although there were to be five permanent members, 'the determination of the Lord President shall be final. . . . There is no magic in the word [Board]. If we could ask at once for an Education *Minister*, the difficulty would be at an end. . . . It is not intended to make the whole Board perform the work of each person. Each member is to do the duty of his separate department. Omit the term "Board" if it is objected to: but simply say that so many persons are to perform the duties, subject to a general power of consultation.'[53] A similar point was made in a plan for the reform of naval administration. The Board of Admiralty should continue, but the First Lord should 'decide . . . without reference to any vote or equality which may exist under the present board system'.[54]

MINISTERS AND THEIR OFFICIALS

The pressures which compelled ministers to take responsibility for boards, forced them also to take responsibility for individual officers in their departments. It has been said that 'the whole training of the civil servant renders him anonymous and teaches him that it is never for him, as a person, to take responsibility, which is always higher or in another department; and if unfortunate things happen as the result of the system, his own conscience is clear'.[55] Whatever may be the case today, many officials in mid-nineteenth-century Whitehall were not like that. They stemmed from a different tradition, that of the public officer. 'These . . . were appointed and known individually by name . . . and their duties were mostly imposed upon them directly by the law and enforced by the courts.'[56] As such, they often felt a strong sense of personal responsibility, though they do not always seem to have been very clear to whom that responsibility was owed—whether to parliament, to society at large, or to nothing

[53] Disraeli Papers. B IX/B/1. Unsigned printed paper on the constitution of the Education Office, 1867.
[54] ibid. B VII/8. Printed confidential paper on the administration of the navy, by R. M. Bromley, January, 1862.
[55] Allen, 187.
[56] W. A. Robson (ed.), *The British Civil Servant* (1937), 12.

less than the human race itself. It was difficult for them to accept the idea that the minister should be the sole channel between themselves and those to whom they felt an obligation. They wished also to report direct to parliament, to publicize their views in the press, to work through Select Committees and interest groups. The idea of anonymity was alien to them and they only slowly came to accept it; there were 'formidable divergencies in the behaviour of eminent officials from anything that could be called neutral or anonymous'.[57]

In the 1840s no issue was more controversial than Free Trade. Yet, by 1842, 'there was no senior official in the Board of Trade who was a neutral in the controversial problems of economic policy'. Consider, for example, the aim of two of them, Deacon Hume and MacGregor, in putting up a sympathetic M.P. to move for a Select Committee on import duties in 1840. 'They thought that it would be for the public interest if those who were, or who had been, in office at the Board of Trade could be transferred for a short time from their homes, or from their private offices in Whitehall, into a committee room of the House of Commons, for then, not only would their evidence be given publicly, but it would be ordered to be printed, and circulated through the country.'[58] Two points are noteworthy here. In urging the cause of Free Trade, these civil servants believed that they were, not merely advocating their private views, but promoting the public interest. They held, moreover, that their responsibility would not be adequately discharged by advising their minister to adopt a free-trade policy. They believed that it was their duty to go outside their department and try to influence a wider circle. Four leading officials of the Board of Trade gave evidence to the Select Committee and 'a careful reading of the minutes of evidence suggest that the form and character of their statements . . . had been previously concerted between them and the chairman'.[59]

Board of Trade officials were not alone in their attitude. It was shared by the great Trevelyan himself. In one respect, he was nonpartisan. Though 'a keen Whig' he did not vote at elections: 'He thought this was the only correct conduct for a senior civil servant.'[60] But he was also indiscreet. In 1843 he visited Ireland, during O'Connell's last campaign. On his return he reported to Peel and Graham. In October, when the government was watching apprehen-

[57] G. K. Clark, 'Statesmen in Disguise', *Historical Journal*, ii (1959), 30.
[58] L. Brown, *Board of Trade and the Free Trade Movement, 1830–1842* (Oxford, 1958), 29. C. Badham, *Life of James Deacon Hume* (1859), 241.
[59] Brown, 142.
[60] J. Hart, 'Sir Charles Trevelyan at the Treasury', *EHR*, lxxv (1960), 109.

sively the situation caused by O'Connell's arrest, Trevelyan wrote a long open letter to the press on Ireland. He used a *nom de plume*, but proclaimed his authorship to a junior Treasury minister. Graham was indignant. 'Have you seen,' he enquired of Peel, 'in the *Morning Chronicle* today a letter about Ireland containing all Mr Trevelyan's information in the very words which he used to us? Surely it is highly improper that a Secretary of the Treasury should thus communicate to an Opposition paper intelligence which he made known to the government as of official importance? Think of that blockhead, Trevelyan, boasting . . . of his letter to the *Morning Chronicle* as a great public service!!' Peel agreed. 'How a man,' he wrote to Graham, 'after his confidential interview with us could think it consistent with common decency to reveal to the . . . world all he told us is passing strange. He must be a consummate fool.'[61] Was Trevelyan's action 'highly improper' or was it a 'public service?' If he disagreed with his political superiors it was clearly not because he was a 'blockhead' or 'a consummate fool'. The incident was not a breach of a settled rule, but a conflict of views as to the proper behaviour for a civil servant prior to the establishment of the modern convention.

A much less-well-known official was also airing his views on Ireland at the same period. The post of Inspector-General of Railways at the Board was at that time held by Major-General Charles Pasley, R.E. Although he claimed that he had 'always made a point of not interfering in the internal politics of the country, which, as a military man not possessed of landed property, I consider unbecoming and unnecessary', he did not hold that his post at the Board of Trade in itself precluded him from doing so. In Irish affairs, anyway, his rule did not apply. He wrote to *The Times* of the 'unaccountable supineness of the present ministers of this country, whose measures are a disgrace to them as individuals and collectively'. Even though the letter was not meant for publication, it was an extraordinary outburst by twentieth-century standards of official rectitude. A dinner at the Institution of Civil Engineers gave him a chance to declare his views, which he seized, 'reprobating O'Connell and the inactivity of the government'. Far from regretting his words, he was disappointed when, on looking into the press, he found no report of them 'as I would have wished my sentiments to appear'. He discussed politics with M.P.s and—most surprising of all—spoke on Irish affairs in Dublin while on official business.[62]

Sir Henry Cole was in the 1840s an official in the Public Record

[61] Brown, 33. Clark (1959), 31.   [62] Parris (1965), 34.

Office. A leading question of the day was whether there should be a standard gauge for the country's railway system. Most of the lines were built in the narrow gauge, championed by George and Robert Stephenson, and most notably exemplified on the London and North-Western Railway. But one very important company, the Great Western, had adopted the broad gauge, on the advice of their brilliant engineer, Brunel. The narrow-gauge party favoured uniformity, because they felt confident that their system would become standard. The broad-gauge party opposed uniformity, since they could hardly hope to see their system generally adopted: hence standardization would, they feared, mean the end of their bold experiment. Cole published a pamphlet on the subject in 1846. 'After the publication of this pamphlet, the proprietors in the London and North-Western Railway engaged my services to create a public opinion to support uniformity of gauge as best for national interests, and I spent over two years in this work ... The aid of pictures to represent the inconvenience of break of gauge was called in, and the *Illustrated London News* ... inserted graphic scenes at Gloucester ... Thackeray accompanied me to witness the reality at Gloucester, which he satirized by two papers in *Punch*.'[63] In all, Cole wrote or commissioned sixteen pamphlets on the question, whilst continuing his work in the Public Record Office. Both parties had strong political backing. Yet no harm to Cole's official career appears to have ensued.

Chadwick was another official of the period who made extensive use of the press. Alexander Bain, who served with him briefly as assistant secretary of the Metropolitan Sanitary Commission, wrote: 'In supporting Chadwick's various schemes we had frequent recourse to the newspapers which it was his custom all through his career to inspire on topics that he was pushing forward. I had to take a considerable part in this work, and to write leaders on such papers as we had access to, chiefly the *Globe* evening paper and the *Observer* weekly.'[64] Besides the press, Chadwick secured other allies. He would instigate M.P.s to bring items of business up for him, and work with them against his opponents in the public service. The reports of Royal Commissions and other bodies in which he had a hand were used as ammunition to push his schemes or to thwart his enemies. It became public knowledge that certain lines of policy were his, as distinct from policies adopted by his political superiors. He was on occasion criticized in public by ministers he claimed to serve.

[63] Sir H. Cole, *50 Years of Public Work* (1884), i, 82–3.
[64] q. Clark (1959), 31–2.

He was capable of opposing in secret Bills his chiefs were likely to promote. Chadwick did recognize some limits to what a man in his position could do. He would not join the Health of Towns Association, though he helped it from behind the scenes. Recognizing that he could not directly answer his adversaries, he contended that he should be immune from attack. To attack a civil servant, he declared, was like hitting a woman.

Sir Rowland Hill, the postal reformer, was another civil servant whose activities transgressed the bounds of anonymity. Considering that his official superior, Colonel Maberly, the Secretary of the Post Office, was impeding his efforts he intrigued to remove him. He approached a number of back-benchers in the Commons, asking them to put pressure on the Chancellor of the Exchequer to move Maberly. Like Chadwick he had some notion of professional ethics. When Cobden advised him to circularize all M.P.s who might be interested, he declined to do so on the grounds that it would be a breach of faith. Nevertheless, he did approach a large number. He also promoted motions that would help his policy through his friends in the House and enjoyed close relations with *The Times*.[65]

It is surprising what these men, and others, were able to get away with. Sir James Stephen, of the Colonial Office, on the other hand, was subject to bitter attacks. The *Spectator* alleged that he was the 'real' author of the government's colonial policy, not Glenelg, the Secretary of State. He was dubbed 'King Stephen', 'Mr Over-Secretary Stephen' and 'Mr Mother Country'. This was not fair to Stephen personally, but there was a genuine constitutional problem. Hitherto ministerial responsibility had been personal responsibility. 'In England the ministers who are at the head of the several departments of the state, are liable any day and every day to defend themselves in Parliament; in order to do this they must be minutely acquainted with all the details of the business of their offices, and the only way of being constantly armed with such information is to conduct and direct those details themselves.'[66] The existence of servants of the Crown so influential as Stephen seemed to many of their contemporaries to undermine this concept. Even if it was not genuinely believed to do so, it made a good stick with which to beat the government dog. Did the Colonial Secretary tender personal advice to the Crown? Or did he in many cases retail Stephen's advice at second hand? In the latter case, could the Colonial Secretary claim that the advice was his? If not, what was his title to retain his

[65] ibid., 32–3.
[66] Palmerston to the Queen, February 25, 1838. q. Benson and Esher, i, 136.

office? 'The King's servants must be his [advisers], or they cannot remain his servants.'[67] Those who thought in such eighteenth-century terms saw men like Stephen as 'ministers behind the curtain'. Such hidden counsellors must either be sent packing or made honest men of. The King must 'determine who shall be his [advisers], either those who are now his servants, or to make those his servants who are now his favourite [advisers]'.[68]

THE DOCTRINE OF ANONYMITY

In fact, Stephen did not deserve such onslaughts. He was one of the first to realize, as early as 1833, that permanence would imply anonymity. The date is noteworthy because 'it is difficult to carry the history of the exclusive responsibility of ministers and the irresponsibility of [the] civil service behind 1830, because before that date conditions tend to be very different'.[69] The great difference was, of course, that in the earlier period, permanent officers had virtually no share in the formation of policy. 'Practice largely coincided with the constitutional convention that decreed that the policy for which ministers assumed responsibility should be entirely their own.'[70] Stephen's department was, in fact, one of the first where permanent officials took part in policy-making on something like the modern pattern. This development dated from the 1820s. Stephen saw that if the permanent official was to have real security of tenure, he must be shielded from attack. If he was to be so protected, he must also forgo public praise. It followed that the public must be prevented, so far as possible, from being in a position to link his name with particular measures emanating from his department. All this comes out clearly in a letter from Stephen to Howick written in 1833. The latter was about to publish a document and to attribute to Stephen 'the composition or the authorship of certain parts of it'. Stephen objected. 'As I fill,' he wrote, 'no substantive or independent station [i.e. hold no political office], I have no just claim to arrogate to myself any part of the credit of any measure in the preparation or maturing of which I may have been employed. Exempted as I am from all public responsibility, it would be unjust were I to assume any share of the honour due to those [i.e. the political heads of the department] who have rendered themselves responsible for my compositions.'[71]

---

[67] Duke of Newcastle, 1746, q. Pares, 95. [68] ibid.
[69] Clark (1959), 27. [70] Young, 1.
[71] q. E. Hughes, 'Sir James Stephen and the Anonymity of the Civil Servant', *Public Administration*, xxxvi (1958), 30.

Between Stephen's enunciation of the doctrine and its general acceptance several decades were to elapse. Civil servants sometimes displayed bad consciences when they helped individuals or groups outside their departments. For example, in 1839 a Factory Inspector supplied information from official sources for the use of the Anti-Corn Law League with the warning: 'You are at liberty to make whatever use you choose of any information you may give provided you do not make use of my name, or state that it comes from any official individual.'[72] Bromley, Disraeli's correspondent in the Admiralty, was aware of the dubious propriety of a senior official communicating with a leading member of the Opposition. 'Be good enough not to let my handwriting be seen,' he wrote, 'as it is my intention to work this matter with you without *anyone* knowing what I am doing.' 'I may have over-stepped the strict rules of propriety in unburdening myself to you.' Or again: 'That which I ought not to divulge will never escape from me, yet ideas may haunt a man which it may be a relief to him to communicate to one who may use them for his country's good without reflection upon his honour.' He was, clearly, quite certain that he was promoting the public interest rather than merely ventilating private speculations. Yet Bromley could not see what Stephen had perceived so clearly two decades earlier—the civil servants who are to enjoy permanent status must forgo public praise. 'To be mentioned favourably by the Leader of the House of Commons cannot fail to add to a man's reputation,' he declared, referring to a compliment paid him by Disraeli during the latter's spell of office in 1852.[73]

This example is a reminder that it takes two to make a convention. If civil servants were slow to accept anonymity, it was partly because of the lack of guidance they got from politicians. The Factory Act of 1833 delegated extensive powers to the Inspectors themselves, by-passing ministers. Hence, for some years uncertainty prevailed as to which minister was responsible for them. Even after that doubt had been resolved in favour of the Home Secretary, doubt persisted as to the status of their reports. In 1846, Graham wished them to exclude certain information. Instead of simply instructing them to refrain, he told his Parliamentary Under-Secretary to write as follows: 'If their Joint Report is intended for the information of the Secretary of State, it is unnecessary to insert in it letters sent to them from the Home Office or other documents, of which the Secretary of

[72] N. McCord, *The Anti-Corn Law League, 1838–1846* (1958), 187.
[73] Disraeli Papers. Bromley to Disraeli, November 24, 1854, June 30, 1855, January 28, 1856.

State has knowledge before he receives their report. . . . If on the other hand their report is intended for the information of parliament and the public, it would be irregular and inconvenient that it should contain the correspondence of the Secretary of State with the Inspectors, or documents which they have received from him—the propriety of publishing such correspondence or documents being a matter for the consideration of the Secretary of State.'[74] But which of these two purposes were the reports in fact intended to serve? That was too difficult a question for a junior minister and he declined 'to express an opinion as to the form in which it will be advisable for the Inspectors to prepare their reports'.[75] The responsibility was thrust back on them.

As late as 1859, Northcote, in spite of having been an official himself, and in spite of having recently carried out important enquries into the civil service, revealed a complete unawareness of the doctrine. In July of that year, Gladstone had just become Chancellor of the Exchequer under Palmerston, who had succeeded Derby. Northcote had been Derby's Financial Secretary to the Treasury. He challenged Gladstone in the House of Commons. 'The Chancellor of the Exchequer had said that he would not have proposed this arrangement unless he had been assured by the heads of the revenue department that there would be no practical difficulty in carrying it out. Now . . . they must have very recently changed their opinion; because when the matter was discussed a few months ago they thought its working would be attended with serious embarrassment.'[76] Gladstone tried to prevent Northcote going on in this vein 'by a prolonged shaking of his head'. Later he explained to Northcote that he had not meant to deny the fact. His gesture 'was intended to intimate that references from the Opposition bench to the opinions of the permanent officers of the government, in contradiction to the opinion of the minister who is responsible in the matter at issue, were contrary to rule and to convenience'.[77]

THE LOWE CASE

Probably the last occasion when M.P.s seriously asserted that civil servants were directly responsible to parliament was the Lowe case of 1864. The point at issue was the status of reports from H.M.

[74] Thomas, 256. [75] ibid.
[76] 3 *Hansard*, clv, 225, July 21, 1859.
[77] Gladstone to Northcote, July 25, 1859, q. A. Lang, *Life . . . of Sir Stafford Northcote, etc.* (1890), i, 160.

Inspectors of Schools. If Inspectors were personally responsible for these reports, they had the right to choose their own words, free from editorial control in the department. Equally, M.P.s had a right to assume that the reports put before them represented fairly the Inspectors' views, free from amendments made in the department. If, on the other hand, the minister—Robert Lowe, in this instance— was expected to take responsibility for the reports, he had a right to call on Inspectors to revise their drafts prior to presentation. Otherwise, in an extreme case, he might have found himself required to take responsibility for two contradictory things; say, the Revised Code of 1862 and a criticism of it from one of the numerous Inspectors to whom it was anathema. Parliament had to decide which form of responsibility would give it the most effective control of administration. If permanent civil servants 'were relieved from subordination to any superior . . . a system of irresponsible administration would be introduced'. If, on the other hand, responsibility was always in the hands of a minister, subject 'to the general rule of retiring from office when he ceased to possess the confidence of parliament',[78] the latter would have an indirect, but effective, control of those in his department. In fact, Lowe's resignation in 1864 appears to be the earliest arising out of a minister's responsibility for those under him, as distinct from his responsibility for advice to the Crown. Hence, it was 'no arbitrary rule, which requires that all holders of permanent offices must be subordinate to some minister responsible to parliament, since it is obvious that, without it, the first principle of our system of government—the control of all branches of the administration by parliament—would be abandoned'.[79]

Unlike their Factory colleagues, H.M. Inspectors of Schools had no statutory powers. They had been appointed to advise ministers on the administration of grants. There was, therefore, no obvious reason why the practice should ever have grown up of their reporting directly to parliament. Nevertheless, it had. Inside the office, too, the status of the early H.M.I.s was odd in the light of twentieth-century ideas. They met annually in London for the discussion of any matters relating to education, and the conference gradually assumed something of a collegiate character. By 1857 votes were taken even on issues of the department's policy. On at least one occasion, the Lord President had to announce a vote of the meeting adverse to his policy.[80] This practice was stopped in 1859.

[78] Grey, 172.   [79] ibid., 171.
[80] J. Leese, *Personalities and Powers in English Education* (Leeds, 1950), 42.

The previous year, Adderley, the Vice-President, had proposed to drop the publication of the full reports, and merely to print extracts in future. The result was a 'Grand Remonstrance', drawn up by an H.M.I. and signed by almost all his colleagues, which was followed by a debate in the Commons. The complaint was that 'henceforth, the reports of the Inspectors would not be given to parliament, but would be made use of as materials for the reports of the Education Department. This was open to great objection. . . . If the Committee of Education undertook to select passages from these reports for publication, they would be regarded as responsible for whatever they inserted'.[81] The implication was clear; responsible Inspectors were preferable to responsible ministers. Adderley gave way. The full reports would continue to appear. But they would 'be prepared henceforth in accordance with instructions. . . . If there was anything in the report which did not fall under one or other of these [instructions], he would send it back to the Inspector for excision.'[82] A minute of 1861 laid down that 'Inspectors must confine themselves to the state of the schools under their inspection and to practical suggestions for their improvement. If any report, in the judgment of their Lordships, does not conform to this standard it is to be returned to the Inspector for revision, and if, on its being again received from him it appears to be open to the same objection, it is to be put aside as a document not proper to be printed at the public expense.[83] A year later, there was more trouble in the Commons, when Lowe refused to publish two of three reports on Roman Catholic schools, because their authors declined to omit certain passages.

In 1864, Lord Robert Cecil—the future Marquis of Salisbury and future Prime Minister—moved 'that in the opinion of this House the mutilation of the reports of Her Majesty's Inspectors of Schools, and the exclusion from them of statements and opinions adverse to the educational views entertained by the Committee of Council, while matter favourable to them is admitted, are variations of the understanding under which the appointment of Inspectors was originally sanctioned by Parliament'.[84] Lowe denied the allegation. While he was speaking, however, copies of the reports in question with red marks in the margin were circulating among back-benchers. The resolution was carried, and Lowe resigned. A Select Committee later vindicated his conduct. Owing to his bad eyesight, he had had the reports read to him, and so had never seen the marks.

[81] 3 *Hansard*, clii, 696–7, February 22, 1859.   [82] ibid., 713.
[83] q. Leese, 44.   [84] q. ibid., 95.

However, Lowe's personal honour is a red herring in the present argument. Cecil rightly insisted that the issue at stake was one of responsibility and asserted that there was a direct link between the M.P. and the civil servant. 'I do not admit that the Committee of Privy Council have a right . . . so to alter . . . reports intended for the use of this House as to change their meaning. . . . I cannot admit that . . . matter which differs from the opinions of their superiors on questions of policy . . . is rightly excluded from these reports.' Such an attitude, Lowe contended, was incompatible with ministerial responsibility. 'It is quite open to the House to express an opinion that the Inspectors should report directly to parliament, and not go the Privy Council, and thus exonerate us from all responsibility in the matter.'[85] Palmerston took a very strong line. Cecil and those who had acted with him should not even have been put on the Select Committee appointed to investigate the affair. 'They have . . . been guilty of practices which give them a strong interest in discrediting the department in order to rehabilitate themselves. To entrust them with such an enquiry is already to decide a point against us, that is, that there is nothing in the conduct of a M.P. who suffers himself to be made the tool of traitors in an office, and who circulates documents which he dares not produce, disqualifying him from the most important enquiries, nay, to prevent him sitting in judgment on a department which he has betrayed and under-mined by circulating papers unknown to it.'[86]

THE SCUDAMORE CASE

In 1864, then, ministerial responsibility for civil servants was still a controversy rather than accepted doctrine. A very different atmos-phere pervaded the Scudamore affair of 1873. Frank Scudamore was on the staff of the Post Office. Following the purchase of the telegraphs by the state in 1868 he was put in charge of the take-over and of welding them into a national system. Since he was guilty of financial irregularities on a heroic scale, it is important to make one point at the outset. He never made, or sought to make, one penny of private profit out of the transaction. His failing was not that he put private interest before the public interest, but that his zeal for the public interest made him impatient of established rules. A colleague of his predicted that when 'the history of that extraordinary time . . . is written, the public will read with wonder of the desperate unflagging

[85] 3 *Hansard*, clxxvi, 2080–1.
[86] Palmerston Papers. Palmerston to Granville, May 26, 1864.

energy by which it was carried through by the man who had planned it, and his devoted band of followers, who sat up night after night, denying themselves rest, comfort, almost food, in order that the compact with the government might be duly executed'.[87]

Scudamore's 'desperate unflagging energy' enabled him to push ahead with the scheme faster than had been anticipated, with the result that he exhausted the credit voted by parliament. Impatient of the delay that must ensue pending a further vote, Scudamore devised an ingenious system for turning aside Post Office revenues from their established route to the Exchequer into the telegraph purchase account. For a surprising period his ruse went undetected. In 1873, the scandal broke. £800,000 had been diverted. Scudamore made a clean breast of the whole affair. Sir John Lubbock told the Commons: 'Mr Scudamore had frankly taken the responsibility. "I did it," he said, "and I am alone responsible for it."[88] But, as R. Bernal Osborne pointed out, it was "all nonsense, and worse than nonsense, ... to put the onus on a Second Clerk in the Post Office. Mr Scudamore, no doubt with a chivalry that does him honour, ... says "Say it was I", and takes the whole responsibility on himself; but is that sufficient for this House? This House has nothing to do with Mr Scudamore. He is not responsible to us. We ought to look to the heads of departments; for if we are to shuffle off these questions by saying that a clerk in the Post Office, however distinguished and disinterested he may be, is to take the burden and the blame on his shoulders, there is an end to parliamentary government.'[89] And no one contradicted him.

The civil servant stood in a relationship to his minister not unlike that which existed between the minister and the Crown. Both were advisers on the exercise of power. But in another way the relationship differed. Ministerial advisers were expendable, while the Crown remained. At the lower level, the pattern was reversed. The advised were transitory, the advisers permanent. Parliament and public opinion were slow to adjust to the new situation. Hence the violent and persistent abuse of men like Stephen and Chadwick. Their detractors could see that such men were not merely executing policy laid down from on high, and jumped to the conclusion that they were abusing their position in a sinister way. It would have been interesting had someone—Col. Sibthorp perhaps—started proceedings to impeach Chadwick. If advice to the Crown originated with a permanent official, what was the proper course for opponents

[87] Edmund Yates, *Recollections and Experiences*, ii, Chapter V.
[88] 3 *Hansard*, ccxvii, 1209.   [89] ibid., 1223–4.

of that policy to take? To attack the minister would miss the target. If, on the other hand, they attacked the official, they would not be able to get rid of him, because of his permanent status. The difficulty was eventually resolved by an extension of the doctrine of ministerial responsibility. In extreme cases, ministers resigned while officials stayed on. Maitland pointed out that 'royal immunity is coupled with ministerial responsibility'. Lowell turned the coin over to read the inscription on the other side: 'The permanent official, like the King, can do no wrong.'[90]

[90] A. L. Lowell, *The Government of England* (New York, new ed., 1926), i, 193.

CHAPTER IV

MINISTERS IN THEIR DEPARTMENTS

'In every department of state there is a permanent element, and also what may be termed a progressive and political one. The permanent public servants preserve all the traditions of the office, and carry on the ordinary business. They are the advisers of, and to a certain extent, a check upon, the new political chiefs who come in without experience; while, on the other hand, the tendency of all permanent officers is to get into a certain routine, and a change of the heads, from time to time, checked by the permanence of those who are always in office, tends very much to produce an improved system of administration of any department.'

Sir Charles, Wood, 1861

The early-nineteenth-century minister, if he was also a 'man of business', bestrode his department like a colossus. His duties were both political and administrative, but he worked within a system which enabled him to give much time to the latter. Palmerston was probably the last survivor of the species. He did not think of himself as a party man, nor did he habitually behave as one. He regarded himself as a follower of Canning until the latter's death, and so had the simpler loyalty to a man as his guide, rather than the more complex loyalty to a party. During the early part of his career, he represented a constituency on the single condition that he never went near the place. Hence relations with his constituents can scarcely have taken up much of his time. Before 1830, he rarely spoke in parliament, and had no reputation there, save for competence in moving the estimates for his department, the War Office.

Yet the office of Secretary of War, which he held from 1809 until 1828, was anything but a sinecure. The judgment passed by one of his biographers on his whole career applies without modification to this stage of it. 'A remarkable talent for concentrating details . . . was his peculiar merit as a man of business, and wherein he showed a masterly capacity. No official situation, therefore, found him unequal to it.'[1] Since he dealt personally with much of the routine business, his

[1] Bulwer, i, 3.

106

'duties involved a mass of the most petty and tedious routine'.[2] Examples of the kind of business to which he gave his personal attention were: 'Trying vainly to secure from the Army Medical Board information that would enable him to pass on the appointment of an army surgeon for service on the Continent . . . informing the Adjutant-General of mistakes made in the shipping of arms . . . instructing the Storekeeper-General to forward clothing (even to a single overcoat) according to careful specifications regarding size; . . . writing to the Commissary-in-Chief for accounts of food supplied in order that the secretary might next instruct the Paymaster-General to deposit funds in payment at the bank . . . [discussing] the amount of pay due to a single veterinary surgeon, and even . . . the disposal of one unserviceable horse.'[3]

When he went to the Foreign Office in 1830, he ran it in a similar way. He told the House that he read 'every report, every letter, and every despatch received . . . down to the least important letter of the lowest vice-consul'.[4] What is more, he answered them. Greville reported the view of the Foreign Office staff who 'said that he wrote admirably . . . that his diligence and attention were unwearied—he read everything and wrote an immense quantity'.[5] Brougham praised him for using 'his pen better and more quickly than almost anybody'.[6] Other statesmen took equal trouble. Aberdeen 'believed his written instructions [to Lord Amherst, Canada, 1835] to be among his best compositions'.[7] Grey at the Colonial Office had to produce two papers, one on the Orange River sovereignty question, and the other on representative government for Cape Colony. He wrote: 'I am left to write the whole of one report and a great portion of the other myself.'[8] Palmerston contrasted the industry of British ministers with the slackness of their Continental counterparts, who were more than ready to delegate. 'To such an extent is this carried, that Viscount Palmerston believes that the Ministers for Foreign Affairs in France, Austria, Prussia and Russia seldom take the trouble of writing their own despatches, except, perhaps, upon some very particular and important occasion.'[9]

He only achieved this with great effort. He described his work at the Foreign Office as 'more intense and uninterrupted labour than almost any man ever went through before' and that he felt 'like a

[2] H. C. F. Bell, *Lord Palmerston* 2 v. (1936), i, 28.
[3] ibid.   [4] ibid., 258.   [5] q. Bell, i, 198.   [6] q. ibid.
[7] Lady F. Balfour, *Life of . . . Aberdeen* (n.d.), ii, 20.
[8] PRO 30/22/8. Grey to Russell, December 14, 1849.
[9] Benson and Esher, i, 136. Palmerston to Q. Victoria, February 25, 1838.

man who has plumped into a mill-race, scarcely able by all his kicking and plunging to keep his head above water'.[10] Nevertheless, he made it a matter of pride that business was never more than one day in arrears. He explained to the young Queen Victoria that the British system of government forced ministers to run their departments as he did: 'The ministers who are at the head of the several departments of the state are liable any day and every day to defend themselves in parliament; in order to do this they must be minutely acquainted with all the details of the business of their offices and the only way of being constantly armed with such information is to conduct and direct those details themselves.'[11] That this was a real danger is shown by the experience of Palmerston's colleague, Stanley. One of O'Connell's techniques to discredit the latter as Irish Secretary 'was suddenly to ask a question in parliament on some minor Irish occurrence concerning which Stanley would be forced to confess his ignorance'.[12]

But the bulk of business and the demands of parliament were both growing so fast that Palmerstonian administration was becoming impossible. Aberdeen was struck by this when he took over from Palmerston in 1841: 'The business of this office has increased beyond measure since I was here before [i.e. 1830] and I know not how it is to be overcome.'[13] Aberdeen had the advantage of being in the Lords, with a peer as Under-Secretary, and Peel to handle foreign affairs in the Commons.

When Palmerston returned to the Foreign Office in 1846, he tried to run things as before, but business got into arrears, at least during the Parliamentary session. At the end of August 1849, he wrote to the Consul-General at Alexandria: 'In working up the chaotic arrear which accumulates during a session of parliament, I have come upon your letter of the 10th May.'[14] At the beginning of September the following year he wrote: 'I have been more entirely swamped by business during the whole of this last session of parliament than I ever was at any time, and I have not even yet been able to work up the arrear of various matters which has accumulated by the regular overflowing of almost every day.'[15]

In 1853 he found the Home Office 'on the whole . . . a much easier

[10] Bell, i, 190–1.
[11] Benson and Esher, i, 136: dated February 25, 1838.
[12] W. D. Jones, *Lord Derby and Victorian Conservatism* (Oxford, 1956), 20.
[13] E. Ashley, *Life of . . . Viscount Palmerston, 1846–1865* (1876), i, 130.
[14] ibid., 228.
[15] ibid., ii, 9.

office than the Foreign, and, in truth, I really would not, on any consideration, undertake again an office so unceasingly laborious every day of the year as that of Foreign Affairs'.[16] But although easier, the Home Office left little time for detailed administration, at least while parliament was sitting, because 'the whole day of the Secretary of State, up to the time when he must go to the Commons, is taken up by deputations of all kinds and interviews with Members of Parliament, militia colonels, etc'.[17] At this stage of his life he still did a surprising amount of work himself—copying documents, for example[18]—which could have been delegated. Perhaps he did not fully trust even his private staff, for Lady Palmerston was believed to copy 'such of her husband's papers as were too confidential to be shown to any secretary'.[19] Nevertheless, he had learnt to delegate far more than he had ever done at the Foreign Office. His view had become the reverse of what it had been when he wrote to the Queen in 1838. Then he had vaunted the superiority of the British system as compared with Continental bureaucracy. 'There are . . . in all the public offices abroad a number of men who have spent the greater part of their lives in their respective departments, and who by their long experience are full of knowledge of what has been done in former times, and of the most convenient and easy manner of doing what may be required in the time present. This affords to the chiefs [a] motive for leaning upon their subordinates, and gives to those subordinates . . . real influence. This class of subordinate men has, from the fact of its being possessed of so much power, been invested with the title of "bureaucratic" '.[20] At that time, moreover, his practice had conformed to his preaching. Even 'the Under-Secretaries . . . were no more than clerks and did not interfere in matters of policy'. One of them wrote: 'Lord Palmerston . . . never consults an Under-Secretary. He merely sends out questions to be answered or papers to be copied . . . and our only business is to obtain from the clerks the information that is wanted.'[21] The Permanent Under-Secretary was required personally to supervise the copying of despatches, not merely in exceptional cases, but several hundreds every year.[22] When Granville, later to be Foreign Secretary himself, served under Palmerston, he complained that he had nothing more

---

[16] ibid.   [17] ibid., i, 328.   [18] Bell, ii, 253.
[19] Benson and Esher, i, 137.
[20] ibid., 136.
[21] Sir Charles Webster, 'Lord Palmerston at Work, 1830–1841', *Politica*, i, (1934–5), 137 and n.
[22] Bell, i, 201.

responsible to do than correct drafts, which was absurd since those who prepared them were men like James Bandinel, of the slave trade division, who was old enough to be his grandfather, and had been concerned with the slave trade all his working life.

In 1854, however, Palmerston told a very different tale. He informed the Commons that it was 'impossible to overrate the advantage to the public service of having in each department of the government a permanent secretary, not belonging to any political party, not swayed by passion or feeling . . . but a man who, being the depository of the lore and knowledge belonging to the particular department was able . . . to give the newcomer into that office information as to past events, as to the principles regulating the department, as to the knowledge of individuals, and as to the details of transactions, without which it was impossible for any man, let him be ever so able and ever so expert, to perform his duties with satisfaction to himself and advantage to the public'.[23]

THE NEW MINISTERIAL STYLE

Palmerston's change of view is of more than biographical importance. It indicates a change in the structure of central departments which originated at the beginning of the nineteenth century and was more or less complete by 1850. The personal style had given place to one in which work was delegated to inferior levels. The basic reason why ministers had to do this was the pressure of political life. 'My days are short for doing business for they finish at half past three. I must be in the House of Commons soon after four and I must dine before I go down.'[24] Stanley was said to spend his 'mornings . . .not in going through that twentieth part of the business allotted him as Colonial Minister which it is possible for the most laborious of human beings to accomplish, but in excogitating sound pummellings for Cobden, stinging invectives for O'Connell, and epigrammatic repartees for Lord John Russell.'[25] Though unfair to Stanley personally, the gibe pinpoints the conflict of duties in which all ministers found themselves.

Meanwhile the bulk of business continued to increase. Dickens made fun of the practice of measuring government activity by counting documents. 'When that admirable department [the Circumlocu-

[23] 3 *Hansard*, cxxix, 825, q. Roberts, 127.
[24] Add. MS. 48580. Palmerston to Clarendon, March 4, 1856.
[25] q. A. P. Martin, *Life and Letters of the Rt. Hon. Robert Lowe, Viscount Sherbrooke* (1893), i, 256–7.

tion Office] got into trouble, and was . . . attacked . . . as an institution wholly abominable and Bedlamite; then the noble or Right Honourable Barnacle who represented it in the House would [state] . . . that within the short compass of the last financial half-year, this much-maligned department (cheers) had written and received 15,000 letters (loud cheers), had made 24,000 minutes (louder cheers), and 32,517 memoranda (vehement cheering). Nay, an ingenious gentleman connected with the department, and himself a valuable public servant, had done him the favour to make a curious calculation of the amount of stationery consumed in it during the same period. . . . The sheets of foolscap paper it had devoted to the public service would pave the footways on both sides of Oxford Street from end to end, and leave nearly a quarter of a mile to spare for the park (immense cheering and laughter); while of tape—red tape—it had used enough to stretch, in graceful festoons, from Hyde Park Corner to the General Post Office.'[26] This attitude was shared by some who knew governments from the inside, as Dickens did not. 'If you are to judge the duties of men according to the quantity of business done under their direction, the Secretary at War ought to have twice as much to do as the Home Secretary, for he employs three times the number of clerks: but the duties of the one are completely insignificant to those of the other.'[27]

Nevertheless, an increase in the mere bulk of paper could result in a change of administrative style. Up to a point, an able and industrious minister could make virtually every decision himself. Beyond that point, delegation became a necessity. What was the minister to delegate? Clearly, what was unimportant. But who was to decide whether any given case was unimportant? Sometimes business came before the minister in such a way that he had to decide personally how it should be handled. In 1842, for example, G. R. Phillipps, M.P., complained to Gladstone, as President of the Board of Trade, that the Great Western Railway Company had made an agreement with a coach proprietor which in effect gave him a monopoly of the business between Oxford and Steventon, then the nearest station to the city. Gladstone's next step was to endorse the letter: 'Refer to Railway Department. Acknowledge and ask for any information as to the reasons alleged by the Company in justification. W.E.G.'[28] But no minister could have given even this modest amount of attention to all the business of his department, especially as the

---

[26] C. Dickens, *Little Dorrit*, Book 2, Chapter VIII.
[27] PRO 30/22/8. Ellice to Russell, June 16, 1850.
[28] Parris (1965), 41.

tide of paper continued to rise. The figures for the Colonial Office will serve as an example:

Year	Documents received	Documents sent
1830	8,150	4,587
1850	10,956	8,241
1870	13,541	12,136

Source: H. L. Hall, *The Colonial Office* (1937) 24.

If the minister had set himself to bestow on each item only so much attention as would enable him to determine what to delegate, and to whom, the mere labour of sifting would have been so herculean that no time would have remained for deciding on any cases at all.

THE HIERARCHY OF DECISION-MAKING

In the new administrative style, the fundamental discretion which a minister had to delegate was the discretion to distinguish cases which were important enough to be worth his attention from those which were too trivial to merit his notice. This discretion extended right down to officers near the base of the hierarchy. As the clerk inserted his paper-knife in each letter of the morning's mail, he could not know whether the envelope contained a routine request for a printed form, which he could deal with himself in thirty seconds, or the political scandal of the century. Such storms begin as clouds no bigger than a man's hand. It was for the official to decide whether or not to refer each item to his superior, and of course mistakes were sometimes made. Forster's private secretary once failed to recognize that a letter signed 'J. Ebor' had come from the Archbishop of York. He 'did not think it was worth troubling Mr Forster with, so acknowledged it in the usual way, and stated that the matter would receive attention'. The reply was addressed to 'J. Ebor, Esq.,York'. Not unnaturally, His Grace replied in turn and 'thought it gross ignorance for anyone in the position of a private secretary not to know the usual signature of the Archbishop of York'.[29] Such ignorance was, indeed, so gross as to be exceptional. But no matter how far experience, regulations or office custom might guide the clerk, some discretion still remained with him. His superior did not thank him if he were bothered with items which the underling should have decided on his own responsibility. So it went right up the

[29] Sir Algernon West, *Recollections* (1899), ii, 122–3.

scale. At each level, most issues were decided, but some referred higher.

Such a pattern was established in the Railway Department of the Board of Trade by 1854. 'The management of the details is entrusted to an Assistant Secretary, who examines the correspondence of the day, prepares the information necessary for arriving at a decision, and brings the whole of the important business in a convenient shape before the Chief Secretary, who gives him instructions upon which it becomes his duty to act. The Assistant Secretary disposes, on his own authority, of matters of smaller moment, and takes such intermediate proceedings in preparing a question for the decision of the Chief Secretary as his experience suggests.'[30] The Chief (i.e. permanent) Secretary in turn had to decide whether or not to submit railway items referred to him to the minister for decision at the highest departmental level.

The Education Department was organized, according to its Secretary, in a similar way. At the bottom were 'the clerks who are employed merely in copying and drafting letters'. Above them were 'a certain number of officers called examiners; the letters of the day are divided among these officers, and they make upon them the minutes which the cases seem to require; perhaps three out of four . . . require only the despatch of a certain printed form . . . In other cases, letters may have to be written'. One of the examiners recorded many years later how such decisions were taken. 'The work of the examiners was . . . mainly discharged by directing that sundry numbered paragraphs taken from a book of "precedents" should be sent as replies to letters. The "precedents" were originally taken from letters minuted by the Secretary, whose views were always supposed to be infallible, and as incontrovertible as the laws of the Medes and Persians.' The Secretary went on to explain that, where there was any uncertainty, cases were 'referred to two Assistant Secretaries, and if they feel any doubt about them, they send them on to me. . . . In the same way, I take on any letters about which I have any doubt to the Vice-President'.[31]

Thus the permanent head of a department stood at the gate from the administrative to the political level. At the Treasury, Hamilton used to decide what to let through 'by putting it to myself whether the decision is such as can be questioned in parliament. If it is, I consider that the judgment of one of the political officers, the

[30] P.P. 1854, xxvii, 166.
[31] P.P. 1865, vi, 30. Sir G. Kekewich, *The Education Department and After* (1920), 13.

Chancellor of the Exchequer or the Financial Secretary, should be exercised upon it'.[32]

In every grade, the civil servant required judgment, so that his superiors could rely on all those matters, but only those matters, which justified their personal attention being brought before them. Where these conditions existed, officials could be entrusted to speak in the name of the department. As a witness told a parliamentary committee in 1850: 'The permanent under-secretaries of the great departments of state are empowered in all official correspondence to make use of the name of the department, as they would a common seal. They do so upon their own responsibility; and if they abuse or misuse their trust, an appeal can be made to the chief, who is really as responsible to the Crown or to parliament for the act of his subordinate as if he had signed the document himself.' But the principle extended lower down the hierarchy, as shown in this dialogue between a Select Committee and the Secretary of the Education Department:

'Was that done in the name of My Lords?'

'Yes; every letter that leaves the office is written in the name of My Lords.'

'So that, when a letter appears to be from My Lords, there is not even a guarantee that it has been seen by you?'

'No; if it has not been signed by me, the probability is that I have not seen that letter . . . [and] it may be merely the decision of some subordinate in the office.'[33]

Palmerston had pointed out to the Queen how any degree of delegation was to some extent a delegation of power. 'Your Majesty will see how greatly such a system must place in the hands of the subordinate members of the public departments the power of directing the policy and the measures of the government; because the value and tendency, and the consequences, of a measure frequently depend as much upon the manner in which that measure is worked out as upon the intention and spirit with which it was planned.' Taylor, drawing on his Colonial Office experience, showed how even the discretion necessarily allowed to a copying clerk—to work fast or slow, accurately or inaccurately—could influence policy. 'The want of smoothness and celerity in this part of the operations of a statesman's official establishment constitutes a most important defect—a defect much more important than it might at first sight

[32] Hamilton to Stansfeld, October 25, 1869. I owe this reference to Dr M. Wright.
[33] q. Todd (1887–9), ii, 614. P.P. 1865, vi, 30.

appear. Measures upon which the fate of individuals or the material interests of communities may be said in some sort to depend will sometimes be obstructed, neglected, and delayed, owing to this defect; and men in authority are often (to the credit of their personal dispositions) so averse to giving trouble to those about them, or to the appearance of throwing away trouble which has been given, that measures and alterations of measures, in cases in which the sort of trouble in question ought to weigh no more than as the dust of the balance, sometimes turn upon the want of easy action in this part of the system of an office.' A case in point came up in 1849. 'I am very anxious,' wrote Hobhouse, 'that all the honours should be settled before the next mail of the 7th of June. But there is an awful Mr Smith at the Colonial Office whose formalities forbid all hope of dispatch.'[34]

Delegation could enable a minister to cope with the sheer quantity of business, but was not always possible. 'I am sensible that the load of business and responsibility,' wrote Grey, 'which now presses upon me is beyond what I have strength to bear, and that . . . many things are not attended to as they ought to be, and much business is very imperfectly performed.' Grey had always shown himself willing to delegate, when the staff was available. But the problem here was the quality of staff, not the quantity. Indeed, he would have been glad to clear out some of the men he had in order to make room for new blood. Unfortunately, 'you cannot get rid of those of the clerks in the office who are ordinary good men of business, however little they may possess the superior qualifications which are required for efficiently conducting affairs of so much importance. I firmly believe . . . that if we had in the office five or six men such as Elliot or Taylor and the necessary copyists the work would be infinitely better done and somewhat more cheaply than at present'. Sad to say, he did not get them. A year later, he was writing: 'Unfortunately the person into whose hands Merivale put the task of preparing the summary you required did not prove equal to the task, and though I have been daily promised . . . that I should have the paper the next day, and though I have continued to press for it most urgently, I only got it three nights ago and when it came it proved . . . little better than rubbish.'[35]

[34] Benson and Esher, i, 136. Sir H. Taylor, *The Statesman* (1836), Chapter 23. PRO 30/22/7. Hobhouse to Russell, May 28, 1849.

[35] PRO 30/22/8. Grey to Russell, September 22, 1849 and November 22, 1850.

ADVISING THE MINISTER

Grey's difficulty resulted from the fact that business was not only growing in bulk, but also in complexity. The minister needed continual advice from his civil servants in intricate problems. For example, following the repeal of the Navigation Acts in 1849, the question was raised whether foreign-built ships be granted British registry. Labouchere's instinct was to temporise. 'My first impression was to state . . . what the provisions of the Act were and to add that we were in communication with the President of the US on this subject and that at present we could give the parties no assurance with regard to the course which we might consider expedient to follow.' But a discussion with two of his officials cleared his mind. They 'both thought that we had better at once assume that we should admit foreign-built ships to a British registry, as there can be little doubt but that this is what we shall do. I believe that they are right and am therefore disposed to sanction the draft of an answer . . . which Northcote has drawn up, and which I send you . . . But this is a question which I ought not to decide without your concurrence'.[36] Briefing ministers in this way became one of the most important tasks of the civil servant. In 1850, Grey sent Russell a paper on colonial affairs, apparently for the latter to use in the Commons. The section on the West Indies, he explained 'was written for me by Taylor'.[37] Disraeli referred a letter from the Home Cattle Defence Association to Helps, of the Privy Council Office, which had been responsible for dealing with the Cattle Plague of the 1860s. The first line of Help's reply indicates Disraeli's purpose in doing so: 'In order to enable you to speak plausibly and safely at the Royal Bucks Agricultural Association next Wednesday, I am afraid I must trouble you with rather a long letter.'[38]

The ideal was that civil servants should submit for the minister's personal decision exactly those cases which he would have selected himself had he had the time. The remainder were settled at lower levels without his knowledge. For example, the Ambassador to France recommended to the Foreign Secretary in 1857 the purchase of a chapel at a cost of £9,000. The Foreign Office endorsed the request and passed it to the Treasury, which approved it. When the matter came up in parliament, the Chancellor of the Exchequer wrote: 'The whole of it was decided in the Treasury without com-

[36] PRO 30/22/8. Labouchere to Russell, November 1, 1849.
[37] ibid. Grey to Russell, January 9, 1850.
[38] Disraeli Papers, GC. Helps to Disraeli, September 13, 1867.

munication with me, and I had no knowledge of the circumstances until the matter was debated.'[39] In such cases, the minister needed to feel sure that his staff would decide as he personally would have decided, since he had to take responsibility for their verdicts.

This was not always the case, however, and it was possible for a minister to approve a draft without fully grasping its implications. Palmerston gave an account of how this would have happened but for his intervention: 'When I was carrying on the business of the Colonial Office during Molesworth's illness I had to deal with a flagitious attempt on the part of a clique of tenants in Prince Edward's Island to do what has been attempted but frustrated in Ireland, namely to transfer property from the lawful owner to the dishonest tenant. I decidedly repelled this attempt at spoliation. It was, however, renewed afterwards under Labouchere, and as I had taken an interest in the matter, he shewed me an intended dispatch which had been prepared for him by some of the clerks in the office which, under the modest and unpretending phrase of "Extinguishing Titles", would have carried into effect the [same] schemes. ... I drew his attention to the wrong which would thus be committed and the titles of the landowners were not extinguished.'[40]

Ministers who had grown up to believe that they should do the donkey work of administration themselves found it hard to delegate. Peel, for example, complained of the burden of office: 'No artificial helps of memory, not even that of private secretaries, could be relied on. You must trust your own memory, both for the facts and arguments by which any measure was to be supported or opposed, and also for the correct performance of all engagements and the twenty different things you had to look after on each day.'[41] This was just the way *not* to do the job, wrote Ellice: Clarendon, as Lord Lieutenant of Ireland 'talks of his personal labour in deciding multitudinous cases—nine-tenths of which ought to be decided by his secretary, or other subordinate authority—difficult and exceptional cases, with a general supervision, only being reserved for him—and of the local experience and knowledge, which peculiarly qualify him for the dispatch of such business. It is a bad habit for statesmen to mistake their avocation of directing an administration for that of undertaking the details of its execution—a habit increasing sadly of late years—and which savours more of jealousy, and want

[39] Palmerston Papers. Lewis to Palmerston, August 11 [1857].
[40] ibid. Palmerston to Newcastle, June 30, 1863.
[41] PRO 30/22/8. Extract from Lord Hatherton's Journal, dated March 28, 1850.

of confidence in subordinate instruments (often more able than themselves) than of the greater qualifications required for their high station. It always reminds me of an observation I overheard Sheridan make to Whitbread, that if he had been born a dray-horse, he would have insisted on doing all the work of the hundred kept in the brew-house ... I admit it to be true that all Secretaries of State are over-worked; or rather, that they overwork themselves'.[42] Sometimes ministers gave way beneath the burden. Godley wrote to Sir Charles Adderley in 1858 that Lytton 'is literally half-mad about his responsibilities, and fancies he is going to reform the whole colonial empire. He gets up in the middle of the night to write despatches, and is furious if they don't actually *go* in twelve hours.' It is not surprising therefore that he broke down under the strain.[43]

Bagehot pointed out 'how wrong is the obvious notion which regards [the minister] as the principal administrator of his office. The late Sir George Lewis used to be fond of explaining this subject. He had every means of knowing. He was bred in the permanent civil service. He was a very successful Chancellor of the Exchequer, a very successful Home Secretary, and he died Minister for War. He used to say, "It is not the business of a cabinet minister to work his department. His business is to see that it is properly worked. If he does much, he is probably doing harm. The permanent staff of the office can do what he chooses to do much better, or if they cannot, they ought to be removed. He is only a bird of passage, and cannot compete with those who are in the office all their lives round." Sir George Lewis was a perfect parliamentary head of an office, so far as that head is to be a keen critic and rational corrector of it'.[44] Yet Lewis still did things himself he could have delegated to a private secretary. 'I have prepared a memorandum on reform for the Queen,' he wrote, 'which I will send you by today's post, if I have time to copy it out before post-time; if not, I will send it tomorrow.'[45] And even Disraeli wrote enough in his own hand to lead him to exclaim 'my hand is by no means so bad as my handwriting would imply; the scrawl is the consequence of the wretched cheap hucksters' ink, supplied by that miserable department, the Stationery Office'. 'What do you think of the ink they give us? Is it detestable? Or is it this fat, woolly paper, which they think so fine? The ink is not so bad on my own paper. ... I can't think it is the pens. Bad stationery

---

[42] ibid. Ellice to Russell, June 16, 1850.
[43] H. L. Hall, *The Colonial Office* (1937), 57.
[44] Bagehot, Chapter VII.
[45] Palmerston Papers. Lewis to Palmerston, December 22, 1859.

adds much to the labour of life; and whether it be the ink, the pens, or the paper, it seems to me, when in office, I never can write like a gentleman. It's a serious nuisance.'[46]

Ministers should bring into the office, not more talent of the kind which permanent officials already had, but talent of a different kind. The success of a ministry, declared Bagehot, 'depends on a due mixture of special and non-special minds—of minds which attend to the means, and of minds which attend to the end. . . . But this utility of leading minds used to generalize, and acting upon various materials, is entirely dependent upon their position. They must not be at the bottom—they must not even be half-way up—they must be at the top. . . . The summits . . . of the various kinds of business are, like the tops of mountains, much more alike than the parts below—the bare principles are much the same; it is only the rich variegated details of the lower strata that so contrast with one another. But it needs travelling to know that the summits are the same. Those who live on one mountain believe that *their* mountain is wholly unlike all others. The application of this principle to parliamentary government is very plain; it shows at once that the intrusion from without upon an office of an exterior head of the office, is not an evil, but that, on the contrary, it is essential to the perfection of that office. . . . It is he, and he only, that brings the rubbish of office to the burning-glass of sense.'[47]

W. S. Gilbert made fun of this trend in *H.M.S. Pinafore*. Sir Joseph Porter, his First Lord of the Admiralty, has no experience whatever of the sea or of the Navy. He had come into politics from an attorney's firm and his 'partner*ship*' was the 'only ship I ever had seen'. But though the Savoy audiences laughed at Sir Joseph, history was on his side. Had any aspiring politician taken Gilbert's implied advice to prepare for high office by profound study of naval architecture and navigation, it is extremely unlikely that the investment would have paid off. Porter's own advice, taken literally, was much wiser: 'Stick close to your decks and never go to sea and you all may be rulers of the Queen's Navee.' More of the ministerial arts were to be learnt behind a desk than on the bridge of a ship.

THE QUALITIES OF A MINISTER

In the new conditions, what qualities did a minister need? Above all, he must be able to speak. In the eighteenth century, one or two

[46] Moneypenny and Buckle, ii, 214–15.
[47] Bagehot, Chapter VII.

orators in the Commons had sufficed. The majority of all ministries sat in the Lords, and for a peer speaking 'was not necessary (Rockingham could hardly open his mouth, even as Prime Minister, and Portland was remarkable for his monumental silences)'.[48] Prime Ministers therefore came to value parliamentary talent in choosing their ministers rather than the ability to get through mounds of paper-work. At the same time, the mere fact of being a minister tended to make a man a more effective parliamentarian. 'A man speaks with more effect from the Treasury Bench when performing a duty than from the upper bench under the gallery when the House is roaring for a division.'[49] In so far as administrative gifts remained important, one of the main things required was the art of keeping a team working effectively together. 'My object all along, and indeed the only one for which I have felt that I could be in any degree qualified, has been to smooth differences, and conciliate tempers.'[50] The minister could listen to the advice of his officials, but it was up to him to put policy over—'to make things *go down* with Senates, Boards, and bodies of men'.[51] As Morpeth put it to Chadwick: 'Whenever I may be inclined upon any occasion, such as I hope and believe will be rare, not fully to go along with you, it will probably arise from a wish to temper too sudden a strain after perfection by what I may feel to be the most practicable modes of dealing successfully with parliaments and bodies of men.'[52] Harcourt's well-known dictum—'The value of the political heads of departments is to tell the permanent officials what the public will not stand'[53]—is a variation on the theme. (Although, paradoxically, civil servants sometimes showed greater political sensitivity than their masters. Lewis gave an example in a letter to Palmerston. The Bishop of London had asked for a contribution from the government to a church building fund. The Crown rental in the area was £133,000. 'I proposed to Charles Gore to take one per cent on the rental, and to give a sum of £13,000 to be paid by annual grants of £2,000. He says truly that this plan would multiply debates, and he proposes £10,000 to be paid immediately.')[54]

So long as the minister was thought of as the key administrator in his department—a norm to which a surprising number conformed—

[48] Pares, 82.
[49] Palmerston Papers. Palmerston to Westbury, September 10, 1863.
[50] PRO 30/22/8. Carlisle to Russell, September 15, 1849.
[51] Lewis, 159.
[52] ibid., 184.
[53] A. G. Gardiner, *Life of Sir William Harcourt* (1923), ii, 587.
[54] Palmerston Papers. Lewis to Palmerston, October 25, 1855.

it was clearly desirable that he should have first-hand knowledge of its business. Prior to 1830, 'long tenure in office during a period of political stability made ministers familiar with the administrative machinery in all aspects; they themselves, and not the permanent officials, were the chief repositories of the knowledge and experience of the affairs of their departments'.[55] This attitude to qualities required in ministers lingered on. On the separation of the War and Colonial Offices at the time of the Crimean War, it was suggested that Palmerston should take the former because of his 'experience in the last war and from his familiarity with the military department'. Sir George Grey should replace him at the Home Office since he was 'conversant with the affairs of that Office'.[56]

But political conditions since the first Reform Bill have not usually permitted politicians to acquire much knowledge of individual departments. The Board of Works, for example, and its successor departments, has had fifty-one ministerial heads in not much more than a century. 'It is . . . not surprising that within a period of office which seldom lasts more than two years, a minister has difficulty in getting to know the full extent of his responsibilities.'[57] Since permanent officials had come to supply the element of continuity, frequent ministerial changes were not necessarily a source of weakness. Indeed, they could be beneficial. 'There is a great deal of good in the changes which take place from time to time and introduce new ideas . . . into the departments.'[58] The pace of change in nineteenth-century Britain made such new ideas especially necessary. 'The immense importance of such a fresh mind is greatest if a country may be governed by an unalterable bureau for years and years, and no harm come of it. If a wise man arranged the bureau rightly in the beginning, it might run rightly a long time. But if the country be a progressive, eager, changing one, soon the bureau will either cramp improvement or be destroyed itself.'[59]

Once it had been accepted that the minister had a role distinct from that of the official, requirements changed. If, in Bagehot's words, 'at the summit all mountains are very much the same', it followed that ministers should be chosen primarily for their ability to survive at high altitudes. They could do so without any special knowledge of the subject matter of a particular department. 'Good

[55] Young, 2.
[56] BM Add. MS 43200. Molesworth to Aberdeen, June 3, 1854.
[57] Sir Harold Emmerson, *Ministry of Works* (1956), 13–14.
[58] PRO 30/22/8. Wood to Russell, September 1, 1849.
[59] Bagehot, Chapter VII.

Mr Layard,' counselled *Punch*, apropos of his refusal of a Colonial
Office post in 1855, 'be warned and instructed. Take any office;
fitness comes after it. Even as the milk flows to the mouth of the
baby, so does knowledge flow from office. Be assured of it; in this
motherly way does the State suckle her youngest—and sometimes
oldest—ministers.'[60]

The author of the article—Tom Taylor—had good reason to
know how the minister's deficiency would be supplied, for he was a
civil servant as well as a journalist. When Derby asked Disraeli to
take the Exchequer in 1852, the latter 'demurred, as [it was] a branch
of which I had no knowledge'. Derby replied: 'You know as much
as Mr Canning did. They give you the figures.'[61] An example will
show how this was done. In 1859, the Colonial Secretary asked for
more information before introducing a Bill, and his plea is worth
recording. 'I am sorry to give so much trouble but the papers before
me are of no aid. ... The Office, on its judgment and experience,
asks me to erect Moreton Bay into a separate colony, and to go before
parliament with a Bill as to the division of it, but in doing the latter,
parliament will expect me to state why I do the former. I desire to
do so succinctly. And I ask the Office what are the reasons why
Moreton Bay should be made a separate colony; give me these
reasons so as to be plain and intelligible to the House of Commons.
Warn me of the argument against it, and prepare me with the
answers.'[62] Departmental knowledge could be at least as valuable,
politically, as the personal knowledge of the old-style minister. As
early as 1851, Disraeli wrote that 'the usual and almost inevitable
doom of private Members of Parliament ... [is to have their]
statement shattered by official information'.[63]

THE JUNIOR MINISTERS

Junior ministers separated out from the category of public men—
the *sous-ministres*, the 'Treasury Jesuits'—who had performed both
administrative and political functions. In earlier days it had been
possible to make a satisfying career at this level, doing the work of
a department presided over by a grandee. As permanent secretaries
gradually took over that work, parliamentary secretaries were left
with an ambiguous role to play. Each department normally needed

[60] q. G. Waterfield, *Layard of Nineveh* (1963), 262.
[61] Moneypenny and Buckle, i, 1160.
[62] Hall, 63.
[63] Moneypenny and Buckle, i, 931.

a junior minister. 'The certainty of election and re-election is very much diminished in these days, and a few accidental failures might be very inconvenient indeed if they fell on one department. . . . If you leave one officer . . . in parliament you are exposed to risk . . . Good officers in the second rank prevent any mischief from the change of heads.'[64] But, though necessary, the job was not satisfying in itself.

Nevertheless, it was the first rung of the ladder. As Aberdeen wrote when he chose Gladstone to be his Under-Secretary in 1835: 'He has no easy part to play in the House of Commons but it is a fine opening for a young man of talent and ambition and places him in the way to the highest distinction.'[65] Hence a man who had got so far was reluctant to give up hopes of going further. In 1846, Benjamin Hawes was made Parliamentary Under-Secretary for the Colonies. His appointment 'was a compliment to the Radicals. It did not, however, entirely please the electors of Lambeth that any representative of theirs should hold office'. (Shades of the 'influence of the Crown!') Hawes was, in consequence, defeated at the general election of 1847. He crept back a few months later as Member for Kinsale where he 'was proposed by the Government interest, and elected . . . upon a narrow majority' of 97 to 94.[66] By 1850 he had resigned himself to the fact that his political career would end at the next election. Ellice suggested him for a permanent post then vacant at the Board of Trade, 'from a fear I always have of such men being left in the lurch by unforeseen accident'.[67] By the following summer, the forthcoming shipwreck of Russell's government was neither unforeseen nor accidental, and Hawes realized that if his friends were to do anything for him, now was the time. He was found a permanent berth in the War Office. 'And now, my dear Lord,' he wrote to Russell, 'I am about to cease to be a member of your government and leave the House of Commons. I own a melancholy feeling creeps over me as I realize the change. It was, however, inevitable and I only now advert to it, to say how gratefully I feel your kindness in giving your sanction to my filling the office I am about to hold. Had better fortune awaited me I should have preferred taking the chance of public life, and being a follower of yours in or out of office. I should have liked to have won the only honour I ever coveted. But I do not repine, since I have had the privilege of holding office under

[64] PRO 30/22/8. Sir Charles Wood to Russell, September 1, 1849.
[65] Balfour, ii, 18.
[66] *Gentleman's Magazine* (1862), 102: Hawes' obituary.
[67] PRO 30/22/8. Ellice to Russell, October 19, 1850.

one who [*sic*] for years I looked up to, and who [*sic*] I never dreamt of knowing or serving—but who, [*sic*] having known, having served under, I can join in Lord Sydenham's admiration of, in almost the last words he uttered.'[68]

Where the head of the department was in the House of Lords, his junior was at least his deputy in the Commons. 'You know,' wrote Melbourne, 'how entirely a minister, who is himself in the House of Lords, is in the hands of him who represents him in the House of Commons.'[69] When a commoner replaced a peer at the head of a department, the junior's post might become less attractive. As one of them put it: 'My position at the Admiralty is now entirely altered by Sir F. Baring's appointment. His business habits and vigorous mind have already enabled him to master the details of the system which he has to administer. . . . I see now that he does not *want* me. In a little time, I shall be *de trop*; for there can be no division of labour between the First Lord, and the Secretary, in the House of Commons. He has responsibility. He has the power; and to do his duty with comfort to himself, when next year's estimates came on, he must do, beforehand, nearly the whole of the work, that has hitherto devolved upon me.'[70] As the century wore on, a higher proportion of cabinet ministers came to sit in the Commons, reducing the junior's role to insignificance (if in the same House) or to relative obscurity (if in the Lords).

This consideration lay behind Palmerston's choice of Cardwell to succeed Newcastle in 1964. There was 'growing dissatisfaction . . . at finding so many important departments represented in the House of Commons by Under-Secretaries . . . It was strongly represented to me that if the Colonial Office should become vacant it ought to be brought into the House of Commons, and if any other arrangement were to be made some adverse motion might be proposed which might very probably be carried.'[71] But, he had been asked: 'Have you thought of what is to become of Chichester Fortescue? He will probably not like to remain Under-Secretary with his chief in the House of Commons. He has done the work of his office very well, and is the only Irish member except the Irish Attorney-General whom you have in your government.'[72] Palmerston recognized the

[68] PRO 30/22/9. Hawes to Russell, October 25 [or 29?], 1851.
[69] Grey Papers, 2nd Earl. Melbourne to Grey, January 5, 1834.
[70] PRO 30/22/7. H. G. Ward to Russell, March 23, 1849.
[71] Palmerston Papers. Letterbook: Palmerston to Newcastle, April 2, 1864.
[72] ibid. Grey to Palmerston, March 24, 1864.

difficulty. He hoped that Fortescue would carry on 'although his position will of course not be quite so prominent as it has been while he had a chief in the Upper House'.[73]

Occasionally a minister would delegate specific responsibilities to his second in command, who was thus given a more satisfying role to play. Gladstone entrusted the railway business of the Board of Trade to Dalhousie in this way in 1844, on the eve of the Railway Mania—a step which moulded the whole remaining course of the latter's life.[74] 'The office of Civil Lord of the Admiralty,' wrote Palmerston, 'as [the First Lord] has now arranged its duties, his become a very important one. . . . In former times the lay Lord of the Admiralty had nearly a sinecure, his duties being confined to passing a couple of hours a day in the Board Room doing little or nothing.' (Palmerston spoke with knowledge—he had held the post himself.) But now 'to investigate and control the dockyard expenditure is a duty requiring not only much labour and   time but also much sagacity in its performance and some parliamentary ability to enable the officer to satisfy the House of Commons in discussions upon naval expenditure which are every session becoming more frequent'.[75] Again, an Under-Secretary might possess special qualifications which gave him a distinctive part to play alongside his chief in the House. 'It was of great importance for Sir George Grey to have in the House of Commons the assistance of an Under-Secretary practically conversant with legal matters,' wrote Palmerston, explaining the selection of a new incumbent of the office.[76]

A scheme to make the Vice-Presidency of the Board of Trade 'more considerable . . . [by] giving to the Vice-President certain definite functions apart from those of the President'[77] was under consideration in 1866, but it is not clear what, if anything, came of it. But this was not the whole answer. 'The position of an Under-Secretary of State in a great department—even where specific and prescribed duties are allotted to him—is somewhat difficult and anomalous. He feels not unfrequently that he is neither fish nor fowl nor good red herring. His use and wont, his authority and responsibility, his enjoyment of and interest in his post, depend in a very large degree on his chief.'[78]

[73] ibid. Letterbook: Palmerston to Newcastle, April 2, 1864.
[74] Parris (1965), 62–4.
[75] Palmerston Papers. Palmerston to Gladstone, September 21, 1865.
[76] ibid. Palmerston to Strafford, November 18, 1862.
[77] Disraeli Papers: MC. Derby to Disraeli, December 3, 1866.
[78] Hall, 51. q. Buxton in L. Wolf, *Life of the 1st Marquess of Ripon* (1921), ii, 323.

Within the department there was not necessarily any clear distinction between the work done in a department by its Parliamentary and its Permanent Under-Secretary. At the Foreign Office in the '30s, the two Under-Secretaries performed functions so nearly identical that they were able to stand in for one another when one was away from London. As Palmerston himself put it: 'Backhouse and Strangeways are very much like the two figures in the weather house and rusticate and labour alternately.'[79] Thirty years later a similar arrangement seems to have obtained at the Home Office; letters relating to police matters were normally signed by one of the Under-Secretaries, but it seems not to have mattered which of them signed any particular letter.[80] In the Foreign Office at the same period, the Parliamentary Under-Secretary retained the supervision of certain divisions—though they were fewer and less important than those under his permanent colleague.[81] But the junior minister was necessarily at a disadvantage as compared with his permanent colleague because he had less experience. Even Layard, who knew far more about foreign affairs than the average junior minister, complained. 'My position is not a comfortable or satisfactory one,' he wrote. 'Our friend Hammond is so determined to have his own way that it is impossible unsupported to fight against him. . . . Hammond monopolizes the whole work of the office and renders it impossible for the Parliamentary Under-Secretary to do anything or almost to have a voice in any matter. . . . When you have to defend a policy to which you may not agree, and in the carrying out of which you have had no voice at all, the position becomes a very painful one.'[82]

THE GREY EMINENCE MYTH

Before going on to consider the role of permanent officials, it may be worth while to dispose of one persistent myth of public administration, which may be called the 'grey eminence' theory. Chadwick, for example, was seen in this light. 'To many M.P.s and journalists the highly informed and persuasive Chadwick was the grey eminence behind the ministry.' Lord Lyndhurst believed that George IV's private secretary, Sir William Knighton, played a similar role. 'Knighton, very pale—the real king of this country—did everything —wrote all the King's letters. When a weak or indolent person in a

[79] Webster, 137–8.
[80] H. Parris, 'The Home Office and the Provincial Police, 1856–1870', *Public Law* (1961), 235.
[81] Anderson, 230–7.   [82] ibid., 249–50.

high situation once admits the assistance of an inferior, he soon becomes a slave. What is occasional becomes a habit,'[83] Robert Lowe—himself a future minister—relied on the theory to argue that the 'real ruler' of Australia was not the Queen, nor the Colonial Secretary, nor parliament, but an obscure clerk in the Colonial Office. 'Let us trace a dispatch from this colony and its answer. The dispatch is opened by Mr Gardner (the clerk in Downing Street for the Australian group). If it does not strike him as of any consequence, he puts it in a pigeon-hole, and it is heard of no more; if otherwise, it is forwarded to Mr Secretary Stephen, who is generally the *ultima linea rerum*. Few, very few, are the dispatches which he deems necessary to submit to Lord Stanley's eye. When this event does happen, his Lordship, not having seen the dispatches to which this is the sequel, requires to be crammed as to the previous transactions ... Thus the Under-Secretary may be, and frequently is, made the tool of his clerk, and the Principal Secretary the tool of his Under-Secretary. ... Is it not transparent that we are governed, not by the responsible Secretary of State, nor yet by the irresponsible Under-Secretary, but by the doubly irresponsible, because utterly unknown and obscure, clerk?'[84]

Herbert Spencer carried the proposition into the realm of high theory. 'Those who watch the working of administrations, no matter of what kind, have forced upon them the truth that a head regulative agency is at once helped and hampered by its subordinate agencies. In a philanthropic association, a scientific society, or a club, those who govern find that the organized officialism which they have created, often impedes, and not infrequently defeats, their aims. Still more is it so with the immensely larger administrations of the state. Through deputies the ruler receives his information; by them his orders are executed; and as fast as his connexion with affairs becomes indirect, his control over affairs diminishes; until, in extreme cases, he either dwindles into a puppet in the hands of his chief deputy or has his place usurped by him.'[85] Sclater-Booth is a specific case of a minister who is alleged to have become such a puppet in the hands of his Permanent Secretary, John Lambert. 'Mr Sclater-Booth ... whose mental acquirements were not of a high order ... was dominated by the intellectual superiority of his

---

[83] D. Roberts, *Victorian Origins of the British Welfare State* (New Haven, 1960), 238. [Moneypenny and Buckle, i, 391.]

[84] Martin, i, 257. The passage was written for an Australian newspaper in 1845.

[85] H. Spencer, *Political Institutions* (1885), 357.

subordinate, and obediently spoke from his brief without venturing outside it.'[86]

The assumption, which is still widely current in the popular mind, is that civil servants exercise an improper influence on policy, and that they are able to do so only because ministers are often weak, whereas civil servants are strong. On this view, a minister is much like a ventriloquist's dummy, speaking only the words which others have put into his mouth and acting only when manipulated from outside. The minister is made out to be a complaisant nonentity, the civil servant a ruthless master-mind.

Did the British system of government make for weak ministers? It is true that new responsibilities sometimes reveal unsuspected weaknesses. When a man reaches the top of any tree, a relaxation of character may set in, and defects show themselves that had been kept in check during the climb. *Consensu omnium capax imperii nisi imperasset.* The fault may lie, not with the man himself, but in the superior who put him in a position for which his talents were not suited. But these cases are exceptions. In general, ministers in British government went through a series of tests of character before attaining office. They must normally gain and keep the support of a constituency party. They must make a mark in the House of Commons —or, less often, in the House of Lords. They normally served an apprenticeship in a junior post before becoming the head of a department. Sometimes weakness is a filterable virus. But in general, British politics was a school for strength, not for weakness. Complaisant nonentities rarely survived long enough in politics to reach ministerial level; and if occasionally one did, he was not likely to stay long. 'I have heard an eminent living statesman of long experience,' wrote Bagehot, 'say that in his time he only knew one instance to the contrary. And there is the best protection that it shall be so. A considerable Cabinet minister has to defend his department in the face of mankind; and though distant observers and sharp writers may depreciate it, this is a very difficult thing'.[87]

The minister could, of course, have his officials near him in the House. As early as 1833, Stephen referred to 'the seat appointed for me under the gallery of the House of Commons'.[88] In 1847, Kay-Shuttleworth arranged that one of his staff named Harrison 'should be in attendance during the debate on Monday evening' when

[86] H. Preston-Thomas, *Work and Play of a Government Inspector* (1909), 52 and 56.
[87] Bagehot, Chapter VI.
[88] Hughes (1958), 30.

education was to come up.[89] Ryan, one of the non-parliamentary Commissioners of Railways, was 'seen daily plying below the Bar of the House of Lords to take Granville's order or to feed him with railway figures and other facts'.[90] In 1851, Lingen (a future Permanent Secretary of the Treasury) functioned as Harrison had four years ealier. 'I have . . . told him that he may as well be under the gallery on Friday when the [education] vote will probably come on.'[91] When Sclater-Booth was carrying the Public Health Bill through the Commons in 1875, Lambert 'was always at his elbow'.[92] Nevertheless, Bagehot's judgment remains true. 'A fool, who has publicly to explain great affairs, who has publicly to answer detective questions, who has publicly to argue against able and quick opponents, must soon be shown to be a fool. The very nature of parliamentary government answers for the discovery of substantial incompetence.'[93]

If ministers on the whole were not weak, were civil servants strong, in the distinctive sense assumed in the 'grey eminence' myth? Occasionally they were, as appears from Palmerston's account of an interview with Sir Rowland Hill. 'I clearly perceived from what he said to me that he entirely misunderstands the relative positions of a secretary and the head of the department. He appeared to imagine that he ought to be Viceroy over his chief, and the substance of his complaint was that Stanley acted upon his own opinions instead of being invariably governed by his. I told Sir Rowland that I considered Stanley quite right in the matter, and that I have always acted myself on the same principle. That I have been in several offices, and that in each I have always been willing to hear and to consider the opinions of my subordinate officers when they differed from my own, but that as I, and not they, must be held responsible for what was to be done, I acted upon my own decision when deliberately taken. Rowland Hill had no doubt the great merit of suggesting the penny postage, but he seemed to me to be the spoilt child of the Post Office, and he ought either to make his mind up to be what he really is, a subordinate officer, or to retire from a post which his own notions of his personal importance make it unpleasant for him to hold. As to leave of absence, if I was Stanley I would give it him *sine die*.'[94]

---

[89] PRO 30/22/6. Kay-Shuttleworth to Russell, April 25 [1847].
[90] PRO 30/22/8. Brougham to Russell, March 17, 1850.
[91] PRO 30/22/9. Wood to Russell, July 8, 1851.
[92] Preston-Thomas, 56.
[93] Bagehot, Chapter VI.
[94] Palmerston Papers. Letterbook: Palmerston to Gladstone, May 21, 1863.

But was this normal? Was a Permanent Secretary often able to mould his official chief to his machiavellian will? Did he often want to? As with the minister, the formative influences of his career must be taken into account. A civil servant may list 'power' among the attractions of the job,[95] but this cannot be taken very seriously, at least so far as the vast majority is concerned. The civil service had little attraction to a young man with strong views about the policies he would wish to promote. True, he knew that, thirty years after entry, he might be in a position to influence policy. But he knew with far more certainty that for many years he would be no more than a cog in the machine, and might remain one all his days. In other occupations, he could set about realizing his ideas right from the start. The recruitment pattern of the civil service acted as a filter to exclude the vast majority of potential grey eminences.

If the civil service was unlikely to attract masterful types in the first place, its routine for junior members was unlikely to make them so. The one kind of strong belief that might be fostered was enthusiasm for some particular device encountered in the course of normal work—organic sewage, perhaps, or prefabrication as a method of school building. But as the future Permanent Secretary rose, he moved from one kind of work to another, and such enthusiasms normally died in the process. If they did not die of their own accord, they might be killed by a change of minister. In any case, the 'grey eminence' myth envisaged something more extensive than attempts to convert a minister to a different system of school building!

The sort of Permanent Secretary postulated by the myth is, then, likely to be as rare as the weak minister. However, he could happen, just as a weak minister could, Suppose, moreover, a conjunction of the two; the Prime Minister appoints a weak minister to a department which has a strong Permanent Secretary. Is the latter delighted? Not a bit, for civil servants prefer a strong chief. They would echo Rogers' praise of Granville: 'His merits as a chief were . . . that he saw his way clearly and would act vigorously in what may be called ministerial as distinguished from departmental policy, and he was ready to act with promptitude and authority in matters which none but a chief could handle, matters requiring action in the House of Lords or the Cabinet or the Treasury.' It was 'a great recommendation to a chief in the eyes of his subordinates' if he was 'not the least afraid of the House of Commons,'[96] and as for the Cabinet, that was

---

[95] N. Walker, *Morale in the Civil Service* (Edinburgh, 1961), 201.
[96] G. E. Marindin (ed.), *Letters of Frederic, Lord Blachford* (1896), 263–4.

one of the weaknesses of the wretched Glenelg. 'Unfortunately, Glenelg has not the art of fairly laying before [the Cabinet] the opinion of [his permanent officials] or the information necessary for determining what is to be done on important matters.'[97] The department's battles had to be fought outside—in the Cabinet, in parliament—on fields where civil servants had no belligerent status. They must be fought mainly by the minister. With a strong minister, civil servants may not get all they think the department needs, but they get something. With a weak minister, they will get less, and perhaps nothing at all. In the struggle for finance, for Cabinet support, for parliamentary time, the weak minister will be pushed under by more energetic colleagues, and his civil servants will be unable to prevent it.

Such a minister earned only the contempt of his officials. Kekewich's view of the Duke of Devonshire will serve as an example: 'From the day he assumed [his] position to the day he vacated it, he was profoundly ignorant of the system the department had to administer, of its routine, and of its duties. . . . When he had been about six years Minister of Education, I happened to be one day in his room, and he asked me to tell him something about training colleges, . . . I told him everything I could think of. . . . The Duke did not make a single comment nor ask a question, but sat perfectly silent and stared into vacancy. But at the end . . . he suddenly turned to me and uttered these memorable words, "What *is* a certificated teacher?" I had been teaching reading to a pupil who did not know his alphabet. . . . [He] never was capable of "picking out the plums" from a document, and he always read steadily from the beginning until he was tired or completely fogged. Then he used to knock off, and annex the document, as he said, for further consideration. I never knew what became of it afterwards unless some decision was urgently required. But how he arrived at it I know not. He usually managed it, I think, by endorsing whatever recommendations I had made. Writing "I agree" gives little trouble.'[98]

PARTNERSHIP BETWEEN MINISTERS AND CIVIL SERVANTS

From the period—1780–1830—when the two groups, ministers and permanent officials, first separated, the relationship between them has been one of partnership. Their roles have been different but complementary. Bromley, Disraeli's correspondent in the Admiralty,

[97] Melbourne Papers. Howick to Melbourne, December 27, 1837.
[98] Kekewich, 93–4 and 95.

held that the relationship between politicians and officials should be like that between the two branches of the legal profession. Ministers should resemble the leading counsel, 'political secretaries' should correspond to junior counsel, while the 'Head Permanent Officers' would be solicitors. 'You will see that my aim is to incur a *real* general responsibility in the minister, with a *nominal* responsibility in matters of detail. This is not theoretical but *practical* and will work if clearly laid down as the rule of action for the political and permanent service.'[99]

The strength of the higher civil servant did not derive, save in rare and exceptional cases, from personal domination over his minister. It was the natural result of his longer experience of the office and its work.

Frequently changing governments—'deciduous governments' Henry Taylor called them—made ministers dependent on the permanence of their civil servants. On going into a department for the first time, they had to look to the latter to show them the ropes. 'The frequency of change . . . throws the political heads of departments into more necessary dependence upon the subordinate assistance.'[100] As in every sphere of life, it was possible to have too much of a good thing. 'One word on the question of permanence. I do think it well that the Second Secretary should be so far permanent as not to be removed on the occasion of every change of government, but I think that permanent occupation in the narrow sense is anything but an advantage. Ten or a dozen years or even more may be well but forty is too long a tenure.'[101] But generally there was a grateful awareness of the advantages of continuity. Brooksbank, Chief Clerk in the Revenue Room, was said to be 'the only depository at the Treasury of that *lex non scripta* which is not to be collected from books and on which so much of official and parliamentary business depends'.[102] After him, 'the elder Dwight . . . now that Mr Brooksbank is dead, is better acquainted with our technical finance than any person living'.[103] Such continuity was often a slender thread in the small offices of the nineteenth century, since often it depended on a single man. Pasley used this as an argument in pressing for the appointment of an Assistant Inspector of Railways in 1844. It would

[99] Disraeli Papers: GC. Bromley to Disraeli, December 1, 1855.
[100] Taylor to Hyde Villiers, April 2, 1832. See Parris, *Political Studies*, ix (1961), 186.
[101] BM Add. MS. 40458. Haddington to Peel, January 17, 1845.
[102] Melbourne Papers. Spring Rice to Melbourne, October 4, 1839.
[103] Disraeli Papers. B/IV/C/13a. Trevelyan to Disraeli, December 1, 1852.

'perpetuate professional knowledge in this Department . . . [other-wise] all the knowledge and experience . . . that I have acquired would be lost to my successor'.[104] Continuity did break down in the Home Office in 1850. The problem was how a Vice-Chancellor in the Court of Chancery should be appointed. 'No record can be found in the Home Office as to who moved the Secretary of State to issue the warrants for the appointment of Vice-Chancellor Shadwell in 1826, or for Vice-Chancellors Bruce and Wigram in 1841.' Unfortunately, the matter seemed to have been left in the hands of non-permanent officers. 'As the communications between the First Lord of the Treasury and the Secretary of State are generally kept by private secretaries, there is no official record here.' Unfortunately, the man who could have cleared up the whole matter in a few minutes had lately died. 'Poor Plasket could have given the whole history of the matter, I have no doubt.'[105]

Permanence is the basis of the influence—the proper influence—which civil servants exercise on ministers. In the formation and realization of policy, neither could act without the other.

[104] q. in Parris (1965), 112–13.
[105] PRO 30/22/8. Waddington to Russell, October 31, 1850. Grey to Russell, November 11, 1850. Undated memorandum: [1850?].

CHAPTER V

THE PERMANENT OFFICIALS

'The new minister is at once called on to enter on the consideration of questions of the greatest magnitude, and at the same time of some hundreds of questions of mere detail, of no public interest, of unintelligible technicality, involving local considerations with which he is wholly unacquainted, but at the same time requiring deci-sion . . . His Parliamentary Under-Secretary is generally as new to the business as himself . . . Thus we find both these marked and responsible functionaries dependent on the advice or guidance of another; and that other person must of course be one of the per-manent members of the office.'

Charles Buller, 1840

The student of administration is interested in permanent officials in much the same way that the ornithologist is interested in birds. In-dividuals do not concern him very much, but he prides himself on being able to identify the species. What were the civil servants of the nineteenth century like? If they were not all alike, what main types can be distinguished? There are many difficulties in the way of answering that question. The size of the population is so large that a sample must be chosen. But what kind of sample? A stratified sample would be impossible because of lack of information about the general characteristics of the population to be studied—age of entry, age of retirement, etc. A random sample could be chosen, but most of its members would be so obscure that it would probably be impossible to collect the most basic evidence—dates of birth and death, social origin, education, and the like. In any such enquiry, moreover, there is a bias against the obscure that can be foreseen, but not satisfactorily allowed for. Sons of Earls, educated at Eton and Christ Church, tend to leave more traces of their passage through the world than sons of farmers, educated at village schools.

The course adopted here is, first of all, to concentrate on the higher civil servants. This is partly through necessity. Reasonably complete evidence about them survives. But it is a necessity of which a virtue can be made. Higher civil servants were those who, by and large, created the constitutional problems. But even with this restriction, there would be some danger in plunging straight in. It would be easy to select those individuals, without being aware of doing so, who most exemplify preconceived ideas. The second stage, therefore, is to examine the careers of *all* Permanent Secretaries at three dates: 1830, 1850, and 1870. This preliminary survey of an objectively defined group provides guide-lines for a wider study of higher civil servants in the concluding part of the chapter.

PATRICIANS AND PLEBEIANS

In 1830, there were eleven ministerial departments (excluding the Irish Office, which is beyond the scope of this study). Two—the Council Office and the Board of Trade—had joint officers of Permanent Secretary status. There was one death during the year, and as the vacancy was immediately filled, there were fourteen men of Permanent Secretary status to be taken into account. They fall fairly neatly into two groups of equal size—the patricians and the plebeians.

The seven patricians were:

Hon. William Bathurst. Council Office, in succession to Buller. Second son of the third Earl Bathurst. Educated at Eton and Oxford. Eventually succeeded to the title as the fifth Earl.

James Buller. Council Office. Son of John Buller, M.P., sometime Lord of the Treasury. Died, November 14, 1830.

Charles Greville. Council Office. Grandson of peers on both sides. Educated at Eton and Oxford.

Robert Hay. Colonial Office. Nephew of tenth Earl of Kinnoull. Educated at Oxford.

Samuel Phillipps. Home Office. Son of Thomas Phillipps, of More Crichel, Dorset, and Garendon Park, Leicestershire. Educated at Charterhouse and Cambridge.

Hon. James Stewart. Treasury. Son of the seventh Earl of Galloway Educated at Charterhouse and Cambridge.

Laurence Sulivan. War Office. Son of Stephen Sulivan, of Ponsborne Park, Hertfordshire. Educated at Edinburgh and Cambridge.

As for professional training and experience, Bathurst, Phillipps and Sulivan were barristers, while Stewart had served in the army, reaching the rank of lieutenant-colonel. Bathurst and Buller had sat in Parliament, while Bathurst, Greville, Hay, Stewart and Sulivan had held other public appointments before becoming Permanent Secretaries.

Some of these patricians exemplify the old taunt that the public service was the outdoor relief department of the British aristocracy. Greville gave his verdict on his colleague Buller in describing a slip he made at the accession of the new King. 'My worthy colleague, Mr James Buller (the best but stupidest of men) began to swear Privy Councillors in the name of "King George IV—William, I mean", to the great diversion of the Council.'[1] In the judgment of one of his parliamentary colleagues, Hay was 'totally unfit for the situation he holds, and the position in which he is now placed is one in which no man ought to be suffered to remain. While he fills a most important and confidential office, he is not in the slightest degree trusted by, nay, scarcely has any communication whatever with his official superior. He is so little allowed to do the duties of the place he still nominally holds that although he ought to have been the person to manage under Lord Glenelg's direction the whole correspondence with the Cape of Good Hope, he had never seen the dispatch on the Caffre War when it was taken to Brighton, and had never been in any manner consulted or even spoken to on the subject. No one can doubt that it was quite right not to trust this business in his hands, knowing as we do that it is to his incompetence that all the grievous errors in the management of that colony, and the disasters which they have produced, are mainly to be attributed. But I think that if he cannot be trusted with the duties of his office, he ought not to be allowed to continue in it.'[2]

But patricians were not all as bad as that and the most celebrated of them—Greville—will serve as an example. In spite of his distinguished connections, he was a fifth son and had to be provided for. He came down from Christ Church without a degree at the age of eighteen to become private secretary to Lord Bathurst at the Colonial Office. Through the influence of the Duke of Portland, to whom he was related on his mother's side, he was appointed to the sinecure Secretaryship of Jamaica—a colony he never found it necessary to visit—and also to the reversion of a Privy Council clerkship. On the other hand, any acquaintance with his justly celebrated diary conveys the impression of a man of considerable ability and strong opinions. If his duties were light, it was not entirely from choice. In 1830 reform was in the air and there was no knowing whether even the Council Office would be proof against it. 'In these times,' he wrote, 'it will not do to be idle and I told Lord L[ansdowne] that I was anxious to keep my emoluments, but ready to work for them, and proposed that we Clerks of the Council should be called upon

[1] Greville, ii, 2–3.
[2] Melbourne Papers. Howick to Melbourne, December 22, 1835.

to act really at the Board of Trade, as we are, in fact, bound to do.'[3] The success with which new duties in fields so diverse as education and public health were grafted on to the Council suggests that the basic stock was sound and for that Greville must deserve much of the credit.

The evidence relating to the plebeians is partly negative in character and, to that extent, unsatisfactory. The obscurity of the evidence about their origins and education suggests that origins and education were themselves obscure, but does not establish the point. Hence other details will be given in each case. The seven men were:

John Backhouse. Foreign Office. He was born in Liverpool, the 'son of one of the oldest merchants in the town and was intended to follow the same respectable profession'. Instead he became a sort of lobbyist, or parliamentary agent, for the borough and as such, attracted the notice of Canning, who then represented Liverpool. Canning made him his private secretary and later secured him a permanent post.

Sir John Barrow. Admiralty. Born and educated at Ulverston (Town Bank Grammar School). Left school at about the age of fourteen. Worked in a foundry, on a whaler and as a teacher, before entering the public service.

Richard Byham. Board of Ordnance. Nothing known of parentage or education. Main evidence of obscure origin in the fact that he must have entered the service in very early youth, having completed almost sixty years' service in the same department at the time of his death in 1849.

Sir Francis Freeling. Post Office. Born in Bristol. Nothing known of parentage or education. At the age of twenty-one 'on the establishment of the new system of mail coaches ... he was appointed to aid the inventor, Palmer, in carrying his improvements into effect'.

James Deacon Hume. Board of Trade. Son of James Hume, Secretary of the Customs. Educated at Westminster School. Entered Customs service about the age of seventeen.

Benjamin Jones. Board of Control. Nothing known of parentage or education. Entered the service of the Board as a clerk on its establishment in 1784. Retired in 1834, aged sixty-five, after fifty years' service.

Thomas Lack. Board of Trade. Nothing known of parentage or education. Entered the Board as a clerk at about the age of fifteen and completed fifty years' service there.

[3] Greville, iii, 84. December 12, 1830.

Byham, Freeling, Jones and Lack spent all their service in one department; the remaining three transferred from one branch of the public service to another on their way up. All seem to have been at least competent. Barrow and Deacon Hume, on the evidence of their published works, were a good deal more.

Of course, the categories are not watertight. It might be better to exclude Deacon Hume from the category of plebeians in view of his parentage and education. Certainly one of the patricians differed so markedly from the rest in educational and professional background as to make him seem a forerunner of future types. This was Samuel Phillipps, of the Home Office. He was not merely educated at Cambridge, but had a distinguished career there, was eighth wrangler, and won the Chancellor's medal. He then entered the Inner Temple, and was called to the Bar. Though he never practised, he achieved a position of esteem as a legal writer before taking the post of Permanent Under-Secretary at the Home Office in 1827.

By 1850, the picture had become a good deal more confused. Allowing for one additional department (the Poor Law Board), two positions jointly held (Council Office and Board of Trade), and one change during the year, there are fifteen men in all to be accounted for. Three of the patricians—Bathurst, Greville and Sulivan—were still there and Maberly of the Post Office was of the same type. He was the son of John Maberly M.P., of Shirley House, Surrey, and had been educated at Eton and Oxford. After serving in the army, and reaching the rank of lieutenant-colonel, he had sat in parliament for fifteen years before joining the Customs Board in 1834. He had succeeded Freeling two years later. None of the plebeians of 1830 had survived, but Byham's successor, George Butler, and Hugh Stark, of the Board of Control, belong in that category. Le Marchant, of the Board of Trade, typified the hybrid politico-administrative type of public servant which will be discussed further below.

PROFESSIONALS AND ZEALOTS

Seven of the eight who remain may be divided into two groups—the professionals and the zealots. The professionals were those whose training and experience were directly relevant to the work of their departments, namely:

Henry Addington. Foreign Office. Nephew of first Lord Sidmouth. Educated at Winchester. Entered the diplomatic service at about the age of seventeen and rose to be British representative in Madrid.

James Booth. Board of Trade. Educated at Cambridge. Barrister. Counsel to the Speaker.

Captain William Baillie Hamilton, R.N. Admiralty. Grandson of ninth Earl of Home and cousin of tenth Earl of Haddington.

Horatio Waddington. Home Office. Son of Rev. George Waddington, vicar of Tuxford, Lincolnshire. Educated at Charterhouse and Cambridge. Eighteenth wrangler. Barrister. Recorder of Warwick and Lichfield.

In the case of Booth and Waddington, the relevance of their qualifications and experience to their civil service appointments is not, admittedly, so clear as in the other two cases. Many young men went to the Bar in the nineteenth century as part of their general education. But in view of the legal appointments held by these men, it is reasonable to suppose that they were well-established members of their profession, and that those who appointed them Permanent Secretaries must have seen some advantage in having their knowledge of the law on hand. All four differed from the twentieth-century image of the higher civil servant in their professional training and experience, so unlike the general education and experience in administration which is said to provide the ideal background for the top administrator. Among the permanent secretaries of 1850 were three zealots:

Sir George Nicholls. Poor Law Board. Educated at the parish school, and Helston Grammar School, Cornwall. Worked in the Merchant Navy, in banking and in canal management. Achieved a reputation as a Poor Law reformer. One of the first Poor Law Commissioners under the 1834 Act.

G. R. Porter. Board of Trade. Son of a London merchant. Unsuccessful businessman but achieved reputation as a statistician.

Sir Charles Trevelyan. Son of Rev. George Trevelyan, Archdeacon of Taunton. Educated Taunton Grammar School, Charterhouse and Haileybury. Distinguished career in East India Company's service.

Trevelyan is a striking example of a man utterly unlike the 'mandarin' stereotype of a civil servant. Macaulay, his brother-in-law, first met him in India a year or two before he went to the Treasury. 'Trevelyan is a most stormy reformer. Lord William [Bentinck, then Governor-General] said to me . . . "That man is almost always on the right side in every question; and it is well that he is so, for he gives a most confounded deal of trouble when he happens to take the wrong one." He is quite at the head of that active party among the younger servants of the Company who take the side of improvement. In particular, he is the soul of every scheme for diffusing education among the natives of this country. . . . His face has a most characteristic expression of ardour and impetuosity . . . He has no small talk. His mind is full of schemes of moral and political improvement, and his zeal boils over in his talk. His topics, even in courtship, are steam navigation, the education of the natives, the equalization of the sugar duties [and] the substitution of the Roman for the Arabic alphabet in the Oriental languages.'[4] Nor surprisingly, a man of so ardent a temperament often chafed under the restraints inherent in his position at the Treasury.

Porter, at the Board of Trade, was a pale shade beside Trevelyan. Nevertheless, in a quiet way, he too was a zealot. Listen to him assessing the prospects for Free Trade, following Russell's failure to form a government at the end of 1845: 'The turn which things have taken is to me most satisfactory. The Whig party would have entered upon their task with great doubt of success. Some of them were (I fear) unwilling converts to the cause and some would even think more of the advantages of office than of the task to be accomplished and for the accomplishing of which alone they would have been called to office.'[5] It is no wonder that, in successfully urging his claim to a Joint Secretaryship in 1847, he used the argument that his appointment would be popular with the business world because of his known belief in Free Trade.[6]

The last in the 1850 group, Herman Merivale, defies classification. His background was in the professional upper middle class. His father was a barrister, and his grandfather had been Headmaster of Harrow. He was educated at Harrow and Oxford, and called to the Bar. For five years he was Professor of Political Economy at Oxford and was Recorder of three boroughs in Cornwall. Clearly he would have made a modest success of his career even if he had not been jerked out of it, when over forty, to succeed Stephen at the Colonial Office. It also seems reasonable to suppose that had he been born in the open examination era he would have succeeded in that test also.

THE 1870 SCENE

By 1870, further changes had created an administrative scene very different from that of 1850, and still more, that of 1830. The Board of Ordnance had been abolished, the Board of Control had given

---

[4] Sir G. O. Trevelyan, *Life and Letters of Lord Macaulay*, Chapter VI.
[5] McCord, 199. [6] Parris (1965), 114.

way to the India Office, and one new ministerial department, the Board of Works, had come into being. There were no joint appointments and no changes during the year. Thus, twelve men only have to be accounted for, of whom only one (Merivale) was a survivor from 1850, and he had transferred from the Colonial to the India Office. George Russell, of the Board of Works, is perhaps the most obscure of all the Permanent Secretaries. So little is known about him that he cannot be even tentatively placed in any category. The patricians and the zealots had died out, but there was one plebeian Permanent Secretary, Sir John Tilley, of the Post Office. He was the son of a London merchant. It is reasonable to suppose that he was not in a substantial way of business, or he would surely have taken his son into the firm instead of putting him into the Post Office as a junior clerk at the age of sixteen. He rose step by step to succeed Sir Rowland Hill in 1864. He was, in the view of one of his staff, 'a shrewd, caustic, clever man, bred in the Post Office service, and knowing it thoroughly; by no means a crotcheteer, but, with his public office experience, tempered by plenty of worldly knowledge and as unimpressionable as an oyster. An excellent public servant, had he not been a *sic volo*, *sic jubeo* gentleman—one who never allowed anything or anyone to stand in his way; who was accustomed to do as he liked without being called upon for his reasons.'[7]

There were also two professionals, Liddell of the Home Office, and Lugard of the War Office. The Hon. Adolphus Liddell was a younger son of Lord Ravensworth, educated at Eton and Oxford, and a barrister. He became Permanent Under-Secretary at the Home Office at the age of forty-nine, retaining the position until his death in 1885. Thus, he continued the tradition, established by Phillipps and Waddington, that the senior civil servant at the Home Office should have a legal rather than an administrative background. Sir Edward Lugard, Permanent Under-Secretary for War, 1861–71, was the son of an army officer and himself a professional soldier. He had seen active service in Afghanistan, India and Persia, and was over fifty when he became Permanent Under-Secretary.

Three members of the group are hard to fit into any category. Henry Fleming, of the Poor Law Board, was brought in as a personal friend of Charles Buller's, during the latter's Presidency of the Board. He was 'advanced to the office of Permanent Secretary by Lord Palmerston. . . . But Mr Fleming was a great deal more than this. . . . His tact and fidelity made him a useful go-between in many private negotiations . . . and his great knowledge of official business

[7] Yates, ii, 193.

gave him great influence over successive Poor Law Commissioners.'[8] One who worked under him confirmed the general impression, though in less respectful terms. 'Henry Fleming [was] a curious old beau . . . well known by his soubriquet of "The Flea" . . . and . . . a famous adjuster of social disputes.'[9] This makes him sound like a patrician. But, on the other hand, nothing seems to be recorded about his parentage or education—not even the date of his birth.

Sir Arthur Helps, of the Council Office, was the son of Thomas Helps, of London; educated at Eton and Cambridge (thirty-first wrangler) and called to the Bar. He was private secretary to two Whig statesmen, and must have made a certain amount of money by his numerous writings, before becoming Clerk to the Council at the age of forty-six. Vernon Lushington, of the Admiralty, was the son of Rt. Hon. Stephen Lushington, M.P., who later became a judge in the Court of Admiralty. The son was educated at Cambridge (President of the Union) and became a barrister. He took silk and became a Bencher of his inn before being appointed Permanent Secretary to the Admiralty in his late thirties. Like Merivale, these men would probably have achieved some distinction had they never had the chance to enter the civil service. Like him also, they would probably have done well in the open competition age, had they been obliged to make their way in it. But Lushington differed markedly from the other two if the pattern of his entire career is looked at. Viewed as a whole, his life was in the law, since he left the Admiralty in 1877 on his appointment as a County Court judge, a post he retained until his retirement in 1900. Thus he spent thirty-five years in law as compared with eight as a Permanent Secretary. It is doubtful how far it is permissible to infer from a single case in what esteem his last and penultimate positions were held. Certainly it would come as a shock today to learn that a Permanent Secretary had taken a post as a County Court judge.

FORERUNNERS OF THE ADMINISTRATIVE CLASS

Lastly, there remain four men in whom the lineaments of the Administrative Class civil servant can be faintly made out. Those in this group were of upper-middle-class origin; highly educated; entered the service young; enjoyed a status from the start above that of the clerk; but reached the top only after working their way up the hierarchy and, in two cases, changing departments. Among their predecessors of 1830 and 1850, there was no one whose ascent had

[8] *Annual Register, 1875*, Part II, 134.   [9] Preston-Thomas, 54.

been marked by all these features. Those who had worked their way up had started as menial clerks with little education. Those who had had a good education had entered the civil service in mid-career. The Administrative Class prototypes were:

Thomas Henry Farrer. Board of Trade. Son of Thomas Farrer, solicitor of Lincoln's Inn Fields. Educated at Eton and Oxford (Hons. II). Barrister. Entered Board of Trade in late twenties. Secretary of new Marine Department of the Board, 1850. Permanent Secretary, 1865–86. Bart., 1883. Raised to the peerage, 1893.

Edmund Hammond. Foreign Office. Son of George Hammond, of the Foreign Office. Educated at Eton, Harrow and Oxford; Scholar and Fellow of his college. Entered Foreign Office. Served on missions with Sir Stratford Canning. Head of Oriental Department, 1830. Permanent Secretary, 1854–73. P.C., 1866. Raised to the peerage, 1874.

Ralph Lingen. Treasury. Son of Thomas Lingen, manufacturer, of Birmingham. Educated at Bridgnorth Grammar School, Rugby and Oxford: Scholar of his college (Hons. I). Ireland and Hertford Prizes. Fellow of Balliol. Barrister. Entered Education Office in his late twenties. Succeeded Kay-Shuttleworth as head of the Office, 1849. Permanent Secretary to the Treasury, 1869–85. C.B., 1869. K.C.B., 1879. Raised to the peerage, 1885.

Frederic Rogers. Colonial Office. Son of Frederic Rogers, of the Audit Office. Educated at Eton and Oxford. Double First. Craven and Vinerian Scholarships. Fellow of his college. Barrister. Entered public service as Registrar of Joint Stock Companies. Permanent Under-Secretary for the Colonies, 1860–71. P.C. and raised to the peerage, 1871.

These men were, of course, examples of recruitment by patronage. But it is reasonable to assume that they would have done well, or even brilliantly, in open competition. The Administrative Class of the British civil service was born in the period 1830–70, though it was not to grow to maturity—or even acquire its name—until much later.

One striking feature of the Permanent Secretaries of 1870 is that seven of the twelve were barristers. In this they continued a trend which had been apparent since 1830. During the four decades, there were twenty-one barristers among the fifty-eight men who achieved that rank. Moreover, the proportion had risen. In 1830, it had been three of fourteen; in 1850, four of fifteen. In the modern civil service, the small number of barristers is contrasted with the very much larger number of people who have continued with their general education to an advanced level. But in the 1830–70 period, only twenty-seven of the fifty-eight Permanent Secretaries had had higher education of any kind, so the domination of the lawyers is even more remarkable. Of course, it only seems so by contrast with other periods of British administrative history. On the Continent, it has long been assumed that those who are to be responsible for administering the law should be educated in it. Nevertheless, since lawyers did fill so many of the key posts in 1870, it is curious that the idea of legal training as a prerequisite for the higher civil service did not take root in this country. Presumably, open competition was responsible, since it faced the young graduate with the choice of civil service or the Bar. Those who chose the latter might later, as briefs came slowly, regret their decision. But the civil service bolt-hole would normally be closed. Even if age regulations and the like permitted them still to compete, they would probably be trodden down by the hungry generations of bright young men fresh from the university.

CIVIL SERVANTS IN THE HONOURS LIST

One point on which there is a clear contrast between the Permanent Secretaries of 1830 and those of 1870 is in the honours which were bestowed on them. At the earlier date, there seems to have been no customary honour considered suitable for holders of the position. The highest honours in fact conferred were baronetcies for Barrow and Freeling, in both cases prior to their retirement. The most obvious thing they had in common was their exceptionally long service. Freeling received his title after thirty-one years, and Barrow after thirty years, as Permanent Secretary.

It was recognized that honours had many uses in the management of the civil service. When Rowland Hill was reappointed to the Post Office in 1846, the Permanent Secretary's nose was put badly out of joint. 'Maberley is in a sad way at the disgrace and dishonour (he will call it) which he considers we inflict upon him by appointing Rowland Hill so soon after your speech at the close of the session. Nothing but a baronetcy, it seems, will heal his wounded spirit. . . . There is no doubt Rowland Hill's appointment is a sad blow to him and will affect his credit in the country. If you can repair it, it will be a good deed.'[10] But, as a general rule, honours were valued for the positive enhancement of status they conferred. A civil servant, thank-

[10] PRO 30/22/5E. Clanricarde to Russell, November 26, 1846.

ing Disraeli for his K.C.B., wrote 'such spiritual rewards are truly appreciated by the class in which I move, and I assure you, tend materially to secure the *heart* service of a large body of men'.[11] But they could also be useful. Helps thought more civil servants should be made Privy Councillors. 'Waddington was, and he was most useful. My Lords used to be delighted to confer with him and to have the advantage of his great experience.'[12]

Permanent Secretaries in 1870 could reasonably aspire higher than their predecessors of 1830. Four of them—Farrer, Hammond, Lingen and Rogers—reached the House of Lords. The cynic could argue that this may have resulted from a cheapening of honours rather than a rise in the status of the civil servant. But in fact the trend began during a period of relatively few creations. It seems reasonable to conclude that there was some significance in the more generous grant of honours.

The men studied so far provide but a slender basis for generalization about the civil service as a whole. Permanent Secretaries are, by definition, exceptional men, outnumbered many hundreds of times by junior clerks, customs officers and the like. On the other hand, because they were exceptional they counted for more, and so merit more attention here. What can be done is to probe a little and see how far characteristics of Permanent Secretaries applied lower down the scale also.

SOCIAL STATUS AND ORGANIZATIONAL BEHAVOIUR

The patrician status of many civil servants was a fact of the first importance. It set the tone for relationships inside departments. 'Our little commonwealth is a pure democracy. The sense of social equality gets the better altogether of the sense of official inequality. No man gives *orders*, in the proper sense of the word, because no man thinks of himself as one on whom orders may be properly laid. Living apart from the junior members of this Office, I find the difficulty of breaking up this feeling almost insuperable. Living daily with them, Mr Blackwood and his brethren of the first class, must, and certainly do, feel the difficulty so strongly that any attempt to govern by authority is, I am well convinced, neither made nor thought of by them. In fact your Lordship's authority is the only one which can silence controversies on any question of Office regulations.'[13]

[11] Disraeli Papers. Bromley to Disraeli, September 7, 1858.
[12] ibid. B/IX/B/9. Helps to Disraeli, December 1, 1868.
[13] Stephen to Stanley, 1842. q. Young, 99.

The social standing of civil servants was also an important factor in their relations with ministers. If it was inferior, it was likely to curtail their influence. If it was equal, easy co-operation was facilitated. It might even be superior. This was alleged in the case of Henry Fleming. 'He was a welcome member of society which his official chiefs could often not aspire to enter. . . . During the long reign of Lady Palmerston he was a constant guest at Cambridge House.'[14] He was even supposed to advise on dress. 'When Stansfeld became President, Fleming undertook the task of introducing him into society, and a story was current that after The Flea [Fleming] had insisted on his getting clothed by a fashionable tailor, the President was one day caught standing on an official table opposite the looking-glass gazing with surprise and admiration at the unwonted figure which he presented.'[15]

Patrician status also gave links with the outside world. Maberly, for instance, 'liked his status at the Post Office, he liked the salary which it gave him, he was fond of money, and he went through the work; but he was an Irish landlord . . . and his mind was running on whether Tim Mooney would pay his rent, or Mick Reilly the bailiff would get a good price for the heifer'.[16] Sometimes a change of family fortune forced a man to choose between two ways of life. In 1850, Northcote was a highly thought of official, marked out for early promotion. But he unexpectedly became heir to his grandfather, a baronetcy and the family estates. 'We are probably about to lose him at the Board of Trade in consequence of the apprehended death of his father which will make a rich man of him.'[17] His father did die, and Northcote did resign. Ironically, a Permanent Secretaryship fell vacant shortly afterwards. Northcote's old chief thought there was an outside chance of getting him back by using it as bait. 'I should like to try [him] though I believe that it is very unlikely that he would be tempted.'[18]

Northcote did not return. But he had not found the decision to quit the civil service easy. During his father's last days he wrote to a colleague about it from the family home. 'What is doubtful is, whether I ought or ought not to make arrangements for giving up my official position, and living here permanently. . . . I do not see very clearly what could be done here if I did not come to live here. . . . The only [alternative] would be to allow my uncle and his family

---

[14] *Annual Register, 1875*, Part 11, 134.
[15] Preston-Thomas, 54n.   [16] Yates, i, 99–100.
[17] PRO/30/22/8. Labouchere to Russell, January 1, 1850.
[18] ibid. Labouchere to Russell, September 27, 1850.

to come and live here permanently, and to come myself as a visitor only. But I cannot make up my mind to this. It would be cutting myself off from all real connexion with the place. Besides, I shall in a few years have the undivided responsibility of looking after this place, and I have given so very little attention to country matters, that I am sure I ought to lose no time in studying them, and preparing myself.

'The obvious objection . . . is that I ought not to give up a profession in which I am making some progress. I am in a position which ought not lightly to be abandoned. . . . I have some aptitude for official business, and I am afraid I have very little for country pursuits. . . . I think that, on the whole, if I must absolutely choose between the two, the life of a country gentleman is better than the life of an official. I do not abound in ideas, but I see many things which I think I could do in the country, and which perhaps another would not do, whereas I see nothing that I could do in official life which will not be just as well done by others. Without being Utopian I think I may reasonably expect that if I live here among the farmers and the poor, and pay attention to their ways and wants, I may do something towards improving their intelligence, or raising their standard of comfort, which an agent or a steward would certainly not do; whereas I do not believe that one useful measure of government will suffer in the smallest degree by my place being taken by another. Any man of equal qualification could do all that I could in the Board of Trade; but no man of howsoever superior qualifications could do what my position would enable me to do here. Therefore, although I believe (to speak highly of myself) that I am spoiling a good red-tapist and converting him into a very indifferent country gentleman, yet I think I am doing the republic a service by turning such advantages as I possess to account in the quarter where aid is most wanted. . . . I am not in the least influenced by any sense of weariness of official life; on the contrary, it is daily becoming more pleasant to me, and were the question simply one of preference, I cannot tell which life I should prefer.'[19]

THE CAREER PROBLEM: ADMINISTRATION OR POLITICS?

In retrospect, it can be seen that the distinction between political and permanent office was pretty well settled by 1830. Taylor's prescription for a ministerial department shows that the more perceptive recognized it at the time. 'In this country an establishment of this

[19] Lang, 83–7.

kind is commonly formed as follows: 1st. There are one or more political and parliamentary officers subordinate to the minister, who come and go with their principals or with the government to which they belong, but have not seats in the Cabinet. They go by the name of Under-Secretaries of State in the three Secretaries of State's offices, Vice-President of the Board of Trade, Secretaries and junior Lords or junior Commissioners at the Board of Treasury, the Board of Admiralty, and the Board of Control. 2nd. There is an officer of similar rank, who is not in parliament and holds his office by a more permanent tenure, without reference to changes of ministry. 3rd. There is the minister's private secretary, who of course comes and goes with his principal, whether the change extends to the government or not. 4th. There are some twenty clerks, more or less, also permanent, divided into three or four grades of subordination.'[20] But the distinction was not experienced like that. One of the difficulties of life is that it has to be lived forward. A young man entering parliament might end his career in a permanent post—say Chairman of one of the Revenue Boards. Another, starting as a civil servant, might go on to make a political career for himself.

The ambiguity persists throughout Sir Henry Taylor's *The States-man*. It is a satirical—some would say cynical—guide to success. But success in what career? Does it tell the ambitious young man how to become a Permanent Secretary or how to get a seat in the Cabinet? To the modern reader, Taylor never seems quite to make up his mind. 'At many points in his exposition the author does not trouble to distinguish between the qualifications necessary for the politician and those required by the permanent official.'[21] The reason was that he never thought he had to. To him, statesmanship was a career embracing politics and administration—though he distinguished between the two branches: 'Every minister ... charged with a particular department of public business should be provided with four or six Permanent Under-Secretaries instead of one, and all of those four or six should be efficient closet-statesmen.' Elsewhere, he calls the administrators 'indoor statesmen', implying the existence of 'outdoor statesmen' or politicians. Young men could still begin as clerks and wind up in the Cabinet. 'One of the most important benefits which a statesman can render to his country is ... to place ... in all offices belonging to the establishment where his own business is transacted under his own eye, young men of promise, who may be bred up in them to the business of statesman-

[20] Taylor, Chapter 22.
[21] C. H. Sisson, *The Spirit of British Administration* (1959), 31.

ship, and thereby feed the state with a succession of experienced men competent to its highest employments.'[22] Equally they might start as M.P.s and reach their highest status as Permanent Secretaries.

Trollope's novel *The Three Clerks* is set in the same world. There is an M.P., the Hon. Undecimus Scott, eleventh son of an impecunious Scottish peer, who has struggled into Parliament on his wife's modest fortune. His aim is a place on the payroll of the state. 'He then set himself studiously to work . . . by placing his vote at the disposal of the government. Nor had he failed of success in his attempt, though he had hitherto been able to acquire no high or permanent post.'[23] He is contrasted with Alaric Tudor, an able and ambitious young civil servant, who chafes at his department's narrow room. One day he may be the permanent head of his department; but will it 'ever be worth his while' to fill 'the secretary's chair? . . . The secretary at the Weights and Measures had, after all, but a dull time of it, and was precluded by the nature of his office from parliamentary ambition and the joys of government'. So when Scott prophesies: 'The time is quickly coming when you will address me in the House', Tudor is 'not ill-pleased at the suggestion that he also, on some future day, might have a seat among the faithful Commons'. By the time Tudor gets a chance to come forward as a candidate, he has been promoted to a position not lightly to be sacrificed. Sir Gregory Hardlines—Trollope's code-word for Trevelyan—very reasonably asks why he is thinking of throwing up £1,200 a year. Tudor replies 'that it might be possible that he should get into parliament without giving up his seat at the Board'. How could that be? Surely it was an 'office of profit under the Crown'? But that venerable doctrine is full of anomalies, and Tudor is allowed to know that the Prime Minister and the Chancellor of the Exchequer are in doubt as to his ineligibility; 'Alaric was well aware that their doubt was as good as certainty to him. The truth was that the Prime Minister had said to the Chancellor of the Exchequer, in a half-serious, half-jocular way, that he didn't see why he should reject a vote when offered to him by a member of the civil service. The man must of course do his work—and should it be found that his office work and his seat in parliament interfered with each other, why, he must take the consequences. And if — or — or — made a row about it in the House and complained, why in that case also Mr Tudor must take the consequences.'[24] Tudor is portrayed as an able, ruthless opportunist, prepared to sacrifice anyone and anything to

[22] Taylor, Chapters 22 and 23.
[23] A. Trollope, *The Three Clerks* (1858), 83.   [24] ibid., 89, 124, 335, 354.

his own advancement. But, by the standards of a twentieth-century civil servant, his conduct seems rash and foolish rather than cold and calculating. Why forsake permanent status, his successor might well ask, to go into politics, when by sitting tight he would probably have reached the top of a tree at least equally eligible, if not more so? Tudor behaves differently from his descendants partly because the implications of permanence have not sunk into his bones. He does not have faith that proven administrative ability will itself bring advancement. He has not been 'made constantly to feel that [his] promotion and future prospects depend entirely on the industry and ability with which' he discharges his duties.[25] On the contrary, he feels that he must render some political service to get to the top. Nor does he think of administration as an independent realm, with its own ascents and summits. For him, getting to the top means quitting administration for politics. Observing the subordination of administrators, he infers the superiority of politics to administration.

Many public men had careers like that of Alaric Tudor except for the scandal. Administration served as a spring-board into politics. In an age when parliamentary ambitions were so widely diffused, the desire to exchange a stool in a public office for a seat in the House of Commons was not uncommon. Many politicians started their careers in this way. Charles Jenkinson, first Earl of Liverpool, began in the office of a Secretary of State.[26] George Rose, Pitt's Secretary of the Treasury, was originally in the Record Office, whence he transferred as Secretary to the Tax Office before finally entering parliament.[27] William Huskisson spent several years in public offices as a young man before entering parliament, where he retained his Under-Secretaryship. The career of J. C. Herries (1778–1855) is a good example of the type. He entered the Treasury in 1798 as a copying clerk, volunteered for more onerous duties and soon made himself useful to William Pitt. From 1801 he held a succession of private secretaryships, and in 1811 became Commissary-in-Chief. For the next five years, he handled the extremely complex finance and supply problems of Wellington's army. Some £42 million passed through his competent and thrifty hands. In 1816 he became the first Auditor of the Civil List. But in 1823 he crossed the divide between administrative and political appointments to become Financial Secretary to the Treasury with a seat in the Commons. Four years later he was Chancellor of the Exchequer.[28] He last held office as President of the Board of Control in 1852.

[25] q. Fulton, 111.   [26] Jucker, vii.   [27] Ward (1953), 156.
[28] I owe this account of Herries' career to Dr H. Roseveare.

Until almost the end of the century, civil servants could stand for parliament without giving up their posts. Indeed, when one of the Inspectors of Railways offered to resign on becoming a candidate in 1852, the Board of Trade persuaded him to postpone doing so 'for the convenience of the public service' and at 'some personal inconvenience to himself'. When, having been elected, he did quit, he did so, not on the ground that there would be anything improper in continuing, but because his duties in the House 'would interfere too much with those of an Inspector of Railways to permit me to retain that appointment either with satisfaction to myself or advantage to the public service'.[29] Northcote concluded that, while his position in the civil service did something to advance his parliamentary ambitions, the status of a resident country gentlemen would do more. 'I do not see that after all I am doing an unwise thing for my own advancement even in a parliamentary sense. If, in a few years' time, I have made myself master of my duties here, and established my position in the country, and learnt practically something of the wants of my own class and of my neighbours, I think I should come into parliament naturally and with much more strength than if I were a mere official adventurer.'[30] At the same time, having been in the civil service was a recommendation. During the campaign that eventually led him to a seat at Westminster, Northcote wrote that part of his strength lay 'in my having been at the Board of Trade, and being able to take the character of "a man of business." '[31] In 1871, when Gladstone knew that he would soon have to replace the government Whip, he suggested to his civil service private secretary, Algernon West, that he should enter the House of Commons and succeed to the office. West declined, for domestic reasons. 'But it took many moments and many days to put out of my head a proposal which, had it been practical, would have given me and my wife the greatest pleasure—for parliament then represented the height of my ambition.'[32]

Traffic the other way depended on the availability of posts to which politicians could be appointed directly at a high level. No one would apply for the Chiltern Hundreds as a step to a mere clerkship. These conditions subsisted throughout the greater part of the century. As shown above, there were Permanent Secretaries in 1870 who had never held any inferior civil service post. There was, of course, nothing to wonder at in such appointments in an age of political patronage. But it should be noted that some saw positive merit in

29 Parris (1965), 130.   30 Lang, 86.
31 ibid., 109.   32 West, ii, 1–2.

them. 'Permanent Under-Secretaryships of State and the corresponding situations in other departments . . . are very properly regarded as
not falling within the regular course of promotion. The members of
the department where the vacancy occurs are not ineligible for these
appointments, but are not regarded as having any preferential claim
to them; and in general they are given to men not previously in
public service. This ought to continue to be the practice, not only
because a wider field of selection is thus given to the government in
filling up situations of great importance, but also because other
pursuits in life are more likely than the training of a public office, to
produce men well fitted for these employments.'[33] It should be
remembered that, when those words were written, young civil servants
were obliged in many departments to devote the early years of their
careers to mechanical duties—copying and the like—which tended
to stultify them rather than to fit them for the highest posts.

HYBRID CAREERS: BOWRING AND LE MARCHANT

A good example of the career cutting across the two branches of the
public service was that of John Bowring (1792–1872). He first
attracted public notice in 1822 when he was arrested in France while
carrying a message to warn the Portuguese of the Bourbons' intentions
to invade the Peninsula. On his release from prison, he established
himself in Benthamite and Radical circles. He took a leading part in
the work of the committee set up in London to support the Greek
nationalists. On the foundation of the *Westminster Review* in 1824,
he became joint editor. He was very close to Bentham during the
last years of the latter's life and later edited his collected works. His
first employment in public service was in 1828, when he carried out
investigations on the Continent for the Finance Committee of that
session. It was the first of many similar tasks, mostly carried out for
the Board of Trade, over the next decade, though he never held a full-
time post in the civil service.[34] In 1835 he entered parliament and
sat for two years. In 1841, he returned to the House of Commons.
There seems no doubt that he would have liked to stay in politics,
but by 1846 had doubts about the wisdom of doing so. 'An election,'
he wrote, 'cannot be far distant. And it now becomes me seriously
to consider whether I ought to walk away from public life altogether,
or still keep my parliamentary post, or look in one of the departments
to which my attention has been specially directed, that of public
accounts . . . or in the Board of Trade . . . for some fixed position of

[33] Grey, 187. [34] Brown, passim.

usefulness. . . . I am not without the desire and the ambition to be enabled officially to aid reforms, with which my public history has been associated and which are important to the public weal.'[35] He re-entered government employment in 1847, as Consul at Canton. His action following the *Arrow* incident in 1856 led to war with China. There was widespread criticism of his conduct, but, thanks to Palmerston's support, he survived. He retired in 1859.

The case of Sir Denis Le Marchant (1795–1874) was similar. He began life as a barrister, was private secretary to Brougham, 1830–4, held a legal appointment, 1834–6, and entered the civil service at the top as Joint Permanent Secretary to the Board of Trade in 1836. His duties included liaison with the press on behalf of the government.[36] Five years later, he became a junior minister at the Treasury without a seat in parliament; any possible difficulties in such a transition were resolved by Melbourne's resignation shortly afterwards. He sat briefly in the Commons, 1846–7, and was 'political' the term 'parliamentary' is clearly not applicable—Under-Secretary at the Home Office, 1847–8. He returned to the Board of Trade as Joint Permanent Secretary, 1848–50. But he still seemed to be hankering after politics, for when he accepted the post of Chief Clerk to the Commons in 1850, he wrote: 'Political employment would have suited me better and would have been more to my taste but a combination of obstacles having dashed my hopes in that direction, there was no office that I coveted so much as either of the parliamentary clerkships.'[37] He never returned to Whitehall.

QUALITIES OF A CIVIL SERVANT

The qualities of some nineteenth-century civil servants were in significant ways not merely different from, but opposite to, those of their modern counterparts. Sisson, writing as a civil servant, stresses the ideal of cool detachment. 'In the British conception, it would be better if the administrator did not exist at all. He does in fact exist and cannot be wished away, but at least his education and training are such as are appropriate to a man who is supposed to have no pretensions to play a positive role.'[38] The official does not 'commonly face situations in which the turpitude of one course shows up grimly against the radiant goodness of a practicable alternative. No doubt such choices come unexpectedly, and Pontius Pilate was perhaps

[35] PRO 30/22/5. Bowring to Ellice, November 5, 1846.   [36] Bell, i, 257.
[37] PRO 30/22/8. Le Marchant to Russell, September 24 [1850].
[38] Sisson, 38.

taken off his guard. The steps he took to still a particular local clamour were more or less what the service required, and he washed his hands with a civilized regret.'[39] Such a temperament is at the antipodes from Chadwick. 'Although his mind when it was open was more open that most, it was never open for very long, and once he had formulated an opinion from his mounds of facts and statistics the sedulous judge turned into the ferocious advocate. From that moment he became positive and dogmatic to a degree. The source of his failures and successes alike was his insuperable conviction that he was right. He never confessed to an error and rarely to an omission, and once set upon a course he pursued it with unrelenting tenacity. Furthermore he was passionate, and so eager as to be almost hasty; certainly always headstrong, importunate, and impatient of delay and opposition. To make matters worse he had . . . far less than the average degree of compassion, honour or sympathy. . . . It is doubtful whether he ever understood a human being, . . . the paradox of this busy, scheming, restless man is that his colossal egotism was undeviatingly and passionately devoted to public objects.'[40]

Chadwick was, of course, the supreme example of the zealot in official life. The term is not intended solely to signify a readiness in some nineteenth-century civil servants to work themselves to death, or very near it, though some were, in fact prepared to do just that.

William Hill, the Treasury's second Permanent Secretary, died 'burnt out' at the age of fifty.[41] Kay-Shuttleworth went on sick-leave through overwork in 1848, and never returned—arguably, the greatest single misfortune in the country's educational history. His chief reported that he was 'not the only person (there have been two more—examiners—both strong men) who have been overpowered by the mass of increasing details, which the progress and very success of the system had produced'.[42] His successor fared no better. 'Poor Lingen, I am sorry to say, is as ill as Shuttleworth though in a different way. The labour of the situation, thanks to the insatiable appetite of the clergy for finding or making difficulties, is overwhelming.'[43] Disraeli's Admiralty correspondent, Bromley, reported during the Crimean War that his chief clerk had 'broken down'.[44] The Cattle Plague was a period of extreme pressure. 'We have often

---

[39] ibid., 125. [40] Finer (1952), 2–3.
[41] For this information, I am indebted to Dr H. Roseveare.
[42] PRO 30/22/7. Lansdowne to Russell, December 9, 1848.
[43] PRO 30/22/8. Lansdowne to Russell, September 16, 1849.
[44] Disraeli Papers. Bromley to Disraeli, November 19, 1855.

been engaged from early in the morning until late at night, and I do not believe that a greater burden ever fell with more suddenness and force upon a public department, and has been met with more zeal and energy on the part of those who have had to deal with it. I can say for myself that for a long time I was made the sole Local Authority for the metropolis, independent of the Council Office, and that I never went through so much work in my life.'[45]

Over and above the willingness to work as hard as three or four ordinary mortals, the true mark of the zealot was belief in a cause and single-minded devotion to its realization. Such a temperament was by no means rare. Leonard Horner, the most remarkable of the early factory inspectors, had it. He had held a post in the University of London but 'his imperious temper brought him into conflict with the authorities ... and he resigned. ... His strong mouth and determined jaw proclaimed a man of ruthless energy and deep conviction—ideally fitted for the part he was called upon to play'.[46] He told his wife that he revived his spirits during the drudgery of his job by recalling 'that I am the instrument of making the lives of many innocent children less burthensome'.[47] Edward Gulson, when applying for a post with the Poor Law Commission, promised ' "at all times to do my utmost to serve our general weale." This was no idle assertion, for it came from a man who had given, with no pay, two years of full-time work as Coventry's Director of the Poor'.[48] Inspectors as a body tended to the zealous type. They 'hoped for much from the moral improvement of the working class, but no more than what they demanded of themselves and the upper classes. Hard and exacting as they occasionally were, they were not hypocrites. Their character did not belie their pious sermons on middle-class virtues. ... Their industry was prodigious—and their integrity apparently incorruptible. ... The picture is formidable to an age of easier manners and more lax standards, formidable in particular because of the men's passion to do good'.[49]

But inspectors have received, perhaps, more than their due share of attention from administrative historians. Zealots were also found in the normal hierarchy of the offices. Stephen is a striking example. He gave up a good practice when he became a full-time member of the Colonial Office staff. Had he remained at the Bar, there is little doubt that he would have become a wealthy man. His motive in renouncing so much was largely that he believed he would be able

[45] ibid. Helps to Disraeli, September 13, 1867.
[46] Thomas, 98n.   [47] Roberts, 174–5.
[48] Ibid., 174.   [49] ibid.

to do more for the abolition of slavery from within than he could without. Opposition to slavery was, of course, a family tradition. Joseph Hume attacked his appointment on these grounds. 'Nothing could be more objectionable to the colonies than such an appointment. He was the son of the person whom the colonists supposed to be their greatest enemy; and to put him in an office in which every communication to and from the colonies must pass through his hands was highly objectionable. The appointment had outraged the feelings of the colonists more than any other act of the government.'[50]

Rowland Hill was a zealot to the point of monomania. 'He found it somewhat hard . . . to understand how anyone could be indifferent to the statistics of penny postage, and help watching the rise in the number of letters and the postal revenue with as much interest as Englishmen, on a wet day, watch the rise in the weather-glass.' Of his unique meeting with Garibaldi, at a dinner in Fishmongers' Hall, he recorded: 'I had some conversation with Garibaldi about the state of the Italian Post Office; but it was evident that he felt but little interest in the matter.' To this, his brother retorted: 'I was . . . very much amused to find that you consulted Garibaldi on Italian penny postage. When you go to heaven, I foresee that you will stop at the gate to inquire of St Peter how many deliveries they have per day, and how the expense of postal communication between heaven and the other place is defrayed.' His biographer portrays him thus: 'He longed for power, but it was for the power to carry through his great scheme. . . . His strong mind was made up that it should succeed. He looked upon it with all the fondness and the pride with which a father looks upon his only boy. Take it from him, and his life was done. . . . He had not the fault of most enthusiasts, who look in others for a zeal as ardent as that which animates themselves. . . . But . . . he did look for the same carefulness, the same exactness, the same integrity, and the same constant thought for the public good. . . . He failed to make due allowance for the weakness of man's nature. By asking too much from men he got from them, perhaps, less than they might otherwise have given.'[51]

What became of the zealots? In the nature of the case, the type tended not to perpetuate itself. 'Once the service machine has been adapted to the new responsibilities and functions, men of restless energy tend to become impatient at the slow pace of development and the limitations within which they have to work.'[52] MacGregor,

[50] 3 *Hansard*, xiv, 1081. March 3, 1826. q. Young, 85.
[51] G. B. Hill, *Life of Sir Rowland Hill, etc.* (1880), ii, 412–17.
[52] R. K. Kelsall, *Higher Civil Servants in Great Britain* (1955), 195.

for example, retired from the Board of Trade at the age of fifty to enter the House of Commons and his going was described in the following words: 'On the repeal of the Corn Laws, he threw [his post] up.'[53] The implication is clear. He regarded the position in a missionary light. Once the mission had been accomplished, he had no interest in remaining simply as an administrator. MacGregor's successor was Porter—another zealot. But more typically 'their places are taken by senior officials more cautious in temperament, more content to play second fiddle even to ministers whose sole claim to office may be that they were good party men'.[54] Though these words refer to a later period, they refer to a process exemplified when, for example, Lingen succeeded Kay-Shuttleworth as secretary to the Committee for Education.

Matthew Arnold—himself on H.M.I.—left a sketch of Kay-Shuttleworth. He possessed 'a thorough knowledge of popular education . . . [and] he knows it in the only way in which this subject can ever be known, because he loves it. Statesmen—and among them Lord Lansdowne deserves to be named first—who perhaps did not share his zeal, were yet wise and open-minded enough to see the benefits which might be wrought by it'.[55] But without Kay-Shuttleworth's devotion, his statesmanship and the excellent relations he built up with his staff and everyone concerned in the management of schools, the policy would not have realized itself. Lingen resembled him in ability and industry, but lacked his ardour. Arnold attributed the Department's troubles under Lingen to 'the presence in the heart of the Education Department, of this want of love for the very course which such a department is created to follow'.[56] Admittedly, Arnold heightened the contrast to make his case; but it was striking enough even when reduced to bare essentials. Under Lingen, the inspectors felt handicapped in their work by the dictatorial tone of the office in dealing with managers. Many of the most influential and enthusiastic among the latter were alienated by the tone of the correspondence they received. Some withheld their schools from inspection because they 'refused to crawl up the back-stairs of the Education Department to ask for grants'. A clergyman, who had lost his temper at the pomposity of several letters from the Department, wrote to Lingen: 'First you blunder; and then you bully.'[57]

Again, Sisson holds that 'there is no need for the administrator to be a man of ideas'. Laski's complaint that no Home Office official had ever made a serious contribution to penology or criminology merely showed 'a mistaken view of the sort of animal the official is.

[53] *D.N.B.*   [54] Kelsall, 195.   [55] q. Leese, 93–4.   [56] ibid.   [57] ibid., 98–9.

... His distinguishing quality should be rather a certain freedom from ideas. The idealisms and the most vicious appetites of the populace are equal before him. He should be prepared to bow before any wisdom whose mouth is loud enough.'[58] In one of the very fields cited by Laski—penology—there were notable examples to the contrary among nineteenth-century civil servants. (Whether Laski did not know of them, or overlooked their contribution as not being serious, is another matter.) In the great debate on the 'separate' versus the 'silent' system, it was William Crawford's report of 1833 on his visit to American prisons which carried the day. Two years later he became one of the first Inspectors of Prisons. Far from being a man without ideas, he was 'an inflexible dogmatist, typical of an age which had complete faith in a few comprehensive and apparently simple reforms'.[59] Sir Edmund du Cane, the first Chairman of the Prison Commissioners, was another Home Office penologist. His views may be studied in *Prevention and Punishment of Crime* (1885).[60]

Chadwick was, of course, another notable 'man of ideas'. 'His intellectual powers were formidable but of a peculiar order. . . . Every element in each of his plans was borrowed; but he combined diverse ingredients so ingeniously as always to produce a completed scheme of striking originality. He reached his conclusions by an overpowering blend of strict logic and massive inductions.'[61] Chadwick's co-worker in public health was similar in type. 'I will tell you . . . what . . . the claims of Dr Southwood Smith are for the vacant seat at the Board of Health. . . . I consider him the originator of the whole sanitary movement; he first prominently called the attention of the public and the government to the whole subject—devoted his time, energy and practice to it. Without him and Chadwick it would never . . . have assumed shape or substance. When the Public Health Act first passed the immediate arrival of cholera enabled the government to appoint a paid medical member of the Board. He seemed naturally designated . . . for the situation, and he was immediately appointed. He continued for more than a year and a half sharing and bearing not certainly the least laborious part in all these proceedings. . . . In the preparation of [the Metropolitan Interment] Bill, Dr Smith took the chief labouring oar: he almost entirely drew up the report on which it was founded. Even upon the mere ground of expediency, I think it desirable that the person most *steeped* in the subject should be charged with the working of it. . . . Certainly I, and I believe . . . Ashley, would feel ourselves disgraced if Dr

[58] Sisson, 23.   [59] W. L. Burn, *Age of Equipoise* (1964), 178n.
[60] ibid., 190 and n.   [61] Finer, 2.

Southwood Smith should not have the first paid situation at the Board. I believe also that the indignation among all the promoters of sanitary reform would be intense.'[62]

THE EMERGENCE OF THE GENERALIST

What became of the five types of civil servant considered in this chapter? Patricians and plebeians lived in a symbiotic relationship with one another. The former were often incapable of getting through the business of their offices. They needed the latter to lean on. As the quality of upper-class recruits improved, however, there was less room at the top for those of lower-class origins. Zealots, as noted above, tended not to perpetuate themselves; though they continued to crop up from time to time. (Sir Robert Morant was a notable example.) The professionals, on the other hand, have proliferated, but only at intermediate levels. It has been exceptional since 1870 for them to reach the heights touched by such a man as Sir John Simon in the middle decades of the nineteenth century. They have been subordinated to generalists. When the Local Government Board was set up in 1872, Lambert (a generalist) became its first permanent head while Simon (a professional) suffered a drop in status.[63] The incident symbolizes the fate of professionals in the British civil service. By 1870, it was clear that men like Farrer, Lingen and Rogers were prototypes of the future higher civil servant. Upper-middle-class origin, Oxbridge education, proficiency in literary studies: such were the marks by which they were known. The Administrative Class type was not created by Open Competition. Open Competition served to perpetuate a type which had already come to the top.

[62] PRO 30/22/8. Carlisle to Seymour, July 17, 1850.
[63] Lambert, 518ff.

CHAPTER VI

LAW AND ADMINISTRATION

'It is not only necessary that the legislature should make provision in the laws for their due execution; it is also desirable that the executive agency should work towards new legislation on the same topics. For the execution of laws deals with those particulars by an induction of which the results to be aimed at in legislation are to be ascertained; and the generalization from those particulars can only be well effected when the lowest in the chain of functionaries is made subsidiary to the operations of the highest in a suggestive as well as in an executive capacity—that is, when the experience of the functionary who puts the last hand to the execution of any particular class of enactments is made available for the guidance of the legislature.'

Sir Henry Taylor, 1836

'Policy is secreted in the interstices of administration.'

Old saw

Ilbert pointed out long ago that the first Reform Act was a turning point in the relationship between law and administration. 'The net result of the legislative activity which has characterized, though with different degrees of intensity, the period since 1832, has been the building up piecemeal of an administrative machine of great complexity which stands in as constant need of repair, renewal, reconstruction and adaptation to new requirements as the plant of a modern factory.'[1] Such a relationship has three implications, none of which was true in the eighteenth and early nineteenth centuries. These are:
1. that administrative changes, central or local, stem mainly from Public General Acts
2. that such Acts will include, when required and as a matter of course, provision for administrative machinery to put them into operation
3. that it is part of the responsibility of every government to carry

[1] Sir C. Ilbert, *Legislative Methods and Forms* (Oxford, 1901), 212–13.

a programme of legislation, initiating administrative changes, in every normal session of parliament.

Whereas the characteristic nineteenth-century statute was public, national and obligatory, in the eighteenth century, much legislation, particularly in the social and economic sphere 'was private, local and facultative, setting up local agencies, such as turnpike, paving, enclosure, or improvement commissioners where such things appeared to be desired by preponderant local interests'.[2] A volume of eighteenth-century statutes is very bulky. 'Apparently parliament got through much more work then than it gets through in our own day. But on inspection we find that anything that in the strictest sense can be called legislation, any alteration of the general rules of law, was much rarer than . . . in the days of the first three Edwards.'[3] It was the practice for many measures originating under private Bill procedure to be declared Public Acts to relieve the promoters of the heavy fees which would otherwise have been required.[4] Maitland took the statutes of 1786 and concluded that 'fully half of the public Acts are of [a] petty local character'.[5] A decade later, the picture was much the same. One hundred and eighty public Acts received the Royal Assent in the session of 1796–7. They included Acts relating to canals at such places as Bodmin and Grantham, Acts for the improvement of Ipswich and Northampton, Acts relating to harbours at places as far apart as Rye, Barmouth and Aberdeen, and Acts for purposes so diverse as fisheries on the Tweed, drainage in Lincolnshire, water-supply at Weymouth, Milbrooke Parish Church, Southampton, and the road from Wem to Bron-y-Garth. In all there were seventy-seven Acts of a 'petty local character', a rather lower proportion than in Maitland's sample. But 1796–7 was a period of war, and the total was swollen by twenty-eight Acts relating to defence. If allowance is made for these, it will be seen that the proportion was very much the same in the two sessions.

Many of the private Acts of 1796 had still more the character of *privilegia*, relating as they did to particular individuals and places. There was an Act to dissolve the marriage of William Townsend Mullins with Frances Elizabeth Sage; another for exchanging lands between the Guardians of the Poor in the City of Canterbury and Thomas Barrett, Esq.; a third for dividing the estates of Thomas Leacroft, Esq., and John Leacroft, Gent.; a fourth to enable Evelyn Meadows, Esq., and others after his death, to grant building leases in Whitechapel; other Acts again conferred the necessary powers

[2] Pares, 3.
[3] Maitland, 382–3.
[4] C. Hughes, *The British Statute Book* (1957), 100.
[5] Maitland, 383.

for enclosing common lands at Sixpenny Hanley and Nether Wallop; yet another naturalized Petrus Wilhelmus Aloysius Pottgeisser. Maitland called the eighteenth century 'the century of *privilegia*. It seems afraid to rise to the dignity of a general proposition; it will not say, "All commons may be enclosed according to these general rules," "All aliens may become naturalized if they fulfil these or those conditions," "All boroughs shall have these powers for widening their roads," "All marriages may be dissolved if the wife's adultery be proved." No, it deals with this common and that marriage. We may attribute this to jealousy of the Crown: to have erected boards of commissioners empowered to sanction the enclosure of commons or the widening of roads, to have enabled a Secretary of State to naturalize aliens, would have been to increase the influence and patronage of the Crown, and considering the events of the seventeenth century, it was but natural that parliament should look with suspicion on anything that tended in that direction'.[6]

'As time has gone on parliament has become much less suspicious of the Crown, because "the Crown" has come to mean a very different thing from what it meant in the last century. The change is a gradual one, but I think we may say that it becomes very apparent soon after the Reform Act of 1832. Parliament begins to *legislate* with remarkable vigour, to overhaul the whole law of the country ... but about the same time it gives up the attempt to *govern* the country, to say what commons shall be enclosed, what roads shall be widened, what boroughs shall have paid constables and so forth. It begins to lay down general rules about these matters and to entrust their working partly to officials, to secretaries of state, to boards of commissioners, who for this purpose are endowed with new statutory powers, partly to the law courts.'[7] As the nineteenth century wore on, private Bill legislation declined in importance, relatively to Public General Acts. And with the exception of divorce, which became a matter for the courts in 1857, this decline was accompanied by an increase of administrative responsibilities in corresponding fields. An Act of 1844 delegated to the Secretary of State the power to issue certificates of naturalization, and this procedure, administered by the Home Office, superseded naturalization Acts. Statutory Commissions were created to deal with enclosures, changes of tenure (e.g. substitution of freehold for copyhold) and commutation of titles. The Home Secretary took the responsibility from 1834 onwards of introducing an annual Turnpike Acts (Continuance) Bill, which reduced the need for road commissioners to promote separate

[6] ibid.   [7] ibid., 383–4.

Bills of their own. In the field of local government, Public General Acts, starting with the Poor Law (Amendment) Act of 1834, and the Muncipal Corporations Act of 1835, became the standard mode of procedure, in place of the old method whereby bodies of improvement commissioners for particular towns, each with its special powers, were set up by private Act.[8] Of course, local authorities continued, as they do today, to seek special powers. But even here, the introduction of the Provisional Order made it often possible for them to secure the powers they needed from central administration rather than from parliament. In one field—railways—private Bill procedure remained of prime importance. But there was a great difference in the attitude of government, as compared with its attitude towards the road, navigation and canal Bills of the eighteenth century. 'The expansion of railways brought more clearly than ever before into the consciousness of parliament the conception that in private legislation there was an aspect of public, as well as one of private, interest, to which no government could be indifferent.'[9] From the 1840s onwards, promoters of private Bills 'were frequently in communication with the Chairman of Ways and Means, or the Chairmen of the Lords' Committees'.[10] Public General Acts, too, delegated to ministers powers to authorize companies to proceed by certificate, instead of by private Act, in certain cases.[11]

The cumulative effect of private Acts had been enormous. Vast changes in such fields as highway administration and local government had resulted from them. The turning point in their decline was, of course, the 1830s, and it is possible to see in the form of the great measures of that decade an importance secondary only to that of their content. 'What was revolutionary about the Reform Act of 1832 and the Municipal Corporations Act of 1835 was that they proceeded by public Bill. . . . The interesting thing about the Reform Act is that it was a Public General Act, that it did not follow the procedure of piecemeal reform, . . . It ushered in a spate of highly important Public General Acts, the destruction of the old machinery of local government being the most radical of them all.'[12] Even statesmen of the old school could see the power of the new procedure —although there is something in Palmerston's way of spelling out his proposition that suggests he regarded it as novel even as late as

[8] S. and B. Webb, *Statutory Authorities for Special Purposes* (1922).
[9] O. C. Williams, *Historical Development of Private Bill Procedure and Standing Orders in the House of Commons* (1948–9), i, 67.
[10] T. Erskine May, q. Williams, i, 122.
[11] Parris (1965) 48–9.   [12] Hughes (1957), 45 and 112.

1854. 'I have often thought,' he wrote, 'that it might be well to pass a Bill investing every municipal council with the powers of a local Board of Health if they chose to exercise them. Such a Bill would supersede in many cases the necessity for provisional orders and special Acts of Parliament.'[13] His correspondent, who belonged to a younger generation, spoke much more roundly. 'I not only intend,' he replied, 'to give [statutory] powers to every municipality but I shall endeavour to establish a Local Board [of Health] in every parish and district in the kingdom with very extensive powers. I shall not give them the *option* of having these powers, but shall confer them for exercise. I think it will be an acceptable imposition.'[14]

The notion that government needed administrative machinery to enforce the law, outside certain fields such as the collection of the revenue, was foreign to the thought of eighteenth-century Britain. In the traditional view, law enforced itself through such agencies as common informers, grand juries and interested parties. 'The eighteenth-century notion of *ubi jus ibi remedia* in practice made the enforcement of the law depend on suits brought, for the most part, at the instance of private individuals: a cumbersome, intermittent and costly process.'[15]

There was not even a police force. The Gordon Riots of 1780—to go no further back—had put the problem on the agenda, as it were. The radical movements of the revolutionary and Napoleonic periods, coupled with such symptoms of industrial unrest as Luddism, kept the ruling class in a continual mood of insecurity. The obvious solution would have been administrative—the creation of a police force. Yet in fact, as Dicey pointed out, 'the revolutionary movements of 1795 and 1815–20 were combated, not by departmental action but by parliamentary legislation. The suspension of the Habeas Corpus Act, the passing of the Libel Act, and of the "Six Acts" of 1819, were severely coercive measures; but they contain no evidence of any attempt to give a Continental character to administration. In so far as individual liberty was destroyed, it was destroyed by and in pursuance of Acts of Parliament.'[16] The turning-point here, of course, was the setting up of the Metropolitan Police in 1829, followed by the requirement in the Municipal Corporations Act of 1835 that boroughs should provide themselves with police forces. When the next great threat to public order arrived, in the form of

---

[13] Palmerston Papers. Palmerston to Hall, August 20, 1854.
[14] ibid. Hall to Palmerston, August 23, 1854.
[15] Finer (1952), 15–16.
[16] J. Redlich and F. Hirst, *Local Government in England* (1903), ii, 240.

Chartism, the action proposed was very different. 'When parliament was required to strengthen the hand of the executive, it was asked to do so in a manner very different from that of the age of Pitt and the age of Sidmouth. Not by tightening up the law, not by introducing new offences, not by taking away civil liberties was the threat of disorder met, but by improving the means of enforcing the existing law: the formation of a police force rather than the suspension of Habeas Corpus was the action sought from the legislature.'[17] The result was the Act of 1839, empowering counties to set up constabularies.

In the field of prison reform, the investigations of Howard and (later) Elizabeth Fry revealed the urgent need that something should be done, and Parliament was willing to go to the length of passing laws on the subject. An Act of 1779 (19 Geo. III, c. 74) authorized the building of a penitentiary but it was never erected.[18] The first general Prisons Act was passed in 1791. But a contemporary commented: 'It is not so much for want of GOOD LAWS, as from their INEXECUTION, that the state of prisons is so bad.'[19] The 1824 Act went further. It was 'the first attempt ever made to formulate a national policy for prisons, provided for the classification of prisoners, hard work for convicts, and regular reports to the Home Office on committals and prison discipline. Parliament, *having established no machinery to administer it*, saw the Act go largely unenforced'.[20] More than half a century of experience had proved beyond doubt the futility of passing elaborate statutes without administrative machinery for enforcing their provisions, before the lesson at last bore fruit in the Act of 1835 (5 and 6 Wil. IV, c. 38).[21]

A similar pattern was to be seen in the field of mental health. There had been an Act for Regulating Private Madhouses (14 Geo. III, c. 9) but 'the provisions for enforcing the regulations contained in this Act were so ineffectual that it remained almost a dead letter'.[22] The 1828 Madhouse Act (9 Geo. IV, c. 41), on the other hand, created administrative machinery within the metropolitan area at least, in the form of paid inspectors, and led to considerable improvement. In 1842 the system was extended throughout the country, for a trial

[17] F. C. Mather, *Public Order in the Age of the Chartists* (1959), 33.
[18] S. and B. Webb, *English Prisons under Local Government* (1922), 39–40.
[19] A. Wedderburn, *Observations on the State of Prisons* (1794), q. in R. S. E. Hinde, *British Penal System, 1773–1950* (1951), 42.
[20] Roberts, 56. (My italics.)
[21] Webb (1922), 110–11.
[22] K. Jones, *Lunacy, Law and Conscience, 1744–1845* (1955), 37–8.

period of three years. The report of the inspectors on this experiment led to its becoming permanent in 1845.[23]

In the sphere of railways, the Liverpool and Manchester Railway Act, 1826, provided for a reduction in the company's charges if it paid a dividend in excess of ten per cent.[24] Thus was enacted, at the dawn of the railway age, a principle over which much ingenuity was later to be expended. But it was never operative because no procedure was laid down for enforcing it. Since the following section states that the dividends and revised tolls shall be declared to the Clerks of the Peace in neighbouring counties and published in the local press, there is perhaps an implication that individuals should seek redress, in case of the company's default, from the local Justices. But no clear guidance was given and in particular 'no security ... was taken ... for a public audit which would have ascertained what profits were really made'.[25] The turning point in the public regulation of railways was the Act of 1840, which delegated powers to the Board of Trade and authorized the appointment of inspectors.[26]

From these examples, it is clear that around the year 1830 a profound change was occurring in the public mind as to the relation between the law and administration. It has been said that 'a statute-book crammed with lovely things is pointless without the means to carry them into practice. Indeed it is a sign of a softening of the brain to tolerate such a state of affairs'.[27] If this is true, then almost all British legislators in the period 1770–1830 or thereabouts were addlepated. However that may be, it came to be assumed as easily as it had previously been rejected that legal change would often imply administrative machinery for the purpose of enforcement. *The Times* made the point clearly in comparing the two Factory Bills that came before Parliament in 1833, one a private Member's Bill sponsored by Ashley, the other a government measure founded on Chadwick's report. Neither was new in principle—there were five Factory Acts on the Statute Book already, all largely ineffective for want of enforcement machinery. There were a number of differences between the two Bills; in the ages of children to be protected, for example, and in the hours they could work. *The Times* brushed such details aside. 'The most important distinction lies in two circumstances which would be great measures in themselves and contain the seeds

[23] ibid., 142, 171, 175 and 191.
[24] 7 Geo. IV, c. xlix (Local and Personal), s. 128.
[25] F. Clifford, *History of Private Bill Legislation* (1885–7), i, 123.
[26] Parris (1965), 28ff.   [27] Sisson, 139.

of mighty changes in our domestic policy, independently of the regulation of the hours of labour in our factories ... Their measure was nearly destitute of *executory machinery* (if we may be allowed the expression) and would soon have been forgotten or abandoned like the previous Bill for regulating cotton factories ... The ministerial Act, on the contrary, provides an important class of new officers, called "inspectors", who shall have the authority of magistrates for enforcing its execution.'[28]

GOVERNMENTAL RESPONSIBILITY FOR LEGISLATION

If the power of the Public General Act as an instrument of administrative change was recognized by the 1830s, it did not at once follow that each government, year after year and as a matter of course, would take responsibility for a programme of legislation leading to such changes. Prior to 1830, 'the King's service very seldom required legislation—except, of course, financial legislation'.[29] Ministers were 'obliged to pass revenue Acts, mutiny Acts, and other Acts which were necessary to the conduct of the executive government. ... And though such emergencies as the rebellion of 1745 might lead to important domestic legislation initiated by the government, for the most part the initiation of legislation for the purpose of effecting reforms in the law was left to individual peers or Members of the House of Commons'.[30] As a result, very few of the reforms which look the most important in retrospect were Cabinet measures. 'Parliamentary reform was not, though Pitt and Richmond would have liked to make it so. The abolition of the slave trade was not ... Fox and Grenville only did, in 1806, what Pitt is so much blamed for doing—they tried to get a measure agreed by a cabinet for the abolition of the slave trade, but when they found they could not, they brought in a Bill as individuals. Wellington sat for many years in cabinets which had agreed to consider Catholic Emancipation as an "open question" because they did not consider it as a matter of government and there were so many other matters of government on which they did agree.'[31] It is noteworthy that many of the great measures of the decades preceding the first Reform Bill are known by the names of their proposers: Sir John Barnard's Act, Gilbert's Act, Hardwicke's Marriage Act, Jervis's Act, Lord Chesterfield's Act for the reform of the calendar, Fox's Libel Act.[32]

---

[28] *The Times*, September 21, 1833, q. Finer (1952), 65–6. [29] Pares, 164.
[30] Sir W. Holdsworth, *History of English Law (1903–1966)*, xi, 371.
[31] Pares, 164. [32] Holdsworth, xi, 371–2: Foord, 414.

Until about 1840, 'ministries . . . regarded themselves as primarily charged with administrative responsibility, and not with the execution of a political programme endorsed by the electorate'.[33] The attitude in fact persisted a good deal longer. In 1848, the government suffered in public esteem through the failure of its Bills. Lord John Russell defended his administration as follows: 'There have been in the course of the last thirty years very great changes in the mode of conducting the business of the House . . . When I first entered parliament it was not usual for government to undertake generally all subjects of legislation . . . [But] since the passing of the Reform Bill it has been thought convenient, on every subject on which an alteration of the law is required, that the government should undertake the responsibility of proposing it to parliament.'[34] At the end of the session, replying to Disraeli, he returned to the theme. 'I must remind the . . . House that the supposed duty of the members of a government to introduce a great number of measures to parliament and to carry those measures through parliament in a session, is a duty which is new to the government of this country. Let me call the attention of the House to the fact that the Ministers of the Crown are chiefly appointed to administer the affairs of the Empire.'[35]

Palmerston at least retained this attitude until his death. In February, 1864, the young Goschen, who had been chosen to second the motion on the Address, called on the Prime Minister to discuss the Queen's Speech. Having dealt with foreign affairs, Goschen asked, 'What is to be said about domestic affairs and legislation?' Palmerston 'gaily replied, rubbing his hands with an air of comfortable satisfaction: "There is really nothing to be done. We cannot go on adding to the Statute Book *ad infinitum*. Perhaps we may have a little law reform or bankruptcy reform; but we cannot go on legislating forever." '[36] Private Members did not necessarily disagree with him. A backbencher had written to him a few years earlier: 'In my opinion the fewer measures you bring forward, and the fewer new laws upon any subject we have, the better.'[37]

Such negativism was not, however, the whole story. Russell was defending himself against a charge; had there been no foundation for the charge, he would have ignored it. Palmerston's attitude impressed Goschen precisely because it seemed to him long out-

[33] Keir, 407.
[34] 3 *Hansard*, xcvii, 969. March 24, 1848.
[35] q. S. Walpole, *Life of Lord John Russell* (2 e., 1889), ii, 96.
[36] A. R. D. Elliot, *Life of G. J. Goschen, etc.* (1911), i, 65.
[37] Palmerston Papers. Drummond to Palmerston, December 22, 1856.

moded. In retrospect, those years were seen to be abnormal. 'Lord Palmerston's last ministry (1859–66) was a period of exceptional barrenness in legislation.'[38] As early as 1822, the Cabinet had begun to consider its legislative policy before the Parliamentary session began. 'I candidly concur with you,' wrote Peel in October of that year, 'in the policy of fully considering, while we have time properly to consider them, all those subjects which during the session will in all probability be pressed upon the notice of parliament, many of which it would be proper for the government to take into their own hands, and on almost all of which it would be most desirable to be enabled to pronounce a decided and well-considered opinion.'[39] The Treasury circulated departments, asking for drafts of Bills by February 10, 1823, and the Cabinet met on January 22, 1823, 'for the purpose of considering the several measures and subjects to which the attention of parliament is likely to be directed soon after its meeting'.[40]

In the session referred to, that of 1823, ministers introduced eighty Bills as compared with fifty-two brought in by private Members. And whereas seventy-two of the ministerial measures passed, only twenty-two of those sponsored by private Members did so: ninety as against forty-two per cent.[41] It is true that numbers do not tell the whole story. Some private Members' Acts were more important than most government measures: e.g., the Repeal of the Combination Acts (1825) and the Repeal of the Test and Corporation Acts (1828). Nevertheless, as time went on, government came more and more to dominate the legislative programme.

The reality was recognized even by such distinguished private Members, as Peel and Graham. The former 'was disposed to think the principle an excellent one, so far as independent Members were concerned, that the duty of preparing measures of legislation should in all cases of general interest be undertaken by ministers'.[42] Graham's view occurs in a report of a conversation he had about a Commission on which he had served. His interlocutor, Walpole, observed that 'the Commissioners should have given us the draft of a Bill to carry out their suggestion'. 'Ah!' replied Graham, 'that we have left to executive government. It is for them to determine whether they will take the whole or what parts of it they will adopt.' 'And then he

---

[38] Ilbert (1901), 212n.
[39] P. Fraser, 'Growth of Ministerial Control in the Nineteenth-century House of Commons', *EHR*, lxxv (1960), 454n.
[40] ibid.   [41] ibid., 455n.
[42] 3 *Hansard*, cviii, 974. February 18, 1850.

added, [continued Walpole] rubbing his hands . . . "I should like to see the man who will draw the Bills." ' And whether or not private Members approved the principle, they accepted the fact. As one of Palmerston's correspondents put it, writing about arterial drainage, 'an Act would be required . . . and although I have been much urged to introduce one, I know too well the fate of individual exertions on such subjects to attempt it. You must do it'.[43]

This accords very well with the view recorded by Sir Charles Wood in 1855. 'When I was first in parliament, twenty-seven years ago, the functions of the government were chiefly executive. Changes in our laws were proposed by independent Members, and carried, not as purely party questions, by their combined action on both sides. Now, when an independent Member brings forward a subject it is not to propose himself a measure, but to call it to the attention of the government. All the House joins in declaring that the present state of the law is abominable, and in requiring the government to provide a remedy. As soon as the government has obeyed, and prepared one, they all oppose it. Our defects as legislators, which is *not* our business, damage us as administrators, which *is* our business.'[44]

The new attitude found authoritative expression in a book by the third Earl Grey. 'Those to whom the executive authority is entrusted, have also the duty of recommending to the legislature the measures it should adopt, and must retire if their advice is not generally followed. By this arrangement the executive government is able to act with the vigour which the assurance of having its policy supported when necessary by legislation can alone give to it. . . . Constantly the executive government of a great nation is compelled to apply to the legislature for new powers, or new laws, to meet exigencies that arise. How greatly its action would be crippled, if it could not depend upon obtaining the assistance of this kind which it requires. . . . This is a duty which has been imposed upon the advisers of the Crown only by degrees, and chiefly since the passing of the Reform Acts of 1832. Formerly ministers took little charge of the proceedings of parliament on all matters not immediately connected with their executive duties. This led to much unwise legislation and to the habitual neglect of all systematic endeavour to effect improvements in our laws as occasion for them arose. A different system has of late years grown up, and the ministers of the Crown are now justly regarded as responsible for bringing forward

[43] Disraeli Papers. Walpole to Disraeli, July 15, 1852. Palmerston Papers. Drummond to Palmerston, December 22, 1856.
[44] q. Ilbert (1901), 82–3.

such measures as are required, and for opposing any objectionable proposals from other quarters.'[45]

In spite of these bold words, arrangements for drawing up the list of measures to be supported remained very loose. A distinction was drawn between a Bill introduced by a minister acting for the government, and one introduced by a minister acting for a Select Committee over which he had presided. The Railway Regulation Bill of 1840—the foundation of government supervision of railways in Britain—originated in the recommendations of a Select Committee. It was introduced by Lord Seymour (who held office) and by James Loch (who did not). Both had been members of the Committee. So far from assuming that Seymour's position guaranteed government support, Loch wrote to Melbourne specifically to entreat such support. 'Let me beg of you to look to Lord Seymour's Railway Bill. It deserves the attention and the support of the government. I beg to assure you that the entire internal communication of the country is about undergoing [sic] the most rapid and wonderful revolution which ever was effected. The carriage of passengers has been accomplished, that of goods is about being effected [sic]. Also both will be transformed to powerful monopolies, which if not now attended to, will be immensely too powerful for legislation, if they are not so already. Pray give the matter some of your attention.'[46] Gladstone's Railway Bill of 1844 was treated by his Cabinet colleagues in a comparable way. Though they did not veto it, they certainly gave him no promise of positive support.[47] Even so important a measure as the Public Health Bill of 1848 might, it seems, never have been considered by the Cabinet prior to its introduction, had not the Home Secretary thought it desirable. 'Before it is brought in I think the Cabinet should know more about it and give it their sanction.'[48] Ministers' reactions to private Members' Bills—which might, of course, lead to their being taken up by the government—were not always co-ordinated. In 1853, Palmerston, as Home Secretary, took a stand opposed to that of his colleague, the Lord Chancellor, over a Trade Union Bill introduced by a private Member.[49] Palmerston recognized that, even by moving an amendment to a private Member's Bill, a minister put his foot on a slippery slope. 'I have read your speech,' he wrote to Milner Gibson, 'against Ewart's

[45] Grey, 16–17, 19–20.
[46] Melbourne Papers; 46. Loch to Melbourne, July 4, 1840.
[47] Parris (1965), 56.
[48] PRO 30/22/6. George Grey to Russell, December 23, 1847.
[49] Bell, ii, 77–8.

fanciful pedantic Bill with more pleasure than your subsequent undertaking to make it a government measure by yourself proposing amendments to his Bill.'[50] A minister in the Lords, with a junior colleague in the Commons, might think it desirable specifically to ask the Leader of the House to find time for a departmental measure. 'I have taken a very great interest,' wrote the Duke of Richmond, 'in the Railway Regulation Bill of which Cave has now the charge in the House of Commons. I hope you will be able to give him a day to get it through, as I think it will be a very useful measure.'[51]

DRAFTING GOVERNMENT BILLS

Grey had understood that a government's responsibility for legislation began before the introduction of a Bill into the House. 'In order that such laws may be passed as are required for the welfare of the nation,' he had written, 'the ministers should be held responsible both for preparing and carrying these measures.'[52] During the greater part of the nineteenth century, the machinery for preparing Bills was in fact very imperfect. The main defect of eighteenth-century statutes was their 'excessive individuality'.[53] Hence the main need was co-ordination of draftsmanship. There were official draftsmen, but very little co-ordination. Arrangements for drafting Bills in the Treasury were among the first matters looked into by the Reform government in 1830. The Solicitor and Assistant Solicitor could draft Bills, with help from consultants, but there were also two 'standing counsel to the Treasury'. One of them, William Harrison, had been a government draftsman for over forty years. He had been brought in by Pitt to help with proposed reforms of titles and Poor Law, which came to nothing. He drew fiscal Bills, and Bills connected with the army and the militia. At first he was assistant to one Lowndes. But on the latter's promotion in 1798, Harrison succeeded him. Much of his work was for other departments. For the Foreign Office, he had drawn Bills setting up slave courts abroad. He had also been responsible for Bills relating to the Church and the residence of the clergy. 'I receive the Minute of instructions from the Chancellor of the Exchequer; I put the Minute into heads, with details for revision and approbation, and then I prepare the Bill.'[54]

The other Treasury counsel, Sir Thomas Tomlins, had been counsel to the Chancellor of the Irish Exchequer, and had been 'taken over'

[50] Palmerston Papers. Palmerston to Milner Gibson, April 5, 1864.
[51] Disraeli Papers. Richmond to Disraeli, July 9, 1868.
[52] Grey, 19.   [53] Holdsworth, xi, 372.   [54] Ilbert (1901), 80–1.

in 1816 when the Irish Exchequer ceased to exist. 'The practice hitherto has been to employ either Sir Thomas Tomlins or Mr Harrison to draw the Treasury Bills.'[55] But the Solicitor and Assistant Solicitor had been responsible for 'overlooking some of the revenue Bills drawn by the direction of the inferior Boards. The Solicitors . . . have been also much employed by other departments of government'. There was in addition a parliamentary agent, named Dorrington.

Tomlins gave an account of his own duties. 'The officers of the several subordinate departments (Customs, Excise, National Debt, etc.) communicate with him, under the orders of the Treasury; and the officers in Ireland under orders from the Chief Secretary through . . . Sir C. Flint, the resident Under-Secretary. It is utterly impossible for Sir Thomas to particularize the whole of the duties performed by him during the last five years. . . . The general nature of his several duties may, however, be understood from the following detail:

1. The drawing of all Bills (where relating to government or revenue) for which instructions were sent to Sir Thomas either as relating to the United Kingdom or Ireland respectively.
2. Perusing or settling Bills drawn, or prepared by the counsel, or officers, of any and every Department.
3. Advising on the necessity of introducing Bills.
4. Preparing and correcting (in consultation with Mr Dorrington, of the House of Commons) the resolutions requisite to be proposed, previous to the introduction of Revenue Bills.
5. Attending the progress of all Bills referred to him from the first introduction into parliament to the final passing, preparing amendments for the committees on such Bills and in [sic] all other stages of their progress.
6. Advising on the operation of all existing Acts (British or Irish).
7. Giving opinions on the construction of the Statute and Common Law, and on the agreement or discrepancy of the law in Ireland and Great Britain.
8. Answering in writing or verbally (and immediately) all questions and references relating to any point of law on any subject whatever.

'To perform these duties Sir Thomas has, during every session, been continually in attendance at a minute's notice; and generally

[55] Grey Papers: Second Earl. 56/1. Memo. on payments to lawyers for Treasury business, n.d. unsigned, from which all quotations in the following paragraphs are taken.

at all times of the year is known to be where he can speedily be sent for: during the session he has been (generally speaking) daily employed from six to eight hours, and during the recess of parliament has had Bills to draw or consider for the ensuing session. He has also prepared the *Index* of Acts relating to Ireland, the whole of which is annually reprinted, so as to shew the complete state of the Statute law, as relates to that part of the United Kingdom, from the Union to the end of the session preceding each annual [edition]. He has also prepared the report on the expiring laws introduced in the House of Commons at the commencement of each session.'

Much of his advice had been verbal. For example, 'on Sunday week: Sir C. Flint sent to him (between three and four o'clock) a note requesting information, whether as the *Commissions of the Peace in Ireland* expired in consequence of the demise of the Crown, they might be continued by proclamation or Act of Parliament. Sir Thomas sent an answer referring to three Acts of Parliament (two British and one Irish). . . . On considering the question it occurred to Sir Thomas as probable that the measure of a continuing Act would be required . . . He prepared a short Bill accordingly, and sent it to Sir Charles, . . . and it was introduced into the House of Commons on Monday, and is now in progress'.

The trouble was that there were too many cooks, and they spoilt the broth. 'Throughout our enquiry concerning the parliamentary business of the Treasury, we have been struck with the apparently needless multiplicity of opinions and revisions, to which a Bill to be brought in upon a Treasury matter is usually subject.' Individual responsibility was thereby lessened. For example, the Bill for Consolidating the Customs of Great Britain and Ireland (4 Geo. IV, c. 23) 'was drawn up by Mr Hume of the Customs', revised by the Customs solicitor, recast by Tomlins and 'prepared with great labour for the House' by Dorrington. The Stamp Regulation Bill had been drawn up by Timms, the Solicitor to the Board of Stamps, inspected by Harrison, recast by Tomlins, and was then with Dorrington 'to be finally prepared for the House'.

But this was not the worst of it. Many Bills were drafted outside the Treasury altogether. James Stephen was at that time counsel to the Colonial Office and the Board of Trade. In 1830, for example, he was drafting a Truck Bill, and the following year, reducing a plan for the salaries of the clergy into the form of a Bill.[56] At the Home Office, William Gregson had been counsel since 1822. He had

[56] Grey Papers: Second Earl. 54/18/18. Melbourne Papers: 61. Senior to Melbourne, January 31, 1831.

prepared most of the criminal law reform Bills, and had a hand in the Reform Bill of 1832.[57] But for so politically sensitive a measure, the government relied also on a lawyer outside the public service, but of known attachment to the party. This was H. Bellenden Ker, who later wrote: 'I was employed, without any claim for remuneration, both in advising on the Reform Bills and Boundary Bill and the Boundary Commission, and in some other [measures] during Lord Grey's administration.'[58] Brougham confirmed his story. 'He gave up his conveyancing business for above a year to work out our great Reform Bill and Boundary Commission.'[59]

Other Bills were drafted in a variety of ways. James Booth, Counsel to the Speaker, was responsible for the Clauses Acts of 1845, with the aid of his opposite number in the House of Lords. A little later, Russell wrote to his Lord Chancellor, Cottenham, that something should be done about a recommendation from a Lords' Select Committee on burdens on land. One way would be to set up a committee of lawyers 'to frame the heads of Bills'. Another would be 'to frame with the assistance of Lord Campbell and other able men whom you may consult Bills for ... for carrying into effect the recommendations of the Lords' Committee'.[60] The implication was that it was appropriate to work through the Lord Chancellor when technical legal reforms were in question. In 1849, Carlisle was urging a Public Health Bill for London not 'wholly concocted by' the Board of Health. 'The same course should be pursued which answered extremely well in the general Public Health Bill, that the Attorney-General should be directed to superintend the drawing up of a Public Health Bill for the metropolis' with leave to 'devolve the duty' on someone else. 'I think it very desirable,' he went on, 'that any measure of this difficult and complicated nature which is to be brought into Parliament should be so with the knowledge and approval of the Government's legal advisers.'[61] There is a reference to Bills in the hands of Romilly a few weeks later.[62] A little later again, Counsel to the Speaker was once more pressed into service. 'In concert with the Speaker, and Charles Wood, I have arranged that Mr Rickards

[57] J. A. Gulland, 'History of the criminal law reforms of the period of Peel's Home Secretaryship, 1822–7', *Bulletin of the Institute of Historical Research*, viii (1930–1), 183.

[58] Melbourne Papers. Ker to Melbourne, May 9, 1835.

[59] PRO 30/22/8. Brougham to Russell, n.d. [probably December 1849].

[60] PRO 30/22/5E. Russell to Cottenham, November 6, 1846.

[61] PRO 30/22/8. Carlisle to Russell, August 3, 1849.

[62] ibid. George Grey to Russell [?], December 18, 1849.

... together with Mr May, should during the recess prepare a Bill consolidating all the laws relating to the election of Members.'[63]

All these expedients were used during a period when counsel to the Home Office held a general responsibility for drafting government Bills. Following the retirement of Harrison and Tomlins in the '30s, the office of counsel to the Treasury had been allowed to lapse, and their mantle fell on the shoulders of their Home Office colleague, William Gregson. When he retired in 1835, there seems to have been an interregnum until the appointment of J. E. D. Bethune in 1837. He 'was a person of great intelligence, but he never drew a Bill before he was appointed to this office, except . . . the [Municipal] Corporation Bill'.[64] By a Treasury Minute of 1842, he was made responsible for drafting Bills for twenty-three departments. But he was a stickler for protocol. 'He declined to draw Bills unless they were sent to him by the Secretary of State.'[65] The Gauge Regulation Bill, for example, was drafted at the Home Office in Bethune's day.[66] He was also involved in drafting the abortive Public Health Bill of 1847.[67]

When Bethune was promoted to a higher post in 1848, he was succeeded by Walter Coulson, who 'had been in his youth an amanuensis to Jeremy Bentham, was a friend of Charles Lamb and Leigh Hunt, and became a very successful newspaper editor before he abandoned journalism for the legal profession and was called to the Bar.'[68] He had 'to draw Bills for all the departments. Any department may send a Bill to Mr Coulson to be drawn'.[69] Immediately before Palmerston's defeat in 1858, Coulson was working on an India Bill, and drafted that which Derby's government carried later in the same year.[70]

When Coulson died, in 1860, his successor was Henry Thring. In a passage of autobiography, he described how he formulated his principles of draftsmanship as a young man. 'Briefless, and therefore with much leisure, I devoted a great deal of time to the study of the contents of the statute book.' He found many defects in it and worked out a plan which he felt certain would give better results. 'In the year 1854 I had at last an opportunity of putting my new system in

[63] Lewis to Russell, November 17 [1851].
[64] P.P. 1847–8, xviii, 284.
[65] ibid., 283.   [66] Parris (1965), 101.
[67] PRO 30/22/6. Morpeth to Russell, June 23, 1847.
[68] Sir Courtenay Ilbert, *Mechanics of Law Making* (New York, 1914), 63.
[69] P.P. 1847–8, xviii, 283.
[70] Palmerston Papers. Palmerston to Lewis, January 2, 1858. Disraeli Papers. Stanley to Disraeli, June 28, 1858.

practice. Mr Cardwell was anxious to make a great reform in the merchant shipping law. Following in some degree the example of the American codes, I divided the Bill into parts and then divided the parts under separate titles, arranging the clauses of the Bill in a logical order so that a glance at the table of contents would convey to the reader a correct idea of the effect of the Bill.'[71] The result was 'a Bill which was the pioneer of the new style of drafting'.[72] Thring continued to be employed in drafting Acts of Parliament during his private practice at the Bar till 1861, when, following Coulson's death in the previous year, he became counsel to the Home Office.

In 1869, the title of Parliamentary Counsel to the Treasury was revived in his favour. The Treasury Minute appointing him sets out the reasons for the new development. 'The increase of late years in the number of Bills which have in every session to be introduced into parliament by H.M. government is so great, and the attention which some of the more important require during their progress, so onerous, that . . . it has become necessary to call in other professional gentlemen of the highest eminence. To such gentlemen . . . large fees are of course paid and in consequence the cost . . . has become a considerable item.'[73]

It was Thring who laid down the principles of the government draftsman's office as it still exists today. Enough has been said to show that, in the middle of the nineteenth century, although talented individuals were employed, there was no system. In 1860, the situation remained as Lord Langdale had described it fourteen years earlier. Langdale, as Master of the Rolls, had decline to help the Lord Chancellor with a scheme for the registration of deeds, although he personally approved of it. 'The government is in want of proper and adequate machinery,' he wrote, 'for the management of this sort of business. Surely the government of England might afford . . . a regular Board or Committee of Council, or some such authority, in which the ministry might entirely confide, to assist constantly [as parliamentary draftsmen]. In these matters the government has no adequate help, it is *magnas inter opes inops*. [Given] a good head to such a Board, thoroughly confidential, I am persuaded that government would be relieved from many unnecessary difficulties and perplexities, and the country would have better security than it has ever yet had for the enactment of well-framed Acts of Parliament.'[74]

[71] Lord Thring, *Practical Legislation* (new e., 1902), 2, 4–5.
[72] Hughes, (1957), 63.
[73] PRO T29/614. Minute 2245. February 8, 1869.
[74] PRO 30/22/5E. Langdale to Cottenham, November 13, 1846.

Thring worked towards the principle that all government Bills should, except in special circumstances, pass through his hands. Special circumstances did apply to the Reform Bill of 1867 and the outcome shows how the new system worked. The first draft was prepared by Dudley Baxter, a Conservative election agent. Thring 'expressed ... an opinion unfavourable to the Bill as drawn. This opinion was repeated to Lord Derby who sent for me to the House of Lords. ... Lord Derby said it was too late to take any steps to alter the Bill to the extent which I wished, and I undertook at his request to communicate with the draftsman and to tell him to proceed with his work'.[75] But Derby thought again. 'What have you done,' he asked Disraeli, 're Thring v. Baxter? It is very unfortunate, for [one] has done all the work, and the [other] has all the real knowledge and experience on his side. But if Baxter refuses to communicate with Thring, I do not see on what ground we can support him. Thring is a very safe man, a good draftsman, and a fair politician; and as he is employed in all other government Bills, I do not see how we can set him aside, without pledging ourselves to all the points of difficulty which may occur between him and Baxter, in which it is quite possible he may have the best of it.'[76]

Thring recorded that he had 'returned to my office and was actually engaged in writing the letter [to Baxter] when Mr Disraeli's secretary ... came in and told me as an instruction from Mr Disraeli to entirely redraft the Bill'.[77] Baxter resented the criticism and refused to communicate with Thring.[78] The latter, 'working with two short-hand-writers from 10 till 6, ... completed it. The Bill was printed during the night and was laid before the Cabinet three days after Thring had seen it for the first time'.[79]

THE MIKADO EFFECT

However well drafted an Act may be, weaknesses may still show up when the new law is put into operation. Maitland complained long ago that this aspect of legal history had been neglected. 'Some people seem to think that a Bill loses all its importance at the very moment when it becomes law, that it ceases to be a subject for constitutional history, or indeed for history of any kind, when the last division has

---

[75] Thring (1902), 7.
[76] Disraeli Papers. Derby to Disraeli, March 14, 1867.
[77] Thring (1902), 7.
[78] Moneypenny and Buckle, ii, 252.
[79] Thring (1902), 7. Cf. Moneypenny and Buckle, ii, 252n.

been taken.'[80] The administrative historian must go further and examine what may be called the Mikado effect. 'That's the pathetic part of it. Unfortunately, the fool of an Act says "compassing the death of the Heir Apparent". There's not a word about a mistake, or not knowing, or having no notion, or not being there. There should be, of course, but there isn't. That's the slovenly way in which these Acts are always drawn. However, cheer up, it'll be all right. I'll have it altered next session.'[81]

That was all very well for Titipu. But who, in the system of government obtaining in nineteenth-century Britain, was to take the responsibility for any defect in the law and 'have it altered next session'? Sir Henry Taylor felt that the lack of any such sense of responsibility was a grave weakness. 'With the narrow limits which opinion ... assigns to the duties of the executive government ... responsibility for defect of law falls nowhere; or if it be held to fall upon the legislature, it is so diffused over that numerous body as to be of no force or effect. When evil manifests itself ... there is no member of the government ... who does not think that his case for non-interference is complete, so soon as he makes out that the evil is owing to a fault in the law. The question whose fault is it that the law is faulty, is asked of no man, and naturally no man asks it of himself. But that must needs be regarded as an imperfect system of administrative government which docs not lay these faults at the door of some individual functionary.'[82] Taylor realized that the people best placed to point out defects in the law were those who had the responsbility for administering it—though he thought that they did not in fact do so. But it could be done 'by a system of filtration. The lowest classes of functionaries, whilst they may be assumed to have the largest knowledge of facts, must also be taken to have the least power to discriminate and to gencralize. They cannot be expected to distinguish barren from fruitful facts; those which are mere specialities from those which lead to general conclusions. What is wanted is that the crude knowledge collected in the execution of the laws should pass upward from grade to grade of the civil functionaries intrusted with their administration, more and more digested and generalized in its progress; and, lastly, should reach the legislature in the shape of a matured project of law, whereby what was superfluous in the legislation in question might be abrogated; what was amiss might be amended; what was insufficient, enlarged; what was doubtful, determined; what was wanting, added'.[83]

[80] Maitland, 537. [81] W. S. Gilbert, *The Mikado*.
[82] Taylor, Chapter 27. [83] ibid.

FEEDBACK FROM ADMINISTRATION TO LEGISLATION

Unperceived, apparently, by Taylor himself, just such a process developed in many departments. Acts of Parliament delegated powers and set up machinery. Those appointed to exercise those powers and to operate that machinery soon became aware of inadequacies. Their first instinct was to try persuasion. Nevertheless, the administrator's blandishments derive much of their effectiveness from the knowledge that the alternative to falling in with his wishes may be an application to parliament for fresh powers. An official of the Railway Department voiced this threat when urging a company in 1843 to accept voluntarily a suggested change in management practice. 'If the directors do not think proper to attend to this recommendation, it will only remain for their Lordships to take the first fitting opportunity of applying to parliament for the necessary power to enforce what they believe to have been the spirit of the Acts relating to railways, and the intention of the legislature.'[84] Administration became one of the main sources of legislation. 'Since . . . the officials got to know more about the subject-matter in hand than anyone else, future legislation was necessarily founded upon their expert knowledge.'[85] In such fields as public health, lunacy, education and factory regulation, the 'impulse for reform came from the investigation and reports of government inspectors'.[86] An example may be taken from the correspondence between Graham and Peel. 'With respect to schools in the manufacturing districts, I have framed some clauses for insertion in a Factory Bill. They have been prepared under my direction by Mr Horner, who has influence with the dissenters, and by Mr Saunders, who has the confidence of the Bishop of London; and they are both Factory Inspectors.'[87] It was, of course, true that 'government inspectors could . . . not pass laws; they could give the impetus but could not carry through the reform.'[88] Nevertheless, their disclosures carried much weight with legislators. In 1844 Benjamin Hawes announced that he voted for Ashley's Ten Hours Bill on 'the authority of the reports of the Factory Inspectors'.[89]

As an example of feedback from administration to law, the Railway Regulation Act, 1889 (52 and 53 Vict. c. 57) may be cited.

[84] Parris (1965), 49.
[85] G. K. Clark, *Making of Victorian England* (1962), 109.
[86] Roberts, 72.
[87] C. S. Parker (ed.), *Sir Robert Peel from his Private Papers* (2 e., 1899), ii, 549.   [88] Roberts, 72.   [89] ibid., 227.

Its most important provisions were contained in Section 1: 'The Board of Trade may from time to time order a railway company to do, within a time limited by order, and subject to any exceptions or modifications allowed by the order, any of the following things:

(a) to adopt the block system on all or any of their railways;
(b) to provide for the interlocking of points and signals on or in connexion with all or any of such railways;
(c) to provide for and use on all their trains carrying passengers continuous brakes complying with the following requirements:
  (i) the brake must be instantaneous in action, and capable of being applied by the engine-driver and guards;
  (ii) the brake must be self-applying in the event of any failure in the continuity of its action;
  (iii) the brake must be capable of being applied to every vehicle of the train, whether carrying passengers or not;
  (iv) the brake must be in regular use in daily working;
  (v) the materials of the brake must be of durable character, and easily maintained and kept in order.'

Where did all this come from? From the brain of the minister? From the recommendations of a Select Committee? To answer this question it is necessary to recount the history of the Armagh accident and certain of its consequences.

On June 13, 1889, a heavy train of the Great Northern Railway of Ireland struggled up an incline near Armagh, but failed to reach the top. The majority of its passengers were children on a Sunday-school outing. Because of its weight, the train was then divided, so that the engine could take on the first part, and return later for the second. Meanwhile, the intention was to leave the rear coaches on the incline, held stationary by their non-automatic vacuum brakes. The brakes failed, the coaches ran backwards out of control, and collided with an on-coming train. There were 340 casualties, seventy-eight of them fatal. It was the most serious accident which had, until that time, occurred on any railway in the British Isles. The usual Board of Trade enquiry was held, and the Inspecting Officer reported that 'this terrible collision would in all human probability have been prevented had the excursion train been fitted with an automatic continuous brake instead of (as it was) with only a non-continuous brake'.[90]

The report was dated July 8, 1889. Even before that, Sir Michael Hicks Beach, as President of the Board of Trade, had given a conditional pledge to amend the law relating to rail safety. A Member

[90] P.P. 1890, lxv, 91.

had suggested that the accident had been a result of lack of automatic brakes. The minister had replied: 'If the opinion pointed to in the Hon. Member's question should be borne out by [the Inspecting Officer's] report, I will certainly consider whether it may not be possible to deal with the subject during the present session.'[91]

In making such a statement, Hicks Beach knew he was on firm ground. Regular returns, made under an Act of 1878,[92] had supplied his department with detailed information about the types of brakes in use on British railways. The Member who put the question about the Armagh incident had documented his argument with Board of Trade statistics on the subject.[93] The returns showed that some progressive companies had gone a long way of their own accord to equip their trains with the most effective brakes available. Any statutory obligation would bear mainly on a backward minority of companies. The 1878 Act was a result of the brake trials, suggested by the Royal Commission on Railway Accidents, and conducted under official auspices in 1875. The attention given by the Royal Commission to the question of brakes was, in turn, the result of the publicity given to the issue by accident reports from Inspecting Officers of the Board of Trade. Continuous brakes had figured in the Board's *Requirements*[94] since 1862.[95] Ultimately, Board of Trade interest in the problem of continuous brakes can be traced back to the '50s. 'When each brake requires a separate man to work it, the number of brakes . . . forms an important element in the expense of the train, and an increased number of brake vans, beyond the number actually required for parcels or luggage, causes additional unproductive weight. Several plans have therefore been tried for . . . giving the engine-driver from his tender, or the guard from his van, control over brakes on passenger carriages. . . . The principle . . . is thoroughly sound; and . . . should be adopted . . . at least for [fast] trains.'[96]

The provisions of the 1889 Act relating to block working and interlocking arose from administrative experience in a similar way. Lack of the former had, indeed, been a complicating factor in the Armagh accident. 'With regard to the block telegraph system, had it been in operation on the line . . . it would, no doubt, have considerably mitigated the fatality attending the collision.'[97] The argu-

---

[91] 3 *Hansard*, cccxxxvii, 119.
[92] Railway Returns (Continuous Brakes) Act, 41 and 42 Vict., c. 20.
[93] 3 *Hansard*, cccxxxvii, 118.
[94] See p. 194. [95] Parris (1965), 201n.
[96] P.P. 1856, liv, 306. [97] P.P. 1890, lxv, 91.

ment was that the second train would not have been allowed to start while the block in which the stoppage had occurred was occupied. Hence the runaway train would have left the steep gradient, and lost momentum through running for a considerable distance on the level, before meeting the second train. The impact would have been further reduced because the second train would have been at rest when the collision took place.

Information about the extension of these two devices on existing railways had been accumulating in the Board of Trade for more than fifteen years. Under an Act of 1873,[98] companies were required to make annual returns showing what progress they had made with interlocking of signals and the introduction of block working. The intention was, as with the Act of 1878 referred to above, that the publicity would encourage the progressive and shame the recalcitrant. Since 1872, interlocking and block working had figured in the Board's *Requirements* as conditions for the opening of new lines. Interlocking of signals originated technically, as well as legally, in administrative experience, since the key invention was made under the direct stimulus of the Board, as far back as 1859.[99] The history of the Board's encouragement of block working goes back even further. As early as 1854, an Inspecting Officer reported on an accident which showed 'how impossible it is . . . to preserve trains from collisions, when their safety depends alone upon the interval of time which elapses between the *starting* of the trains; and it adds another argument to the many which already exist in favour of adopting a system of working all trains, in which the interval . . . is one of distance . . . instead of an interval of time'.[100]

Thus, the Railway Regulation Act of 1889 reflects more than three decades of administrative experience. It illustrates a process described by a modern civil servant. 'The administrators' general practice, in this country, had been to shun legislation where other means can achieve his ends. He prefers to see things taking shape in the real world before he invents an elaborate legal construction, because he knows that with such a construction, devised *in vacuo*, nothing may ever correspond. In an obscure way, he is not unfriendly to the old conception of law as custom, and where the subject-matter of the business allows he may try to stimulate a habit of behaviour and recommend legislation only when the habit is widely enough diffused to bring effective enforcement

[98] Railway Regulation Act (Returns of Signal Arrangements, workings, etc.), 36 and 37 Vict., c. 76.
[99] Parris (1965), 188.   [100] P.P. 1854, lxii, 201.

reasonably within sight.'[101] This is to put a philosophical interpretation on what was, perhaps, an unnecessarily long-drawn-out process. Some civil servants wished to move faster but ran up against resistance from cautious ministers or colleagues. 'We do not codify,' wrote Lewis to Russell in 1851, 'but make laws to meet existing evils. We do not profess systematic and logical legislation, when a new and unforeseen evil arises. We meet it by a special measure, limited to the evil; we provide a plaster for the wound, but we do not make it larger than the wound.'[102] A celebrated parliamentary draftsman, Sir Mackenzie Chalmers, used to tell a story with a similar moral. In this enthusiasm for the improvement of the statute-book, he urged a high official to agree to the orderly rewriting of a long and untidy series of statutes dealing with the sale of food and drugs. 'Why trouble about that?' he was asked, 'we know all about the law inside the department and the public finds out in the police court.'[103]

THE ADMINISTRATION LEGISLATES THROUGH PARLIAMENT

At the beginning of the nineteenth century, parliament was in a very real sense a legislature. It actually made the laws, with the minimum of help from ministers. Moreover, it performed many acts which elsewhere were the responsibility of the executive. It was parliament, not a minister of the interior, which authorized the construction of roads and the paving of towns. By the end of the century, however, it was possible to write that a 'leading characteristic of English legislation is the control exercised over it by the executive government. . . . The parliament of the present day has largely reverted *in substance* to the practice . . . of the first Edwards, under which the king, by his ministers, made the laws. . . . It is largely led, and virtually controlled, by the executive power'.[104] Bills had to pass through parliament to become Acts, just as they required the Royal Assent. But to say that the administration legislated through Parliament is not to say that Parliament legislated. Only in form was parliament a law-making body: in substance the law was made elsewhere.

[101] Sisson, 72.
[102] Lewis to Russell, March 4, 1851. q. G. P. Gooch (ed.), *The Later Correspondence of Lord John Russell* (1925), ii, 62.
[103] Sir C. Carr, *Concerning English Administrative Law* (1941), 127.
[104] Ilbert (1901), 213 and 219.

CHAPTER VII

THE MINISTER'S POWERS

'To a very large extent indeed England is now ruled by means of statutory powers which are not in any sense, not even as strict matters of law, the powers of the King. . . . This is the result of a modern movement, a movement which began . . . about the time of the Reform Bill of 1832. . . . We can no longer say that the executive power is vested in the King: the King has powers, this minister has powers, and that minister has powers. . . . But of this vast change our institutional writers have hardly yet taken account. They go on writing as though England were governed by the royal prerogatives, as if ministers had nothing else to do than to advise the King as to how his prerogatives shoud be exercised.'

F. W. Maitland, 1888

The phrase 'the minister's powers' implies a discussion of a number of devices such as delegated legislation and administrative tribunals. But before going on to consider them, it is necessary to look at something even more basic, namely, the minister's power to enforce the law through the courts. The point to emphasize is that this obvious mode of proceeding was of limited value to the administrator. Take, for example, the spirit in which Sir Arthur Helps, as Clerk of the Privy Council, handled the cattle plague crisis of 1865-7. The emergency threw up a great many legal problems, and Waddington, Permanent Under-Secretary of the Home Office and himself a barrister, advised him: 'You ought to have a lawyer always at your elbow.' But Helps was doubtful. 'One of the shrewdest men in my office said to me: "We shall not find a lawyer of such great assistance. We shall have much to explain to him upon every occasion; and, in the end, he will come to you to decide the matter, especially as all our proceedings are of somewhat doubtful legality." I have already found that this has proved to be the case where I have consulted a lawyer.'[1] Helps may well have been thinking of a problem which had arisen a few weeks earlier, relative to an attempt to exclude the disease from Ireland by banning the importation of cattle from Great Britain. On

[1] Palmerston Papers. Helps to Palmerston, October 4, 1865.

this point, the lawyers gave contradictory advice. In Waddington's summing up, the administrator in him predominated: 'I cannot think that, if you consider it right and expedient to prohibit the importation of cattle from Great Britain to Ireland during the prevalence of the plague, you need be deterred by the *legal* difficulties. I am very much inclined to agree with the Irish Law Officers, that this may be done by Order in Council in strict conformity with the law, but at all events the question is one which may be fairly argued, and there can be no doubt whatever that such an Order would be obeyed generally.'[2]

In a situation like this, recourse to the courts was of little use. 'In cases relating to prosecutions ... knowing how weak our law is, I must restrain inspectors, and be very prudent, only authorizing prosecutions where I am sure of getting convictions.'[3] But administrators found that over a very wide field prosecution was a blunt instrument, to be used very sparingly. Their approach differed from that of a forthright politician like Palmerston. In 1854, as Home Secretary, he 'urged his inspectors to prosecute every violation of the Factory and Mining Laws. Penalties on mill-owners, he told the inspectors, "should never be remitted, it is difficult enough to get them imposed," and he told the mining inspectors to prosecute even when the evidence was slim, for "it is right to do everything in our power to protect these poor people".'[4] In the early days, some at least of the factory inspectors acted in the Palmerstonian manner. But as their authority grew, the number of prosecutions fell, until one of them could write: 'In the inspection of factories it has been my view always that we are not acting as policemen, that it is our object to be the friend of the manufacturer as much as the friend of the employee and the friend of the parent, and that in enforcing this Factory Act ... we do not enforce it as a policeman would check an offence which he is told to detect. We have endeavoured not to enforce the law, if I may use such an expression, but it has been my endeavour since I have had anything to do with factory administration that we should simply be the advisers of all classes, that we should explain the law, and that we should do everything we possibly could to induce them to observe the law, and that a prosecution should be the very last thing that we should take up.'[5]

The Railway Department of the Board of Trade acted in a similar spirit. Declining to prosecute in one case, they told an informant that

[2] ibid. Waddington to Palmerston, August 24, 1865.
[3] ibid. Helps to Palmerston, October 6, 1865.
[4] Roberts, 293.   [5] q. Thomas, 259.

they would first 'require to be satisfied not only that the Act in question has been violated but that it will be for the public advantage that the company should be restrained from acting in violation of the Act'.[6] In this case, a favourable verdict would probably have been obtained. But the problem of forcing the defendant to comply with it might still remain. Since defendants were usually collectivities, this was sometimes difficult; it is impossible to imprison a railway company. Fines were often ineffective, since they could be paid out of the corporate purse, and did not hurt the individuals responsible. The Board of Trade pursued one company through the courts for five years, with very little to show for it, in spite of favourable judgments.[7] To let slip the chance of a successful prosecution was only to lose a battle. To suffer a defeat in the courts might be to lose a campaign, if it set a precedent and in effect changed the law. 'Judges will decide adversely on factory cases submitted to them, and thus legalize relays,' wrote Shaftesbury in his diary in 1850. 'The Attorney-General said to me this afternoon: "They will give judgment, not according to law, but on policy. Judge Parke," he added, "observed to me 'I have no doubt that the framers of the Act intended that the labour should be continuous, but as it is a law to restrain the exercise of capital and property, it must be construed stringently.' " Might not this judge have said and thought, with equal justice and more feeling: "This is a law to restrain oppression and cruelty, and alleviate an actual slavery under a nominal freedom. I will, therefore, construe it liberally!" '[8] Shaftesbury's fears were realized, but in this case, parliament was persuaded to reverse the verdict of the court. However, the difficulties of persuading the minister to take up such a question, of getting parliamentary time, and of carrying a new measure through parliament, were enough to give an administrator pause. They help to explain why 'the British administrator on the whole avoids law-making when he can, though it may be thought, from the look of the bulging statute-book, that his efforts have been singularly unsuccessful'.[9]

APPEAL TO THE COURTS

Of course, the choice whether to go to court or not did not always lie with the administrator. Sometimes he had to appear to defend a decision against an objecting plaintiff. Naturally, administrators

---

[6] Parris (1965), 150.   [7] ibid., 164–6.
[8] E. Hodder, *Life and Work of . . . Shaftesbury* (1886), ii, 199.
[9] Sisson, 72.

chafed against such a right of appeal. 'Chadwick rejected . . . judicial review . . . of administration. The courts could clog administration by defeating regulations on verbal or technical grounds. They were ill-informed on the public policy of the law. They were concerned with the individual plaintiff and not with "large classes of cases and general and often remote effects, which cannot be brought to the knowledge of judges".'[10] Yet, paradoxically, although the immediate effect of an adverse judgment in the courts is to restrict the operation of an Act, ultimately the administrator's scope may be widened, since parliament may grant more extensive powers.[11] Something of the sort was happening in 1832, when Melbourne sought the opinion of the Lord Chief Justice on a Bill which was then before the House of Lords. The Bill, he wrote, 'confers powers upon the Commissioners of Sewers, which I am informed are new, and which I am sure are extraordinary. It was brought into the House of Commons by Mr Hodges, the Member for Kent, and I am informed that some immediate legislative provisions upon the subject are rendered necessary by some decision recently pronounced by your Lordship upon the construction of the statute of Henry VIII'.[12]

ORIGINS OF MODERN ADMINISTRATIVE LAW

With this caution in mind, that administration was not simply a matter of enforcing of the law through the courts, the battery of devices which was developed during the nineteenth century will now be described. Writers on law have not always been very helpful here. Ilbert, for example, could write in one place 'there is no administrative law, and there are no special administrative courts'.[13] Yet elsewhere he says 'the later volumes of the Statute Book are far more concerned with public or administrative than with private law. Nine-tenths of each annual volume of statutes are concerned with what may be called administrative law'.[14] The explanation is probably semantic in character. In English, there is only one word—'law'—to cover two ideas which are very different, and for which distinct terms exist in many languages; *le droit* and *la loi* in French, for example. When Ilbert said Britain had no administrative law, he appears to have meant, no *droit administratif*—a self-evident proposition. When he directed the attention of his reader to the Statute Book, on the other

[10] Chadwick to Russell, March 7, 1840, q. Finer, 88.
[11] Hughes (1957), 70–1.
[12] Melbourne Papers, 23. Melbourne to Lord Chief Justice, August 4, 1832.
[13] Ilbert (1901), 4.   [14] ibid., 6.

hand, he was saying that a great many of the *lois* which emanate from Westminister had to do with administration—a statement which can hardly be disputed. This interpretation is consistent with a later stage of Ilbert's argument. 'When the authors of books of juris-prudence write about law, when professional lawyers talk about law, the kind of law about which they are usually thinking is that which is to be found in Justinian's Institutes, or in the Napoleonic Codes, or the new Civil Code of the German Empire'.[15] If this passage had to be translated into French, *le droit* would be the appropriate term throughout. But parliament, Ilbert goes on, has never been much interested in *le droit*; it is much more at home with *les lois*. 'The substantial business of Parliament as a legislature is to keep the machinery of state in working order. . . . Take up a file of the public Bills for a session, or an annual volume of the public general statutes, and it will always confirm this statement. . . . The bulk of the Statute Book of each year will usually consist of admini-strative regulations, relating to matters which lie outside the ordinary reading and practice of the barrister. This has probably always been a characteristic of English legislation, but it has been so in a marked degree during the period which has elapsed since the Reform Act of 1832.'[16]

The limited resources of the English language leave no alternative but to say that there was administrative law in the nineteenth century, since there were so many administrative laws. In exploring it, there are two contrary dangers to bear in mind. One is the anti-quarian fallacy which, recognizing that the Henry VIII clause is comparable with a power conferred in the reign of Henry VIII, assumes that it is a perennial feature of English law and therefore raises no problems for the twentieth century. The other is the failure to perceive that English administrative law has any history whatever. This was the trap that Lord Hewart fell into, for example, in his comment on the Rating and Valuation Act, 1925, 'which contained the egregious provision that the Minister might, if he thought fit, actually modify the provisions of the Act itself'.[17] The historian of administrative law can point to examples of a like power being delegated in the early nineteenth century.[18] But 'such laws were not lawyers' laws; lawyers did not study them'.[19] Hence they accepted, in some cases, the argument that such powers originated in a

---

[15] ibid., 209.   [16] ibid., 210.
[17] Lord Hewart, *The New Despotism* (1945 ed.), 53.
[18] Sir Cecil Carr, *Delegated Legislation* (1921), 8: and (1941), 41.
[19] Carr (1941), 21.

189

conspiracy of power-hungry civil servants. In administrative history, as elsewhere, one swallow does not make a summer. The problem is, not to collect and date isolated examples, but to indicate the period when such administrative tools as delegated legislation, administrative tribunals, inspection, and exchequer grants, came into general use.

That period was the 1830s, when the 'beginning of novel relationships between central and local authorities, and between both sets of authorities and the people, created problems of what is vaguely called "administrative law" which are with us still. . . . There they were, in full view . . . —central government replacing a loose local administration, the paid professional superseding the unpaid amateur delegation of the legislative power, the possibility of appeal from administrative decision, the strictness of judicial interpretation, the well-intentioned bureaucrat's outpacing of public opinion, and so on'.[20] The reactions of contemporaries varied from the phlegmatic to the prophetic. It would be hard to imagine anything more matter-of-fact than Althorp's notes on the sweeping powers proposed for the Poor Law Commissioners: 'Commissioners to frame rules for management of workhouses, appointment of paid overseers, guardians, etc., and for relief to the poor. These rules to be binding unless disapproved by Privy Council.'[21] (The last point is fascinating. Had it been carried into effect, would the Privy Council have developed a jurisdiction analogous to that of the Conseil d'Etat?) James Stephen's exclamation was far more profound. 'Surely such an accumulation of authority—judicial, legislative, administrative and financial—with such an amount of patronage, uncontrolled by any specific checks, is a trust such as never yet was devolved on any British subjects, nor, in truth, on any British sovereign.'[22]

The contrast with the immediate past was striking. 'If we go back . . . to the years 1819 and 1820, we find plenty of talk of "regulations" in Acts of Parliament, but they were regulations actually contained in the Acts, not regulations to be made by some other authority. Thus in the factory and workshop legislation a century ago the ages of employees in cotton mills were specified; the hours of work were fixed; there was a definite time for breakfast and a definite time for dinner.[23] There was no margin for elasticity; nothing was left

[20] ibid., vii and 8.
[21] Melbourne Papers: 23. Althorp's notes, dated 1833, on Poor Law Amendment Bill.
[22] Stephen to Senior, April 12, 1834, q. in Finer (1952), 79–80.
[23] 60 Geo. III, c. 66.

190

to be arranged by departmental order; we were not yet so elaborately administered. The Acts of the period were full of almost grotesque detail for want of the practice of entrusting minor matters to subordinate legislation.'[24] This style of law-making found an occasional critic. In 1821, George Holford, M.P., speaking on the Prisons Bill (which was later enacted as 4 Geo. IV, c. 64) argued that there were too many regulations in the Bill, which should be confined to general principles.[25] But generally, jealousy of the executive made parliament keep the detail of legislation in its own hands. 'Parliament was still able to do itself almost all the legislating that the country required.'[26]

DELEGATION OF POWERS

In 1832, however, 'the "great and extraordinary" and "very arbitrary powers" delegated to the Privy Council by the Prevention of Cholera Act, for the prevention of the epidemic and for the care of the afflicted, were granted by Parliament with enthusiasm. Lord Althorp, the minister in charge, thought that "the exigency of the case ... was such as to justify it in the eyes of all rational men." One member declared that "all the powers which were necessary ought to be given" while another ask the Privy Council to "consider themselves fully authorized to act even before the Bill passed through parliament." Sir Robert Peel "suspected no abuse of the powers which it was proposed to confer, and therefore thought it better to give a discretionary power to the Privy Council than for parliament to attempt to define the precise nature of the measures to be adopted".'[27] The preamble to the Act conveys the new approach strikingly. 'Whereas it has pleased Almighty God to visit the United Kingdom with the disease called the cholera ... and whereas, with a view to prevent as far as may be possible by the Divine Blessing the spreading of the said disease, it may be necessary that rules and regulations may from time to time be established within cities, towns or districts affected with or which may be threatened by the said disease, but it may be impossible to establish such rules and regulations by the authority of parliament with sufficient promptitude to meet the exigency of any such case as it may occur.'[28]

[24] Carr (1921), 49.   [25] Hinde, 69–70.   [26] Carr (1921), 50.
[27] Chih-Mai Chen, *Parliamentary Opinion of Delegated Legislation* (New York and London, 1933), 43–4.   [28] 2 and 3 W. IV, c. 10.

DELEGATED LEGISLATION

where were occasional protests, but in general delegated legislation Tent unnoticed. By 1865, Helps could write: 'it has been the practice of late years, and a very judicious practice it is, to insert in Acts of Parliament, a provision that the Queen in Council shall settle all manner of matters of detail'.[29] And a text-book of government could state confidently: that 'experience has proved that certain subordinate powers of legislation must be entrusted to almost every leading department of state'.[30] Perhaps the most weighty statement on the subject was that of Thring himself, first drawn up as part of his instructions to draftsmen in his own office,[31] and later published. 'Procedure and matters of detail should ... be left to be prescribed by a ... department of the Government ... The system of confining the attention of parliament to material provisions only, and leaving details to be settled departmentally, is probably the only mode in which parliamentary government can, as respects its legislative functions, be satisfactorily carried on. The province of parliament is to decide material questions affecting the public interest, and the more procedure and subordinate matters can be withdrawn from their cognizance, the greater will be the time afforded for the consideration of the more serious questions involved in legislation.'[32]

Law-making by the executive was not limited to the exercise of delegated powers. It was held to be a legitimate exercise of the prerogative for the Crown to regulate the conditions of employment of its own servants. Hence the law of the civil service developed mainly in the form of Treasury Minutes. The trend was recognized by well-informed observers. 'Treasury Minutes may do much— either for good or evil—but I doubt whether in a constitutional point of view they may not be carried too far and become dangerous weapons and serious rivals to Acts of Parliament.'[33] But there was a case for regulating the conditions of the public service in this way. No Act of Parliament 'could define the misconduct or incompetence for which offices now regarded as permanent might be taken away, in such a manner as to allow the tenure of these offices to be made legally during good behaviour, without the risk of having the executive government paralysed by the passive resistance of persons

[29] Palmerston Papers. Helps to Palmerston, October 6, 1865.
[30] A. Todd, *On Parliamentary Government in England* (1867–9), i, 291.
[31] Ilbert (1914), 99.
[32] Lord Thring, *Practical Legislation* (n.d.) [1877?]
[33] Disraeli Papers. Bromley to Disraeli, April 1, 1856.

holding these situations, and by the obstructions they would be able to throw in the way of ministers they wished to oppose. So great is the authority of opinion, that no minister now ever thinks of dismissing a public servant from those offices which are regarded as permanent, unless for gross misconduct; but at the same time he has the power (and opinion would support him in using it) of dismissing such a servant for misconduct, which it might be impossible for any law to define beforehand, and of which there might be no legal evidence, though there was a moral certainty. An attempt to embarrass the government by passive resistance, and by those difficulties which might so easily be thrown in its way by its permanent servants, if they were independent, would be precisely the kind of misconduct which would be most dangerous, and of which either a legal definition beforehand, or the proof by legal evidence, would be most difficult'.[34]

QUASI-LEGISLATION

Perhaps the most subtle, and not the least influential, means of action possessed by central government is what a writer of the 1860s called 'quasi-legislation'.[35] This means a statement by a department of the terms on which it proposes to exercise a discretion in a specified field. The power to issue such statements had not explicitly to be conferred; it resides implicitly in any delegation of administrative discretion. For example, the Railways Act of 1844 required companies to carry their Parliamentary passengers in 'carriages ... provided with seats and ... protected from the weather ... in a manner satisfactory to the [Board of Trade]'.[36] The Board could have decided each case on its own merits and in isolation. But that is not the way of an administrator. His instinct is to work by precedent, and to decide each case in the light of what was done last time. Hence after a few weeks' experience a rule was adopted for general enforcement, 'that my Lords cannot certify any carriage for the cheap third-class train to be sufficiently protected from the weather, in the sense of the Act, unless it is capable of being entirely closed when necessity may require, with provisions for the admission of light and air'.[37] This was in effect a regulation under the Act, although the Act gave the Board no specific power to make regulations. Of course, the standard embodied in this minute, being higher than that required on a literal interpretation of the Act, could not be enforced in the courts, as a

[34] Grey, 190–1.
[35] Todd (1867–9), i, 288.
[36] 7 and 8 Vict., c. 85, s. 6.
[37] Parris (1965), 96.

case which arose in 1845 showed. The Board refused to pass the carriages of the Edinburgh and Glasgow Railway because there was 'no provision . . . for the admission of light when the carriages are closed'.[38] In other words, they had no windows. The Board considered a prosecution but the Lord Advocate put his finger on the weakness of the case. 'On looking into the statute,' he wrote, 'I do not observe anything as to "light and air".'[39] No action was taken. But what is much more significant is the fact that the great majority of companies complied with the requirements of the Board, rather than test them in the courts.

The Board of Trade eventually built up an elaborate quasi-legislative code in the form of its *Requirements* for the opening of new lines. It had power under an Act of 1842 to postpone the opening of a line if it 'would be attended with danger to the public using the same, by reason of the incompleteness of the works or permanent way or the insufficiency of the establishment'.[40] One of the *Requirements* was, for example, that platforms should end in ramps, not in steps. No doubt ramps were safer, but it is hard to see how they could be brought under the heading of 'incompleteness of works or permanent way' and they clearly had nothing to do with 'insufficiency of the establishment'. Yet again the remarkable thing is that the great majority of companies complied. Indeed the *Requirements* may have been more effective than statutory regulations. Had they been exercises of delegated power, the courts could hardly have avoided considering the question of *ultra vires*. Since they were not, it would have been difficult to persuade a court to acknowledge their existence, let alone to scrutinize them. If the Board did not prosecute for a breach of the *Requirements*, neither did any company challenge them in the courts.

Probably the most important examples of quasi-legislation were the Minutes of the Committee of Council on Education, together with the Codes into which they were collected, and the supplementary rules which accompanied them. They formed the basis on which exchequer grants were distributed from 1839 until the first Education Act of 1870. There was a process of feedback from administration to quasi-legislation, as there was to legislation proper. 'These rules represent the generalization of decisions which have arisen in the daily practice of the Education Office.'[41] A new Minute 'would usually arise from either an apparent need of a greater measure of assistance to schools, or from the need of settling some question

[38] ibid., 98.
[39] ibid., 98–9.
[40] 5 and 6 Vict., c. 55, s. 6.
[41] Todd (1887–9), ii, 701.

which had provoked a great deal of correspondence. . . . The Lord President . . . would give instructions, probably to the Secretary, to draw up the draft of a Minute, which would be confidentially circulated among the Members of the Committee, and very often remarks would be made upon it, and when finally settled a Committee would be called at which that Minute would be passed, and then laid upon the table of the House of Commons.'[42] In practice, the procedure was sometimes less formal. The instruction might come from the Vice-President rather than the Lord President, and the meeting of the Committee was sometimes dispensed with.[43] The very important Revised Code was laid before parliament on August 6, 1861—the very day of prorogation![44] It rested with the office whether to lay a Minute or not. One of 1861, which introduced the new principle that Inspectors must not question the department's policy in their reports, was not laid before parliament at all.[45] Robert Lowe, who was Vice-President at the time, made no secret of his attitude. 'I think that the legislative, or I may call them the *quasi*-legislative, functions of the office, must be carried on . . . in the Department itself; the business is too technical to be carried on in the House of Commons.'[46]

Why did parliament tolerate such an attitude? Why did it hand over large sums of money each year to be disbursed by such a department? The explanation given in a text-book of the time does not go very far. 'As its connection with various schools is entirely voluntary on the part of their managers, and the [Committee] possesses no compulsory powers, it was not constituted by Act of Parliament, nor had it received any power from parliament beyond that impliedly conferred by the annual appropriation of a sum for the purposes of education.'[47] As early as 1842, Peel had perceived that power conferred by implication could do more than statutory power. 'My own belief,' he wrote to Graham, 'is that a more rapid advance in promoting good could well be made by the cautious and gradual extension of the power and pecuniary means of the Committee of the Privy Council than by the announcement of any plan by the government.'[48] There was probably a good deal of truth in a statement made by the Committee's own secretary in 1855. The nation wanted education. Parliament wanted education. But the nation did not want parliamentary control of education. Extra-statutory

[42] P.P. 1865, vi, 16.   [43] ibid., 17.   [44] Todd (1887–9), i, 466.
[45] P.P. 1864, ix, 16 and 59.   [46] P.P. 1865, vi, 47.
[47] H. Cox, *The Institution of the English Government* (1863), 653.
[48] q. Parker (1899), ii, 533.

administrative regulation was a lesser evil, and parliament tolerated it. 'The public with which the Department deals is not a political but a religious one, and a religious one in fragments. Take each fragment by itself, Church, Wesleyan, Roman Catholic, etc., and talk to any one of their leading men and you see in a moment how they dread and shrink from any system which subjects the congregation to any civic and undenominational power; no matter whether that power be the Vestry, Town Council, Board of Guardians, or the House of Commons. "Find us the money and leave us to ourselves" is the prayer of each and all of them. Now this system can be, and has been, carried on by an office not so directly represented in, or communicating with, the House of Commons as to involve a clash between the political and religious systems. I do not think myself that the two could proceed in very close contact on the present footing. The schools are so purely Church, Roman Catholic, Wesleyan, etc., in their character and in their management so little educational, that I think the relations of the government with them require to be manipulated by passionless hands such as belong rather to bureaucracy than to parliamentary ministries.'[49]

ADMINISTRATIVE TRIBUNALS

As with delegated powers so with administrative tribunals, examples can be found before 1830. The Commissioners of Excise, for example, had long exercised such a jurisdiction. It was alluded to in one of Dr Johnson's most spirited definitions. Excise was 'a hateful tax levied upon commodities and adjudged not by the common judges of property but wretches hired by those to whom excise is paid'. But just as in the twentieth century, 'it is not at all certain that administrative tribunals are unpopular',[50] so the Excise jurisdiction found defenders two centuries ago. 'It saved the defendants much expense,' declared a Colonel Phipps in 1789, 'and it enables them to state all their grievances at once fully and fairly. For his part, he believed that the summary processes were administered with as much justice as any species of process whatever.'[51] But such tribunals were rare at that time. Once again 1830 was the turning point.

The term 'administrative tribunal' is here used in a wide sense to include any organ through which the administration exercised judicial or quasi-judicial functions. Such functions sometimes ori-

[49] q. P. H. J. H. Gosden, *Development of Educational Administration in England and Wales* (Oxford, 1966), 7–8.
[50] Carr (1941), 100.   [51] Hughes (1934), 333.

ginated in statutes which did not expressly delegate them, as Dicey pointed out towards the end of his life. 'The imposition upon the government of new duties inevitably necessitates the acquisition by the government of extended authority. But this extension of authority almost implies, and certainly has in fact promoted, the transference to departments of the central government ... of judicial or quasi-judicial functions. ... There is a great convenience in leaving to a government department, which deals with any business in which large numbers of persons are interested ... the power to decide questions which are more or less of a judicial character.'[52] Dicey was speaking of the early twentieth century, but the trend was in fact apparent much earlier. He did not really add much to what Sir Henry Taylor had said eighty years earlier. 'In every question there are two or more parties interested. A large portion of the questions which come before a minister arise out of disputes and complaints on which it is his business to *adjudicate*. His functions in these cases are quasi-judicial. His office is for these purposes a Court of Justice, and ought to be a Court of Record. Every step of his procedure, and every ground upon which he rests every step, should appear upon the face of producible documents. ... In all cases of individual claims upon the public and public claims upon individuals, in short in all cases (and such commonly constitute the bulk of a minister's unpolitical business) wherein the minister is called upon to deliver a quasi-judicial decision, he should on no consideration permit himself to pronounce such decision unaccompanied by a detailed statement of all the material facts and reasons upon which his judgment proceeds.'[53]

In this broad sense—which any reader is welcome to reject if he so wishes—Gladstone, conducting an enquiry prior to the issue of a certificate under the 1842 Railway Regulation Act, was a tribunal.[54] The company wished to widen a cutting so as to reduce the slope and so reduce the risk of landslips on to the line. To carry out such work, powers of compulsory purchase were needed. Ripon, as President of the Board of Trade, was 'cautious and adverse to taking people's land'. Gladstone was deputed to hear the objectors, and succeeded in bringing them to an understanding with the company before issuing the desired certificate. As such enquiries became more common, ministers could not afford the time to conduct them personally. It came to be the normal procedure to appoint an

[52] A. V. Dicey, 'The Development of Administrative Law in England', *Law Quarterly Review*, xxxi (1915), 149.
[53] Taylor, Chapters 8 and 22.   [54] Parris (1965), 48–9.

197

inspector to hold an enquiry on the spot, and for the minister to decide in the light of the inspector's report—the procedure of the local enquiry, much as it exists today. Chadwick was mainly responsible for developing the technique and in his hands it became 'an adaptable instrument of infinite flexibility, which, while paying due respect to local idiosyncrasies, would bring the local authority firmly into line with the policy of the central department'.[55] Here, for example, is an inspector's account of an enquiry under the 1848 Public Health Act: 'On my arrival in Hexham, I found the town in a state of ferment as to the inquiry, the bell-man was perambulating the streets summoning the ratepayers to a meeting to oppose the inquiry. .... The inquiry had to be adjourned to a large room as there was a full and rather formidable attendance. I commenced the inquiry by a short statement of the proceedings which had brought me down—and then glanced rapidly over the powers contained in the Act—taking up one by one the objections which I had been informed the promoters of the opposition had made. I then requested any persons having evidence to offer either for or against to come forward and tender it. The opponents entered most resolutely into the arena, declaring that Hexham was well supplied with water; and was, in all other respects, a perfect town. ... I then called the Medical Officers and the Relieving Officers and soon got amongst causes of fever, small-pox, and excessive money relief. I then traced disease to crowded room tenements, undrained streets, lanes, courts and crowded yards, foul middens, privies, and cesspools. The water I found was deficient in quantity and most objectionable in quality, dead dogs having to be lifted out of the reservoir. ... By this time the eagerness of the opponents had somewhat subsided, the body of the meeting had come partially round, and so I entered into an examination of the promoters who came willingly forward. At the termination of the inquiry several of the opponents came forward and stated that I had removed their objections and they wished the Act could be applied immediately.'[56]

Another kind of administrative jurisdiction was exercised by any officer who had power to issue a licence for carrying on some trade or occupation. Under an Act of 1855, the runners who were at the centre of the abuses of the North Atlantic emigrant traffic had to be authorized by an emigration officer. They were employed by shipping agents and lodging-house keepers, and met every Irish steamer, touting for business among those seeking passages to North America. 'Once he was in the runner's hands, it was almost inevitable that the

[55] Lewis, 102.   [56] ibid., 280–1.

emigrant should be cheated. . . . Runners worked hand-in-glove with brokers and lodging and shopkeepers, and extorted a commission from them on all transactions in which an emigrant whom they had introduced took part.'[57] Hence, the licensing system was justified, yet at the same time it raised 'issues of first importance which could not be avoided by any reasonably conscientious officer; and although in carrying out such duties, he could not but affect people's livelihoods—even to the extent of destroying them upon occasions—no appeal from his decision was allowed'.[58] Similar problems were raised by the power of the Education Office to revoke a teacher's certificate. A former official invited his readers to imagine the teacher's feelings under 'payment-by-results', 'when he looked over the Inspector's shoulder and saw the failures being recorded wholesale, and knew that his annual salary was being reduced by two and fourpence for each failure . . . But he knew more than that. He knew that when the report got to the office, the ruthless Lords of the Privy Council would dock the grant still further . . . Moreover, he was apprehensive for his certificate, which at that time was heartlessly suspended or cancelled on very slight provocation. I remember that once, after I had suggested a deduction of two-tenths of the grant, Mr Lingen, who happened to see that recommendation, sent for me and reproved me for not inflicting a larger fine. He then took his pen and wrote: "My Lords have ordered a deduction to be made from the grant of five-tenths for faults of instruction, and have suspended the certificate of the teacher." He added, addressing me: "There, I think that will do for them!" I should think it probably did'.[59]

Powers such as these raised the question of whether there should be any appeal to the ordinary courts. Such a course did not invariably recommend itself. 'During the drafting conference on the [Poor Law (Amendment)] Bill somebody suggested a right of appeal from the decisions of the Commissioners. Lord Althorp said it was an absurd idea; the appellate court, whether consisting of judges or the Secretary of State or the Privy Council, would be quite incompetent to deal with the issues involved. The Act did, however, eventually provide that rules, orders, and regulations should be removable by *certiorari* into the King's Bench court. In one of its annual reports the Poor Law Board observes that the courts interpreted this jurisdiction strictly.'[60]

Nineteenth-century lawyers showed little awareness of administrative jurisdiction, but at least one civil engineer did. Called in to

[57] O. MacDonagh, *A Pattern of Government Growth* (1961), 35.
[58] ibid., 302–3. [59] Kekewich, 10–11. [60] Carr (1941), 5.

advise a railway company about a line whose opening had been postponed by the Board of Trade, he wrote: 'The annoyance and loss to which the N.E.R. Co. have been exposed . . . justifies [sic] me in making a few remarks beyond the ordinary range of a professional report.' But there was no remedy. 'The law affords you none! There is no appeal against . . . an inspector's report except to the tribunal of which he was an officer and which may feel itself bound to uphold his report.'[61] Was appeal to the minister necessarily appeal in vain? Experience suggests otherwise.[62] The managers of a Manchester school carried on a correspondence about a cut in their grant until they got a letter which said: 'My Lords decline any further correspondence upon the subject.' They then wrote to the Lord President 'and in two or three days they got their money'.[63]

INSPECTION

Inspectors have figured prominently in this narrative already. It is now time to indicate the date when they came on the scene. There were government inspectors in the early nineteenth, and even in the eighteenth century. But their function was limited to the supervision by central agencies of their own field services—in revenue collection, for example. The characteristic of the new inspectors, on the other hand, was that they were given the function of regulating activities outside the sphere of central government altogether, in local government, industry, and voluntary work. The principle of inspection, in the new sense, was incorporated in Bills dealing with mental asylums which passed the Commons in 1816, 1817 and 1819; each was rejected by the Lords.[64] Robert Owen's original draft of the Factory Act, 1819 (59 Geo. III, c. 66) made provision for paid inspectors,[65] but the clause was amended. George Holford, M.P., speaking on the Prisons Bill of 1821, recommended an inspector to be appointed by the government, [66] but the proposal was not adopted. The turning-point came in 1828, with the appointment of inspectors of lunatic asylums under an Act passed in that year (9 Geo. IV, c. 41).[67] This was the first of the many inspectorates which proliferated during the succeeding years. By 1854, there were sixteen of them.[68]

The second group with comparable functions were the emigration officers, the first of whom started work in Liverpool early in 1833.

[61] Parris (1965), 138-9.   [62] ibid., 91 and 139.
[63] P.P. 1865, vi, 158.   [64] Jones (1955), 108.
[65] B. L. Hutchins and A. Harrison, *History of Factory Legislation* (1926), 24.
[66] Hinde, 70.   [67] Jones, 142.   [68] Roberts, 106n.

Their chronicler makes the valid point that the term 'inspector' conveys an inadequate—even a misleading—idea of what these men did. He suggests the term 'field executive' instead,[69] and the expression does give a fuller indication of the scope of the activities of, say, the first factory inspectors appointed under the Act of 1833. 'In each division, the inspector possessed tremendous powers. He inspected the factories and mills; he made rules and regulations to carry out the Act; he performed the judicial function of deciding factory cases when they were brought before him; he had to see that enough good schools were established and maintained in his division for the education of factory children. He reported to the Home Secretary twice a year; . . . the four original inspectors wielded in their hands overwhelming powers, administrative, legislative and judicial; they were not so much under the restraint of their superiors as the factory inspectorate is now.'[70] Not only had they wide powers, but were unrestrained by tradition in the use of them. The original inspectors were 'men who had no previous experience of the public service. The whole conception of inspectorial control was new; standards of vigilance, propriety, and personal relationship were governed by no precedent, and it was the duty of the Inspectors to shape the plans and devise the machinery that were essential to the due enforcement of the law. There was as yet no tradition to guide them, no corpus of minutes and decisions upon which they could rely—all this had to be worked out slowly and painfully, and there were many setbacks, for [they] had still to establish a code of professional conduct'.[71]

Assistant commissioners constituted the 'field executive' of the New Poor Law under the Act of 1834. Her Majesty's Inspectors of Schools played a similar role in education from 1839. 'Among the assistant poor-law commissioners . . . there were great differences in family position and education.'[72] Twistleton, educated at Oxford and the Middle Temple, was the grandson of a peer. Gulson, a fell-monger of Coventry, was a Quaker and had served his time as an apprentice. A'Court and Clement were brothers of peers. They had little in common with Mott, a London poorhouse contractor. Five of the assistant commissioners were baronets and four were listed in Burke's *Landed Gentry*. They had the most rural and aristocratic colouring of any of the new departments. 'These men worked together in agreeable harmony. Their co-operation illustrated the fusion of the different segments of England's complex middle class

[69] MacDonagh (1961), 332.
[70] T. K. Djang, *Factory Inspection in Great Britain* (1942), 33–4.
[71] M. W. Thomas, 108–9.   [72] Roberts, 154.

that gave to the nineteenth-century governing [class] its strength and its dominant social philosophy.'[73] 'The education inspectorate enjoyed a greater uniformity of social background than did the assistant commissioners.'[74] None was a baronet and none was connected with the peerage. All but one were university men, and he had studied law at Lincoln's Inn. They mostly came from professional backgrounds—six from clerical families, and the rest were the sons of doctors, solicitors and school-teachers.

Unlike their colleagues in most other departments, the inspectors of the General Board of Health were not salaried but 'were paid by the day, and were free, once they had completed an engagement for the Board, to undertake private commissions'. Strange as it may seem in the light of modern assumptions, 'they might in their official capacity examine and report on the sanitary condition of a place under the Public Health Act, and then as private individuals put in a bid to carry out the works they had recommended. And very often the Local Board, as it nervously faced up to its programme of sanitary construction, sought the services of the inspector, who had the advantage of professional competitors that he had already surveyed the ground and had indicated authoritatively the works that would be required'.[75]

Whether in mental health or emigration, factories or poor law, education or public health, or indeed in any of the sixteen inspectorates which had come into existence by 1854, the great majority of these men had one thing in common. They were zealots, in the sense defined in Chapter V above. In this respect they differed profoundly from the typical civil servant of the present day. They 'did not interest themselves in certain things simply because they were servants of the state; rather, they were servants of the state because they were interested in those things, because they had formed opinions which an official position allowed them to translate into action. However good the case might be for open competition for all civil service appointments, it could not produce men more dedicated than Tremenheere and Crawford [or] John Allen'.[76]

It is easy to picture the inspection process as a clash of interests necessarily opposed. It is also very misleading. Inspectors could secure the respect, and even the affection, of the inspected. When

[73] ibid., 155.   [74] ibid.   [75] Lewis, 297.
[76] Burn, 223–4. H. S. Tremenheere (1804–93). H.M. Inspector of Schools, 1840–2. Assistant Commissioner of Poor Law, 1842. Inspector of Mines, 1843–59. William Crawford (1788–1847). Inspector of Prisons, 1835–47. Rev. John Allen (1810–86). H.M. Inspector of Schools, 1839–47.

Matthew Arnold came to Kidderminster it was like 'the admission of a ray of light when a shutter was opened in a darkened room. . . . He brought with him a complete atmosphere of culture and poetry. He had something to tell of Sainte-Beuve's last criticism, some new book like Lewes' *Life of Goethe* to recommend, some new political interest to unfold, and, in short, he carried you away from the routine of everyday life with his enthusiasm and his spirit. He gave me most valuable advice as to the training of pupil teachers. "Open their minds," he would say, "take them into the world of Shakespeare, and try to make them feel that there is no book so full of poetry and beauty as the Bible." He had something to tell me of Stanley and Clough, and it is really difficult to say what a delightful tonic effect his visits produced'.[77] When Darlington Training College appointed a new principal who had no experience of teacher training, Canon Tinling H.M.I. took her to see a demonstration school in London. In the autumn of her first year, his visit 'for the annual inspection proved most helpful and encouraging'. He was, she wrote, 'so considerate and encouraging and gave me so many suggestions as to my future management of the College that I took fresh heart'. Indeed, 'of all the visitors in the early years of her reign [she] looked forward most to the annual visits of the Inspectors . . . [she] regarded the Inspectors as friends and advisers to whom "one and all we owe a debt of gratitude for their wise suggestions, kindly criticisms, and often expressed appreciation of our work".'[78]

EXCHEQUER GRANTS

Inspectors of schools derived much of their influence from the fact that money was given or withheld on the basis of their reports. Education was the first important service in Great Britain to receive grant aid. Indeed, the first state intervention in this field derived not from a statute, but from the grant of £20,000 in 1833 for school buildings. Until the Act of 1870, the 'law' of education consisted of the minutes regulating the administration of the various grants voted by parliament. 'The history of elementary education finance is rich in the kind of grants designed to achieve particular purposes. The central theory [was] . . . that they . . . should be directed to inducing local agencies to provide those additional facilities which at particular times seemed most necessary or most desirable . . . From 1833 there was a long series of *ad hoc* fertilizing grants designed to

[77] q. Leese, 157–8.
[78] O. M. Stanton, *Our Present Opportunities* (Darlington, n.d.), 52.

stimulate the particular crops in the field of education. . . . At first, the problem was felt to be the provision of school buildings . . . thirteen years later (1846) it became clear that while schools were being built they were in a large number of instances inadequately staffed, and so a new grant was given in aid of teachers and their apprentices. In the following year, a small grant was made towards the cost of lesson-books and maps for scholars, and text-books for teachers, all of which were at that time inadequate. Grants based on average attendance were started about this time, designed not only to give general financial assistance but also to encourage regular attendance. . . . In 1853 a policy of paying capitation grants was adopted in respect of rural areas and subsequently extended to all areas in 1856.'[79]

Lessons of grant aid soon accumulated. It was agreed that it achieved results. The money laid out during the first five years of the school grant 'trifling as it is, has done more to advance education and to stimulate private charity than any steps heretofore taken by parliament'.[80] 'We may not have had the full value of our money, but we have derived great value from the outlay.'[81] But, since the aim was to stimulate activity in others, it was a branch of government expenditure peculiarly difficult to control. 'As to education—[one of the three] main sources of increased expenditure—the increase has arisen from the working of a self-acting system.'[82] One-hundred-per-cent grants were, of course, the most 'self-acting' of all, since they sapped the motives of local economy. Hence they were to be avoided. In 1850, the President of the Poor Law Board thought that 'the charge for pauper lunatics . . . might usefully be transferred from local to public funds'. The Home Secretary did not object, especially since 'the amount . . . is not very large. It would, however, increase considerably if the whole charge was taken by the Treasury and it might be advisable to leave a portion of it payable from local funds'.[83] 'All or nothing' grants were also to be avoided. In case of inefficiency, power to withhold part of a grant was more effective. In the 1850s, for example, it was a condition of the education grant 'that if the inspector reported that properly qualified teachers had not been provided, the whole amount of the grant would be withheld. The harshness of the penalty caused the inspectors to hesitate to penalize a school if the departure from grant conditions was only minor'.[84]

[79] D. N. Chester, *Central and Local Government* (1951), 148, 156–7.
[80] Melbourne Papers. Spring Rice to Melbourne, September 5, 1838.
[81] Ashley, ii, 222.   [82] ibid.
[83] PRO 30/22/8. Grey to Russell, December 27, 1850.   [84] Chester, 148.

Recipients of grants became, at least potentially, interest groups, with the consequence that it was extremely difficult to discontinue them. 'John Russell . . . now seems conscious of the opposition which the church will raise to his education scheme. . . . Russell's present notion is to withdraw the grant altogether. Now this strikes me as being a very ill-judged proceeding. . . . Besides which I think we should most assuredly be beaten. Churchmen and dissenters, both eager applicants for aid, would combine against us, and I know not how we could resist a vote founded on the principle on which we ourselves have acted for the last five years.'[85]

Eager applicants for aid were not necessarily passive recipients of aid. Delicate negotiations took place as to the terms on which educational bodies would accept public money. 'The clause in question was suggested, not prescribed, by the National Society, but their having acted in the matter arises from no answer having been given by the Committee of Council to a letter of theirs of May 12. Then they thought themselves bound to do something. Shuttleworth and I agree that the best course will be for him to see you forthwith, and, if you approve, to give a dilatory answer to the applicants pointing out the objectionable words and asking if they object to the old form—but Shuttleworth should see the Bishop of London in order to ascertain if he cannot manage the withdrawing of the objectionable words—and that an endeavour should be made to agree on clauses with the common consent of Council and Society. We must be very quiet and discreet or we may be on the verge of a quarrel which would be a great pity.'[86] On the eve of 'payment by results', Granville feared such pressure might make it difficult to change the conditions of grant. 'Up to this time, the Privy Council has had to pay the grants to each master and pupil teacher. . . . If the plea of vested interests has any strength now, it will get stronger every day and no one can be ready to declare that we are irrevocably bound to the details of the present system.'[87] It is easy, against such a background, to see why 'the government has found it very difficult to withdraw from the relations implied by a grant'.[88]

The principle of a police grant was under discussion even before there were, outside the metropolis, police forces to be aided. As early as 1833, Althorp saw a case for helping the Metropolitan Police alone,

[85] Melbourne Papers. Spring Rice to Melbourne, September 5, 1838.

[86] PRO 30/22/5G. Charles Wood to Russell, n.d. [probably September 1846].

[87] Palmerston Papers. Granville to Palmerston, October 13, 1861.

[88] Schaffer (1956), 446.

on the grounds that it was 'of great general utility, both as an example and as a means of checking and discovering crime in all parts of the country, and the preservation of tranquillity of the metropolis is certainly a public object beyond the immediate local advantage'. At the same time, he saw that it might be the thin end of the wedge. 'There appear to me sufficient reasons for confining public aid to this particular force, but it is impossible to conceal from one's self, that if it is given in this instance, it will be claimed and expected in others.' Other forces should be established and aided. 'I think that after the first object of defence from foreign enemies, the next [object] to which the public funds should be applied, is the establishment of internal security, but the adoption of this principle now would involve a considerably expense which it may be doubtful whether we can afford. It is melancholy to consider what enormous funds are devoted in this country to the production of evil, for I cannot consider the Poor Law as having any other tendency, whilst we are squeezed so close with respect to measures of undoubted advantage and utility.'[89]

In spite of this, the Whig government went on to lay the foundations of the borough and county forces without introducing police grants. But the possibility remained in the back of ministers' minds. 'If we were to take half the expense of the police whenever it was placed on an efficient footing it would greatly encourage the establishment of such a force.'[90]

The whole question of grants in nineteenth-century government is full of curious paradoxes. Radical reformers favoured them, as a means of promoting policies—e.g. education—which they favoured. But conservatives also favoured them, especially after the repeal of the Corn Laws, as a means of relieving the burdens on land. Charles Wood analysed the problem in these terms in 1850: 'Two different causes are now co-operating towards the same, and ... as I think, most mischievous end. Our philosophers are all for centralization, our country declaimers are all for throwing expenses on the central funds, which inevitably leads to central appointment and control. He who pays must ultimately do both. ... I am against any large relief (as it is miscalled) of agriculture by assuming local burdens.'[91] In any case, government could not afford it. Any possible sum would produce 'positive evil on one side, and be laughed at for [a] *ridiculus mus* by the squires'.[92] That such expectations were well grounded is

[89] Melbourne Papers: 23. Althorp to Melbourne, September 30, 1833.
[90] PRO 30/22/8. George Grey to Russell, December 27, 1850.
[91] ibid. Wood to Russell, December 31, 1850. [92] ibid.

shown by the language of Disraeli's biographers. Compensation for the repeal of the Corn Laws in 1846 'turned out to be a trivial readjustment of expenses between the counties and national exchequer'. While in 1851, government 'conceded, though in a minute fashion, the principle against which they had so obstinately contended, by proposing a grant-in-aid of £150,000 to be handed over to local authorities for the maintenance of pauper lunatics'.[93]

Disraeli did not forget the principle—indeed, his followers did not allow him to do so. 'The Poor Rate had long been so high that agricultural property bore much more than its fair share of the burden of direct taxation and during the '50s and '60s there was a steady increase in the volume of complaint, as new burdens were imposed on the rates at the behest of Parliament. The problem was most acute in counties which had adopted the Highways Act of 1862, but was serious (by nineteenth-century standards) in any county where the central government had insisted that the magistrates build new prisons, lunatic asylums, or militia barracks.'[94] It should be remembered that, prior to 1888, the county authority was Quarter Sessions, and it was thought that Justices of the Peace, lacking the support of a popular constituency, were peculiarly susceptible to pressure from Whitehall. Hence, 'two possible reforms were advocated: one called for a reform of county government, and the other for Treasury grants to local authorities'.[95] In the words of the *Colchester Mercury*, 'the management of the county finances by the magistrates is not looked upon with any degree of suspicion, but it is thought that the ratepayers would have greater powers of resistance to extravagant schemes which government inspectors and departments required should be carried out'.[96] However, long before county administration was reformed, something was done to increase financial aid. 'Conservatives were [not] averse from granting considerable powers to the central government provided that they received a financial *quid pro quo* for them.'[97] Following Disraeli's return to power in 1874, the pauper lunatic and police grants were increased, and prisons were transferred altogether from local authorities to the Home Office. In so doing, a prophecy made a quarter of a century earlier was fulfilled. 'If . . . we were to take on ourselves the whole charge [of prisons] . . . we must at the same time supersede local management . . . The whole of the appointment of

[93] Moneypenny and Buckle, i, 757 and 1100.

[94] H. J. Hanham, *Elections and Party Management: Politics in the time of Disraeli and Gladstone* (1959), 36.   [95] ibid.

[96] *Colchester Mercury*, June 6, 1868, q. ibid., 36n.   [97] Burn, 172.

the prison officers would also be taken into the hands of the government.'[98]

Hence, though grants were useful in 'smoothing difficulties with the country gentlemen'[99] the basic question was not one of finance but of the country's administrative structure. Sir Charles Wood declared himself 'opposed to such a step altogether, on grounds not financial. I do not mean that the financial reasons against it are not strong, but my own opinion [is] . . . political rather than financial. . . . There is nothing in the world which I think is so much to be deprecated in this country as discouraging country gentlemen in the performance of those duties which they now execute throughout the country. . . . This tendency is most dangerous. We have hitherto been for the most part locally governed. Responsibility has been very much distributed; and I believe it to be indispensable for the future stability of government in this country that it should be so. In old times if twenty overseers starved twenty paupers, they were corrected or punished: but nothing was shaken of the administration of the country. It was quite right to mend this. But how much unpopularity attached to Melbourne's government on account of the new Poor Law administration? . . . We should [provide] as few fields for attacking the government of the country as we can help. Heaven knows there are plenty, and the universal disposition now, is to hold them responsible for matters hitherto beyond their province altogether. This is . . . the black cloud on the horizon, that we are gradually approaching the state of Continental countries, where the government is responsible for everything, for whatever goes wrong the government is blamed. That which twenty years ago might have changed a parish vestry may change a ministry and the nation be involved in difficulty from some petty local grievance.

'I am against doing anything to forward this tendency. If country gentlemen are not to have some power and responsibility, they will not act. Why should I visit a gaol, if I have no authority? Why should I attend a grand jury, if my verdict is of no use or effect? Acting as a magistrate is not the easy work that it was. We are watched by sharp-eyed attornies. Lazy gentlemen cannot make out *mittimus* etc. after the fashion of Sir Roger de Coverley. A far better race of justices now do the work, but they are actuated by a desire to do the duty of the business of the counties, and have naturally the pleasure and enjoyment of the exercise of power, but if you supersede them in this you will leave them no motive for mere routine, and you will

[98] PRO 30/22/8. Grey to Russell, December 27, 1850.
[99] ibid. Wood to Russell, December 31, 1850.

have then to administer the counties by *prefets* and *sous-prefets* and the bureaucratic [machinery] which prevails abroad.'[100]

On the face of it, there seemed to be a simple test of what local expenditure should be grant aided and what should not. A community should provide for its own needs. But where national functions were carried out locally, the exchequer should pay. Lord John Russell seems to have been of this opinion. Wood did not agree. 'You say Manchester water is a local concern. It is paid by Manchester. The punishment of offenders is national. It is paid by the nation. So far you have your way. But I do not admit that everything that is a public concern, i.e. that which concerns more than the locality, ought therefore to be borne by the nation. I somewhat doubt the wisdom of having taken on the public the whole expense of the punishment of offenders. The result has been a very considerable increase of expense, with no more efficiency. The obvious cause is that the local magistrates have ceased to exercise a careful check on the expenditure, in defraying which they had no longer so immediate an interest. It does not seem to me that there is anything inconsistent or contrary to principle that the charge of providing for *public* objects within given districts should be charged on those districts, instead of on the whole country—e.g. the maintenance of roads, of churches, etc. I think that the question whether a charge should be general or local . . . is to be determined not *only* by the nature of the benefit derived . . . but also . . . by a consideration of the most advantageous way of raising the money and checking the expenditure . . . But I go myself still further, and I think that in many cases where the charge might be taken on the general [budget], it is better to leave it on a district, in order to cultivate that, on which I believe the real stability and prosperity . . . of this country depends, the habit of self-government. I would sacrifice a good deal to attain this end.'[101]

MISCELLANEOUS POWERS

Another power wielded by central government was that of granting a provisional order in place of a Local Act of Parliament. The procedure was attractive to promoters of local schemes because it was simple and cheap. The first example of such a power is to be found in the Inclosure Act of 1845 (8 and 9 Vic., c. 118)[102] but the main development of the procedure lay in the field of local government.

[100] ibid.   [101] PRO 30/22/8. Wood to Russell, January 6, 1850.
[102] F. J. Port, *Administrative Law* (1929), 133.

Provisional orders required confirmation by parliament. From the point of view of the development of local administration, the central government's power of audit has, of course, been of the first importance. As early as the 1830s, Lord Melbourne confessed that 'it has always been to me a matter of very great surprise [that the Poor Rate] should have been so long left to be imposed, levied and expended by the parochial authorities and the Justices of the Peace without any examination, check or control upon the part of the government of the country'.[103] Audit by officials responsible to Whitehall was in fact introduced as part of the New Poor Law administrative package, but from the present point of view, calls for little notice, because of its negative character. It 'can frighten a local authority into avoiding certain expenditure but not into undertaking new developments. If anyone should doubt this, the history of poor law between 1834 and 1929 stands as a record for all time'.[104]

The default power, by use of which a central department can supersede a local authority, sounds extremely stringent but in practice is much more limited in its scope than it might appear. It was first conferred by the Sanitary Act, 1866. The Home Secretary was authorized, on receipt of a complaint that a local authority had failed in its duty in relation to water-supply or sewage, and after due enquiry, 'to order the performance within a fixed time of the neglected duty'. So far the power could be regarded as analogous to the writ of *mandamus*, issued by the executive instead of the judiciary. If, however, the default continued, the Secretary of State could appoint a person to remedy it and direct the expenses to be paid by the defaulting authority. The Sewage Utilization Act, 1867, went further and provided that a person who had been appointed to act in default should have all the powers of the defaulting authority except that of levying a rate. The device lacked teeth, however, because the Secretary of State lacked the power to raise the cash to pay for the work carried out by the person appointed. The Sanitary Act, 1868, therefore, took the logical step of empowering his representative to levy a rate and even to raise a loan. 'As a result, action was taken in a number of cases where complaints had been received.'[105]

The requirement that local authorities should obtain the sanction of central government before raising loans may seem somewhat trivial as compared with the power of grant aid. But in Chadwick's hands it became the most powerful weapon wielded by the Central Board of Health, implying, as it did, the scrutiny by the central department of all local improvement schemes. 'The bitterest objec-

[103] Melbourne Papers, 54.   [104] Chester, 101.   [105] ibid., 67.

210

tions to sanitary reform were raised by property-owners who feared that drains and water meant heavy additional burdens upon themselves. Thomas Cubitt, the building contractor, spoke for this class when he declared that "the public" were not prepared to go to the extent of putting a water-closet in every house: "I think that if people were obliged to put them, it would be considered a very severe tax upon them." Chadwick's reply was to demonstrate that, if the charge were spread over thirty years, the cost of fitting new house-drains, closets, and water-pipes would dwindle to a weekly payment of $1\frac{1}{2}$d., which was within the means of even the poorest tenants, and was considerably cheaper then the cost of the existing privies, cess-pools and stand-cocks. It was good arithmetic and good economics; but it fought a slow battle with the "landlord fallacy" that stinks and damp formed part of the tenant's risk, and the equally powerful ratepayers' fallacy that fever nests were cheaper than public works.'[106]

The purpose of this chapter has been to outline some of the legal means available to administrators for the realization of policy. But it would be misleading to end with the implication that administration could be reduced to law. 'For the administrator the law is an instrument. It is one of a number, not always the best, sometimes quite unusable.'[107] Sometimes feedback led officials to the conclusion that those who were breaking the law were in the right, and that the law needed to be changed. This happened in the early days of the Poor Law Commission. 'To remove the stinking refuse and stagnant pools which were breeding the diseases, the East End Unions were forced to spend their money, although this was illegal. When the auditors disallowed such payments, the matter was brought to the Commission's very doorstep. Chadwick defended their policy.'[108] This does not mean, of course, that ministers and those who serve them are above the law. What it does mean is that it is necessary to distinguish, as the Treasury once did in negotiations with the Local Government Board, between duties undertaken in minimum compliance with the letter of the law and duties 'in excess of those imposed by parliament which can be attributed to administrative zeal on the part of the chiefs of the office rather than to legislation.'[109] Administrative action may precede legislation, as well as follow it. 'It is an excellent practice to test out a field for possible legislation by seeking to encourage voluntary agitation and action within it, and to legislate only when, by the measure of what has in this way been done, it is possible to judge the practicability

[106] Lewis, 101–2.   [107] Sisson, 139.   [108] Finer (1952), 155.
[109] R. M. McLeod, *Treasury Control and Social Administration* (1968), 22.

211

and usefulness of the legislation proposed.'[110] The Poor Law problem mentioned above led on to Chadwick's first enquiry in the field of public health. Chadwick stressed its origin in administrative experience: 'In directing the enquiry, the Commissioners were influenced by the circumstances which appeared before them in the course of the business of the day and by no representation of . . . any person whatever.'[111] Ministers and civil servants were not mere creatures of statute, endowed with no powers other than those conferred by specific Acts of Parliament. Over and above—or perhaps, behind and beneath—such powers lay a wider responsibility for guarding and promoting the public interest. Confronted with a situation requiring action, an administrator could not plead as a valid excuse for doing nothing that the law did not tell him precisely what he should do. Within the limits, which were normally wide, of what the law said he must *not* do, he was expected to suggest the course which, in the light of his experience, was most conducive to the general welfare.

[110] Sisson, 139. [111] Finer (1952), 157.

CHAPTER VIII

SOME DEPARTMENTS AND TREASURY CONTROL

'The English offices have never, since they were made, been arranged with any reference to one another; or rather they were never made, but grew as each could.'

Walter Bagehot, 1865

Pooh-Bah 'Speaking as your Private Secretary, I should say that, as the city will have to pay for it, don't stint yourself, do it well.'
Ko-Ko 'Exactly—as the city will have to pay for it. That is your advice.'
Pooh-Bah 'As Private Secretary. Of course you will understand that, as Chancellor of the Exchequer, I am bound to see that due economy is observed.'

W. S. Gilbert

It has been shown how the departments were recruited and what was the effect of ministerial responsibility on the respectives roles of ministers and civil servants. The structure of departments has been explained, and in particular, the hierarchy of decision-making within them. Categories of permanent officials have been indicated. A reconnaissance of the border country between administration and law has been made, and attention has been drawn to the feedback from administrative experience to legislation. The battery of legal powers available to officials for the enforcement of policy has been sketched out. But one thing essential to an understanding of nineteenth-century administration has not been done. None of the departments has been shown at work. The interaction of the various factors has not been demonstrated. This chapter aims to make good the omission. Diverse as are the departments chosen, two broad themes run through them. In the first place, there is the determination of the central government to enforce policies believed to be in the public interest on individuals and collectivities scattered throughout society: businessmen and firms in the case of the emigration service and alkali inspection; local authorities in the case of vaccination and police. In the second place, the relevance of science and

213

technology to administration stands out. Both themes were paralleled many times in departments not studied here. Both were highly characteristic of the new administrative pattern that developed after 1830 and merit a prominent position in any account of it.

A. THE EMIGRATION OFFICERS

To regulate the North Atlantic traffic was a particularly difficult administrative problem. The annual average had risen from 25,000 in the period 1815–20 to over 70,000 in the early thirties. The great majority of the emigrants were Irish, but the main port of embarkation was Liverpool. They were almost all poor and ignorant, and an easy prey for the 'runners' who met every packet from Ireland. 'It was the runners who . . . led emigrants into the traps which had been prepared. . . . [They] met every Irish steamer as it docked and laid hands upon the disembarking passengers. . . . Before he could understand what was happening, the emigrant, or his baggage, was seized. . . . Once he was in the runner's hands, it was almost inevitable that the emigrant should be cheated. . . . The runner could . . . exchange the emigrant's little stock of gold greatly to his own advantage, or persuade the emigrant that he would not be allowed aboard without liquor, telescopes, bowie knives or whatever rubbish he had to trade. But worse than individual and petty fraud was the fact that runners worked hand-in-glove with brokers and lodging and shopkeepers, and extorted a commission from them on all transactions in which an emigrant whom they had introduced took part.'[1] This commission was rarely less than seven and a half per cent and might be considerably more. The emigrants had normally bought their passages in Ireland, a custom which opened the way for a further range of abuses. They might find themselves delayed weeks beyond the appointed sailing day, or transferred to a different vessel, or simply defrauded of their passage money. Delay meant that passengers had to put up in lodging-houses, where they were often exposed to infection, and forced to eat into their stock of food for the passage, since prior to 1842 emigrants were responsible for feeding themselves on board ship. Once on board, they found themselves for six weeks or more in vessels not designed for passengers. Most shipowners regarded emigrants as a kind of ballast, or as a means of reducing overheads when no cargo was available. Hence, toilet and cooking arrangements were almost always extremely primitive. If winds were adverse, drinking-water often ran short; and if the

[1] MacDonagh (1961), 34–5.

emigrants' own food ran out, they often starved. In case of illness—
a real risk, since many passengers brought infection on board with
them—medical help was rarely provided. Mortality was high; over
ten per cent for an entire season; more than forty per cent for single
voyages. When land was sighted, the passengers might find themselves hundreds of miles from the port to which they had booked.
Yet the system flourished, because not one in a thousand ever came
back to accuse those who maintained it.

These evils first attracted notice in 1827, and in the following year
a Passenger Act was passed. Its execution was left to the customs
officers, and in practice it was not enforced. Protests and complaints
to the Colonial Office led to the appointment of the first emigration
officer, stationed at Liverpool, in 1833. 'Emigration is now becoming
so extensive and systematic,' wrote Stanley, the Secretary of State,
'that it is very desirable to afford any facilities for it on the part of the
government, and to check, as far as we can, the frauds which are
practised on the lower description of emigrants by the agents . . .
Their interest being to secure as many passengers as they can for the
ships for which they are engaged, they deceive them by all sorts of
misrepresentations as to the time of vessels sailing, etc., and keep
them loitering about the port till the whole of their little stock of
money is exhausted . . . The experiment might be tried at Liverpool.'[2]
Within a fortnight, Lt. Robert Low, R.N., was appointed emigration
officer at Liverpool.

Two of Low's earliest cases illustrate the difficulties he had to
contend with. Despite his protests, the *General Brown* sailed with
fifty-four passengers, their luggage and sea-stock in a living space
250 square feet in area and only five feet, seven inches high. The
Cumberland carried eighty-six passengers with luggage and provisions in a space of 600 square feet by five feet, six inches high. This
vessel, though only 336 tons, carried also 479 tons of cargo, dan-
gerously stowed. Low was reluctant to grant a clearance certificate.
But the owners refused to make any alternative arrangements for the
passengers, who were all the while eating into their provision. Had
any of them subsequently died of starvation, he would have been
blamed. Hence, Low finally let her sail. A fortnight later she came
back. Cargo, provisions and luggage had all been jettisoned to save
the ship. The owners were under no statutory obligation to provide
compensation in such a case. In this instance, they did ultimately
provide another ship. But she foundered, and the passengers found
themselves back at Liverpool a second time. What could the emigra-

[2] ibid., 92.

215

tion officer do in such a situation? James Stephen, Low's superior, ruled on the point. 'The executive government, and those whom it employs, must enforce the law as they find it, looking to the legislature for further powers when necessary, but acquiescing in the defectiveness of the law, so long as it continues unremedied by Parliament.'[3] As for enforcing the law, emigration officers as such had no statutory powers. In any case, the law was silent on a number of points, such as the stowing of cargo, which were material to the safety of passengers. Not surprisingly, Low fell back on the alternative indicated by Stephen. He looked to the legislature for further powers.

Within a few weeks of his appointment, Low drew up a series of recommendations for a new Passenger Act, which showed a shrewd power of diagnosis. Typical of his approach was the suggestion that in future passage-brokers should be responsible for providing all food for the voyage, from the time fixed for departure, even if the actual sailing were delayed. This would have, firstly, the obvious advantage of guaranteeing an adequate diet. Secondly, it would reduce the suffering caused by delays in sailing, or time lost on the voyage. Thirdly, it would make possible a thorough inspection by the emigration officer, to satisfy himself that the stock of food was in fact adequate. This was not feasible so long as responsibility for providing food was shared among the emigrants themselves. The emigration officer was to be the sole judge of the quantity and quality of the victuals, and also the sea-worthiness of the vessel, the adequacy of its berths and fittings, and the stowage of its cargo. He would have statutory power to refuse clearances. Such refusal would carry with it a sort of fine, since the broker would be put to the expense of feeding his passengers until the certificate was granted. He also recommended that adequate lifeboats and cooking places should be provided, segregation of the sexes, and a minimum area for each berth. Passenger agents should be licensed. Again, a penalty—the withdrawal of the licences—is implied.

Low's plan, though prophetic, bore no immediate fruit. There was a new Passenger Act in 1835, but it was not based on administrative experience. Meanwhile, the corps of emigration officers grew. Appointments were made to seven further ports in 1834, and more followed. Low got an assistant. All were half-pay naval officers. The corps acquired a head in 1837, with the appointment of T. F. Elliot as agent-general for emigration. He quickly perceived, not only that new legislation was needed, but that it should reflect the experience

[3] ibid., 105.

of those who were administering the old. But Elliot's duties were extensive, and he might well have taken a long time to prepare a Bill had he been left to himself. He was not left to himself, however. In 1839, the Durham Report attracted wide publicity for a severe (though unfair) indictment of the existing pattern of regulation. The emigration officers, it alleged, 'exercised no effective supervision over the arrangements for the passage of emigrants, and [leave untouched] all the old evils of filth, inadequate accommodation, inferior and insufficient food'.[4] Emigration became a live issue. In 1840, the Colonial Land and Emigration Commission was set up, with Elliot as one of its members. One of its first duties was to be the preparation of a new Passenger Bill. As the Colonial Secretary put it, 'the [present] Act frequently proves much less effective than could be desired. The difficulty of dealing with this subject is to determine the line between, on the one hand, unduly encroaching upon the liberty of individual action in persons desiring to emigrate, and also exacting so much as to raise the cost of passage to a prohibiting price, or, on the other hand, failing that general protection which is on every account proper. . . . An extensive body of notes for the amendment of the present statute has been collected in the office of the agent-general, and will, of course, receive your consideration'.[5]

The result was the Passenger Act of 1842. Its main provision (section 6) was that vessels should supply each passenger weekly with seven pounds of bread or the equivalent. A requirement of this kind had been independently suggested by four of the men employed in regulating the traffic. The quantity had to be kept low, because a more generous allowance would have raised the fares beyond what the great majority could pay. But the aim was administrative as well as humanitarian. While emigrants supplied their own food, it was virtually impossible to ascertain whether the quantity aboard was sufficient for the voyage. 'It is enough to reflect upon the condition of a vessel into which 200 or 300 people are crowding together, each carrying his own box or bag of provisions, in order to feel how impossible it must be to exercise an effectual superintendence under this head.'[6] But the adequacy of a ship's stores could be judged with reasonable accuracy. Food supply, moreover, was the key to other problems. If the passengers were assured of a basic ration, the risks of disease were reduced, and there would be less chance to sell food at extortionate prices to those whose own stock had run out.

The Act went on to prescribe a form of agreement for passengers,

[4] ibid., 131.   [5] ibid., 137.   [6] ibid., 135.

a copy of which was set out in the text. All brokers and their agents were to be licensed, and their licences could be withdrawn for proved misconduct. Passenger lists were to be sent ahead by mail steamer, so that emigrants could be checked on disembarkation. This was calculated to restrain the practice of taking on further passengers after clearance, which had often made nonsense of the emigration officers' attempts to prevent overcrowding. Further stipulations related to the size and structure of berths, the size of water-containers, and the proportion of lifeboats to the size of the vessel. The height between decks was increased to six feet. The emigration officers were for the first time given specific statutory duties. This was no more than right, since ultimately they were the authors of the Act. 'Every clause other than the purely legal had been originally proposed by an executive officer working in the field. Every clause had been submitted to several executive officers for criticism. . . . The Passenger Bill of 1842 was almost exclusively the work of a professional inspectorate and their professional superiors, an "administrative" not a "political" measure.'[7] Gaps in the statute were filled in by quasi-legislation. Emigration officers had no explicit powers over cooking arrangements. But the Commissioners, after complaints, instructed them to insist on at least one grate for every hundred passengers.[8] During the first three years of operation, the Act seemed to have been a remarkable success, and to have gone a long way towards solving the problem of regulating the traffic.

Then came the Irish famine. More people crossed the Atlantic in 1846 than in any previous single year, and the traffic during the four years 1846–50—1,139,000—equalled that for the thirty years prior to 1845. The majority of these were already weak from hunger when they decided to quit, and the long walk to the sea weakened them further. Such was the demand for passages, that all kinds of vessel were pressed into service, many of them even less suitable than those ordinarily used. Passengers embarked at many small ports without emigration officers to inspect the ships, provisions, etc. The high price of food increased the temptation to sail without adequate stocks, trusting to luck and favourable winds for a quick passage. The numbers passing through the controls, which had never averaged more than 300 or so per day for all ports in previous years, reached as many as 3,000 in a day at Liverpool. Small increases in staff were made, but were nowhere near the same proportion. The administrative system broke down under the strain. 'Vessels departed freely without the statutory requirements of food or water or berths;

[7] ibid., 152.   [8] ibid., 159.

many even sailed without a clearance. The plea that passengers would probably starve and certainly contract fever, if detained, could not well be controverted. The departing emigrants came fleetingly into view, were packed off with much haste and little ceremony, and then passed over the horizon to unseen trials and terrors.'[9]

A further Passenger Act was passed in 1847. It did not stem directly from the disasters of the period, nor did it give the emigration officers extensive new powers. Nevertheless, it was a significant measure from the standpoint of legal principle. The Commissioners were granted powers to alter the food schedule. (They had in fact already done so, extra-statutorily, in the previous year.) This was the first example of delegated legislation in emigration regulation. The emigration officers were made responsible for judging the sufficiency and competence of crews. In effect, they became so many administrative tribunals for licensing seamen who wished to work in a specified class of ships. The officers were also empowered to inspect lighting and ventilation. If necessary they could order such 'provision to be made for affording light and air to the between decks as the circumstances of the case may, in the judgment of such officer, appear to require, which directions shall be duly carried out to his satisfaction'.[10] Earlier statutes implied the delegation of discretionary powers. 'It may even be that such powers are implicit in all social legislation of this type.'[11] But nothing which preceded it in this field was so wide or explicit.

Stephen de Vere, nephew of Lord Monteagle, travelled steerage to Quebec so 'that he might speak as a witness respecting the sufferings of emigrants'.[12] His account was all the more scarifying since he made it clear that the vessel on which he had sailed was above, rather than below, the average. Food and water were issued irregularly and in quantities below those specified by law. Passengers sank into disease, repelling every effort to bring them or their bedding up on deck. Hundreds lay cramped in the dark and stifling hold. Even those with fever had scarcely room to turn in their narrow bunks. The ravings of the sick demoralized those who were not infected, and led them to take refuge in drink. The ship's officers sold liquor on profitable terms, in spite of the prohibition imposed by the 1842 Act, under a penalty of £100. After weeks of filth and degradation, de Vere noticed a total loss of self-respect among the passengers. The emigration officer's inspection on disembarkation was a mere farce. The main deficiencies were in food, space, discipline and

[9] ibid., 180.   [10] ibid., 200.   [11] ibid.   [12] ibid., 194.

219

morale. De Vere recommended a large increase in the food allowance; a reduction in the numbers ratio; separate quarters for single men and women; the employment of a surgeon and a chaplain for each vessel; the provision of kitchens and ovens; hospital wards for the sick; and ventilation for the passenger decks. For the first time, the administrators had before them a report on the crossing by an educated observer. It became the basis of future legislation. Attempts were made sooner or later to achieve every one of de Vere's proposals, except the provision of chaplains.

De Vere's influence, as well as that of the emigration officers, is apparent in a further Act of 1848. The space allowance was increased from ten to twelve square feet for every adult. Vessels carrying 100 or more passengers were either to have a doctor, or alternatively, to allow fourteen square feet instead of twelve. Such vessels had also to provide a cook, cooking apparatus, and cooking places to the satisfaction of the emigration officer. Each emigrant was to be medically inspected and certified free of infectious disease prior to embarkation. Further discretionary powers were heaped upon the emigration officers. They were to be the sole judges of the eligibility of ships' doctors, and to fix the fees to be paid by the owner or charterer to the doctor who inspected the emigrants. They were authorized to dispense with the medical inspection and permit a vessel to sail without that precaution under certain circumstances. More of de Vere's suggestions cropped up in an Act of 1849. It forbade the berthing together of single men and women. The food scale was increased and diversified. No longer were the ships to issue breadstuffs alone, but a varied diet including oatmeal, tea, rice, sugar and molasses. Brokers were required to enter into bonds of £200 and provide two sureties resident in the port. They had also to furnish lists of authorized runners. Every agent was to carry written authority from the broker for whom he acted.

There was an element of 'wishful government'[13] in all this. Law-making was cheaper than law-enforcing. The growth in the administrative machinery did not keep pace with the growth in the traffic. 'Whereas the volume of emigration increased fourfold during the 1840s, the executive corps was not even doubled in size. Moreover, the disproportion was worst precisely where additional officers were needed most'[14]—above all, at Liverpool. Still less did the number of emigration officers keep pace with the growth, both in bulk and complexity, of the code they had to administer. Some of their new duties under the 1849 Act may be cited as an example. To see the

13 ibid., 178.   14 ibid., 217.

sexes berthed separately, to check the lists of runners and the agents' letters of authority, to ascertain that supplies of tea, sugar, molasses and rice were adequate in quantity and quality, added hours to a day which was already too short. Discretionary powers were a psychological burden. Was it fair to expect a naval officer to rule on the mechanics of ventilation devices, the type of oven to be used in the passengers' galley, or the qualifications of a physician? 'Although the [doctor's] documents may in themselves be satisfactory, yet, if the emigration officer is aware of any circumstances which in his judgment would render it improper to commit the charge of an emigrant ship to the holder of them, it will be his duty to object to him under the authority conferred by the law.'[15] Most of the officers found such chores embarrassing and they were largely neglected. To enact such measures was a device to quieten consciences and to give the appearance that something was being done. But there was little recognition that a growth in legislative powers implied a growth in the machinery of enforcement. Indeed, it is arguable that a growth in the latter might have done more good without the extensions of power voted in the period 1847–9.

A Select Committee in 1851 revealed how wide a gap remained between what the law enjoined and what the administrators in practice enforced. Fresh legislation ensued in the following session. Perhaps the most interesting feature was the discussion on the question of whether there should be any appeal from the emigration officer's decision. A call for such a right came from the Liverpool Chamber of Commerce, and the associations of ship-owners in Liverpool and Glasgow. Cardwell, one of the Members for Liverpool, supported the demand, Pakington, for the government, replied that 'practically speaking, a sufficient court of appeal existed in the [Colonial Land and] Emigration Commissioners'.[16] He went on to argue that the officers, being naval men, were 'very competent and ... acquainted with nautical matters; and the appeal would probably be to persons less competent to decide and having no knowledge at all'.[17] One of the Members for South Lancashire moved an amendment which would have granted a right of appeal from the emigration officer's decision to the Justices of the Peace. 'Was it right,' he asked, 'to entrust to any individual, without appeal to some competent tribunal, a power which might be abused from caprice, ignorance or vindictiveness?'[18] As for the Commissioners, they would naturally tend to favour their subordinates if appealed to. Henley, who had sat on the Select Committee, spoke against the amendment. A

[15] ibid., 253–4. [16] ibid., 243. [17] ibid. [18] ibid.

government officer was quite as likely to be impartial as a J.P. The sole effect would be 'that both the Justices and the shipmasters would be landed in the Queen's Bench upon such a simple question as whether a cask of biscuits was good or bad'.[19] It was defeated, seventy-three to twenty-five.

In the later years of emigration regulation, the most interesting new feature was the extent to which administrative decisions came to depend on questions of science and technology. Ventilation is a good example. The 1848 Act had made the emigration officers responsible in this field. The Commissioners acquired a good deal of knowledge of the subject from their direct responsibility for assisted emigration to Australia, and Elliot—now Assistant Secretary at the Colonial Office—was able to discuss it in a well-informed fashion with technologists. During the early 1850s the commissioners experimented with various shafts, fans and screws until in 1856 a really satisfactory system was found. Whether impelled by public opinion or by a simple passion for gadgetry, the Commissioners made the pace in this field, in contrast to their usual habit of waiting for events. No fresh legislation was needed to enforce it. An instruction to the officers to guide them in the exercise of the discretion the law had previously awarded them was enough.

The increasing use of iron in the construction of ships, and the increasing frequency of iron cargoes, raised problems about compasses. The Commissioners instructed all officers to require each emigrant vessel to carry an azimuth compass. Elliot recoiled from their audacity in ordering 'very humble officers of the government', by quasi-legislative means, to act where 'parliament has either shrunk from the task, or has not thought it advisable'.[20] The ministerial heads of the office backed the Commissioners, however, and told them to enforce the regulation. Within a week they had to instruct the officers not to refuse clearance to vessels without compasses of the recommended type. The law was uncertain on the point, legal proceedings had been threatened, and they feared actions for damages, resulting from delayed sailings. The section of the Act referring to measures 'promoting the health and safety of passengers' could hardly be stretched to cover the azimuth compass. A further difficulty soon arose. An ordinary compass needed to be 're-swung' both before an iron cargo was loaded and after one had been carried in a vessel. The emigration officers were not competent to do this; a specialist was needed.

The regulation of the emigrant traffic suffered a fate unusual in

[19] ibid.   [20] ibid., 251.

nineteenth century administrative history. It came to an end. As steamships captured more and more of the trade, the worst of the evils dwindled of their own accord. The new ships had many advantages over the old, but what was really decisive was their greater speed. All the problems—overcrowding, feeding, sanitation, disease—had been intensified by the duration of the passage. 'It was the change in the time-scale which was really revolutionary. A two-weeks voyage resolved many of the old difficulties automatically.'[21]

B. VACCINATION AND MEDICAL RESEARCH

Vaccination was the one certain method of preventive medicine known in the middle of the nineteenth century. Government had been directly involved in promoting it almost since its discovery. Jenner had published his paper in 1798. In 1808, parliament had founded, at a cost of £3,000 a year, the National Vaccine Establishment to provide free vaccination in London and to distribute vaccine-lymph to other vaccinators. The first results were not impressive. Local authorities could pay for public vaccination, but did little. Smallpox mortality remained high and reached epidemic proportions in the late 1830s. An Act of 1840 required all Boards of Guardians to provide free vaccination by contracting with physicians. The Poor Law Commissioners were given control of the system. The connection with the Poor Law was unfortunate, but no alternative local machinery existed. A further Act declared the new scheme to be non-pauperizing—it was, in fact, the first national health service for the population at large. A report published in 1853 by the Epidemiological Society created a climate of opinion favourable to further legislation. As a result, parliament passed an Act providing for compulsory vaccination of all infants within three months of birth, under penalty on the parents. Local Registrars of Births were to notify parents of their obligation and to record vaccinations. Specified minimum fees were to be paid to public vaccinators by the Guardians. Parliament thus committed what an anti-vaccinationist called 'the first direct aggression upon the person of the subject in medical matters . . . attempted in these kingdoms'.[22]

The success of the new measure was very limited. In 1854, the proportion of vaccinations to births rose sharply, but fell again the

[21] ibid., 310.
[22] R. J. Lambert, 'A Victorian National Health Service: State Vaccination, 1855–71', *Historical Journal*, v (1962), 3.

following year. The reasons were plain. The registration arrangements were deficient. The Guardians could not prosecute defaulters. The Poor Law Board's supervision was slack and unenlightened. The Epidemiological Society suggested in 1855 that the responsibility should be transferred to the Board of Health, which should be provided with a 'competent and energetic Medical Officer to harmonize the whole system and keep it in constant activity'.[23] Such an appointment was made later that year, when Dr John Simon, Medical Officer of Health to the City of London, transferred to the service of the central government.

The next step in the development of vaccination was the Public Health Act, 1858. (Its main purpose was the abolition of the Board of Health, and the transfer of certain of its functions to the Privy Council.) Section 2 enabled the Privy Council to issue regulations for securing the qualifications of vaccinators, and for securing the efficient performance of vaccination. Simon was 'shocked, utterly shocked ... [that] hitherto no security had been taken that the vaccination so universally and so extensively enforced should be useful or even harmless to the recipient'.[24] Public vaccinators had had no training in the technique, for no medical schools provided it. After trying in vain to get them to do so, Simon made arrangements to fill the gap. Fifteen carefully chosen doctors with special experience in this field were given exclusive authority to grant Privy Council certificates of proficiency. Detailed regulations were issued on the admission of their trainees, the fees to be paid, attendance and the subjects of examination. The Privy Council forbade Guardians to employ as a vaccinator anyone entering the profession after 1860 without the Council's certificate of proficiency. For the benefit of untrained vaccinators already operating, guidance was provided by the two leading authorities, Ceely and Marson. In 1861, Simon took over the National Vaccine Establishment, and replaced its supplies of lymph with those from the Educational Stations. The Stations were subject to regular inspection by the representatives of the Council. In the same year, the Guardians secured power to prosecute defaulters.

Simon's next step was to carry out an enquiry into vaccination arrangements throughout England and Wales. Between 1861 and 1864, four doctors visited nearly 640 Unions. One of them in 1862, for example, conferred with 373 vaccinators and 235 local Registrars. He personally examined the vaccination condition of 46,871 schoolchildren. The standard was appallingly low, and the Guardians

[23] ibid., 4. [24] ibid., 5.

responded 'invariably ... with the warmest co-operation ... with expressions of extreme satisfaction that the Government was stirring'.[25] In these years 'every public vaccinator in England found his work subjected to skilled criticism and was assisted to understand the causes of whatever shortcomings were found in it'.[26] The value of inspection was clearly established in this field as in so many others. Four permanent appointments were made, with the object of inspecting every vaccination authority biennially. Simon now proposed 'to stimulate the public vaccinators by the bestowal of certain gratuities on the principle of payment for results'.[27] His inspectors would recommend the award of a shilling or eightpence for first-class or second-class vaccinations. The payments began in 1866—'a primitive form of grant-in-aid to the local authority'.[28] Between 1867 and 1871, the sums disbursed rose from £1,824 to £9,349. At eightpence per head for a second-class vaccination, this indicates an increase from 54,720 to 280,470 patients treated. Since some payments were at the higher rate of a shilling per head, the actual number of patients must have been somewhat less.

The Council acted up to the limited of its powers against recalcitrant Boards of Guardians. To avoid the delay of going through the Poor Law Board, which was not co-operative, it often struck directly. Stiff letters to, for example, Northampton in 1869 or Brighton in 1870, sufficed to prod Boards into action. Seventy-two such remonstrances went out in 1870. Obstinate Boards received special inspections, of which there were ninety in 1870 and sixty-three in 1871. Such visitations usually overcame local resistance, as at Sheffield. Sometimes the Council had to threaten legal action, in the form of an application for *mandamus*, as in the case of Hastings or Liskeard. Nevertheless, one of the inspectors could claim in 1871, that, except for Spalding, he could 'not remember any case in which what the Privy Council has insisted on has been finally resisted'.[29] This was all the more remarkable since, as Simon put it, 'we have had to change their system very much indeed and to interfere in details; but they have accepted that interference and altered their modes of action'.[30]

In spite of all this, vaccination was still very far from universal. An epidemic which reached its climax in 1871 forced the question on to the public agenda once more. The opponents—an Anti-Vaccination League had been set up in 1866—could claim that the epidemic proved the uselessness of the technique. Its champions, on

[25] Lambert (1962), 7.   [26] ibid., 7–8.   [27] ibid., 9.
[28] ibid.   [29] ibid., 11.   [30] ibid.

the other hand, could argue that only vaccination had saved the country from something a great deal worse. The evidence vindicated the latter. Mortality was less in proportion to population than it had been in the epidemic of 1837–40. It was also lower than in countries without vaccination or in Britain before the vaccination period. The epidemic led to the appointment of a Select Committee which confirmed the principle of compulsion and adopted a list of recommendations put before them by Simon.

Most of these were embodied in the Vaccination Act, 1871. The appointment of paid vaccination officers became compulsory. Boards of Guardians had had the power to establish such posts since 1867 and well over 100 had done so. Registrars were to send them monthly lists of infant births and deaths, and vaccinators were to send certificates of vaccination; by comparing the two and by prosecuting defaulting parents, the officer could ensure maximum compliance with the law. Their returns testify to their success. Between 1872 and 1883, more than ninety-five per cent of all children born were satisfactorily accounted for. This result, despite busy anti-vaccinationist propaganda, defective registration, and the necessity of working through the Poor Law authority with all its disagreeable associations, represents a considerable feat of administration. Vaccination, said The Times in 1874, was 'a type of thorough and effective technical administration'.[31] And the Lancet called it in 1876 'a perfect marvel of successful administration'.[32]

The state's action in regard to vaccination advanced far beyond what English governments have attempted since. No modern government, even when facing a deadly disease like diphtheria and possessing a certain prophylactic, has dared to force such a preventive method upon its civilian population. In intruding 'the parliamentary lancet' between parent and child the nineteenth-century state had fewer qualms. The reason seems to be that the scheme originated in, and was maintained by, organized medical pressure: one of the earliest triumphs of this powerful factor in British politics. Medical opinion was unanimous. The remedy was cheap and certain. (Two factors notably absent from the field of public health.) Governments and parliament could hardly withstand such pressure, and did not, in any case, wish to. In this field, even more than in emigrant regulation, 'experimental science . . . spoke in the imperative mood'.[33]

On most health questions, science could not speak in the imperative mood because it did not know what to say. As Simon put it when talking of cholera, 'our utmost power is but perhaps some very little

[31] ibid., 13.   [32] ibid.   [33] MacDonagh (1961), 252.

ability of palliation'. The answer, as he saw, lay in research, sponsored where necessary, by the government. As Medical Officer of Health to the City of London, he had helped to persuade Sir Benjamin Hall to do so in 1854. Hall was, to use his own words, 'impressed by the necessity of some means by which this department [the General Board of Health] might be enabled to avail itself of the best medical assistance in matters coming within the domain of scientific medical enquiry'.[34] Hence he appointed a Medical Council to investigate the cholera epidemic then raging. It consisted of thirteen eminent practitioners and scientists. Divided into three committees, the Council investigated, fruitlessly, the problem of treatment, compiled useful statistics, and corresponded with foreign scientists. Simon himself served on the Committee for Scientic Inquiries, which was concerned with the causes of the disease. They instituted several lines of investigation—meteorological, microscopical, chemical and medical—concluding cautiously that the determinants of the disease 'belong less to the water than to the air'.[35] They also called for further research into the possibility of propagation by water. The importance of the Council lay not in its work, but in its very existence. 'Science [had] at length been recognized by the state as the ally of civil jurisprudence and as the guide to a more enlightened code of medical policy.'[36] For the first time, the government had promoted and financed medical research of the highest possible calibre.

Simon investigated further the possibility that cholera was a water-borne disease. Snow had already published evidence tending to confirm this theory, and Farr had carried out a pilot analysis of the 1854 epidemic in South London as effected by water-supply. Simon applied the technique pioneered by Snow and Farr in a much more extensive study. It covered both the epidemics of 1848–9 and 1853–4, over an area inhabited by 500,000 people whose drinking-water came from two suppliers, the Southwark and Vauxhall, and the Lambeth Companies. The customers of the two companies, living sometimes in the same street, were homogeneous in all relevant factors except water-supply. The object of the inquiry was to calculate separately the cholera death-rates of the clients of the two companies in each epidemic. At the earlier period, the Lambeth consumers' figure was 125 per 10,000 as compared with 118 per 10,000 for the Southwark group. By 1854, however, the Lambeth Company had transferred its intake-point to the Thames at Ditton —'as good a water as any distributed in London';[37] whereas the

[34] R. J. Lambert, *Sir John Simon, 1816–1904* (1963), 227.
[35] ibid., 228.   [36] ibid.   [37] ibid., 247.

Southwark supply was still drawn, unfiltered, from the Thames at Battersea—'perhaps the filthiest stuff ever drunk by a civilized community'.[38] As a result, the cholera death-rate among those who drank Lambeth water sank from 125 to 37 per 10,000 in the second epidemic; while the consumers of Southwark water died at a higher rate—130 per 10,000 as compared with 118. The enquiry demonstrated the importance of pure water, but the method of transmission of the disease by a specific organism remained undiscovered. Hence Simon insisted that the inquiry only gave more exact knowledge of one factor; it did not preclude the possibility of others.

In the epidemic of 1865–6, Simon enlisted seven eminent London doctors for further research into the treatment, biochemistry, anatomical changes, symptoms and communicability of cholera. He got only £1,500 of the £2,000 he asked for, and part of the programme had to be abandoned. The findings were on certain points worth while but did not constitute a major breakthrough. He recognized that the limits of certain lines of enquiry had been reached.

Meanwhile, he had followed with close interest the work of Pasteur and others on micro-organisms as the causes of disease. It convinced him that the most rewarding discoveries for preventive medicine might now be made in the laboratory rather than in the field. 'The present,' he wrote, 'is a time of the most extraordinary transition and progress in the sciences which are fundamental to medicine; so much so, that scarcely a month passes without raising some new pathological question which bears upon principles of action; and this department, practically considered, would be lagging far behind the knowledge which ought to be represented in its administration and might often be spreading mere obsolete error among persons who look to it for intelligence, if it were not itself able to submit such questions to examination, and thus ... to take part in the scientific reconstruction which is in progress.'[39] From 1865 onwards the department began to divert some of its funds to fundamental research, as distinct from research prompted by special emergencies, such as epidemics.

Simon selected two main areas of study; first, the chemistry of the morbid processes. Biochemical research was of the highest importance, since it was 'unwise to assume that the ends of preventive and curative medicine can be reached till our practical proceedings shall have got to be based on the very chemical formula of the morbid process'.[40] The project was entrusted to Dr J. L. W. Thudichum,

[38] ibid., 247–8.   [39] ibid., 401.   [40] ibid., 402.

who has been described by his twentieth-century biographer as 'the greatest chemist between Justus von Liebig and Emil Fischer and one of the truly original minds in biochemistry'.[41] Thudichum worked under the Privy Council for nearly twenty years. He made fundamental contributions to the chemistry of the pigments of blood, bile and urine, and pioneered the use of the spectroscope in such analysis. He followed this with a pioneering study of the chemistry of the brain. The second area for special study was the etiology of contagion, a problem then attracting the attention of many of the best scientific minds in Europe. A French scientist, Jean-Antoine Villemin, had recently announced experimental proof of the communicability of tuberculosis by a specific organism. Unfortunately he had not been able to isolate the bacillus, and his discovery was greeted with a good deal of scepticism. Simon was impressed, nevertheless. He made time amidst his official work to return to his old laboratory at St Thomas's Hospital, where he carried out a series of controlled experiments on rabbits, using Villemin's technique. In 1867, he read a paper confirming the inoculability of the tubercle bacillus. Thereafter, Villemin was taken much more seriously. The task of carrying on the research fell to John Burdon Sanderson. Simon set him to work on a more elaborate series of experiments, helping out in the laboratory himself. By 1868, the inoculability of the tubercle bacillus received the fullest verification possible. Sanderson went on to carry out a valuable series of studies on the natural history of contagia. By 1871, he had confirmed for the morbid contagia what Pasteur had earlier discovered for putrefactive and fermentatory processes—that each specific contagium was a living, self-multiplying organic form. These advances helped to establish the germ theory in Britain. Studies of wound infection and blood poisoning followed, in which Sanderson identified the agents of pyaemia and septicaemia.

As time went on, Simon's research team grew in size without losing any of its lustre. Baxter ascertained the relative effectiveness of disinfectants against common contagia. Creighton investigated the anatomy and aetiology of cancer. Klein joined Sanderson in the field of bacteriology, which was then the most important development in European research. He identified the pathogenic organism of sheep-pox and claimed to have discovered and described the causal agent of typhoid—though, in the latter case, Simon was not convinced by the evidence. After some work on scarlet fever, he went on to isolate the specific organism of pneumo-enteritis of swine. This was one of

[41] ibid.

the first occasions on which such a thing had been done, and a major step forward in the science of bacteriology.

Generally speaking, these researches were carried on by scientists working on their own premises, and on a four-figure annual budget. Yet in an age of fanatical economy, there were no complaints, apart from an occasional parliamentary question, about this apparently unproductive use of public money. 'That such work should be carried out and published at the national cost,' wrote the *Times*, 'is an admirable illustration of the enlightened manner in which the Medical Department of the Privy Council is conducted.' The medical press took up the chorus. The reports were 'most valuable contributions towards the solution of the deepest problems in practical medicine'. State-sponsored research had made 'discoveries which in the point of physiological interest and practical importance cannot be too highly estimated'. 'Crucially scientific, the whole body of work is unique in sanitary literature.'[42] Simon had set in motion a process which was to lead, decades later, to the setting up of the Medical Research Council.

C. THE HOME OFFICE AND THE PROVINCIAL POLICE[43]

The origin of the police outside the metropolis was the Municipal Corporations Act, 1835, which required each borough to establish a force. Little more than half of them even claimed to have complied within two years of its passing. Most of the remainder alleged that they had done so at intervals over the next fifteen years. But an enquiry during the year 1856–7 showed that thirteen boroughs had never implemented the Act.[44] It was a typical reform of the old type, with no administrative machinery to carry it into effect. Counties were permitted to establish police forces by an Act of 1839. By 1856, almost half had still not adopted the Act, while some of the remainder had done so for only part of their areas. The County and Borough Police Act, 1856, made it obligatory for counties, as well as boroughs, to have forces. It differed from the earlier measures in providing administrative means—inspection and exchequer grants—by which its terms were to be carried into effect. The effectiveness of the new system may be judged by the fact that within two years of the passing

[42] ibid., 404.

[43] H. Parris, 'The Home Office and the Provincial Police, 1856–70', *Public Law* (1961).

[44] J. M. Hart, 'Reform of the Borough Police, 1835–56', *EHR*, lxx (1955), 416. PRO. HO 65/3: circular, January 1, 1858.

of the Act, all the counties but one, and the great majority of the boroughs, not only had forces, but efficient forces.

The Act authorized the payment of an Exchequer grant equivalent to twenty-five per cent of the cost of pay and clothing to an authority whose force was found, on inspection, to be 'in a state of efficiency in point of numbers and discipline'.[45] The Inspectors judged efficiency in numbers primarily by the ratio of constables to population,[46] but a higher ratio was thought necessary in boroughs. In urban conditions, the Home Secretary could 'not give any sanction to the rule that a police force is to be considered sufficient in point of numbers if it is in the proportion of one man to a thousand, and he thinks that although it is possible that in some places that might be a sufficient number, experience has shown that in towns with a large and dense population a larger proportion is requisite'.[47] In practice, approved ratios varied between wide limits: 1 : 558 in the case of Liverpool to 1 : 2,733 in the case of Rutlandshire, for example. The test of efficiency in discipline was that a force should have enough superior officers to supervise the constables on duty continuously and regularly.

The Act provided for three Inspectors of Constabulary. Major-General William Cartwright, a veteran of the Peninsular War and Waterloo, appears to have had no police experience. Lieutenant-Colonel John Woodford, on the other hand, had been Chief Constable of the Lancashire Constabulary since its foundation. Captain Edward Willis, similarly, had been Chief Constable of Manchester. The three men divided England and Wales between them, each taking a distinct geographical district. Equal and independent in status, they were not 'men from Whitehall'. They lived in their districts and worked from their homes. They were capable of setting up administrative machinery apart from that of the Home Office. For example, forces in Cartwright's district sent him information about men dismissed, which he circulated each quarter, 'by which means no constable, found unfit for one force, can enter another'.[48] Moreover, the Inspectors could influence police authorities directly, apart from any action that might follow their recommendations to the Home Secretary. Between 1856 and 1871, for instance, Caernarvonshire was the scene of large-scale disturbances as a result of enclosures. They were eventually brought to an end by forming the disturbed area into a separate police district with an increased establishment

[45] 19 and 20 Vict., c. 69, s. 16.   [46] 2 and 3 Vict., c. 93, s. 1.
[47] PRO. HO 65/3: Letter to Woodford, October 21, 1856.
[48] P.P. 1860. lvii, 534.

and higher rates than the rest of the county. The authority was very reluctant to take this step and 'undoubtedly, the person who prevailed upon the magistrates to take a decision in the matter was Cartwright. He withheld his report to the Home Secretary until he saw what course they would take. In a letter to the chairman of quarter sessions he declared that a special police district was necessary: "Without some understanding that some steps are taken to prevent a repetition of these offences, I cannot report the force efficient" '.[49] Faced with the loss of grant, the magistrates adopted Cartwright's suggestion.

The Home Office staff was so small—less than forty when the Act came into operation—that no elaborate organization for police business was needed. Virtually no decisions were taken below Under-Secretary level, and only unimportant cases at that level. Horatio Waddington was Permanent Under-Secretary during the early years of the 1856 Act. An exchange of minutes makes clear the responsibility entrusted to him. 'These are the fees that are always sanctioned,' wrote an anonymous clerk on a scale submitted by the magistrates of County Durham: 'Then sanction them in this case,' ordered his superior.[50] On occasion, however, Waddington could persuade the Secretary of State to think again. When Cheshire sought permission to train police in the use of the rifle and to supply rifles from the police rate, the Home Secretary was inclined to sanction the training though not the issue of rifles. Waddington commented: 'It seems impossible to deal with this question in one county . . . only. Considered with reference to the whole kingdom it is one of the most serious nature and seems to be to be well worthy of a *Cabinet* deliberation. It has been frequently suggested to organize the Metropolitan Police *militairement* and always repudiated. It seems highly unconstitutional.'[51] The Home Secretary saw the force of this, refused the Cheshire application on both points, and set a precedent which was followed in other instances.

All important cases, and many that were not, went to the Home Secretary for his personal decision. This is not to say, however, that incumbents of that office exercised strong personal influence in this field. Indeed there is no evidence that any of them during the decade or so following the 1856 Act had any clear policy as to the way the police should develop. For example, it was widely held that small boroughs should amalgamate their forces with those of the counties, and many did so. But no Home Secretary made a determined effort

[49] J. O. Jones, 'The History of the Caernarvonshire Police Force, 1856–1900' (unpublished M.A. Thesis, Bangor, 1956), 131.
[50] PRO HO OS 6423.   [51] PRO HO 45. OS 6811.

to persuade them all to take this step. His role was normally to decide on recommendations put before him by others, especially the Inspectors. Most of these called for immediate decision. Each year he had to issue certificates of efficiency in respect of each force which had earned one. Where the Inspector's recommendation was firm either way, it was very unusual for the minister not to follow it. 'How could the Secretary of State report efficient against the recommendation of the Inspector?' reads an anonymous minute in one case.[52] In a sense, this was the simplest thing to do, but when it meant refusing an authority a grant, it required some courage. For authorities could almost always find spokesmen of social standing and political influence—mayors of boroughs, chairmen of quarter sessions, Lords Lieutenant, and Members of Parliament—to protest on their behalf. It is worth noting that Home Secretaries were less ready to follow the recommendations of Inspectors later in the century than during the first years of the Act's operation.[53] When, on the other hand, no immediate decision was needed, Secretaries of State had an easy alternative. They could do nothing at all. Inspectors repeatedly urged legislation to compel boroughs with populations under 5,000 to merge their forces with those of counties. There is no evidence that their proposals were even considered at ministerial level.

There was statutory provision for the establishment of fifty-nine county forces, allowing for separate forces in areas which are today administrative counties, e.g., East and West Suffolk. In a number of instances, however, adjoining counties appointed the same Chief Constable with results similar to those which would have followed a complete merger of the forces. The Soke of Peterborough, for example, appointed the Chief Constable of Northamptonshire to command its force, which in consequence 'worked precisely in the same way ... [there is the] same system of co-operation with adjoining forces ... the office work is done at Northampton ... the regulations are similar to those of the county of Northampton ... [and] the clothing is similar to the county of Northampton'.[54] Other cases of joint appointments were Cumberland and Westmorland; Cambridgeshire, Huntingdonshire and the Isle of Ely; and the Parts of Lincolnshire. These joint arrangements went some way towards eliminating small independent county forces. Rutlandshire remained the most striking example. Many of the Welsh county forces were,

---

[52] ibid. OS 6642.
[53] J. M. Hart, 'The County and Borough Police Act, 1856', *Public Administration*, xxxiv (1956), 409.　　　　[54] P.P. 1859 Sess. I, xxii, 428.

of course, small, but the advantages of amalgamation would have been less because of the large areas involved, the difficult nature of the countryside, and the backward state of communication, particularly railways, as compared with England.

With a single exception every county qualified for grant during the first two years of the Act's operation. Rutlandshire secured its certificate in 1862, and over the next decade few counties were ever in danger of forfeiting the Inspectors' favour. The initial differences turned in almost all cases on the number of police needed. There can be no doubt that the influence of the Inspectors was the main factor in raising the size of establishments. Such influence was often mentioned in correspondence with the Home Office: e.g., in the cases of East Suffolk and Breconshire.[55] Between 1857 and 1869, the establishment of the Caernarvonshire force rose from thirty-five to sixty; the increases were primarily 'the result of pressure from the government Inspectors. . . . Not until 1878 did the justices of their own accord and initiative decide that . . . an increased establishment was necessary'.[56]

It will be shown that a substantial number of boroughs resisted for years the persuasions of the Inspectors to increase the size of their forces. Why were the counties more amenable? Part, at least, of the answer seems to be that in the counties the Chief Constable was sufficiently independent in status to play an important role in negotiations between central government and local authority. When it suited him he was quite capable of siding with the Inspector against his own authority. Such a role is clearly apparent, for example, in a report made by the Devonshire Police Committee to the county justices in 1859. 'The committee have considered the question of the reorganization of the police force, and also the letter from the Government Inspector of Constabularies [sic], relative to the inadequacy of the force which were referred to them at the last quarter sessions, and are of the opinion that the new scheme of the Chief Constable so far as relates to the number and description of the force should be adopted. The Chief Constable informed the committee that he is quite unable to meet the wants of the various localities with the number of constables. The committee therefore recommend an addition to the force of twenty-two constables.'[57] The report was adopted.

---

[55] PRO HO 65/5; letter to E. Suffolk, July 31, 1857. 65/6; letter to Breconshire, January 17, 1863. [56] J. O. Jones, 115–16.

[57] W. J. Hutchings, *Out of the Blue: History of the Devon Constabulary* (n.d.), 49.

It was only a short step from siding with the Inspector for the Chief Constable to use the Inspector for his own purposes, as seems to have been done in Buckinghamshire. There, 'the men were grossly overworked and in 1858, *as a consequence of agitation by Captain Carter* (the Chief Constable), H.M. Inspector of Constabulary attended one of the justices' meetings and said outright that the force was not large enough to work efficiently. . . . It was therefore agreed to increase the force by sixteen men'.[58] The head of a borough force was, of course, so much under the thumb of his Watch Committee that it would have been dangerous for him to attempt a manoeuvre of this kind.

The effect of the 1856 Act on the boroughs was markedly slower. Fifteen years later there were still boroughs with no police forces at all. And there were still boroughs—some of them large and important—which had never qualified for a certificate of efficiency. Was it because the Home Secretary's powers over boroughs were less than over counties? The 1839 Act empowered him to make rules for the county constabularies. Those in force in the fifties and sixties regulated pay, set a maximum age and a minimum height for recruits, and precluded county forces from engaging men dismissed from other forces. Justices also had to get the Home Secretary's approval for changes in establishment and when appointing a Chief Constable. Similar rules for borough forces would, in a general sense, have been beneficial. But they would not have made them efficient 'in numbers and discipline'. Inspection and grant were the means used to raise the county forces to that level. All borough forces were liable to inspection, and all, save those boroughs whose population was below 5,000, were eligible for grant. The question is, why were these devices less effective in the boroughs than in the counties?

The 208 boroughs which had police powers during the first year of the Act's operation, 1856–7, may be divided into three groups: large boroughs—those over 20,000—numbered fifty-seven, rising to sixty-three after the census of 1861; medium boroughs—5–20,000—numbered eight-six, falling to eight-five after 1861; small boroughs —under 5,000—were sixty-five, falling to sixty after 1861.

The development of police in the large boroughs was almost as satisfactory as in the counties. All had forces when the Inspectors first visited them, and the great majority qualified for grant within two years of the passing of the Act. A number were, however, slower

[58] A. G. Hailstone, *100 Years of Law-Enforcement in Buckinghamshire: an Historical Survey* (1956), 12. (My italics.)

to achieve efficiency, and four —Ashton-under-Lyme, Macclesfield, Oldham and Stockport—had still not done so at the end of the period. Three large boroughs announced in 1856–7 that they would not accept a grant from the government. This was an empty gesture on the part of Gateshead, which on inspection failed to qualify for one in any case. But Sunderland and Southampton stuck to their principles even after being found eligible for grant.[59]

Among the medium boroughs, more than half were inefficient in 1856–7; but only fourteen remained so in 1869–70—sixteen per cent. Many forces in this group were consolidated; that is, the boroughs did not exercise their police powers, but had an agreement whereby the county provided police. As shown above, inefficiency among county forces was rare and there was no case of inefficiency among consolidated boroughs during the fifteen years after 1856. The number of consolidated medium boroughs rose from eleven to twenty-one during that period—more than twenty per cent. Among them were towns of some importance, such as Stafford and Gloucester.

The test of efficiency cannot be applied to the small boroughs. The 1856 Act excluded them from grant, and as the Home Office ruled in another context, where no grant was payable, 'it would be immaterial whether the [Inspector's] report . . . were favourable or unfavourable'.[60] Hence, the reports on small borough forces are often so vague that it is impossible to say whether they were efficient or not. In general, however, they were held to be inefficient and incapable of achieving efficiency because of their size. The Inspectors encouraged small boroughs to employ more men and improve discipline; but their comparative lack of success showed that inspection without grant achieved little. With the small boroughs, the Inspectors tried mainly to persuade them to consolidate with the counties.

The number of inefficient boroughs fell from sixty-three in 1857 to eighteen in 1870, largely as a result of the influence of the Inspectors. The case of Tynemouth was typical. In 1862, Woodford suggested an increase as a result of the population increase shown by the census of the previous year. 'This suggestion,' he reported, 'like all others tendered to the authorities of this borough having any tendency to add to the efficiency of their police force, was acted upon without loss of time, and . . . a few days later an augmentation of the force was ordered'.[61] Ready co-operation was the norm. All

[59] PRO HO 65/5. Letter to the Treasury, December 14, 1857.
[60] ibid. Letter to Cartwright, September 29, 1860.
[61] P.P. 1862, xlv, 494–5.

the more striking by contrast was the behaviour of the group of boroughs next to be considered.

There were forty chronically inefficient broughs, i.e., boroughs which failed to qualify for grant during three or more successive years. Had they anything in common besides inefficiency? Firstly, they were very unevenly distributed geographically. Twelve were in the industrial region of Lancashire, Cheshire and north-west Derbyshire, and eight in the three western counties of Somerset, Devon and Cornwall. Moreover, inefficiency was slower to disappear from those regions than elsewhere. Of the nineteen boroughs which remained inefficient in 1870, thirteen were in these two regions.

Secondly, there were two distinct types of inefficiency, corresponding largely to the regions indicated. In the north-west an increase in strength was in almost all cases the one thing wanting to make forces efficient. Congleton, which refused even to provide uniforms for its police until 1890,[62] was an exception, but Woodford's comment on the Bolton force was typical: 'The Inspector had every reason to be satisfied with the state and general appearance of this police force, but ... it is far from being sufficient in number.'[63] Forces elsewhere, on the other hand, and particularly in the south-west, tended to be inefficient generally. Bridgwater, with a superintendent and four constables for a population of over 10,000 was characteristic. 'The superintendent is the only officer who takes day duty, and he is infirm and appears incapable of much exertion. The constables perform night duty; and, with the exception of being seen when going on duty at nine o'clock in the evening, and when coming off duty at six o'clock in the morning, there appears to be scarcely any supervision.'[64]

After resisting for years the blandishments of Inspectors and the seductions of the grant, places like Blackburn, Beverley, Louth and Stalybridge at last yielded, brought their forces up to standard and kept them there. Were there general factors favouring such transformations? Was there, firstly, any connection between the volume of crime and the state of the police? In some cases, it seems, there was. For example, in reporting Barnstaple's force, with five men to a population over 11,000, inefficient, Willis drew attention to several undetected robberies which had occurred in the town. Soon after, the force was increased from five to ten and put under the command of a new superintendent transferred from the Metropolitan Police.[65]

[62] R. W. James, *To the Best of our Skill and Knowledge: a short history of the Cheshire Constabulary, 1857–1957* (n.d.), 115.   [63] P.P. 1867–8, xlvii, 711.
[64] ibid., 762.   [65] P.P. 1861, lii, 735; 1863, l, 275.

It is, however, difficult to show any general connection. If the police are inefficient, it is unlikely that their crime returns will be accurate. In any case, people are less likely to take the trouble to report a crime to an inefficient force. Paradoxically, a rise in efficiency might lead to an *increase* in the crime figures. When Barnstaple reported a significantly larger number of offences than the previous year, Willis pointed out that the 'increase . . . is more apparent than real and attributable to a considerable extent to the increased attention of the police in making records'.[66]

Hence, the Inspectors often supplemented the statistics with a qualitative statement of the volume of crime in a particular area. The proportion of constables to population in Exeter, for example, was well below the average for a large city: 'As, however, crime is light' the force was efficient nevertheless.[67] There had been serious murders in Breconshire and Wiltshire; but they did not detract from the efficiency of those forces, since crime was 'generally light'.[68] Similar comments occur in the reports on chronically inefficient boroughs. In Penzance crime was 'light considering the population'. In Tiverton crime was 'generally light'. In Congleton, 'generally speaking, crime and offences were all of a minor character'.[69] Thus, while there is little significance in the fact that the returns from chronically inefficient boroughs do not show crime there to have been above the average, it is noteworthy that there is some evidence pointing the other way. The most obvious connection between crime and the state of the police is that crime might be expected to flourish where the police were inefficient. But it is equally likely that inefficient police would be tolerated longest where there was least crime. This last statement seems to have been generally true of the chronically inefficient boroughs, and so far as the admittedly inconclusive evidence goes, the prevalence of crime does not seem to have been a general factor making for police improvement in such towns.

Secondly, it is worth considering whether there was any general connection between public order and the state of the police in the chronically inefficient boroughs. Had they been quiet country towns, undisturbed by industrial and political unrest, they might well have been content with small forces. But many of them were not such communities. Lancashire and Cheshire, in particular, had been among the most disturbed areas throughout the first half of the nineteenth century, and were also characterized by weak police forces. For example, of thirteen centres of Chartism in the two

66 P.P. 1863, 1, 275.   67 P.P. 1860, lvii, 612.
68 P.P. 1861, lii, 768, 770.   69 P.P. 1867, xxxvi, 535, 542. James, 117.

counties eight were also chronically inefficient boroughs.[70] The area was also the centre of the Plug Plot riots of 1842.[71] Chronically inefficient boroughs elsewhere had known similar periods of unrest. There had been Chartist rioting at Dewsbury during the winter of 1839–40, while it had been necessary to summon the military to put down bread riots at Tiverton in 1847.[72] There was clearly no natural law by which outbreaks of public disorder led inevitably to the establishment of efficient police forces.

Nevertheless, there seems to have come a point in several of these towns when a riot led the authorities to conclude that an efficient police force was a lesser evil than periodical anarchy. Thus in 1861 Beverley was 'more than once . . . in a state of anarchy, and . . . on October 16 . . . so seriously was the peace of the town threatened, the mayor found himself compelled to call upon the Chief Constable of the . . . East Riding of Yorkshire to afford him the means of preserving order'. The following year the borough implemented the 1835 Act, qualified for grant,[73] and kept it thereafter. At Stalybridge there were serious bread riots in 1863. Contingents of police from Cheshire and Lancashire were called in, as well as military aid. Eighty-three people were charged with rioting. Later in the year, the force was increased from thirteen to twenty-five men, was certified efficient for the first time,[74] and remained so. A riot at Oxford towards the end of 1867 was followed by the promotion of a local Act to amalgamate the forces of the city and the university, and the new force was recognized as efficient in the year 1868–9.[75] *Post hoc*, of course, is not *propter hoc*; but there may well have been some link between public order and police efficiency.

In urging boroughs to consolidate their forces with those of counties, the great argument the Inspectors could use was economy. The cost of policing Devizes fell from £259 to £150 a year on consolidation with Wiltshire, whose Chief Constable declared that if Salisbury, the last independent borough in the county, followed the example of the others, it would be possible to cut its force from eleven to six men.[76] When a similar step was under discussion at Kidderminster, the Inspector reported that the force could be

[70] A. Briggs (ed.), *Chartist Studies* (1959), 52n.
[71] A. G. Rose, 'The Plug Riots of 1842 in Lancashire and Cheshire', *Transactions of the Lancashire and Cheshire Antiquarian Society*, lxvii (1958).
[72] Hutchings, 153.
[73] P.P. 1862, xlv, 482, 495: 1863, l, 240, 252.
[74] James, 122–3; P.P. 1864, xlviii, 676.
[75] P.P. 1867–8, xxxvi, 39; 1868–9, xxxi, 6; 1870, xxxvi, 349.
[76] P.P. 1852–3 (603), 1st Report of the Select Committee on Police, 143–5.

reduced from sixteen to thirteen, because the borough would have 'the assistance of the county force for support'.[77] For very small boroughs, however, there was an even more economical alternative. They could ignore the 1835 Act and have virtually no police force at all. As late as 1870, six boroughs employed only one officer each, the largest being St Ives, with over 7,000 population. Pwllheli's single constable was paid £40 a year, rising to £52 10s. The only other police expenses were uniform and the occasional employment of special constables. The borough's police expenditure can hardly have averaged more than £60 a year from 1857 to 1879, when at last its 'force' merged with that of the county. From that date, three men were stationed in the borough and, even allowing for grant, there must have been some increase in the cost.[78]

The administration of the 1856 Act was remarkably successful. Inspection and grants ensured that the aims of the Act were realized at almost all points within a short period of years. The process was smoothest in the case of the counties. The boroughs presented greater difficulties, but, by the end of the period, chronic inefficiency was a regional rather than a national problem. The greatest failure was the continued survival of a number of small forces not consolidated with the counties. The practical difficulties they caused, were, however, localized. It was the grant of police powers to newly incorporated boroughs that created the twentieth-century problem of small borough forces, rather than the survival of ancient independent corporations. Here the border between administration and policy was reached. The Inspectors showed themselves to be good administrators; and it was from them rather than anyone within the Home Office itself, from the Secretary of State downwards, that the impetus for improvement came. But they did not prove effective advocates of new policies. To check the proliferation of new forces would have required a change of policy, which was not forthcoming until long after.

D. THE ALKALI ACTS

The administrative machinery set up under the Alkali Act, 1863, is an interesting early example of the employment of scientists in the civil service. By the middle of the nineteenth century, much of the countryside around Merseyside and Tyneside had been reduced by the chemical industry to a drab, lifeless, wasteland. 'The sturdy hawthorn,' wrote one observer, 'makes an attempt to look gay every

[77] P.P. 1865, xlv, 456. [78] J. O. Jones, 153, 161.

spring; but its leaves . . . dry up like tea leaves and soon drop off. The farmer may sow if he pleases, but he will only reap a row of straw. Cattle will not fatten . . . and sheep throw their lambs. Cows, too . . . cast their calves; and the human animals suffer from smarting eyes, disagreeable sensations in the throat, and irritating cough, and difficulties of breathing.'[79] The major cause was hydrochloric acid. Since 1823, when James Muspratt had built the first English works for the production of soda by the Leblanc process, the alkali trade had grown rapidly and was becoming the foundation of the heavy chemical industry in Britain. Sodium carbonate was essential for the manufacture of glass, soap and textiles. A by-product was hydrogen chloride gas, which on escaping from chimneys into the moisture of the atmosphere, descended in destructive clouds of acid. In 1862, Derby was persuaded to raise the matter in the Lords, and presided over the Select Committee which was formed. Evidence was given that the only remedy available—an action for damages at common law—was unsatisfactory. 'Partly in consequence of the expense such actions occasion, partly from the fact that while several works are in immediate juxtaposition, the difficulty of tracing the damage to any-one, or of apportioning it among several, is so great as to be all but insuperable; and . . . even when verdicts have been obtained, and compensation, however inadequate, awarded, a discontinuance of the nuisance has not in most cases been the result.'[80] Since the courts were unable to deal with the problem, administrative machinery was needed.

The result was the Alkali Act, 1863. Works were to be required to condense at least ninety-five per cent of the hydrogen chloride gas. The Board of Trade was to appoint an Inspector to see that they did so. Chemical manufacturers did not positively welcome government inspection. If the industry 'in its earlier stages had been subject to a system of inspection, and constant interference had taken place with its chemical experiments, combinations and processes, it would have been so paralysed that it never would have arrived at its present position.'[81] But the Inspector's discretion was a lesser evil than a statutory provision as to the precise mode in which condensation was to be carried out. Evidence had been given to the Select Committee that this was technically possible, but expert witnesses had disagreed as to the best technique. Hence the Act did not prescribe any specific way in which the problem was to be tackled.

[79] R. M. MacLeod, 'The Alkali Acts Administration, 1863–84: the emergence of the civil scientist, *Victorian Studies*, ix (1965), 87.
[80] ibid., 89.   [81] ibid., 89n.

To do so would have been to put a brake on technical progress. The problem was very similar to that of communication on railways a few years later.[82] Manufacturers would feel confident the Inspector would talk their technical language, and that they would be able to persuade him of the merits of any new system they might try. They would not have felt so confident of getting a new Act of Parliament every time a new condensation process was mooted. The Act was passed for five years only, in the first instance.

The first Inspector, Dr Robert Angus Smith, F.R.S., was a chemical consultant in Manchester. He had had a distinguished career, had studied with von Liebig, worked with Lyon Playfair, and taken part in several public inquiries. Four Sub-Inspectors were also appointed. From the start he had a very free hand. As he wrote later: 'I was at first appointed to attend only to [hydrochloric] acid escaping from alkali works but I found that the whole literature of escaping gases at works required to be made, that no one knew what my duties could be and that I had to teach myself as well as others.'[83]

At most works, condensing towers in which the evolving gases were passed over irrigated coke, and condensed liquid hydrochloric acid collected at the base, were put into operation even before inspection began. As Smith put it, 'even before I had the honour of being appointed Inspector I had become familiar with the possibility of complete condensation so that all fear of pressing on an improvement to an impracticable issue was removed from the mind'.[84] Measurement was the main difficulty. But 1865, Smith reported the widespread adoption of a technique developed by himself. The average escape was down to 1·28 per cent—easily within the legal limit of five per cent. Almost overnight, the deposit of acid was reduced from an estimated 13,000 tons to forty-three tons per annum. Twenty-six works were condensing 100 per cent of their gases, while none of the sixty-four works registered under the Act was outside the prescribed limit. Manufacturers began to see positive benefits in inspection when Smith suggested new and profitable ways of turning the former waste material into saleable products. Soon Smith and his colleagues found themselves acting as industrial consultants. Between March 1864 and January 1865 they paid over a thousand visits to the sixty-four works and to non-alkali plants which had gas problems, Smith explained his double role: 'It has been necessary to be very careful not to give such advice as might appear to be an interference; we have no power to decide on the mode of producing the desired result. At the same time, it so frequently happens that the

[82] Parris (1965), 216.   [83] MacLeod (1965), 91–2.   [84] ibid., 92.

necessary improvement is self-evident to those who are experienced, that any hesitation to advise would be unfair and indeed simple pedantry. This is more especially seen when the manufacturer himself has not at all thought on the subject, and is obliged either to seek advice or to remain inactive.'[85] The state was unintentionally providing a service to industry which ultimately reversed the relative economic importance of hydrochloric acid waste and alkali product.

By 1868, then, the original problem was solved, but instead of the Act being allowed to lapse, and the administrative machinery broken up, a new Act was passed without time limit. The reason was that new needs had succeeded to the old. As production increased, and as works multiplied, the escape of even a small proportion of the hydrogen chloride could seriously pollute the atmosphere. In any case, hydrochloric acid was not the only problem. Sulphurous and nitric acids were also serious threats. In 1872, the alkali inspectorate was transferred from the Board of Trade to the Local Government Board, and in that year Smith reported: 'Chemical works generally are greatly on the increase, and the power to repress escapes of gases does not increase with them. . . . The Alkali Act, which was excellent for a time and has done some good, is becoming less valuable daily. When alkali works accumulate in one place they make even one per cent of escape a great evil'.[86] The eventual result was the Alkali Act (1864) Amendment Act, 1874. It contained three innovations which reflected administrative experience. Firstly, it extended to new kinds of works and gases other than hydrogen chloride. Secondly, it substituted a volumetric test for escaping gas (0·2 grain of hydrochloric acid per cubic foot) for the proportionate test (not more than five per cent of the total gas generated). The reason for the change had been explained by Smith. 'The present method of judging by percentages is a great obstruction, because no action can be brought unless the gas going away can be measured into parts of the total evolved. Now all the random and many of the most dangerous escapes are beyond measurement, we may as well attempt to measure the speed of the wind when it has passed us.'[87] Thirdly, it required firms not merely to prevent the escape of gas, but to use the 'best practicable means' of doing so. The significance of this is that it introduced a dynamic element into administration. The original approach had been that the problem was something to be solved once and for all. Now it was recognized that the problems of an industrial society are not of that order. Technical advance makes improved methods available. The Inspectors would have power to

[85] ibid., 93.　　　　[86] ibid., 96.　　　　[87] ibid.

243

press them on manufacturers in place of those already in use. In Smith's words, they would be 'enforcing the acquisition of sustained improvements'.[88] The *Chemical News* sang his praises: 'If the Act is successful the result is mainly due to his zeal, tact, and intelligence. His method has been to lead, not to drive, the interests affected. He does not seek to lay down at once a hard-and-fast line, but as a truly practical man he aims at and effects gradual improvement. We can wish nothing better for the cause of sanitary reform than that all Inspectors who have to deal with "standards" may sit at his feet.'[89]

New sources of pollution continued to arise, however. Sulphuretted hydrogen from the waste heaps of alkali works was one. Since such deposits were not covered by the Act, the Inspectors had no power over them. Cement works were not covered by the Act either. In 1875, Queen Victoria complained that ammonia vapour from one was making Osborne uninhabitable. Smith went down, but could not persuade the owner to remedy the nuisance. Complaints such as these led to the setting up of the Royal Commission on Noxious Vapours in 1876.

The Commissioners reported a paradoxical divergence of attitude towards the organization of inspection. Manufacturers wished it to remain a function of central government. Local inspection, they felt, would be inefficient and would vary in rigour from one area to another. Local officers would have less technical knowledge—essential to the working of the 'best practicable means' test, which was favoured by manufacturers since it gave them scope to experiment. They also feared that local inspection would be partial, vexatious, and not conducive to industrial progress. They had found central inspection not unduly severe. 'These trades,' they argued, 'cannot be carried on with absolute innocuousness. Occasional forbearance will be as necessary a quality in an Inspector as vigilance and firmness, and more likely to be found in a government officer than in a local officer.'[90]

Authoritative spokesmen from Whitehall, on the other hand, wanted to transfer the responsibility to local authorities. For the Local Government Board, both Lambert and Simon argued that local inspection was more effective, and any further legislation should extend the powers of local authorities, not those of the central government. Simon argued that 'the central government should act not as inspector of nuisances, but as inspector of nuisance authorities. ... Any deviation from this principle must, on the one hand, embarrass central government with duties which it cannot properly

[88] ibid., 97.　　　[89] ibid.　　　[90] ibid., 103.

244

discharge, and on the other hand, hinder local authorities from acquiring a proper sense of their duties to the public'.[91] But would a local authority hold the balance even? The typical county, dominated by landowners, would be likely to penalize the manufacturers. A borough, on the other hand, might fall under the control of powerful firms, and turn a blind eye to their shortcomings. The Commission recommended that central control should continue, with more Inspectors and wider powers.

The Alkali, etc., Works Regulation Act, 1881, embodied many of the Commission's recommendations. It provided for increased control in three ways: first, it extended fixed standards to sulphuric and nitric acid; second, it brought more than a dozen new kinds of works under the 'best practicable means' test; and third, it gave the Local Government Board power to establish inspectorial control of cement and salt works by Provisional Order, as soon as feasible means of regulation could be worked out. All works emitting the scheduled acids were required to pay a registration fee. Although the motive here was mainly economy, it constituted also a licensing scheme. It became potentially possible to refuse registration to a defaulting firm, and thus attacked them on a second front. The number of works under inspection rose from approximately 240 to almost 1,000.

One of Smith's priorities under the new Act was to extend inspection to cement and salt works. He instructed his staff to give special thought to the question. In regard to the former, he worked out new principles for the construction of furnaces and a scheme for the achievement of successive stages of purity. Similarly, he set enquiries afoot to discover the 'best practicable means' for salt works. These efforts culminated in a Provisional Order, passed without debate in 1884. Further extensions were made by the same means in 1892 and 1906. The last of these—a consolidating order—is the basis of vapour regulation at the present time.

The Alkali Acts administration led to a significant debate concerning the function of Inspectors. The public, the politicians and the administrators tended to see them as technical policemen with the responsibility of detecting offenders and prosecuting them before the courts. The Royal Commission on Noxious Vapours, for example, noting that only four prosecutions had taken place over fifteen years, went on: 'In the opinion of many of the witnesses, this policy, at first expedient, has been unnecessarily prolonged; and we believe that, although allowance should have been made for the shortcomings of manufacturers honestly striving to render due obedience

[91] ibid., 103n.

245

to the law, more frequent instances of severity exercised towards those known to have been animated by a different spirit, would have been advantageous to the public, and desirable in the interests of the manufacturers themselves.'[92] In consequence, Lambert, Permanent Secretary of the Local Government Board, ordered Smith to take a tougher line. The Inspector reported that the manager of a firm at Widnes had accidentally allowed an escape of gas in excess of the legal standard. Lambert referred the case to the minister. 'You know how often it has been alleged that the Inspector omits to take proceedings, and you will be able to say whether or not Messrs. Snape should be allowed to escape on the present occasion.' Sclater-Booth gave his fiat: 'Let proceedings be taken.'[93] The firm apologized profusely and pleaded that the prosecution should be dropped. Lambert remained unmoved. 'The Board regret the necessity of proceedings in these cases but so much blame has been incurred by the supposed indisposition of the Board to enforce the provisions of the Act that they do not feel justified in dispensing with these actions.'[94] The firm paid the maximum fine of £50 without waiting for the case to open, and further proceedings were dropped.

Smith's conception of his role was entirely different. Legal enforcement seemed to him likely to do more harm than good. As he said to Lambert when forwarding some papers relating to a prosecution pending, 'I forward the papers because, among other reasons, they show the spirit of the alkali-makers and their relation to inspection. To be found fault with causes a most serious commotion. If trials were frequent this delicacy of feeling would disappear.' Two days later, he added: 'I do not think it well to trouble the Board with feelings, but this enclosure is only a specimen of much that I was obliged to hear and perhaps there is no harm in showing the Board for once somewhat of the inner workings of the inspection.'[95] Legal action would threaten Smith's good relations with the industry. Hence, he was reluctant to prosecute, and preferred to do so only on specific instructions from his superiors. 'Having been so much blamed for clemency I have no desire to compensate by an act of cruelty, but as I have been blamed for taking so much responsibility upon myself, I feel inclined in this case to relieve myself if possible of some.'[96] As he saw it, the Inspector must be a technologist, not a policeman. The basis of his influence must be science, not law. As he told the Royal Commission on Noxious Vapours: 'I labour in the . . . field of chemical works, repressing some evil, doing some good, I think, but not so much as I wish, for I see that it is invention

[92] ibid., 102.   [93] ibid., 104–5.   [94] ibid., 105.   [95] ibid.   [96] ibid., 105n.

that is required, and not inspection merely. Invention is slow, and if ideas are quick the [experiments] are not so. Nature with which we struggle is so complex.'[97] The trade appreciated his attitude. A passage from the *Chemical News* may stand as his memorial: 'His thorough knowledge of industrial chemistry, his suggestive and fruitful mind, his tact, courtesy and patience, his clear oversight of the whole field of operations, and of the rival interests to be dealt with, cannot be too highly esteemed. ... His method of leading instead of driving the chemical manufacturers, and of substituting whenever possible, remonstrance and advice for summonses and fines, is perhaps slow, but it is sure. We all know that a part of the British public value remedial agencies and reforms of every kind simply in proportion to the disturbance they create. ... Dr Smith remarks that, "Some of the public would have preferred to see the Inspectors frequently in court with cases of complaint, but I know well that information must grow and habit must grow, and that to torment men into doing what required much time to learn was to return to the old system of teaching by the cane instead of through the intellect'.[98]

E. TREASURY CONTROL

The departments so far considered were ships on a wide sea. Each tended to sail on its own course for long periods of time without coming within hailing distance of another. The Treasury, on the other hand, was in constant contact with other departments over estimates and establishment. What was the nature of this contact? Did Treasury control restrict the growth of administration? The departments grouped in this chapter illustrate different aspects of the question. In relation to the police, the Home Office was eminently a spending department. H.M. Inspectors of Constabulary, in urging police authorities to employ more constables, and to increase the proportion of higher-paid officers, were in effect pressing the tax-payers' money into palms which were not always anxious to receive it. The Treasury seems to have been content that they should do so. The Medical Department of the Privy Council may not have got all the money they wanted, but managed to get a good deal. One factor in their success was Simon's ability to blind administrators with science. Lingen was the last person to give money away without careful scrutiny. Yet he confessed in reference to one of Simon's demands: 'I do not know who is to check the assertions of experts

[97] MacLeod (1965), 110.   [98] ibid., 109n.

when the government has once undertaken a class of duties which none but such persons understand.'[99] The Local Government Board, too, was accustomed to reductions in its estimates for the Alkali Acts administration.[100] But it would be hard to argue that its development was seriously hampered by Treasury control.

Such an argument has, however, been advanced in relation to one department considered in this chapter: the regulation of the emigrant traffic. Apropos of the famine period, for example, MacDonagh writes: 'It may seem extraordinary that the corps was not increased. Even twenty additional officers, quite sufficient to perfect the protective system up to the limit of its statutory capacity, would have cost only £4,000 per annum. But the Treasury of the 1840s strove not only to control public spending but also to prevent, so far as possible, every new expenditure. ... Down to 1842, the executive officers had even to meet many official expenses from their own pockets. Henry at Liverpool was so overwhelmed by inspections and court appearances that he employed a clerk privately to keep his returns and statistics. Friend also employed his own assistant to maintain the Cork office while he visited the outport. Even such items as postage, the printing of handbills and (despite many years of agitation) travelling expenses to meet vessels in distress, were not regularly defrayed by the Treasury. The crowning absurdity came in 1845 when in order to secure a badly needed assistant at Liverpool the Commissioners had to reduce the salary of one of their existing officers from £208 to £120. A species of musical chairs then developed, at the end of which it was the unfortunate Lieutenant Shuttleworth of Sligo, possibly the most overworked of all Irish officers, who was the victim. All of which makes it clear why the climate was unfavourable to any, let alone a sufficient, increase of staff.'[101]

A full account of Treasury control would require a volume in itself. What must be done here is first to stress that it was not a constant influence but developed mainly, like so much else in British central administration, during the middle decades of the nineteenth century. Before that period, the Colonial Office was like many other departments, not 'a unit in an accounting system, ... [but] an independent institution that merely reported its expenditures annually to the Treasury and observed, within limits, the principles of economy that the age enjoined on all departments. It received its own revenue, it paid its own bills. The revenue, admittedly, was not enough to meet all the bills but in drawing on the Exchequer for

[99] Lambert (1962), 16.   [100] MacLeod (1965), 90.
[101] MacDonagh (1961), 168–9; cf. 268, 299, 319, etc.

block grants, the department paid for the services of the clerks of the Exchequer according to a form prescribed centuries before the Treasury assumed the central role among the government departments, and thus, in form at least, it did not prejudice its independent and equal status'.[102] The position of the Mint was similar. 'The expenses of the establishment are now defrayed, partly by profits derived from the silver and copper coinages, partly from the consolidated fund by a grant given to the Mint by an old Act of Parliament, and partly by a sum annually voted upon an estimate.'[103] Nevertheless, Treasury control was growing. In the case of the Colonial Office, 'the appearance of independence [was] to a considerable extent illusory by 1830. The size of salaries and the number of persons receiving them were . . . determined outside the department. By 1830 the awarding of pensions and the determination of their size had also passed out of the hands of the Secretary of State. In addition, by 1830, the provision of accommodation for the office was decided by the Treasury, stationery and printing were obtained through prescribed channels and even the supply of coal had come under Parliamentary scrutiny'.[104] Similarly with the Mint, where the Chancellor of the Exchequer had agreed 'to the introduction of a Bill which will provide that the whole service of the Mint shall in future be regularly voted upon estimate'.[105]

The control exercised by the Treasury over superannuation was a key step in the development of control of establishments. By fixing conditions which it considered desirable, the Treasury was able to move towards standard conditions throughout the civil service. Power to grant superannuation allowances was given to the Treasury by the Superannuation Act (3 Geo. IV, c. 113). To help in the determination of a proper figure and 'to stimulate all public servants to attend constantly to the duties of their offices', each department had to state, with each claim, 'the number of days on which the individual has been absent from his official duties during each of the preceding ten years, distinguishing whether such absence was by leave or without leave or by reason of sickness. In many public offices a record is kept of the attendance of the officers and clerks every day. And in those offices in which either no record is kept or an imperfect one, the Treasury might require a perfect record to be kept in future . . . [thus] a strong stimulus and a constant inducement

[102] Young, 147.
[103] Melbourne Papers. Labouchere to Melbourne, December 20, 1836.
[104] Young, 147.
[105] Melbourne Papers. Labouchere to Melbourne, December 20, 1836.

to regular attendance would be created in all the departments of the government'.[106] The suggestion seems to have been acted upon. But in response to a Treasury circular calling for regular hours for all clerks, which was sent round in 1830, the Colonial Office pointed out that fixed hours would not necessarily mean more work. 'So long as certain definite tasks are required of any public servants as the fixed and indispensable measure of their duty, it will be vain to look to the same persons for any additional voluntary exertions.'[107] The principle was already applied in that department. 'Senior clerks were men of privilege. They had no set hours of attendance, and usually wrote their drafts at home, since the frequent interruptions made composition difficult at the office. Henry Taylor could talk with his Benthamite friends at breakfasts, which sometimes went on until three o'clock in the afternoon, without feeling that he was neglecting his duties; his serious work was done at home in the evenings.'[108] But this was exceptional. So far as the general run of business was concerned, Treasury pressure for regular attendance was clearly justified.

Departments could not ignore it without jeopardizing the prospects of their staff when the time came to retire. For in this sphere, the word of the Treasury was final. The courts would entertain no appeal from its decisions. It is perhaps surprising that this administrative jurisdiction found so few critics. Most people would have echoed the verdict of a Select Committee of the Commons. 'The grant of each superannuation is submitted to a committee of Lords of the Treasury, who determine every case according to its merits and circumstances. Your committee think such a tribunal as effective a one as can be formed for the purpose.'[109]

But from the Treasury windows, the outlook was often gloomy. It was one thing to lay down general principles, quite another to enforce them. Trevelyan's approach to control of establishments, for example, was hard to challenge in principle. 'The revision of office estimates seems to belong in a peculiar manner to the executive government. No investigation by persons who are not connected with the different offices in the daily transaction of business can give them such a hold over the interior arrangements as to enable them to pronounce with confidence that so many offices and such and such rates of salary are required for the proper transaction of the business —and this seems to have been felt by both the finance committees of last session which confined themselves to making general observa-

[106] Grey Papers: 2nd Earl. Finance 14/8/17.　　[107] Young, 92–3.
[108] ibid., 92.　　[109] P.P. 1847–8, xviii, 33.

tions on the establishment submitted to their consideration and remitted the more detailed investigation and revision of them to the executive government. This was expressly done by the civil finance committee in regard to the Treasury and we have accordingly bestowed great pains on the subject.'[110] But how was this to be applied to a simple question like travelling expenses? The conversation between two of Trollope's civil servants, on their way to Tavistock, must have been repeated in essence a thousand times. 'We'll get a chaise at Plymouth,' said Alaric. 'I think there will be a public conveyance,' said Neverbend. 'But a chaise will be the quickest,' said the one. 'And much the dearest,' said the other. 'That won't signify much to us,' said Alaric, 'We shan't pay the bill.'[111] The problem was not wholly fictional. 'My messengers complain of their inferior allowance when they go to Balmoral. It appears that the messengers of the Home Office and Foreign Office get between £4 and £5 for each journey, whereas mine get only thirty shillings, which barely pays their journey. They do not complain of the difference on every other journey, but when they go to the Queen they think they ought to be put on an equality with their colleagues. Pray see into this.'[112] Exceptionally, a Chancellor might get a tip from a department. Bromley of the Admiralty wrote to Disraeli: 'Press for a reduction in the number of seamen and marines . . . If you can carry *this* I would give way to Sir John Pakington [First Lord of the Admiralty] not to reduce either the vote for wages or stores.'[113] With such unusual help forthcoming, it is not surprising to find a correspondent of Disraeli's writing: 'We want a Treasury spy—a Bromley—in each department, to warn us of fraudulent demands and to check the expenditure on the various grants.'[114] But this was a counsel of perfection. Usually it was necessary to rely on Trevelyan's device of investigation by small committees representing the Treasury and the department concerned. They were useful up to a point but their limitations are indicated by the frequency with which such investigations had to be repeated. 'Hunt is in town, as he and Mr Cave are on a Committee of enquiry into the establishment of the Board of Trade which is always being revised and never gets any better.'[115]

[110] PRO 30/22/7. Trevelyan to Russell, March 24, 1849.
[111] Trollope, 80.
[112] PRO 30/22/9. Russell to Lewis, August 14, 1851.
[113] Disraeli Papers. Bromley to Disraeli, January 14, 1859.
[114] Moneypenny and Buckle, i, 1654n.
[115] Disraeli Papers. Fremantle to Disraeli, September 1, 1866.

Proposals for new expenditure needed special caution. Each had to be scrutinized as a seed which might grow into something of large proportions. 'The charge for the magnetic observations began in 1839, and was to last for three years; in 1842 it was extended to 1845, and has since been prolonged. Without wishing to object to this particular vote, your Committee think it right to point the attention of Parliament to the manner in which temporary charges may become permanent.'[116] Pump-priming grants were especially difficult. In education, for example, the object of the grants was to stimulate private expenditure. In so far as the policy succeeded, grants tended to rise. If there were any sign of falling demand for grants, it would have been a danger signal for the policy. 'Does the Treasury exercise any control over the education votes?' The question was put to the Financial Secretary in 1860 by one of his predecessors, Northcote. 'I think I may say no control,' was the reply. 'Certain Minutes of the Council . . . are the conditions of the grant and they constitute a pledge to the public that while those Minutes exist, all who like to avail themselves of them may get the money.'[117] He went on to agree that a simple change, such as reducing the number of days on which pupils had to attend in order to qualify for the capitation grant, might considerably add to the amount of expenditure under the education vote. Such changes did not require Treasury sanction, even on financial grounds. The exchange took place on the eve of the introduction of payment-by-results. But the new system, though radically different from the old, was not any more susceptible to Treasury control.

Exchequer grants were always difficult. When in 1846 the cost-of-prosecutions grant was brought in, which had the effect of transferring the burden from county rates to national funds, expenditure under this head soon rose from £80,000 to £130,000 a year. A parliamentary committee commented: 'The Treasury do not . . . exercise any control over the expenditure or any interference with the rate of payment, provided they do not exceed the usual average. . . . [This] appears to indicate the necessity of establishing some more efficient check upon this expenditure. . . . It might . . . be desirable, that from the opportunity of comparison between the costs of different counties, and the experience of Assizes and Quarter Sessions, some scale of fees and expenses should be prepared and recommended for general adoption.'[118]

Another loophole was the ability of departments to retain balances

[116] P.P. 1847–8, xviii, 28.   [117] P.P. 1860, ix, 504.
[118] P.P. 1847–8, xviii, 23.

from one year to the next. A parliamentary enquiry in the session of 1847–8 had scrutinized what looked like a sharp increase in the education vote over the preceding year. But 'the increase in . . . this estimate is apparent only. The actual sum spent in the year was £125,000; the excess over the vote having been defrayed out of the surplus of the preceding year. This is not the only vote in which your committee have observed this practice, which they think deserves the close attention of the Treasury.'[119] Two years later, the phenomenon recurred. 'Since we determined on taking a vote of £150,000 instead of £125,000 for English education,' wrote Wood to Russell, 'I have learnt that there is a balance of £200,000!!! . . . Of this, £130,000, appropriated as building grants, is liable to be called for, though some probably is forfeited by lapse of time and some may not be called for. It is pretty certain that all will not be called for within the year. However, assuming that the whole sum will be called for, there remains an unappropriated balance of £70,000. I have seen Mr Lingen who cannot put the possible expenditure higher than £160,000. He had reckoned on some balance in his estimate; but they knew so little of their own affairs at the Council Office, that they would not believe that they had a balance of such an amount. I need not tell you that accumulating a balance in this way is contrary to all principle, or that if we acted according to our practice in ordinary cases we should say £160,000 probable expenditure, minus balance in hand £70,000, equals the sum to be voted, £90,000. . . . I think that we either ought not to increase the vote at all, which will be the easiest way *for this year*, or increase it only a little . . . to . . . render subsequent increases easier. . . . Last year Shuttleworth . . . stated the unappropriated balance at £50,000, and as it is now £70,000 it seems to be an accumulating fund.'[120]

A very general complaint by ministers was that Treasury control meant, in practice, control by officers of much inferior status to themselves. Howick alleged that, while the Secretary-at-War could suggest changes, 'very often his recommendations are overruled in the name of the Lords Commissioners of the Treasury by some subordinate person in the department'.[121] One of the historians of the Colonial Office concluded that 'in the Treasury, the permanent staff possessed far more power than in any other department, and we may suspect that Herbert was right when he declared to Lord Derby that "My Lords" often did not see communications from the

[119] P.P. 1847–8, xviii, 25.
[120] PRO 30/22/8. Wood to Russell, March 4, 1850.
[121] Melbourne Papers. Howick to Russell, August 10, 1839.

Colonial Office, and that the staff answered these without any reference to the political heads, and therefore took no notice of anything else but financial considerations'.[122] A former Commissioner of Woods, who must have known what he was talking about, wrote that Treasury control meant 'that most mischievous delays take place, and that the practical power devolves on some subordinate and irresponsible officer in the Treasury, who, assuming the name of "My Lords", procures the signature of some high officer, and thus the supreme authority may be and constantly is exercised with very little knowledge, or without the matters to be disposed of having been considered by any competent or responsible officer ... the practical result of the present system being that the real management is to a great extent conducted by subordinates unknown to the public, as depositories of power and practical control'.[123]

In this situation, it was highly desirable for the department to have a minister who was capable of standing up to the Treasury. 'Now I do think,' wrote Lansdowne to Russell apropos of government support for an Irish railway, 'this is too important a question to be disposed of at once in Trevelyan's room at the Treasury, and trust that you will be able at once to look into it, and if you and Wood cannot take it upon yourselves, let it be submitted to the Cabinet if possible without delay.'[124] Appeal also lay from the Chancellor to the First Lord. When Gladstone pressed Stanley of Alderley to allow the Civil Service Commission to recruit postmen by open competition, the latter went to Palmerston. 'I told [Gladstone] that the Treasury comprehended a First Lord as well as a Chancellor of the Exchequer, and any question as to the mode of appointment of the civil service was more a matter for ... the First Lord than for the Chancellor ... and that I must object to revolutionize the whole system of public appointment without your direct authority.'[125]

For the administrator who enjoyed firm political support, the Treasury held few terrors. 'The Treasury, as a general rule ... gives way when applied to by any board or other department presided over by a Cabinet minister for their sanction to spend money. They may delay at first ... but the Treasury invariably gives way in the end.'[126] For example, when it was desired to appoint a Senior Chief Inspector of Schools, the approval of the head of the department

[122] Hall, 269.
[123] T. F. Kennedy, *Letter to Rt. Hon. Lord John Russell* (1854), 51.
[124] PRO 30/22/8. Lansdowne to Russell, October 15, 1850.
[125] Palmerston Papers. Stanley of Alderley to Palmerston, June 7, 1861.
[126] Todd (1867–9), i, 563.

having first been obtained, 'a letter was . . . written to the Treasury. No answer. Several further letters were sent, with the same result. At last my patience was exhausted, and I went to Lord Cranbrook again and told him that I was quite unable to move the Treasury. He was, happily, a minister of strong character, and he said: "Write to the Treasury, and say that I have determined that this appointment is absolutely necessary, and that if they do not reply I shall have to consider my position." The same day that the letter was sent the Secretary of the Treasury came to my room in some perturbation and agreed, without demur, to give what we wanted'.[127]

Inability to take such a line earned ministers the contempt of their subordinates. This was part of Kekewich's indictment of the Duke of Devonshire. Impressed by what he had seen in Germany, the former 'formulated a . . . scheme . . . to create a great central technological institution in London, and to affiliate to it, in connection with the provincial universities, other institutions which might probably adapt themselves usefully to the industries of particular localities. I explained the scheme in general terms, for of course it would have been premature to have worked out the details, to the Duke. I told him that it was a big proposition, and would cost a good deal of money, that if it was to be of real benefit to our industries, it ought to be carried out at least on the German scale, and that if it was starved financially either as regarded buildings, staff, or equipment it would be useless. The Duke said casually that he thought it "rather a good idea", but that if much money was wanted, there would be a difficulty. I asked him how much he thought he could get the government to give, and he said: "Certainly not more than about £20,000 or £30,000." I replied that such a sum would not even suffice for efficient equipment and apparatus, and that, although I had had no estimate made, the whole capital expenditure would run to some hundreds of thousands of pounds, perhaps even to a million and a half if the thing was to be done well, and that the government would also have to provide a large annual sum for upkeep. The Duke said that such an expenditure *for such a purpose* was out of the question, that he could not possibly ask the Chancellor of the Exchequer for anything approaching it. Of course, I could do no more. . . . As [the Duke] . . . rarely gave himself the trouble of serious discussion, his influence certainly was the reverse of stimulating. He went to sleep, and the office seemed to try to follow his example.'[128]

To return to the emigration service, it was not always a case of the

[127] Kekewich, 69.   [128] ibid., 97–9.

255

Colonial Office asking and the Treasury refusing. The Office itself had inhibitions about money. Elliot, for example, "assumed in his heart that all government intervention *and expenditure* was at best the lesser of two evils'. Some imaginative proposals for regulating the traffic failed to win his support: they 'conjured up visions of such great expenditure as to place them beyond the bounds of serious discussion'. Merivale had an habitual 'reluctance . . . to ask the Treasury for money'.[129] Secretaries of State were not necessarily any bolder. Grey was uncommonly well placed, since the Chancellor of the Exchequer was his brother-in-law. Yet the sums he asked for in the crisis year of 1847 were pitifully inadequate.[130] What Mac-Donagh says about the Commissioners applies to all levels on the Colonial Office side. 'We cannot absolve [them] from all blame . . . It is difficult to believe that [money] would have been unattainable, even in the most hostile circumstances, had a brief been thoroughly prepared and tirelessly advocated. Men of higher calibre in similar situations at this time succeeded in enlarging their departments.'[131] It is pointless to blame the Treasury for turning down requests that were never made.

The Treasury view was by no means unpopular. Its 'attitude towards public expenditure . . . [enjoyed] the hearty endorsement of "public" and politicians alike'.[132] Had the Treasury met the utmost wishes of those working in the service, there was no guarantee that parliament would vote the money. There was, in fact, pressure positively to reduce costs. 'A ranging shot was fired in 1851 when F. Scott objected in the House of Commons to the amount of the Commissioners' estimate; and in 1854 the assaults of the financial reformers began in earnest. Bright demanded an all-round reduction in the Commissioners' staff, and was strongly supported by other radicals and economizers. These demands were repeated in 1855 and 1856 . . . In 1857, 1859, 1860, 1862, 1863 and 1864 the attacks upon the estimates continued, as did indeed the fall in the Commissioners' expenditure.'[133] Parliament was far more ready to pass reform legislation than to set up reform administration. As Sclater-Booth said in another connection, 'one of the reasons why the Alkali Acts had been somewhat restricted had been the difficulty of asking Parliament to provide a larger establishment of Inspectors . . . It was most important that the public should pay for the remedy they

---

[129] MacDonagh (1961), 126, 143, 226. (My italics.)
[130] ibid., 174–5.   [131] ibid., 288.
[132] ibid., 190.   [133] ibid., 284–5.

desired to have applied'.[134] Timidity in the face of public expenditure was nearly universal in the nineteenth century. It was common to the public, to politicians on both sides of the House, whether they sat on the front benches or the back, and to civil servants of all departments. Treasury control was a sympton not a disease.

[134] MacLeod (1965), 107n.

CHAPTER IX

THE NINETEENTH-CENTURY REVOLUTION IN GOVERNMENT

'Many political writers ... have declared that the business of government is simply to afford protection, to repel or to punish internal or external violence or fraud, and that to do more is unsurpation. This proposition I cannot admit. The only rational foundation of government, the only foundation of a right to govern and of a correlative duty to obey, is expediency—the general benefit of the community. It is the duty of a government to do whatever is conducive to the welfare of the governed.'

Nassau Senior, 1847

Any discussion of nineteenth-century government growth must start (as this book did) with Dicey's *Law and Opinion*:[1] 'The best introduction to the interplay between thought and political action' in the period since 1832;[2] 'The classic exposition of individualism and collectivism';[3] 'First in the field, [it] has dominated it ever since.'[4] Most impressive tribute of all, the London School of Economics arranged a series of seventeen public lectures in the academic year 1957–8 to mark the sixtieth anniversary of the course on which the book was based. Given by scholars of distinction, they were 'at once a continuation of [his] work ... and a widening of it'. They have since been published under the title *Law and Opinion in England in the Twentieth Century*.[5]

Yet *Law and Opinion* is a highly misleading book. If strange doctrines about nineteenth-century government growth persist today,

---

[1] A. V. Dicey, *Lectures on the Relation between Law and Public Opinion during the Nineteenth Century* (2 e., 1914). All page references here are to the paperback version of 1962. Dicey himself used the short title *Law and Opinion*: cf. *Memorials of A. V. Dicey*, e. R. S. Rait (1929), 189, etc.

[2] K. B. Smellie, *100 Years of English Government* (2 e., 1950), 331.

[3] Sir Kenneth Wheare's article on Dicey in *Chambers' Encyclopaedia* (1955 ed.).

[4] O. MacDonagh, 'The Nineteenth-century Revolution in Government: a Reappraisal' in *Historical Journal*, i (1958), 55.

[5] M. Ginsberg (ed.) (1959).

they are largely attributable to Dicey. It is odd that in the decades that have elapsed since Jennings first book took scalpel to Dicey's *Law of the Constitution*,[6] no similar reappraisal of *Law and Opinion* has appeared. Jennings commented on *The Law of the Constitution* that 'just as Macaulay saw the history of the eighteenth century through Whig spectacles, so Dicey saw the constitution of 1885 through Whig spectacles:[7] His remark applies equally, *mutatis mutandis*, to *Law and Opinion*. Dicey's career as a political partisan is of the greatest relevance to an understanding of his thought. An orthodox Liberal until 1885, he broke with his party over Home Rule, and devoted much time and effort thenceforth as a speaker and pamphleteer to combating the doctrines and measures of his former associates. *Law and Opinion* is, of course, much more than a political pamphlet. Yet to read it solely as a work of scholarship is to miss much of its significance. Dicey's purpose was not only to describe the consequences of certain trends in Liberalism, but also, as a Whiggish exponent of the true faith, to denounce them.

Three aspects of Dicey's work in particular call for scrutiny. They are: (a) his account of Benthamism; (b) his summary of legislation in the middle decades of the nineteenth century; and (c) his division of the nineteenth century into periods.

Dicey nowhere claims that his account of Benthamism is an account of Bentham's own ideas. 'My objects ... are,' he says, 'to sketch in the merest outline the ideas of Benthamism or individualism *in so far as when applied by practical statesmen they have affected the growth of English law.*' In a footnote, he goes on to explain that the principles he is about to outline 'are not so much the dogmas to be found in Bentham's works as ideas due in the main to Bentham, which were ultimately, though often in a very modified form, accepted by the reformers or legislators who practically applied utilitarian conceptions to the amendment of the law of England'.[8] What Dicey himself understood by Benthamism in this special sense is summed up in three words from the passage quoted above: 'Benthamism or individualism'. Variations on this theme recur throughout the book: 'That faith in *laissez-faire* which is of the very essence of legislative Benthamism,' or, 'Benthamites looked with disfavour on state intervention ... Legislative utilitarianism is nothing else than systematized individualism.'[9] Dicey does not argue that *laissez-faire*

[6] Sir W. I. Jennings, *Law and the Constitution* (1933).
[7] Sir W. I. Jennings, 'In Praise of Dicey' in *Public Administration*, xii (1935), 128.   [8] Dicey, 134 and n. (My italics.)
[9] ibid., 44, 174–5: cf. 39, 125, 145, and 146n.

was the basic principle of the creed. Indeed, he is aware that 'this dogma of *laissez-faire* is not from a logical point of view an essential article of the utilitarian creed'.[10] What he does argue is that 'though *laissez-faire* is not an essential part of utilitarianism it was practically the most vital part of Bentham's legislative doctrine, and in England gave to the movement for the reform of the law, both its power and its character'.[11] To test the validity of this thesis calls, not for a close examination of Bentham's writings, but for a study of legislation during the period when, according to Dicey, Benthamism was the dominant opinion. He has no difficulty, of course, in producing a number of examples in support of his case. All that need be said here about such events as the repeal of the Corn Laws is that their importance is recognized. What is more interesting is to see what he has to say about developments that do not fit into his model; for example, factory inspection, exchequer grants for education, the New Poor Law, and other similar measures.

Dicey is fully aware of the importance of factory legislation for the validity of his thesis: it was here, he tells us, that 'Benthamite liberalism suffered its earliest and severest defeat'.[12] He attempts to explain it (or explain it away) by two lines of argument. First, he attributes it to a current of opinion hostile to Benthamism: 'The factory movement gave rise to a parliamentary conflict between individualism and collectivism.' But he does not seriously argue that such men as Oastler, Sadler and Shaftesbury were exponents of a coherent philosophy of society, comparable with utilitarianism. Indeed, he has already told us that collectivism 'cannot, in England at any rate, be connected with the name of any one man, or even . . . any one definite school'.[13] Secondly, he invokes a force which he labels 'Tory philanthropy'. The Factory Movement 'from the first came under the guidance of Tories. With this movement will be for ever identified the names of Southey, Oastler, Sadler and above all Lord Shaftesbury'.[14] No one will dispute this statement about the men named as individuals, but the attempt to stick a party label on the movement soon fails. Dicey himself quotes Shaftesbury on the hostility of three leaders of his party—Peel, Graham, and Gladstone—to the Ten Hours Bill, while admitting 'nor was there anything in the early factory movement which was opposed either to Benthamism or to the doctrines of the most rigid political economy'. In illustration of this admission, he points to the support of McCulloch (1833), Cobden (1836) and Macaulay (1846).[15]

[10] ibid., 146.   [11] ibid., 147.   [12] ibid., 237.
[13] ibid., 232, 64–5.   [14] ibid., 224.   [15] ibid., 234–5, 221–3.

In discussing the assumption by the state of a share of the responsibility for elementary education, Dicey adopts a different argument. He is quite clear about its relevance to his theme: 'Our present system [of elementary education] is a monument to the increasing predominance of collectivism.'[16] What, then, were the currents of opinion which led to the foundation of this monument? None worth discussing, it seems. Dicey chooses the first exchequer grant for education to illustrate the process by which 'a principle carelessly introduced into an Act of Parliament intended to have a limited effect may gradually so affect legislative opinion that it comes to pervade a whole field of law'.[17] It is true, of course, that the historic vote of August 17, 1833 was passed by a very small House; to suggest, however, that there was anything casual about the interest which such men as Hume and Roebuck were taking in education at the time is to ignore the vital role played by education in the whole system of utilitarian thought. But Dicey was scarcely capable of understanding the part of such a man as Hume. For him, 'no politician was a more typical representative of his time than Joseph Hume. He was a utilitarian of a narrow type; he devoted the whole of his energy to the keeping down or paring down of public expenditure'.[18] Yet Hume criticized the 1833 grant, not because it was too big, but because it was too small. Tiny as the 1833 seed was, by 1869 it had grown into a considerable plant. In that year there was accommodation in schools under government inspection for more than 1,200,000 children.[19] It is generally agreed that the main brake on educational progress had been sectarian tensions. Dicey, however, has another explanation. Although the first grant had been made as early as 1833, 'the assumption of this duty was delayed by the distrust of state intervention which characterized the Benthamite era'.[20]

With all his ingenuity, Dicey found himself in some difficulty when he came to fit the New Poor Law into his chosen categories: 'It may appear to be a straining of terms if we bring under the head of freedom in dealing with property the most celebrated piece of legislation which can be attributed to the philosophic Radicals. The Poor Law of 1834 does not, on the face of it, aim at securing freedom of any kind; in popular imagination its chief result was the erection of workhouses, which, as prisons for the poor, were nicknamed Bastilles.'[21] He recognizes that the effect of the 1834 Act was to

[16] ibid., 277, 279.   [17] ibid., 46.   [18] ibid., 411n.
[19] J. Corlett, *Financial Aspects of Elementary Education* (1929), 47.
[20] Dicey, 277.   [21] ibid., 203.

increase the power of the state: 'The new Poor Law . . . placed poor relief under the supervision of the state.'[22] And again, 'the rigorous and scientific administration of the Poor Law (1834) under the control of the central government . . . limited the area of individual freedom'.[23]

A curious footnote is worth a mention also. It occurs apropos of an assertion that 'confidence in the beneficent effects of state control . . . is utterly foreign to the liberalism of 1832'. 'If anyone doubts this statement,' Dicey suggests, 'let him consider one fact, and ask himself one question. In 1834 the Whigs and Radicals who reformed the Poor Law expected the speedy abolition of outdoor relief; they hoped for and desired the abolition of the Poor Law itself.'[24] No doubt there were doctrinaires who looked forward to the withering away of the entire Poor Law. But to suggest that such a hope was general or typical is surely quite erroneous. To echo Dicey, if anyone doubts this statement let him consider one fact and ask himself one question. All over the country are to be found large solid buildings put up in the late 1830s as Union workhouses. Many are still in use today. If those who built them expected the Poor Law to wither away, why were they so prodigal of the ratepayers' money? It is fitting to correct a misrepresentation of Benthamism by an argument which Bentham himself might have styled 'a simple idea in architecture'.

In conclusion, a minor example of Dicey's mode of argument may be cited. 'Between 1835 and 1844,' he tells us, 'agricultural training schools and model farms were established in Ireland' but they were much restricted by Peel and Cardwell. 'This illustrated both the *laissez-faire* of the day and the attitude of Peel and the Peelites'.[25] What then did their establishment exemplify?

Most of the distortions in Dicey's argument are closely bound up with his determination to demonstrate distinct trends in opinion and legislation before and after 1870. He divides the century into three periods, as follows: (i) Legislative Quiescence, 1800–30; (ii) Period of Benthamism or Individualism, 1825–70; (iii) Period of Collectivism, 1865–1900.[26] Dicey himself was in considerable difficulties about his second turning-point. Speaking of the 'characteristics of law-making opinion in England' he lays down a general proposition that 'the opinion which affects the development of the law has, in modern England at least, often originated with some single thinker or group of thinkers. No doubt it is at times allowable to talk of a prevalent belief or opinion as "being in the air", by which

[22] ibid., 188. [23] ibid., 306–7. [24] ibid., 39n.
[25] ibid., 180n. [26] ibid., 62–4.

expression is meant that a particular way of looking at things has become the common possession of all the world. But though a belief, when it prevails, may at last be adopted by the whole of a generation, it rarely happens that a widespread conviction has grown up spontaneously among the multitude'.[27]

This obviously applies to the role played by Bentham and his school in the transition from the first to the second period. But when Dicey comes to the next point of transition he cannot point to anyone who played a similar part: 'Hence a curious contrast between the mode in which an inquirer must deal with the legislative influence on the one hand of Benthamism, and on the other hand of collectivism. He can explain changes in English law by referring them to definite and known tenets or ideas of Benthamite liberalism; he can, on the other hand, prove the existence of collectivist ideas in the main only by showing the socialistic character or tendencies of certain parliamentary enactments.'[28]

Nor is Dicey any more successful in pointing to the date when the period of individualism gave place to the period of collectivism. Since all division of the past into periods is artificial, it would be reasonable to say that these periods shade so insensibly into one another that no precise turning-point can be fixed. But Dicey does not do that. 'The difference between the legislation characteristic of the era of individualism and the legislation characteristic of the era of collectivism is, we perceive, essential and fundamental. The reason is that this dissimilarity (which every student must recognize, even when he cannot analyse it) rests upon and gives expression to different, if not absolutely inconsistent, ways of regarding the relation between man and the state.'[29] Such a change should be capable of being precisely dated, and in fact when the period of collectivism is first introduced Dicey tells his reader that it began in 1865.[30]

Unfortunately, at other points in the argument a number of other dates are mentioned. 'Socialistic ideas were, it is submitted, in no way a part of dominant legislative opinion earlier than 1865, and their influence on legislation did not become perceptible till some years later, say till 1868 or 1870, or dominant till say 1880.'[31] 'At this point [i.e. the Limited Liability legislation of 1852–62], individualistic and collectivist currents of opinion blend together . . . since the transference of business from individuals to corporate bodies favours the growth of collectivism.'[32] 'In 1854 the opponents

[27] ibid., 21–2.   [28] ibid., 68.   [29] ibid., 300.
[30] ibid., 64.   [31] ibid., 66.   [32] ibid., 201.

263

of Benthamism were slowly gaining the ear of the public.'[33] Collectivist influence is to be seen in housing legislation, dating from 1851; in municipal trading, from 1850 onwards; and in public health legislation, from 1848 onwards.[34] 'At the time when the repeal of the Corn Laws gave ... what seemed to be a crowning victory to individualism ... the success of the Factory Acts gave authority ... to beliefs which, if not exactly socialistic, yet certainly tended towards socialism or collectivism.'[35] 'Between 1830 and 1840 the issue between individualists and collectivists was fairly joined.'[36] Elementary education 'is a monument to the increasing predominance of collectivism': it dates from 1833.[37] Hence, on Dicey's own showing, the era of collectivism began in 1833, only three years after the end of the period of legislative quiescence.

Moreover, this so-called 'collectivism' itself derived from utilitarianism. Dicey called his ninth lecture 'The Debt of Collectivism to Benthamism'. Bentham had admitted that the principle of utility is dangerous to an unjust society. Since 'in any state the poor and the needy always constitute the majority of the nation, the favourite dogma of Benthamism pointed to the conclusion ... that the whole aim of legislation should be to promote the happiness, not of the nobility or the gentry, or even of shopkeepers, but of artisans and other wage-earners'.[38] As a result, 'the legislative tendency was the constant extension and improvement of the mechanism of government, ... the creation of authorities for the enforcement of laws to promote the public health and the increasing application of a new system of centralization, the invention of Bentham himself'.[39] Although earlier Dicey had equated Benthamism with individualism, he now admits that 'Benthamites ... differed among themselves ... as to the relative importance of the principle of utility and the principle of non-interference with each man's freedom. ... [and some] e.g. Chadwick, were practically prepared to curtail individual freedom for the sake of attaining any object of immediate and obvious usefulness, e.g. good sanitary administration.'[40] Dicey's conclusion was paradoxical. 'The Liberals, then, of 1830 were themselves zealots for individual freedom, but they entertained beliefs which, though the men who held them knew it not, might well, under altered social conditions, foster the despotic authority of a democratic state. Benthamites ... forged the arms most needed by socialists. Thus English collectivists have inherited from their utilitarian predecessors a legislative doctrine, a legislative instrument, and

[33] ibid., 33–4.   [34] ibid., 284–5, 291.   [35] ibid., 240.   [36] ibid., 217.
[37] ibid., 276–7, 279.   [38] ibid., 305.   [39] ibid., 306–7.   [40] ibid., 308n.

a legislative tendency pre-eminently suited for the carrying out of socialistic experiments.'[41]

Yet Dicey was a man of ability, learning and wisdom. How could his argument get into such confusion? That he could, on occasion, be wrong, not in small details, but in great matters closely related to his special field, is known from his treatment of *droit administratif* in France and the alleged absence of administrative law in England.[42] In *Law and Opinion* he was working in a field not entirely his own: 'An author who tried to explain the relation between law and opinion during the nineteenth century undertook to a certain extent the work of an historian.' And he recognizes that there are limits to the degree to which 'an English lawyer ought ... to trespass ... upon the province of historians, moralists, or philosophers'.[43] He was aware, moreover, of the special difficulty of his enquiry: 'Few indeed have been the men who have been able to seize with clearness the causes or the tendencies of events passing around them.' Even those who have come nearest to success have usually missed something of first-rate importance: and he instances Bagehot's lack of reference to the importance of political parties.[44] In addition to all this, Dicey candidly admits that he approached his subject in an uncritical frame of mind; his book, he says, 'cannot claim to be a work of research; it is rather a work of inference or reflection. It is written with the object, not of discovering new facts, but of drawing from some of the best-known facts of political, social, and legal history certain connections which, though many of them obvious enough, are often overlooked'.[45]

Dicey, then, writing his lectures at the end of the nineteenth century, made no attempt to go beyond the accepted accounts of what took place two generations before, either in regard to what men were thinking or to what men were doing. He believed that, since he was 'writing of a time not long past, he was almost delivered from the difficulty with which an historian of eras removed by the lapse of many years from his own time often struggles in vain, the difficulty, namely, of understanding the social and intellectual atmosphere of bygone ages'.[46] But he was born in 1835, and on his own admission, his memory of public affairs did not go much further back than 1848.[47] Of all periods of history, the quarter-century preceding a man's twenty-first birthday is likely to be that of which he has least understanding, unless he makes a conscious effort to understand it.

[41] ibid., 309–10.   [42] Cf. Jennings esp. 210ff. and Carr (1941), 21ff.
[43] Dicey, xxiii, 465.   [44] ibid., xxiv–xxvi.   [45] ibid., viii.
[46] ibid., xxiv.   [47] Rait, 1 and 6.

Too remote from his adult mind for him to know of his own know-ledge, they are too near to form part of history, as it is generally taught and learnt. How much understanding of the Second World War is found today in those born in 1941? What would a reader expect of a book about, say, the General Strike by an author born in 1911, who stated at the outset that he had undertaken no original research but had contented himself with 'drawing from some of the best-known facts ... certain connections which ... are often over-looked?'

Dicey's erroneous beliefs about Benthamism and its influence on legislation have helped to perpetuate a myth about nineteenth-century government—the myth that between 1830 and 1870 or thereabouts, central administration in Great Britain was stationary, if not actually diminishing, and that this state of affairs ended when a new current of opinion, collectivism, superseded individualism.

HALÉVY AND THE DECLINE OF PHILOSOPHIC RADICALISM

Another account of the end of Benthamite influence was offered by Elie Halévy in *The Growth of Philosophic Radicalism*.[48] According to Halévy there was an inherent contradiction in the doctrine. In econ-omic affairs, it was assumed that a harmonious pattern of production, distribution and exchange would result from the completely free pursuit of each man's interests. Any intervention by the state would be harmful. The natural identity of interests must be the golden rule. In all other social relations, on the other hand, the unrestricted pursuit of individual ends would result in something much less than the greatest happiness of the greatest number. State intervention in many spheres was not only justified but absolutely essential. Artificial identification of interests should be the watchword. In the period, 1832–52, both principles were at work, operating in opposite directions. The idea of natural identity of interests pushed legislation in the direction of free enterprise, while the principle of artificial identification of interests worked the other way, in favour of state intervention. The conflict was resolved, in Halévy's view, by the triumph of the former principle: 'Thus was developed in England, twenty years after Bentham's death, a new and simplified form of the Utilitarian philosophy. Disciples of Adam Smith much more than of Bentham, the Utilitarians did not now include in their doctrine the principle of the artificial identification of interests, that is, the governmental or administrative idea; the idea of free trade and of the

[48] English e., 1928.

266

spontaneous identification of interests summed up the social conceptions of these new docrinaries.'[49] Certain events in the history of administration (e.g. Chadwick's retirement in 1854) appear to fit this interpretation. Similarly, the abandonment of the Railway Regulation Bill in 1847 marked the turning-point in the trend towards greater public control of railways, which was not resumed for another two decades.[50] It is probably significant that Halévy's summing-up relates to the year 1852—the very year at which his unfinished *History of the English People* breaks off. Had he lived to make a more thorough study of the 1850s and 1860s he might well have reached a different conclusion. The setback to the growth of central administration around 1850 was only apparent. In reality it continued; checks here and there were more than counterbalanced by developments elsewhere.

THE MACDONAGH MODEL

As with Dicey, so with Halévy, everyone knows of facts which do not fit their models. For lack of a theoretical framework, however, they have been treated as mere isolated facts, apparent exceptions to an assumed general rule. The most important attempt to supply such a framework is that of MacDonagh, which has been extensively debated in the trade press.[51] He argues that the administrative changes in the middle decades of the nineteenth century added up to a revolution in government comparable in importance to the Industrial Revolution. The most valuable part of his model is the demonstration that 'internal dynamism' played a crucial role in the process: a 'vital and neglected factor is the momentum of government itself'.[52] This is a useful corrective to those who tend to trace profound changes in structure to particular crises, such as the Crimean War—the Cleopatra's nose of nineteenth-century administrative history.

The MacDonagh model is less satisfactory in its attitude towards

[49] Halévy, 514.
[50] Parris (1965), 99 and 125.
[51] MacDonagh (1958).
  H. Parris, 'The Nineteenth-century Revolution in Government: a Reappraisal Reappraised', *Historical Journal*, iii (1960).
  J. Hart, 'Nineteenth-century Social Reform: a Tory Interpretation of History', *Past and Present*, no. 31 (1965).
  V. Cromwell, 'Interpretations of Nineteenth-century Administration: an Analysis', *Victorian Studies*, ix (1965–6).
[52] MacDonagh (1961), 322–3.

Dicey. The criticism advanced above untouched three of Dicey's chief arguments; that there is a close connection between law and opinion in general; that that connection was particularly close in the case of Benthamism; and that its practical influence dates from around 1830. Although MacDonagh does not explicitly criticize Dicey's views on any of these points, his argument implies a rejection of them. His model allows for public opinion in the ordinary sense of the term; that is, the sort of popular sentiments and attitudes to particular questions of the day that are now assessed by the Gallup poll. But it has no place for opinion, as Dicey understood it, either in general, or in the particular case of Benthamism. 'Broadly speaking, so far as the administrative matters with which we are concerned go, Benthamism had no influence upon opinion at large or, for that matter, upon the overwhelming majority of public servants.'[53]

LAISSEZ-FAIRE AND STATE INTERVENTION

The appeal of the MacDonagh model is that it appears to get round a difficulty that has puzzled many students of the subject. Halévy saw it as a contradiction within the Utilitarian doctrine. He contrasted the principle of artificial identification of interests, on which Bentham founded his theory of politics and law, with the principle of natural identity of interests, which appeared to be the basis of Benthamite economics.[54] Carr was unable to make out 'how the Benthamites could reconcile their theory of law with their natural addiction to the doctrines of *laissez-faire*'. It was 'one of the puzzles of political science'.[55]

Other have perceived contradictions between theory on the one hand, and the course of events on the other. Prouty, for example, in a book sub-titled 'a study of administrative reorganization in the heyday of *laissez-faire*', argues that '*laissez-faire* in early nineteenth-century Britain was never a system. . . . The most determined liberal could not *consistently* argue for *laissez-faire*; he sooner or later found himself advocating a measure which involved the government in the regulation of some part of industry'.[56] MacDonagh is similarly mystified. (One of the peculiarities of his approach is that, while he plays down ideological factors favourable to government growth, he is constantly on the look-out for ideological barriers against it.) Thus he points out that civil servants were inclined 'naturally towards

---

[53] MacDonagh (1958), 65.
[54] Halévy, 490, 514, &c.   [55] Carr (1941), 8–9.
[56] R. Prouty, *Transformation of the Board of Trade, 1830–1855* (1957), 1.

the shibboleths of the day. ... This acceptance of the current orthodoxy did not positively prevent the civil servants from extending the scope of this legislation. They were, rather, Occamists in the matter, keeping their faith in the "broad principles" of *laissez-faire* apart from their consideration of the Acts. None the less, this various outside pressure against the interference of the state must have confused the issues, tied down the imagination and narrowed the field of seeming possibilities'.[57]

Were 'determined liberals' really inconsistent, as Prouty implies, in arguing for *laissez-faire* in one sphere, and public regulation in another? Were civil servants, as MacDonagh suggests, really guilty of preaching one thing and practising another? Prouty concludes that 'the text-book accounts of a government concentrating on the removal of all restraints and regulations on industry perpetuate a myth which is no longer acceptable. In a society fast industrializing and urbanizing, the demands made upon the government to act in the general interest and in the interests of public welfare and safety grew more constant. While *laissez-faire* as a general principle or as an argument against a particular measure might continue to receive wide publicity, it was persistently defeated in practice. ... State intervention may not have been policy but it was the growing reality'.[58] That is to say, there was a contradistinction between men's beliefs and men's actions, they preached free enterprise whilst practising public control. If such was the case, the growth of government was indeed a curious process which calls for a good deal of explanation. But was there in fact a contradiction of the kind implied?

An extreme solution to this problem was propounded by Brebner.[59] His approach to Dicey resembles that of Marx towards Hegel. Dissatisfied with his argument, he sought to correct it by turning it the other way up. Dicey had assumed that the consequences of Benthamism were limited, in practice, to the promotion of *laissez-faire*. Brebner suggests, on the other hand, that '*laissez-faire* was a political and social myth in the sense formulated by Georges Sorel'. Although it 'never prevailed in Great Britain or in any other modern state, many men today have been led to believe that it did. In this matter ... Dicey ... seems to have been the principal maintainer of the myth for others'. *Law and Opinion* 'amounted to an argument against increasing collectivism. The lectures were so passionately motivated as to be a sincere, despairing, and warped reassertion of

---

[57] MacDonagh (1961), 234–5.   [58] Prouty, 1.
[59] J. B. Brebner, '*Laissez-faire* and State Intervention in Nineteenth-century Britain', *Journal of Economic History*, supplement viii (1948).

the myth in terms of legal and constitutional history. . . . In using Bentham as the archetype of British individualism he was conveying the exact opposite of the truth. Jeremy Bentham was the archetype of British collectivism'. *Laissez-faire*, according to Brebner, was a separate current of opinion, deriving ultimately from Adam Smith, and though often in alliance with Benthamism, never assimilated to it.

Valuable as a corrective to Dicey, Brebner's argument is too violent a reaction. *Laissez-faire* and state intervention were equally characteristic of the middle quarters of the nineteenth century and it is not necessary to assume that they were in contradiction to one another. Robbins has shown how they were reconciled in economic theory. Halévy was wrong in supposing that there was a conflict between the assumptions underlying Bentham's theory of law, on the one hand, and classical economics on the other. The latter was not based on an assumed identity of interests. If the classical economists 'assumed anywhere a harmony, it was never a harmony arising in a vacuum but always very definitely within a framework of law . . . they regarded the appropriate legal framework and the system of economic freedom as two aspects of one and the same social process'.[60] They advocated free enterprise as the general rule in economic affairs on the ground that it was the system most likely to benefit the consumer. But they recognized no natural right of free enterprise. Like any other claim to freedom, it had to be justified by the principle of utility. As a rule, it was so justified; but there were many situations where the state should intervene.

Before going on to consider what they were, it is necessary to issue a warning that *laissez-faire* slogans are not always evidence of an articulate creed in the minds of those who voiced them. 'Although the idea of a coherent and dominant *laissez-faire* philosophy cannot be maintained, there was a well-used set of *laissez-faire* clichés which possessed emotional appeal.'[61] These clichés might be invoked in opposition to some initiative of central government by those whose interests were threatened, either absolutely, or relatively to those of some other group. It is much easier to understand the attitude of various religious groups towards educational grants if it is borne in mind that the great majority of the money went to Anglican schools. 'What could be paraded as opposition to centralization *per se* might well be no more than the resentment felt by a self-made nonconformist manufacturer to "centralization" as represented by an inspector or other administrator who was a gentleman and an

[60] L. Robbins, *Theory of Economic Policy in English Classical Political Economy* (1952), 191.   [61] Burn, 289.

Anglican, who held a degree of Oxford or Cambridge and who had connections with the aristocracy or the landed gentry. Conversely, acceptance of centralization might mean little more than a sense that the central government was comfortably in the hands of one's own kind of people or that one was going to receive some kind of benefit in return.'[62] Again, much opposition to state action was inspired by fear of the growth of patronage, through which (it was thought) governments would be able to maintain themselves in power against the wishes of the electorate. 'A . . . general objection to government agency, is that every increase of the functions devolving on the government is an increase of its power, both in the form of authority, and still more, in the indirect form of influence.'[63]

LAISSEZ-FAIRE IN CLASSICAL ECONOMICS

Nevertheless, there was a genuine case for *laissez-faire*, whose advocates did not mean by it doing as one pleased regardless of the consequences to others. Listen for example to Adam Smith disposing of the case against a proposed restriction on bankers: 'Such regulations may, no doubt, be considered as in some respect a violation of natural liberty. But those exertions of the natural liberty of a few individuals which might endanger the security of the whole society are, and ought to be, restrained by the laws of all governments. . . . The obligation of building party walls, in order to prevent the communication of fire, is a violation of natural liberty, exactly of the same kind with the regulations of the banking trade which are here proposed.'[64] No one likes to be taxed. But Bentham would not admit that infringement of liberty was a valid objection to a fiscal proposal. 'It would . . . be a gross error, and an extremely mischievous one, to refer to the defalcation thus resulting from the mass of liberty or free agency, as affording a conclusive objection against the interposition of the law for this or any other purpose. Every law which does not consist in the repeal, total or partial, of a coercive law, is itself a coercive law. To reprobate as a mischief peculiar to this or that law, a property which is of the essence of all law, is to betray . . . a total unacquaintance with what may be called the logic of the laws.'[65] Intervention on behalf of the poor was not necessarily a reduction in freedom. It was cant to talk, for example, of freedom of

---

[62] ibid., 222–3.
[63] J. S. Mill, *Principles of Political Economy* (1848), ii, 511.
[64] Adam Smith, *Wealth of Nations* (ed. Cannan, 1950 e.), i, 307.
[65] J. Bentham, *Economic Writings* (ed. Stark, 1952–4), iii, 334–5.

contract between employer and worker, since they were not equal in strength. A particularly interesting formulation of the argument occurs in a letter by Northcote. He makes no claim to originality, admitting that he has taken it from Mill's *Principles of Political Economy*. But it is significant that a practical politician should try to apply theory to a practical question of the hour. 'Labourers and persons in the employ of others have no real freedom in these matters. . . . The interference of the law is required, not to overrule the judgement of individuals respecting their own interest, but to give effect to that judgment, they being unable to give effect to it except by concert, which cannot be effectual unless it receives validity and sanction from law. There are plenty of cases in which this is done, such as the limitations of the hours of factory labour, the prohibition of the truck system, etc.; but indeed the same might be said of almost every law we have. Every law interferes with the "natural law" of people to do as they choose, and every law which protects the weak against the strong is open to the same kind of objections on the part of the strong as those which you raise against the Sunday Trading Bill when you say that such trading is a matter of mutual convenience and arrangement. Our point is, that it is not a matter of mutual convenience, but of one-sided convenience.'[66]

The entrepreneur of classical economics was an individual—not a firm, or a joint-stock company, or a corporation, but a single man, raising his own capital, investing it as he thought best, bringing together the factors of production in his own way, managing his own works, and selling his own product. Bearing all the costs of the undertaking, he was entitled to enjoy the benefits—and, of course, had to suffer any losses there might be. In a world of such entrepreneurs, it was argued that *laissez-faire* would make for the greatest happiness of the greatest number. Men were hungry and cold, in need of food, clothing and shelter. In supplying them, producers would seek to maximize their profits, and in conditions of free competition, this would mean maximizing their production. At the same time, free competition would prevent them exploiting the consumer. Where these conditions applied, it was thought that public enterprise was necessarily less beneficial to society than private enterprise for two reasons. Firstly, officials would have less interest in the success of an undertaking, since they would only benefit from it personally to the extent of their salaries and would not suffer any of its losses at all. Secondly, officials would have less knowledge of the working of the enterprise than those who had practical experience of it. Officials

[66] Lang, i, 118. Northcote to his wife, July 4, 1855.

of themselves were conscious of these disabilities. 'Goods and passengers find out the best channels,' reads the endorsement on a Colonial Office document, 'the first by the alertness and intelligence of merchants, the second by self-interest enlightened by the copious information afforded by competitors for custom.'[67] This single sentence unites the four assumptions on which the utility of *laissez-faire* was justified. Individual responsibility—'merchants', not firms; free competition—'competitors for custom'; maximum interest—'self-interest'; and knowledge—'alertness', 'intelligence', and 'copious information.'

CORPORATE ENTREPRENEURS

Even in the middle decades of the nineteenth century, these assumptions did not universally apply. Entrepreneurs were sometimes corporations, not individuals. Railway companies first brought the distinction home to the public. In such an undertaking, there was room for diversity of interests. The directors could make money out of a line, while the shareholders lost. The directors could sell land to the company at a profit, draw fees for their services, issue shares to themselves at par and sell them at a premium. Many schemes were promoted by solicitors and engineers who aimed to divert the shareholders' money into their own pockets in the form of fees, and by contractors out to create work for themselves. The growth of corporate enterprise was just as much a supersession of individualism by collectivism as was government growth. Mill made the point, and Dicey quoted the passage with qualified approval. 'Whatever, if left to spontaneous agency, can only be done by joint-stock associations, will often be as well, and sometimes better done, as far as the actual work is concerned, by the state. Government management is, indeed, proverbially jobbing, careless, and ineffective, but so likewise has generally been joint-stock management. ... The defects ... of government management do not seem to be necessarily much greater, if greater at all, than those of management by joint-stock.'[68] Water-supply was a sphere where private companies were not superior to local authorities 'in efficiency, economy, or management. Experience under the Public Health Act had shown that local authorities could supply the lower classes, who were generally neglected by the companies, for 1¾d. a week, and at the same time avoid the risks and losses of a trading body. Moreover, they were willing to undertake the construction of works for complex objects, such as combined

[67] MacDonagh (1961), 234.   [68] q. Dicey, 247n.

273

works for drainage, water-supply and sewage-disposal, which the wary capitalist would rarely touch. The new works exonerated municipal corporations and Local Boards from the charge of incapacity levelled against them, and demonstrated that responsible public bodies could give cheaper and better service than companies actuated by the motive of a trading profit to be levied on individual necessities'.[69]

IMPERFECT COMPETITION AND MONOPOLY

If entrepreneurs were not always individuals, neither was competition always free. The classical economists were not much aware that monopoly can arise through the operation of purely economic factors, but realized very clearly the importance of monopolies endowed by the state—chartered companies, for instance, or companies constituted by private Acts. Although the law treated such privileged bodies as persons, economics regarded them as collectivities. 'The whole spirit of the classical outlook was opposed to monopoly. . . . The classical economists sympathized with the state and with the individual citizens but not with intermediate bodies claiming coercive power. . . . There was nothing in their system to justify any predisposition in favour of groups of producers exercising restriction *vis-à-vis* the rest of the community.'[70] If monopoly was created by the state, the state must take measures against its abuse. So every railway Act, for example, contained provisions to limit the charges companies could exact. This was soon found inadequate. A Select Committee reported in 1840 that 'instances are not infrequent where companies and large capitalists, instead of competing with each other . . . have combined, and entered into agreements, whereby the public have suffered'.[71] It did not 'appear to have been the intention of parliament to give to a railway company the complete monopoly of the means of communication upon their line',[72] since it had been expected that carrying companies would compete with one another subject to payment of tolls to the company owning the line. This was not technically feasible. Even if it had been, it was not desirable. 'The safety of the public . . . requires that upon every railway there should be one system of management. . . . On this account it is necessary that the company should possess a complete control . . . although they should thereby acquire entire monopoly.'[73] In such a situation, there was no guarantee that a company would maximize

[69] Lewis, 307–8.   [70] Robbins, 105.   [71] P.P. 1840, xiii, 175.
[72] P.P. 1839, x, 132.   [73] P.P. 1839, x, 132–3.

its services to the public. At least one railway—the Leeds and Selby —had already increased its income by raising fares and reducing the number of passengers carried.[74] The Committee concluded: 'The absence of any effectual check from the absence of free competition on their respective lines . . . [makes] it advisable to subject this monopoly to some general superintendence and control . . . [which] will be most advantageously entrusted to some department of the executive government.'[75]

If government regulation of corporate entrepreneurs in an imperfect market was justifiable, it did not follow that it was feasible. One of the main limits on effective intervention by a government was its ignorance. 'It may believe its interference to be useful where it is really mischievous. There is no government that does not make such mistakes, and the more it interferes the more liable it must be to make them.'[76] But lack of knowledge was no excuse for inaction. 'Its refusal or neglect to interfere may also be founded on error. It may be passively wrong as well as actively wrong. The advance of political knowledge must diminish both these errors.'[77] Since governments acquire knowledge through the very activity of governing, 'the most fatal of all errors would be the general admission of a proposition that a government has no right to interfere for any purpose except for the purpose of affording protection, for such an admission would prevent our profiting by experience, or even acquiring it'.[78]

Experience of Poor Law administration had already, when Senior wrote those words, afforded sufficient knowledge of public health to justify intervention in housing. 'No one denies the right in the state to interfere to prevent a man from injuring others. It exercises this right when it forbids him to build a row of undrained cottages. But the right of the state to interfere to prevent a man from injuring himself supposes that the legislator knows better how to manage the affairs of an individual than the man himself does. In the present case this supposition is true.'[79] Hence the public authority should disinfect houses, enforce repair of unfit dwellings, or condemn them, as might be appropriate. The accumulation of knowledge in the hands of the state made possible intervention in new spheres. Census data provide good examples. For example, under the Public Health Act, 1848, the General Board of Health could intervene only where the death rate exceeded twenty-three per thousand. Similarly, the

[74] P.P. 1840, xiii, 105. [75] ibid. xii, 173.
[76] M. Bowley, *Nassau Senior and Classical Economics* (1937), 265.
[77] ibid. [78] ibid. [79] ibid., 266–7.

275

County and Borough Police Act, 1856, laid down that the new exchequer grants were to be payable where forces were 'efficient in number',—a test which clearly implied some comparison between the number of officers and the population of the area. Neither provision would have been workable without the census tables to draw on.

GOVERNMENT SPONSORSHIP OF RESEARCH

But the knowledge acquired by the state was not limited to what accumulated in the normal course of administration. There was also knowledge achieved through research. Before going on to consider its importance, it is necessary to show how the expenditure of public money on research was justified by nineteenth-century economic theory. The argument was an extension of Adam Smith's proposition about public works. The third function of the state, after defence and the maintenance of internal order, was 'erecting and maintaining certain public works and certain public institutions, which it can never be for the interest of any individual, or small number of individuals, to erect and maintain; because the profit could never repay the expense to any individual or small number of individuals, though it may frequently do much more than repay it to a great society'.[80] Of course, Adam Smith was thinking of comparatively modest investments in items of infrastructure such as bridges and harbours. Bentham extended it to research. At the head of a list of 'examples of the principal establishments which should or might be set on foot for the purpose of making . . . a positive addition to the stock of national felicity',[81] Bentham placed an establishment for the promotion of knowledge, as distinct from education. The state should sponsor research because 'the amount of profit reasonably to be expected is beyond calculation: while the individuals, among whom it may come to be shared, are equally out of the reach of conjecture. On the other hand, in the character of a source of profit, there is no limited assemblage or class of individuals, to whom the establishment of . . . one of these institutions would at the same time have been practicable, and have afforded a reasonable expectation of payment for the expense'.[82] Investigations to discover why the Dee Bridge collapsed in 1847 were justified in this way. 'The last few years have rendered necessary the construction of a number of

[80] Smith, ii, 184–5.
[81] J. Bentham, *Works* (ed. Bowring, 1843), xi, 133n.
[82] Bentham (1952–4), iii, 338n.

bridges, intended for the use of heavy trains passing at great speeds, in designing which the known laws relating to the strength of materials [are] most probably inapplicable; while the experiments requisite to ascertain those which may be applicable, *are beyond the means of individuals* ... Neither can the solution of this problem be left to time, or to the experience which might be obtained from a number of sudden and frightful accidents; the knowledge is required at once.'[83] The success of the Alkali Acts administration, or the regulation of railways,[84] derived very largely from the fact that the inspectors were at least as well informed as those whom they inspected, and sometimes more so.

SOCIAL COSTS AND STATE INTERVENTION

The 'social costs' argument was relevant to many other government activities besides research. If society at large enjoyed the benefit of an undertaking, society should contribute to the cost. Grant aid to the National Vaccine Establishment was justified on these grounds. Vaccination appeared to be a service for the poor. But it was administered by the Boards of Guardians solely because there was no one else to do so. The real reason why the Establishment merited financial support was that it was 'the only official and authentic source from which a pure lymph is obtained ... rather than only as a means of protecting a certain portion of the poorer classes from small-pox'.[85]

If, on the other hand, society was forced to bear part of the costs of an undertaking, it was entitled to regulate its operation. This was the reasoning behind the interest felt by the Board of Trade in railwaymen's working conditions from 1843 onwards.[86] On the face of it, the Board's concern might seem simply humanitarian, like the concern felt for slaves, for the factory children, or for women and children working in coal-mines. Someone, it might be supposed, was feeling sorry for the railway workers, because they were underpaid, or because they were being made to work excessively long hours, or both. But in fact the chain of reasoning was different. The officials argued that companies could not get good enough men as drivers and firemen at the wages they were offering, and that the lives of passengers would be endangered by entrusting them to the men who were in fact employed. The case in relation to hours was broader. No matter how good the men employed as signalmen (for instance)

[83] Parris (1965), 117–18. (My italics.) [84] ibid., 169ff.
[85] P.P. 1847–8, xviii, 34. [86] Parris (1965), 47–8, 225–6.

277

their reliability must deteriorate through fatigue. Hence if made to work too long at a stretch, the lives of passengers would be endangered. In either case, costs incurred in running a railway for profit were being improperly transferred to society.

The social costs factor was particularly important in public health. As Chadwick put it, 'all epidemics and all infectious diseases are attended with charges ... on the poor rates. Labourers are suddenly thrown by infectious disease into a state of destitution, for which immediate relief must be given. In the case of death, the widow and the children are thrown as paupers on the parish. The amount of burthens thus produced is frequently so great as to render it *good economy* on the part of the administrators of the Poor Laws to incur the charges for preventing the evils where they are ascribable to physical causes, which there are no other means of removing'.[87] Chadwick was thinking only of the physical environment. His successor, Simon, extended the indictment to the economic system in which potential paupers lived. 'If such and such conditions of food and dwelling are absolutely inconsistent with healthy life, what more final test of pauperism can there be, or what clearer right to public succour, than that the subject's pecuniary means fall short of providing him other conditions than those? It may be that competition has screwed down the rate of wages below what will purchase indispensable food and wholesome lodgement.... All labour below the mark is masked pauperism. Whatever the employer saves is gained at public expense ... and it is the public that, too late, pays the arrear of wage.'[88] Simon could logically have gone on to argue in favour of a legal minimum wage. But that would have been too much in nineteenth-century Britain. 'Probably on no point of political economy is there more general concurrence of opinion, than against any legislative interference with the price of labour.'[89] But at least the environmental services should be improved. 'Before wages can safely be left to find their own level in the struggles of an unrestricted competition, the law should be rendered absolute and available in safeguards for the ignorant poor. ... The fact is ... that, except against wilful violence, human life is practically very little cared for by the law.'[90]

[87] Finer, 155–6.
[88] q. O. R. MacGregor, 'Social Research and Social Policy in the Nineteenth Century', *British Journal of Sociology*, viii (1957), 149.
[89] ibid.   [90] ibid.

THE CASE OF EDUCATION

State aid to education was justified on a number of grounds. Most obviously, it was a charity, an act of kindness to the poor. But the social costs argument was also heard. Education cost money, but it was argued that not sending children to school might ultimately be even more expensive. Mill, for example, took this line. 'There are certain elements and means of knowledge, which it is in the highest degree desirable that all human beings born into the community should acquire during childhood. If their parents . . . have the power of obtaining for them this instruction, and fail to do it, *they commit a . . . breach of duty . . . towards the members of the community generally, who are all liable to suffer seriously from the consequences of ignorance and want of education in their fellow citizens.* It is therefore an allowable exercise of the powers of government, to impose on parents the legal obligation of giving elementary instruction to children. This however cannot be fairly be done, without taking measures to ensure that such instruction shall be always accessible to them, either gratuitously or at a trifling expense.'[91] But there was an even deeper reason. The individualism of nineteenth-century Britain rested on the assumption that everyone knew his own interests. Without education this was obviously not true. What Finer said of the Benthamites applied equally to many others. 'Any Benthamite was automatically an educationist, since his philosophy depended on the perfectability of society through the free play of its members' *enlightened* self-interest. . . . Education was desirable because it turned pauper children into productive citizens and prevented them from becoming permanent inmates of the workhouses; because it prevented juvenile delinquency and mendicancy; because it increased a labourer's skill, productivity, and earning power; because it prevented the growth of criminal classes; and because it led the workman to realize that his true interests lay not in "communism" or Chartism, but in harmony with his employers.'[92] Hence, Poor Law led on to education just as, in another direction, it led on to public health. The last words of the 1834 Report were: 'As soon as a good administration of the Poor Laws shall have rendered further improvement possible, the most important duty of the legislature is to take measures to promote the religious and moral education of the labouring classes.'[93]

[91] Mill, ii, 524. (My italics.)   [92] Finer, 150–1.   [93] q. ibid., 151.

HERBERT SPENCER ON PRIVATE AND PUBLIC ENTERPRISE

Burn pointed out that the nineteenth-century 'administrator had no
... set of collectivist clichés to help him and most administrators
would not have used them even if they had been available'.[94] This
is true. But it does not mean that there were no principles of government growth inherent in the opinion—to use the word in Dicey's
sense—of the age. Herbert Spencer is a good witness to call, for he
spent his life in battle against them. As early as 1843, he was com-
plaining that 'philosophical politicians usually define government,
as a body whose province it is, to provide for the "general good".
But this practically amounts to no definition at all, if by a definition
is meant a description, in which the limits of the thing are pointed
out'.[95] Instead of setting bounds to state action, the cry everywhere
was that it should extend to new spheres. 'We hear one man pro-
claiming the advantages that would accrue, if all the turnpike roads
in the kingdom were kept in repair by the state; another would saddle
the nation with a medical establishment, and preserve the popular
health by legislation; and a third party maintains that government
should make railways for Ireland, at the public expense. The
possibility of there being any impropriety in meddling with these
things never suggests itself.'[96] Such meddling was, in fact, highly
improper and harmful. The state should not enter new spheres of
activity and should withdraw from many in which it had long been
active. There should be no Poor Law, no state education, and no
public health. There were 'complex and manifold interests' in society
but they 'require no regulation at all ... they are originally so
arranged as to regulate themselves ... the great difficulties encountered in the management of social concerns, arise from the disturbance of natural laws, and ... governments have been foolishly
endeavouring to maintain, in a condition of *unstable* equilibrium,
things which, if let alone, would of themselves assume a condition
of *stable* equilibrium ... The affairs of the nation are in circumstances
of dreadful embarrassment, and ... it may take some skill to bring
them back to their normal state ... but ... this disastrous effect has
resulted—not from want of legislation but from over-legislation'.[97]

More interesting in the present context than the truth or falsehood
of Spencer's argument is the fact it dates from the so-called heyday
of *laissez-faire*, and that the villains of his piece were the 'philosophical politicians', i.e., the utilitarians. They crop up again in

[94] Burn, 289.   [95] H. Spencer, *The Proper Sphere of Government* (1843), 5.
[96] ibid., 3.   [97] ibid. 37.

Social Statics, published in 1851, as 'a school of politicians, especially claiming for themselves the title of philosophical'.[98] The 'expediency-idea of government'—i.e. utilitarianism—is 'the latest and most refined form assumed by this disposition to exalt the state at the expense of the individual. There have been books written to prove that the monarch's will should be the subject's absolute law; and if instead of monarch we read legislature, we have the expediency-theory. It merely modifies "divine right of kings" into divine right of governments. It is despotism democratized'.[99] To the list of proscribed state functions, a number of items are now added. There should be no regulation of personal health services. 'The invalid is at liberty to buy medicine and advice from whomsoever he pleases; the unlicensed practitioner is at liberty to sell these to whomsoever will buy.'[100] So with housing: 'The New Building Act was to have given the people of London better homes; whereas . . . it has made worse the homes that most wanted improving.'[101] Public vaccination was an abortive measure. 'The measures enjoined by the Vaccination Act of 1840 were to have exterminated small-pox; yet the Registrar-General's reports show that the deaths from small-pox have been increasing.'[102] Municipal authorities should renounce drainage, paving and lighting functions, leaving private companies to fill the gap.[103] Public works should become private works. 'That which is beneficial to the community as a whole, it will become the private interest of some part of the community to accomplish. And as this private interest has been so efficient as a provider of roads, canals, and railways, there is no reason why it should not be an equally efficient provider of harbours of refuge, lighthouses, and all analogous appliances.'[104] Even the Royal Mint and the General Post Office came under Spencer's ban. The provision of currency[105] and postal services[106] should be left to private enterprise. Spencer prescribes *laissez-faire*, but describes government growth. His writings show how far the middle decades of the nineteenth century were from a thorough-going implementation of the principle.

TOWARDS A MIXED ECONOMY

There was a nineteenth-century revolution in government, but there was nothing inevitable about it. The new pattern of central administration which emerged between 1830 and 1870 was an example of

[98] H. Spencer, *Social Statics* (1851), 196.
[99] ibid., 200.   [100] ibid., 373.   [101] ibid., 386–7.   [102] ibid., 387.
[103] ibid., 394.   [104] ibid., 406.   [105] ibid., 400ff.   [106] ibid., 403ff.

the way in which institutions respond to changes in the society around them. The French Revolution and the Hitler régime were others. An essential factor differentiating the three situations was the nature and quality of current thought about society, its problems, and their solution. It would be absurd to argue that the utilitarians revolutionized the British system of government by power of abstract thought alone. Their ideas were influential because they derived from the processes of change going on around them. They were working with the grain. But it does not follow that the same solutions would have been reached had they never lived.

So far Dicey is vindicated. His concept of collectivism, on the other hand, turns out to be a red herring. Utilitarianism was at work throughout—'that current of thought which arises in Bentham at the beginning of the century and flows into Fabianism at its end'.[107] Both *laissez-faire* and public enterprise were justified by its principles. There was a place for each, and no inconsistency in advocating both. This is what Chadwick, for example, did. 'He had great faith in self-interest. He commended it as the spring of individual vigour and efficiency; and it figured prominently in his thought as the most persistent and calculable element in human character. But he saw no evidence at all that social benefits resulted of necessity from its pursuit, and much which persuaded him that without the barriers erected by the law its undirected energies might disrupt society. He put his trust, therefore, not in the rule of some "invisible hand", blending the interests of the individual and society in a mystic reconciliation, but in the secular authority of the state which, abandoning the superstitions of *laissez-faire*, should intervene to guide the activities of individuals towards the desirable goals of communal welfare.'[108] The question was then, as it is today, not private enterprise *or* public enterprise, but where, in the light of constantly changing circumstances, the line between them should be drawn.

A NOTE ON THE CRIMEAN WAR

It is sometimes supposed that the Crimean War was a milestone in British administrative development, as a result of the scandals which it exposed. There seems to be little evidence to support this view. The question has been authoritatively discussed in a recent book.[109]

---

[107] Lewis, 188. [108] ibid., 130.

[109] O. Anderson, *A Liberal State at War: English Politics and Economics during the Crimean War* (1967).

Well before war began, the government had announced its acceptance of the principle of competitive examination for recruitment to the home civil service, as recommended by Northcote and Trevelyan. This was in the Queen's Speech, 31 January 1854. But the outcry was so great, that the scheme might well have been dropped but for the war. As it was, the setting up of the Civil Service Commission in 1855 must be taken as a sop to the administrative reformers, who were then at the highest point of their campaign. But it must always be remembered that the Commission was allowed very little scope until the introduction of open competition fifteen years later. The responsibilities of the Secretary of State for Colonies and War were divided, and the new Secretary for War took over the duties also of the Secretary at War and the Board of Ordnance. But it is by no means clear that the new system was in all respects an improvement on the old. For a time, the commissariat was also transferred from the Treasury to the new War Department; but it is symptomatic that part of its functions was handed back within two years. Above all, the opportunity was not taken to establish, finally and unequivocally, the principle that the Commander-in-Chief should be subject to the control of a minister responsible to parliament. The net result may well have been, not to produce a climate of opinion favourable to genuine administrative reform, but one hostile to administrative growth as such.

CHAPTER X

OUR PRESENT DISCONTENTS

'Few persons have any idea what obligations this country lies under to those who may be termed her unacknowledged statesmen. They sit in their separate apartments in Downing Street, and Whitehall, the unseen sources of many a splendid reputation. They, not unfrequently, both suggest and prepare the particular measures, which are submitted to parliament every session, by the government, and it is to them that we are generally indebted for those judicious and timely provisions, which relieve the nation from some pressing distress, and lend éclat to the favourite of the hour. As the judges of the land are largely assisted in the cases or causes which come before them by the speeches of counsel, who have been giving their attention to every point at issue, so are Cabinets influenced, and Select Committees of the House of Commons instructed and guided, by the advice and information which Under-Secretaries, especially if they should happen to be men of unusual sagacity and intelligence, are capable of affording. They also from time to time supply the Secretaries of State and the Chancellors of the Exchequer with those telling facts which enable them in debate to silence opposition and extricate government from embarrassing positions. . . . If at every change of administration those who hold office in Downing Street were one and all to depart, the question "How is the Queen's government to be carried on?" would not only be asked, but it would also have to be answered.'

Charles Badham, 1858

It is not so long since well-informed people were almost unanimous in thinking that the British civil service was, like the British police, wonderful. Finer's view in 1937 was typical. Britain's 'civil service', he wrote, 'is rightly the envy of the world, for it combines technical efficiency with humane serviceability as no other civil service does. . . . England . . . has, taken all in all, the best civil service in the world'.[1] A decade later, the Fabian Society stated 'that we have in Britain what is probably the best civil service in the world'.[2] In

[1] H. Finer, *The British Civil Service* (1937), 50 and 196.
[2] Fabian Society, *Reform of the Higher Civil Service* (1947), 5.

1956, Gladden asserted that 'civil service' stood for 'an ideal of vocation in public officials who devote their lives to the service of the community. . . . As an institution the civil service in Britain is well known and highly regarded. Its high professional integrity and absence of personal scandal are accepted without question'.[3] Such tributes could be multiplied to a degree that would be tedious. Where the opposite line was taken, as notoriously by Lord Hewart in *The New Despotism*, it was almost always possible to show that the critics were either misinformed or that they had an axe to grind.

In the 60s, however, all has changed. Shore asserts boldly that 'no one can doubt that the poor quality of the official advice tendered to ministers over the past decade has been one of the major causes of our dismal national record. . . . Again and again, in the post-war period, the wrong official advice has been supplied. . . . The advice tendered to successive Chancellors by the Treasury has been abysmally inept, as Britain's stop-go record so clearly illustrates. The record of the overseas departments—Colonial, Commonwealth and Foreign Offices—has been even worse'.[4] Lord Salter writes: 'In the service today a most striking—and perhaps alarming—fact is the increased power of the official in relation to ministers, Members of Parliament, and the public generally, This reflects a current phenomenon observable in a much wider sphere of our national life—the extent to which the centre of real power is different from that of nominal or legal authority. . . . In a wide, though not unlimited, sphere of their action, the power of ministers themselves has . . . to a . . . growing extent, passed to the officials who serve them. . . . Many changes which were inevitable in the circumstances of [the last fifty years] have in their cumulative effect reduced the relative power of ministers and increased that of the civil servants responsible to them.'[5] Nicholson wonders 'how such a picked group of intelligent, educated, agreeable, high-principled and hard-working people can be quite so disastrous for their nation as the record clearly shows the British higher civil service to have been. . . . Apart from a vague tendency to administer Britain like almost the last remaining Crown colony in an otherwise vanished empire, [the Administrative Class] has no real coherence or commanding level of morale commensurate with its indubitable power'.[6]

[3] E. N. Gladden, *Civil Service or Bureaucracy?* (1956), 17.
[4] P. Shore, *Entitled to Know* (1966), 12, 153–4.
[5] Lord Salter, *Slave of the Lamp* (1967), 281–3.
[6] M. Nicholson, *The System: the Misgovernment of Modern Britain* (1967), 464, 470.

The change of tone is remarkable. The earlier tributes all came from writers who were quite prepared to criticize. Indeed the Fabian pamphlet quoted above went on to say that the high quality of the civil service 'should not prevent us from asking how it may be improved'. Nevertheless, the dominant theme was pride in a great national institution. The criticisms now so plentifully current cannot all be written off as the fruit of spleen and ignorance. All the critics are intelligent and well informed. One—Shore—is (relatively) a young man looking forward; the other two—Salter and Nicholson—are old men looking back. Shore is a politician who has since become a Cabinet minister. Salter is an ex-civil servant, Member of Parliament and minister. Nicholson was in shipping control during the Second World War; attended Yalta and Potsdam; advised Herbert Morrison as Lord President of the Council; and headed the Nature Conservancy for fourteen years. 'By all the normal rules of behaviour [he] ought to be one of the ornaments of The System—that bundle of inherited attitudes, policies and institutions that together go to make up the British way of government.'[7] When men like these write as they do, it is reasonable to suspect that something must indeed be wrong.

FULTON AND NORTHCOTE-TREVELYAN

The tide of criticism has reached high-water mark in the notorious Chapter I of the Fulton Report.[8] In the view of the Committee, 'the structure and practices of the service have not kept up with the changing tasks. The defects we have found can nearly all be attributed to this. We have found no instance where reform has run ahead too rapidly. So, today, the service is in need of fundamental change. It is inadequate in six main respects for the most efficient discharge of the present and prospective responsibilities of government'.[9] The new criticism reflects not merely a shift in values but often a reversal of values. Graham Wallas asserted that 'the creation of [the civil] service was the one great political invention in nineteenth-century England'. Nicholson includes the 'new Victorian civil service derived from the Northcote-Trevelyan reforms of the mid-eighteen-fifties' among four groups which 'we are bound to suspect as possible carriers of [the British] sickness.'[10] Finer thought self-effacement should be the rule for officials. 'The first commandment of a civil

---

[7] Rudolf Klein, writing in *The Observer*, September 24, 1967.
[8] Cmnd. 3638. The Civil Service. Vol. 1 Report of the Committee (1968).
[9] ibid., 11.   [10] Nicholson, 52.

servant is "Subservience!" [11] Shonfield, on the other hand, blames them for subordinating themselves, for being 'anxious above all to ensure that the exercise of the new powers of government did not saddle them with the responsibility for making choices, for which they might later be accountable'.[12] Fulton argues in similar vein. For generations Macaulay's praise of the all-rounder has been quoted with approval.'We believe that men who have been engaged, up to one or two and twenty, in studies which have no immediate connexion with the business of any profession, and of which the effect is merely to open, to invigorate, and to enrich the mind, will generally be found, in the business of every profession, superior to men who have, at eighteen or nineteen, devoted themselves to the special studies of their calling.'[13] The Committee see the all-rounder as a liability rather than an asset. The first defect of the service, in their view, is that it 'is still essentially based on the philosophy of the amateur (or "generalist" or "all-rounder"). This is most evident in the Administrative Class which holds the dominant position in the service. The ideal administrator is still too often seen as the gifted layman who ... can take a practical view of any problem, irrespective of its subject-matter, in the light of his knowledge and experience of the government machine. Today ... this concept has most damaging consequences. ... The cult is obsolete at all levels and in all parts of the service'.[14]

Clearly the civil service is not above criticism. But if criticism is to lead to effective reform, it must set the problems to be solved in the dual context of time and of the social framework within which the service functions. Fulton fails on both these counts. To take the historical context first, the Committee's view is summed up in a single sentence: 'The present structure is still fundamentally the product of the Northcote-Trevelyan report.'[15] Everywhere it assumes that many of the present defects can be traced to that supposed fact.

'The disparaging references to the nineteenth-century Northcote-Trevelyan report on the civil service, made by Fulton and gleefully picked up by almost everyone who discussed Fulton, completely ignore the place of that report, and of its consequences, in the wider framework of the changing British political system. ... It is ... misleading to attack the civil service as being the product of the Northcote-Trevelyan report of over a century ago. The report's recommendations, however administratively desirable, were not

[11] H. Finer, 195.
[12] A Shonfield, *Modern Capitalism* (1965), 94.   [13] q. Fulton, 121.
[14] ibid., 11.   [15] ibid., 64.

practical politics at the time or for the next twenty-odd years.'[16] The Northcote-Trevelyan principles were not implemented immediately. Neither have they ever been implemented fully. If certain weaknesses in the present system are in fact due to the principles of 1853–4, it is at least equally true that other weaknesses result from the fact that the reforms proposed at that period have never been wholly carried out. In considering them it is necessary to look at a little further than the Northcote-Trevelyan report itself. As the Fulton Committee recognize, the reformers were much influenced by Macaulay's ideas for the Indian civil service. It is also necessary to take into account Benjamin Jowett's letter of January, 1854, which was printed as an appendix to the report itself. It was the ideas of these three documents which have been at work in British administration ever since, though some of them are still unrealized.

'ALL-ROUNDERS'

The Fulton Committee seem anxious to pose as revolutionaries. A careful comparison of their ideas with those of the nineteenth-century reformers shows, however, many points of resemblance. Fulton's condemnation of the 'all-rounder', for example, revives the nineteenth-century discussion about recruitment policy. Macaulay, as indicated in the passage quoted above,[17] held that young men of wide general education were the ideal recruits. It is not always realized, in these days of specialization, how wide were the terms in which he thought. In his scheme, even a candidate who got 100 per cent in Classics would have had little chance of success, unless well supported elsewhere. And that support might come from mathematics or natural sciences. 'A candidate who is at once a distinguished classical scholar and a distinguished mathematician will be, as he ought to be, certain of success. A classical scholar who is no mathematician, or a mathematician who is no classical scholar, will be certain of success, if he is well read in the history and literature of his own country. A young man who has scarcely any knowledge of Mathematics, little Latin and no Greek, may pass such an examination in English, French, Italian, German, Geology, and Chemistry, that he may stand at the head of the list.'[18]

Jowett's scheme was different. He argued that recruitment examinations should have regard, among other things, to 'the special

[16] W. Plowden, 'The Failure of Piecemeal Reform', *New Society*, July 18, 1968.
[17] See above, p. 287.   [18] q. Fulton, 123.

attainments needed in any particular department of the public service. . . . The special requirements of the higher departments of the public offices appear to be chiefly two, viz., a knowledge of the principles of commerce, taxation, and political economy in the Treasury, Board of Trade, etc.; of modern languages and modern history, under which last may be included international law, in the Foreign Office. In the offices which are principally offices of account, mathematical talent may with advantage be insisted upon'.[19] Therefor, candidates should be examined in four schools:

A. Classical literature
B. Mathematics, with practical applications, and Natural Science
C. Political Economy, Law, Moral Philosophy
D. Modern Languages and Modern History including International Law.

Two schools were to be required of all candidates, and none were to be allowed to attempt more than two. Successful candidates were to be placed in order of merit. Each man would have been able to choose, starting from the top of the list, from the list of vacancies available, 'provided he has fulfilled in the examination the requirements of the office which he selects'.[20] Thus a candidate who had done well in groups B and C would have been able to opt for the Treasury, while another who had good marks in groups C and D might have gone into the Board of Trade.

The majority of the Fulton Committee (there is on this point a powerful dissenting view) advocate a policy very similar to Jowett's. They 'consider that the relevance to their future work of the subject-matter of their university or other pre-service studies should be an important qualification for appointment'.[21] Like Jowett, they envisage the service as requiring two main types of entrant. 'An administrator, at least in his early years, should specialize in one or other of [two] main categories of work—the economic, industrial and financial, or the social. . . . The economic and financial administrators should be men and women who, in addition to their skill in administration, also have appropriate qualifications, experience and training in such subjects as economics, finance, business administration and statistics, especially as applied to government work. . . . Social administrators should . . . have training and experience in the social studies relevant to modern government. These include a knowledge of the social structure, organization and planning of communities and regions; methods of social investigation and the techniques of collecting and analysing information commonly used in public and

[19] P.P. 1854–5, xx, 472–3.   [20] ibid., 474.   [21] Fulton, 20–1.

private inquiries into social problems; and of social administration, especially the structure of the publicly provided social services and the policy problems which arise from their development.'[22] At the same time, the majority do not wish to exclude graduates in subjects such as Classics altogether. A powerful dissenting minority, on the other hand, believe that if recruitment methods 'give preference to those with relevant studies, the field of selection will in practice be unnecessarily narrowed. . . . We do not at all decry the advantage of a previous grounding in a relevant subject. But we think that it can be overrated. A rigorous and disciplined habit of mind, which can be imparted by "irrelevant" as well as by "relevant" studies, is no less important'.[23]

The minority recommendation is in the tradition of Macaulay, but not simply a restatement of his view. With the best will in the world, the Civil Service Commissioners could not begin recruiting all-rounders in the Macaulay sense next year, because the educational system is not producing them. Whatever criticisms can be brought against the Commissioners, no one can blame them for recruiting too many all-rounders in recent decades. The classicists and historians whom they have taken on in such numbers have specialized in their subjects just as engineers or statisticians do. Chapter I of Fulton introduces a red herring when it talks of all-rounders at the recruitment stage, because they are virtually extinct at that level. The choice today, given the development of the educational system over the last century, is as indicated in Chapter IV, between relevant and irrelevant specialisms. It is, of course, true that the Commissioners' requirements influence trends in educational provision. The nineteenth-century reformers sometimes seemed less interested in changes in the civil service for their own sake than for the effects they would have on schools and universities. The Fulton recommendation that greater stress should be laid in recruitment on numeracy and a working knowledge of foreign languages is therefore sensible.[24] Because of competition with other employers, however, it must be recognized that the influence of the Commissioners on syllabuses and methods is much less today than it was a century ago.

What type of recruit does the service need? If it continues to take on young people of high ability, but whose basic education is in 'irrelevant' subjects, will there be useful work for them to do? Fulton suggests a means of answering the question. 'One basic guiding principle should in our view govern the future development of the civil service. It applies to any organization and is simple to the point

22 ibid., 28.   23 ibid., 29–30.   24 ibid., 30.

of banality, but the root of much of our criticism is that it has not been observed. The principle is: look at the job first.'[25] It is by no means easy for an outside commentator to obey this precept. But here and there a breach in the wall of secrecy has been made. Take for example the work of a Principal in the Department of Education and Science in allocating the building programme for primary and secondary schools.[26] The total programme is settled between the Treasury and the DES, and divided between regions by an Assistant Secretary. Then the territorial Principal takes over, with the task of distributing the allocation among the Local Education Authorities of the region. For example, of £75 millions for England and Wales in 1966–7, £12 millions was the share of the North West. 'The next step . . . is for each territorial Principal to select individual projects from amongst all those put to him by local education authorities to the total of his allocation. He therefore examines in detail the projects in the programmes of these authorities.'[27] There is room for negotiation with interested parties but 'the ultimate decision will be that of the Principal.'[28] His task in doing so is anything but a mechanical application of rules. 'Like all decisions of this kind where the evaluation of cases must be made, where written statements vary in quality, where face-to-face discussions take place, and where the demand far exceeds the supply, subjective judgement cannot be excluded. . . . Discretion must be exercised . . . [since often] the need for a new school cannot easily be assessed with mathematical precision.'[29] 'Territorial Principals do, to a large extent, personally make the decisions on allocations to local authorities. . . . They may be under "political" instructions from above in particular cases, and they are consciously seeking to achieve departmental policy. In one sense the contact between Principals . . . and those above is close and continuous. But each is left to make the decisions appropriate to his or her level.'[30]

What sort of person is needed to discharge the duties of a territorial Principal? At present, generalists from the Administrative Class perform this role. Is this satisfactory? Would a specialist of some kind do the job better? The fact that the function relates to education, and to buildings, suggests at first sight that he might. But such a conclusion would be superficial. There is, in fact, nothing in the process that a graduate in Classics (say) cannot do as well as anyone else, so long as he is reasonably numerate. 'The territorial Principal

[25] ibid., 13.
[26] J. A. G. Griffith, *Central Departments and Local Authorities* (1966), 130ff.
[27] ibid., 132.   [28] ibid., 134.   [29] ibid., 135.   [30] ibid., 137.

must be certain that the population increases in the figures submitted by the local education authorities justify new or enlarged buildings. This entails the examination of the movements of age groups through the years, which reveals immigration. For each project, he must consider the numbers on the rolls of the existing schools, and all the other information submitted in the justification statement.'[31] But equally there is nothing in the job which specifically requires a generalist of the traditional type. If an engineer, for instance, or a statistician were available to fill a vacancy, if on other grounds he appeared suitable, and if he wanted the job, there is nothing in the nature of the work itself to preclude him making a success of it. No doubt the scarce skills of such people are usually better employed on specialized duties. No doubt most of them will always prefer to work at their own specialisms. Nevertheless, the example illustrates the scope for mobility among specialists, as advocated by Fulton.

TRAINING AND CAREER PLANNING

To criticize all-rounders in the civil service is not, in fact, to indict the recruitment system. It is to find fault with their training (or lack of it) and the way their careers have been planned (or not planned). Salter, for example, considers the integration of the civil service under the Treasury since 1919 to have been baneful. 'The minister needs from his principal civil servants advice as to the development of policy and not merely an instrument of execution. . . . Under the old system he was assured of receiving it from men who had many years of experience in the actual problems with which his department was concerned, and who were likely to have a strong personal interest in them. Under the new system the principal advisers might be men with as little experience of these problems as himself, and even less interest. . . . The great panjandrums would be the administrators, concerned not so much to achieve the best results as to prevent the office machine from becoming clogged. . . . [They] might even take a kind of pride in having neither specialized knowledge nor long-range policies.'[32] Defects of this kind have very little to do with the relevance or otherwise of the administrator's degree, but a great deal to do with his post-entry training and the planning of his career. So far as training is concerned, of course, Fulton is highly enthusiastic. Too enthusiastic perhaps: training, like everything else, should be costed, and there is no clear recognition of the necessity to relate the cost of training a civil servant to his probable enhanced

[31] ibid., 134. [32] Salter, 17–18.

value during the remainder of his career. But Fulton is not suggesting any radical innovation here. The principle has already been accepted at all levels.

It is in fact a belated implementation of ideas first put forward by the nineteenth-century reformers, but overlooked by Fulton. 'It is ... a grotesque misreading of the Northcote-Trevelyan report to imply that it endorsed or originated the cult of the "amateur". The concern ... was precisely to create a caste of professionals in government administration.'[33] The first question Northcote and Trevelyan asked themselves was 'whether it is better to *train* young men for the discharge of the duties which they will afterwards have to perform, or to take men of mature age, who have already acquired experience in other walks of life? Our opinion is, that, as a general rule, it is decidedly best to *train* young men'.[34] Admittedly, it is left unclear what form such training would have taken, had the reformers been given *carte blanche* to carry out their ideas. But Macaulay was much more specific. It may be literally true that he 'extolled the merits of the young men from Oxford and Cambridge who had read nothing but subjects unrelated to their future careers'.[35] He extolled them, however, not as civil servants, but as *trainees* for the civil service.

The training needed by Indian civil servants was provided at a school, and those who quote Macaulay's arguments often forget that he was talking about the entrance examination to that school. He argued that it should be designed to attract graduates rather than school-leavers and that the subject of the first degree was (in Fulton terms) 'irrelevant'. The examination should not be narrowly based on subjects such as Indian languages, though they could form part of it. It should rather be related to what were then the staples of a liberal education. 'Skill in Greek and Latin versification ... indicates powers of mind, which, *properly trained and directed*, may do great service to the state.'[36] To explain the importance he placed on training, he drew a comparison between the law and the civil service. 'The most illustrious English jurists have been men who have never opened a law book till after the close of a distinguished academical career; nor is there any reason to believe that they would have been greater lawyers if they had passed in drawing pleas and conveyances the time which they gave to Thucydides, to Cicero, and to Newton. The duties of a civil servant of the East India Company are of so high a nature that in his case it is peculiarly desirable that

---

[33] Plowden, loc. cit.
[34] q. Fulton, 111. (My italics.)
[35] Fulton, 9.
[36] q. Fulton, 123. (My italics.)

an excellent general education, such as may enlarge and strengthen his understanding, should precede the *special education* which must qualify him to despatch the business of his cutcherry.'[37] Candidates successful in the entrance examination were to be trained by means of 'serious studies . . . such as have a special tendency to fit them for their calling'.[38] These studies he grouped under four heads:

A. Indian history, geography, natural resources, manufactures, ethnography, religion and government
B. Law—'the general principles of jurisprudence'
C. Economics
D. One or more Indian languages

The course was to last from one to two years.

THE EROSION OF ANONYMITY

Fulton's most serious misrepresentation of the past occurs, however, in its discussion of anonymity. Broadly speaking, the Committee is against it. 'We think that the administrative process is surrounded by too much secrecy. The public interest would be better served if there was a greater amount of openness. . . . Civil servants, and perhaps also ministers, are apt to give great and sometimes excessive weight to the difficulties and problems which would undoubtedly arise from more open processes of administration and policy-making. . . . We suggest that the government should set up an inquiry to make recommendations for getting rid of unnecessary secrecy in this country. . . . The traditional anonymity of civil servants . . . is already being eroded . . . The process will continue and we see no reason to seek to reserve it. . . . In our view, therefore, the convention of anonymity should be modified and civil servants, as professional administrators, should be able to go further than now in explaining what their departments are doing, at any rate so far as concerns managing existing policies and implementing legislation. . . . It would be unrealistic to suppose that a civil servant will not sometimes drop a brick and embarrass his minister. We believe that this will have to be faced and that ministers and M.P.s should take a tolerant view of the civil servant who inadvertently steps out of line.'[19] Although the connexion between anonymity and ministerial responsibility is noticed,[40] there is no adequate recognition of the importance of these twin doctrines in British government, and of the far-reaching consequences for either if the other is relaxed. The

[37] q. ibid., 121. (My italics.) [38] q. ibid., 124.
[39] ibid., 91, 92, 93 and 94. [40] ibid., 93.

failure to place this recommendation in its historical context is particularly unfortunate, since it becomes easier for opponents to stone it to death with precedents. In fact, an historical analysis suggests that conditions have changed so much since these doctrines were formulated that some modification of them is overdue.

The convention of anonymity is, as Fulton says, being eroded. The reason for this is that civil servants come in contact today with so many more members of the public than they formerly did, and it is essential that they should do so. But, of course, it is not contact with the public at large that has wrought the change. Permanent Secretaries could appear on television night after night, explaining their personal views on departmental policy, without the man in the street perceiving any innovation in the constitution. Any discussion of civil servants in the mass, on the other hand, and 'the public' as a whole, on the other, must fail to do justice to the subtleties of the situation. Typically, a civil servant deals, not with the public, but with a public—a section of the population who have an interest in common. Officials of the Department of Education and Science, for example, meet leaders of teachers' unions, College of Education principals, and so on. Those in Agriculture and Fisheries have to do with farmers, while their colleagues in Health deal with doctors, dentists and nurses. These contacts, now so numerous and continuous, constitute further inroads on the concept of anonymity. The traditional form of address, 'I am instructed by the Secretary of State to inform you' gives way to a first-person style. The task of maintaining contact with such specialized publics is now so heavy that civil servants have to take much of the weight off the shoulders of ministers. It has become normal for civil servants to address bodies concerned with the work of their departments. Fulton approves this development and would like to see it go further. 'Administration suffers from the convention, which is still alive in many fields, that only the minister should explain issues in public and what his department is or is not doing about them. This convention has depended in the past on the assumption that the doctrine of ministerial responsibility means that a minister has full detailed knowledge and control of all the activities of his department. This assumption is no longer tenable. The minister and his junior ministers cannot know all that is going on in his department, nor can they nowadays be present at every forum where legitimate questions are raised about its activities. The consequence is that some of these questions go unanswered.'[41]

[41] ibid., 93.

Merely to know a civil servant by name is not, of course, enough to break the convention of anonymity. But once a specialized public knows him by name, it is very likely that it will soon get to know something at least of the ideas he will feed into the policy-making process in his department. In public discussion, particularly abroad, it is not always possible to refer back for instructions every time a new point comes up. To remain silent, on the other hand, would often create an impression of weakness. As a result, attempts are made to pierce the curtain of anonymity and to identify individual members of the service from whom advice to ministers on crucial matters is said to have originated. A good example of the new wave is Samuel Brittan's *The Treasury under the Tories*. He argues that 'the view that senior civil servants are pliant mind-readers, executing policies which they have had no say in making, is absurd. The opposite view, that senior officials blatantly urge one single course of action on minister after minister is equally false, if stated in this crude form. The truth is between the two extremes, although some Permanent Secretaries are nearer one than the other. . . . In this situation the dice are hopelessly loaded against the conventional type of politician; and it is almost inevitable, as Lord Woolton has remarked, that "the civil servants in the Treasury should have a very large, if not dominant, say" '.[42] This approach results in profiles of individual officials such as the following: 'Sir Frank Lee was . . . the first post-war Permanent Secretary to be fully at home in issues of economic policy. He had strong views on policy and, unlike more conventional officials, did not bother to hide them. But his own conduct was imbued with a fiery insistence on sticking to the practical and the politically possible, and woe betide anyone else who did not do so. . . . He saw more competition (he was the driving force behind the Restrictive Practices Act), rather than planning, as the cure for British industry. The conversion of the government to "Conservative planning" was certainly not his work. . . . In the arguments between the financial expansionists and the restrainers . . . Lee had more achievements to his credit than most of his predecessors put together. As one ex-Whitehall knight privately remarked, "Anyone who could persuade the Conservatives to become a low-tariff party must be counted a great man." His main mistakes arose from his bias towards deflation.'[43]

[42] S. Brittan, *The Treasury Under the Tories, 1951–1964* (1964), 38–9.
[43] ibid., 208–9.

MINISTERIAL RESPONSIBILITY TODAY

Even more serious inroads have been made on the doctrine of ministerial responsibility. The doctrine has, as shown in Chapter III above, a number of aspects, and that which is of concern here is the minister's responsibility for the acts of those under him. Is it now proper to talk of 'the myth of total ministerial responsibility'?[44] 'The civil servant is in the last resort subject to the orders of his minister who in turn depends on the support of parliament. But in practice, the fiction that all the actions of a department are the personal responsibility of its minister and that therefore parliament cannot carry its enquiries beyond the confines of a dialogue with the minister, means that there is a considerable, and constantly growing, range of administrative activity which escapes effective legislative oversight.'[45] Even *Punch*—a periodical not noted for preaching political heresy—was moved to comment: 'The whole idea of centralized responsibility is ludicrous. Those at the titular summit of modern affairs . . . cannot, surely, be expected to be masters in every detail of their great empires, or to do more than delegate as ably as humanly possible. Therefore it is . . . quite stupid to expect them to carry the can whenever malefaction produces exceptional emotional response. . . . Centralized responsibility in government departments . . . is a survival from the dark days of Victorian hypocrisy, when stern middle-class fathers liked to pretend that all men set in authority over them lived lives as blameless as they accounted their own.'[46] Ministerial responsibility, writes Beloff, 'is still the accepted doctrine in the political world itself and in the schools. But it bears increasingly less relation to practice or to what the general public thinks. . . . Most people as they read in the press of major instances of government extravagancc and lack of foresight would come to the conclusion that in their personal and professional lives they are wholly at the mercy of a vast governmental machine against whose arbitrary dictates they are quite helpless. . . . Confidence that parliament can protect people is waning—and they are encouraged in their disbelief in its utility by the utterances of an increasing number of its back-bench members'.[47]

To call ministerial responsibility a myth is misleading, since it implies that it does not exist. The institution of Question Time, or the behaviour of a civil servant giving evidence before a Select

[44] Shonfield, 394.   [45] ibid., 395.   [46] *Punch*, August 17, 1967.
[47] M. Beloff, 'Defining the limits of official responsibility', *The Times*, September 11, 1967.

Committee, are clear reminders that it is still very much in being. To call it a fiction, on the other hand, is helpful, if it is understood to imply an analogy with a legal fiction. A corporation is not a single person, but it is convenient in law to treat it as if it were. Similarly, though a minister is not responsible for every act of those under him —'for every stamp stuck on an envelope,' as Herbert Morrison once claimed[48]—in the same sense as he is responsible for his own acts, it may make for good government to pretend that he is. 'The doctrine gives Members of Parliament the right to demand information about any administrative decision from the minister in charge of the department. This . . . enables Members to investigate the grievances and press the claims of their constituents at the highest level. If Members did not have this right, they might be in a much weaker position than they are now to protect the interests of their constituents.'[49] Hence, ministerial responsibility is an important element in the control of a department. Even if the official is working 'with no immediate outlet to minister and Parliament, he will still be working tacitly with the sort of notions of relevance that would mean something to them; he must try so to order things, that, of all that can happen, only those things happen which are susceptible of explanation in the parliamentary context.'[50] Moreover, 'the ability to hold ministers to account for their actions in parliament facilitates the work of the opposition. . . . In this way the opposition can bring the government's weaknesses to the attention of press and public, and so hope to win votes in the next election'.[51]

But how far can the doctrine be taken? Is it true that 'the minister is responsible . . . for every action of his department and must resign if it is seriously at fault?'[52] How effective is the penalty of resignation? In the first place, it is of relatively recent origin. In his study of the question, the earliest case found by Finer dates only from 1864.[53] Secondly, resignations of this type have been few: 'A tiny number compared with the known instances of mismanagement and blundering.'[54] A number of factors operate to mitigate the offending minister's lot. If his colleagues back him up, the doctrine of collective responsibility supersedes that of individual responsibility. His mis-

[48] q. G. Marshall and G. C. Moodie, *Some Problems of the Constitution* (3 e., 1964), 84.
[49] A. H. Birch, *Representative and Responsible Government* (1964), 148.
[50] Sisson, 123.   [51] Birch, 149.
[52] Sir W. I. Jennings, *The British Constitution* (Cambridge, 3 e., 1950), 183 and 145.
[53] S. E. Finer, 'Individual Responsibility of Ministers', in *Public Administration*, xxxiv (1956), 381.   [54] ibid., 386.

deed becomes a question of confidence, and party solidarity carries the day. Again, the Prime Minister may save him by switching him to another post, not necessarily inferior. In practice, a minister resigns only where no party has an absolute majority, or when he has alienated part or all of his own party. Instances do occur. The resignation of Sir Thomas Dugdale in 1954, over Crichel Down, is a case in point. But they are very rare. Hence what remains of the doctrine? 'In its first sense, that the minister alone *speaks* for his civil servants to the House and to his civil servants for the House, the convention of ministerial responsibility has both the proleptic and the compulsive features of a "rule". But in the sense . . . that the minister *may be punished, through loss of office* for all the misdeeds and neglects of his civil servants which he cannot prove to have been outside all possibility of his cognisance and control, the proportion does not seem to be a rule at all.'[55]

Ministerial responsibility has not ceased to exist. Nevertheless, there are grounds for asking whether it will be adequate in the future as a device for securing an administration accountable to society. Firstly, there is the continued growth in the mere bulk of business which constantly increases the fictitious element in the minister's responsibility for his department. 'A ten-fold increase in the work does not mean that the minister takes ten times as many decisions, particularly when it is remembered that his parliamentary and political functions have also increased and that most of these cannot be delegated. It means that the modern minister takes few of the decisions.'[56] Secondly, there is the lengthening time-span of government operations. The Concorde air-liner project is a good example. More than a decade is expected to elapse between the negotiation stage and the entry of the aircraft into service; the agreement relating to it 'was signed long before parliament had become aware of its financial implications'.[57] Even if it were possible, no one seriously argues that governments should act differently. They are far more likely to be blamed for not looking far enough ahead than for excessive foresight. But what will be the situation if the venture fails? A minister will be responsible. But what would be the point of accepting his resignation, even if he offered it? The question is not hypothetical. It arose in 1961 in connection with the findings of the Romer Committee, which reported that poor security at the Admiralty had helped Soviet agents to get secret information. Lord Carrington, the First Lord, offered his resignation, but the Prime

[55] ibid., 394. [56] Jennings (1950), 131.
[57] N. Johnson, *Parliament and Administration* (1966), 107.

Minister refused to accept it, on the ground that the inadequate arrangements had been in force 'over a considerable period of years, dating from before the time when Lord Carrington had become First Lord'.[58]

INDIVIDUAL RESPONSIBILITY AND COLLECTIVE RESPONSIBILITY

One of the major difficulties is that the doctrine of collective responsibility cuts across the doctrine of individual responsibility. It may still be a principle of constitutional government 'that every act of government is either collective—as where a basic question of policy is concerned—or that of an individual department. In the latter case, except under special circumstances of a narrowly circumscribed kind—the minister who heads it has the responsibility for its action and can neither push them downwards on to his permanent officials nor diffuse them among his ministerial colleagues'.[59] But in contemporary British government, the proportion of collective to individual acts is constantly increasing. Take for example the work of a territorial Principal in the Department of Education and Science, who has the task of allocating the school building programme between local education authorities. On the face of it, this appears to be a clearly defined function for which the minister can take responsibility in the traditional way. In fact, for him to do so leads —paradoxically—to a blurred division of responsibilities between ministers. For the object of the school building programme is not educational. Its effect in the vast majority of cases is to restrain the growth in educational provision, not to promote it; to stop local education authorities from building schools they think necessary. 'Building programmes derive from investment programmes. ... Today the figures for school building are a reflection not only of other educational spending but of all other public spending also.'[60] Most people would accept that such restraint is justifiable on grounds of national economic policy. But that policy must be a collective responsibility of the government as a whole. No single minister— and certainly not the minister in charge of education—can take sole responsibility for it.

Of course it is right to relate school building to general economic policy, but the consequences must be faced. 'The traditional notion of a number of discrete ministerial responsibilities for which the

[58] F. Stacey, *Government of Modern Britain* (Oxford, 1968), 260.
[59] Griffith (1966), 130ff.   [60] ibid., 158.

respective office-holders are liable to give an account of themselves to the legislature is obviously threatened to the extent that departmental policies are interdependent.'[61] In this case it creates difficulties for aggrieved parties who wish to use political pressure to change the administrator's decision. Part of the total allocation is kept back against such an eventuality, so that small adjustments can be made, and there is a difference between appealing to an official and appealing to a minister. 'Civil servants are not greatly impressed by special pleading . . . and . . . resent attempts to influence them if they feel that they have already performed a difficult task to the best of their ability. But politicians . . . are willing to make "exceptions" if this will placate a particularly vociferous or a particularly powerful interest.'[62] A local education authority may enlist the help of local M.P.s. But 'the presence of Members of Parliament in the deputation seems to add little to its strength'.[63] The power of a local authority in this context is almost entirely a question of size. The larger ones can normally insist on seeing the minister; the smaller ones are unlikely to get so far. In any case, even a face-to-face confrontation is unlikely to yield results. 'The Department, forced to adjudicate between so many rival claims for a share of limited money, cannot afford to have the reputation of yielding to deputations. The reputation for fairness which the Department have acquired in their school building allocation could be most easily and quickly lost if it were felt that they were weak when faced with a deputation. And the interest of the Secretary of State in supporting the decisions of his civil servants is obvious.'[64]

In short, although the allocation is carried on under the aegis of individual ministerial responsibility, it is hard to see what advantage accrues thereby. In the last resort, the minister can say with truth that, if the programme is not big enough, the fault lies with the Treasury and the Cabinet, not with himself. 'The immersing of individual in collective responsibility transfers every question to the plane on which a government may . . . proceed to the argument that "the electorate must judge." . . . When ministers offer the collective as a substitute for the individual doctrine it is useful to remember the differences between them. . . . If A is individually accountable for B it is assumed that the facts about B are either patent or discoverable and that judgements about ministerial negligence or maladministration can at least in some cases be separated out from judgements reflecting general disagreement about party policy. Neither of these assumptions can be made about the kind of ability

[61] Marshall and Moodie, 190.   [62] Griffith, 141.   [63] ibid.   [64] ibid.

or accountability that is associated with a capacity for winning the next general election."[65]

But this is not the only way in which lines of individual responsibility have become blurred. Ministers also take responsibility —in everyday parlance—for matters in which they have no responsibility in the constitutional sense. For example, territorial Principals in the Department of Education and Science not only allocate the building programme between authorities, but also weigh up the priorities of individual projects. 'The territorial Principal ... does not merely draw a line below one project and above another on each local authority list. It is of course arguable that he should do so— that he should accept the order of priority put to him by the local education authority and decide only how many such projects should be approved. But in practice he considers each project in detail and may engage in lengthy consultation with the local education authorities on its merits or demerits.'[66] The result is that local education authorities find high-priority schemes turned down, whilst lower-priority schemes are approved. Government relations with the aircraft industry provide a further example. The department responsible (until 1966) was the Ministry of Aviation. The minister was able to exert influence both on the suppliers, who needed a market for their products, and on the main customers—the armed services and the public airline corporations. There was a Transport Aircraft Requirements Committee but it was not very successful. It was 'the Minister of Aviation who had to decide what projects to support, often after reference to the Cabinet. His job has been not so much to consider almost unanimous recommendations based on the best technical and commercial advice, but to arbitrate between conflicting advice what projects should get a share of the limited resources available'.[67] The minister was not responsible for the aircraft used by the services. Nevertheless, pressure had been 'brought on the Air Ministry to take civil types in order to help make them economically viable'.[68] Neither was he responsible for the aircraft used by BEA and BOAC. 'Legally they are free to buy whatever aircraft they need, but in practice this freedom has been seriously restricted by government intervention. Ministerial approval for loans is required, and in practice the government has always had to take into account its interest in the aircraft industry. ... BOAC witnesses made no attempt to conceal the pressures brought to bear on them. Quoting Henry Ford, Sir Matthew Slattery remarked that,

[65] Marshall and Moodie, 191–2.   [66] Griffith, 135.
[67] Johnson, 99.   [68] ibid., 100.

"you can have any colour so long as it is black," by which he meant any aircraft so long as it is British (and presumably one which the government has decided to support).[69] The ministry admitted that 'since the corporations' purchases of new aircraft are financed largely by loans from public funds, the minister is bound to take an interest in the economic and industrial implications of the proposed purchase'.[70] Nor yet was the minister responsible for the decisions of private firms as to which types of aircraft to manufacture. Yet his influence with the principal users naturally gave him great influence also with the producers, especially since it was backed up by his power to contribute to the development costs of new civil transport aircraft and civil aero-engines. It was this which made it possible to push through a policy of rationalization in the aircraft industry. The problem of responsibility for school building priorities could be resolved by the DES simply withdrawing from this field. But very few would advocate giving up any attempt to co-ordinate the demand and supply of aircraft. What is clear is that the traditional doctrine of individual ministerial responsibility does not make much sense in this sphere.

If the conventions of ministerial responsibility and the anonymity of the civil servant were adapted to contemporary realities, clear advantages would ensue. Ministries could become smaller, as a result of 'hiving off', and could devote a bigger proportion of their efforts to policy planning. If this were done, one of Fulton's most dubious recommendations would probably no longer be necessary. The report urges that 'in most departments, if not all, there should be a Senior Policy Adviser to assist the minister'.[71] There is, of course, already a senior policy adviser in each department. He is called the Permanent Secretary, and the Committee is not urging his supersession as senior civil servant in each ministry.[72] It is very hard to see how this would work. It is difficult to separate policy and administration at any level, and it is hardest of all at the top. If ministers really relied on their Senior Policy Advisers in the spirit implied, how could these officials fail to acquire considerable weight in administrative questions also? If on the other hand—which is far more likely—ministers continued to take the advice of Permanent Secretaries on questions of long-term policy, the role of the Senior Policy Advisers would be almost bound to decline. In a small ministry, acting as a policy-forming centre for a group of agencies to which blocks of work had been delegated, the problem would be much less likely to arise. The traditional function of the Permanent

69 ibid., 107.   70 ibid., 108.   71 Fulton, 59.   72 ibid., 60.

Secretary would be more likely to survive, whether with that title or another.

If ministerial responsibility were redefined, the anonymity doctrine would adjust itself accordingly. Would less anonymity matter? History suggests not. It is often supposed, for example, that anonymity is a condition of permanence; civil servants would sometimes have to resign if their recommendations and/or party affiliations became known. But the convention of permanence was, in fact, established some decades earlier than that of anonymity. In any case, the civil service could stand a considerably higher rate of resignations on grounds of policy without ceasing to be permanent. It might well be the better as a result. There is something anomalous in a situation where a writer has to go back years to find an example of an official giving up his post on a point of principle.[73] It is accepted that officers of the armed services who advise ministers should sometimes resign if their recommendations are over-ruled. This 'tradition gives the service chiefs a power to persuade ministers which their civilian counterparts do not possess'.[74] Hence, a reduction of anonymity might enhance the influence of senior civil servants. Moreover, the principle has already been accepted that a minister may bring in personal advisers from outside his department, who are expected to go when the ministers go. Fulton approves 'this practice as a means of bringing new men and ideas into the service of the state'.[75] But it must be difficult for anonymous insiders to work as a team with outsiders whose views are known. Hence any relaxation of the convention of anonymity is likely to help non-civil-service advisers also.

THE ACCOUNTABILITY OF ADMINISTRATION TO SOCIETY

Neither anonymity nor ministerial responsibility should be made fetishes of. They are meaningless except as ways of making administration accountable to society. If they do not seem to be working too well, there is no need to despair. Central administration is not unique in operating under social control. Public corporations, the police, and the schools, are under comparable obligations, and it is largely a matter of chance which individuals rank as civil servants. In Britain, railwaymen, policemen, and teachers are not, but this does not relieve them of special obligations to society arising out of

[73] J. D. Kingsley, *Representative Bureaucracy* (Yellow Springs, Ohio, 1944), 178.
[74] *The Guardian*, December 28, 1967.   [75] Fulton, 45.

their calling. Moreover, accountability to society is compatible, paradoxically, with independent status. The independence of the judges does not mean that they can do as they like. Nor does the autonomy of the universities. The Independent Television Authority is similarly subject to restraints. If therefore some parts of central administration were freed from ministerial responsibility, they need not escape from public control altogether. A generation ago it was reasonable to suppose that that was a real danger. 'We are, it would seem, drifting towards something not far removed from what may be called "government by commission." . . . The success or failure of this new tendency will depend ultimately on whether we can evoke the same degree of devotion to duty, public spirit, integrity, and competence from persons engaged in public administration without the spur or menace of ministerial control as we have managed to secure by means of it. . . . All these new and complicated economic functions of the state no doubt make ministerial responsibility obstructive and cumbersome. But we shall have bought flexibility and freedom at too great a price if they bring a return to the nepotism, low standards, and corruptibility of the eighteenth century.'[76] But it is now realized that administration can be made responsible in a variety of ways.

SUPERVISION BY PARLIAMENTARY COMMITTEES

Pride of place should be given, as Fulton recognizes, to making more effective parliament's supervision of the executive. 'We should . . . like to see Members of Parliament more purposively associated with the work of government than they are now. The traditional methods of parliamentary scrutiny have often failed to enlarge parliament's knowledge of what goes on or to secure for it a proper influence; at the same time they frequently impede the efficiency of administration.'[77] A good deal has already been done by setting up parliamentary committees; some with general responsibilities, such as the Select Committee on Estimates; and others of a specialized kind, such as those on the nationalized industries, and science and technology. Until very recently, it was customary to argue against committees of this kind on the grounds that they were alien to the British tradition. Lord Butler's attitude was typical when he said that a proposal to set up a colonial committee 'smacks to me far more of Capitol Hill and the Palais Bourbon than of the parliament in Westminster'.[78] Such statements had for years great emotive force,

[76] Robson, 27–8. [77] Fulton, 92–3. [78] q. Birch, 162.

but were always irrelevant. Parliamentary committees to supervise the executive were in fact a well-established part of British government in the nineteenth century. Their recent revival is a resumption of a tradition which appeared to have been lost. At that time, it was common for civil servants—sometimes holders of relatively minor posts—to appear before parliamentary committees.

Of course, investigatory committees do create problems. But some of them turn out to be more imaginary than real. Beloff, for example, asserts that 'to reorganize parliament around strong well-staffed committees . . . would be to have not only a different kind of parliament but a different kind of parliamentarian. We would have to consider the impact of such changes on what is in our system . . . a still more important function of the legislature, the selection and training of aspirants for ministerial office'.[79] This implies, firstly, that parliamentarians are all of the same type. In fact, the success of the Select Committee on Estimates (at least) has been largely due to its success in attracting parliamentarians of a rather distinctive type: 'Experienced backbenchers . . . moderate in their political ambitions and sometimes moderate too in their party ardour. It has had the support of men who are neither executive-minded nor obstinately prejudiced against the executive, but with a degree of independence which has permitted them to be critical when this was called for.'[80] Beloff's remark implies, secondly, that service on such a committee is not a good training for potential ministers. It might be supposed, on the contrary, that inquiries which bring Members to grips with administrative problems and into contact with civil servants would be particularly valuable as preparation for office.

More seriously, investigatory committees run into difficulties in separating questions of administration from questions of policy. The tradition has been to suppose the distinction clear. 'Policy, [civil servants] might say, is for the minister; ours is the task of providing the machine to execute it. This is of course the orthodox division of function between minister and civil servant.'[81] Nowadays such an approach would be thought too easy. 'Anyone with experience of actual administration knows that the distinction between policy and execution is not such a simple one. In practice policy is developed gradually by current administrative decisions.'[82] The work of the Estimates Committee provides many instances. For example, with the decline of Empire, the work of the Colonial Office has contracted. How best to transact what remains is an administrative question. But to suggest a merger with the Commonwealth Relations

[79] Beloff, loc. cit. [80] Johnson, 25. [81] Salter, 17. [82] ibid.

Office was held to be 'an unwarranted intrusion into policy issues'. The whole incident 'is a good example of how an enquiry into administrative arrangements can lead on naturally to policy matters'.[83] There is real difficulty in drawing a clear 'line between policy and administration in many areas of government action. The Estimates Committee has experienced this in its enquiries. Often it cannot make sense of administrative procedures and organization until it has found out what policies are being pursued. It just cannot avoid intruding into the area of policy'.[84] Nevertheless, the Committee has not been unduly hampered in its work, and there is no reason why other committees should be. The difficulty is real. But it looks a good deal larger in principle than it does in practice. It will continue to bother people with an obsession for tidiness. But such people would be well advised to look elsewhere for it then the British system of government.

'HIVING-OFF'

The difficulty of separating policy from administration also arises in any discussion of 'hiving-off'—a process of which Fulton approves and of which it would like to see more. 'We see no reason to believe that the dividing line between activities for which ministers are directly responsible, and those for which they are not, is necessarily drawn in the right place today.'[85] It is a process which will be exemplified in the near future on a large scale by the conversion of the Post Office into a public corporation. The principle to be followed is fairly clear. If 'all that central government does that is substantive in character—that is to say of a non-judicial or arbitral kind—must be organized within departments whose heads are seated in parliament, and are there amenable to parliamentary inquiry and control',[86] it follows that the judicial and arbitral business can be delegated to other agencies. In education, for example, the recent decision to postpone the raising of the school-leaving age was eminently a substantive decision, and was rightly defended by the Secretary of State in parliament. The allocation of the school building programme, on the other hand, is an arbitral process[87] and nothing would be lost if the task were handed down to a National School Board.

In the light of British experience, would more 'hiving off' work? There is every chance that it would. Until the middle of the nineteenth century, a large part of central government was carried by non-

[83] Johnson, 69 and n.　　　[84] ibid., 162.　　　[85] Fulton, 61.
[86] Beloff, loc. cit.　　　[87] See above, p. 291.

ministerial agencies and new boards continued to come into existence down until the period of the Crimean War. 'The later Victorian era was the golden age of ministerial administration', but since 1906 'boards with all degrees of independence' have flourished once more.[88] The experience of the Poor Law Commission is the exception that proves the rule. In the first place, the policy which it had to carry out was highly controversial—'substantive' rather than 'arbitral'. Secondly, that policy benefited the majority of the political nation at the expense of those without political rights. Hence, it was natural for the latter to use unconstitutional means to express their protest. In any case, the main criticism of the Commissioners is not that they flouted public opinion, but that they were too responsive to it. They never did completely implement the policy of banning out-relief—the main plank of the 1834 platform. At the present time, there is no reason to expect boards to behave less responsibly than ministries. Each operates in close liaison with representatives of its specialized public. 'Trade unions and trade associations do not need any new institutions to represent their interests, for these are already represented in a variety of ways. . . . [Similar] kinds of representation are enjoyed . . . by any organized group which represents a genuine interest. Ex-servicemen are represented through the British Legion, motorists through the motoring organizations, and people who enjoy fox-hunting through the British Fields Sports Association.'[89] The danger is, not that agencies will ride rough-shod over their clients, but that cosy conspiracies will exploit society. If the whole of central administration were conducted in this way, Britain would be well on the way to the corporate state.

DEVOLUTION TO REGIONAL AUTHORITIES

It is not to central agencies alone that responsibilities could be delegated. Decentralization would perform a similar function. Parliamentary control 'necessarily imposes, since parliament is in one place, a high degree of centralization upon the machinery of the national government, even in relation to administration. The forms of parliamentary control . . . make it highly desirable that the answer can be found speedily in the minister's department in London'.[90] The result is to impede the working of the machinery which has been set up at regional level. There is an obvious case for co-ordinat-

---

[88] Willson, 47.   [89] Birch, 113.
[90] J. D. B. Mitchell, 'The Causes and Effects of the Absence of a System of Public Law in the United Kingdom', *Public Law* (1965), 99–100.

the development of highways (for example) with developments in other spheres, such as industry and housing. The Economic Planning Councils, with their Boards of officials, provide the means by which this could be done. The Divisional Road Engineer of the Ministry of Transport consults the other interests, and considers their comments. But the decision what to recommend to headquarters rests with him. 'It is significant that the draft list prepared by the DRE, but not his final list, goes to the Council, so that the Council is not involved in the DRE's advice to headquarters of his own department, and the DRE is not involved in detailed argument with the Council about the departmental view of priorities.'[91] In other words, co-ordination is necessarily ineffective and is bound to remain so within the present framework.

Nor is parliamentary control of this part of the Ministry of Transport's work effective either. The Ministry distributes money to local highway authorities, and 'the basis of [its] control rests . . . in the power . . . to approve or withhold grants'.[92] Very wide discretion is invested in the DREs, who 'have complete responsibility for the selection of schemes costing less than £100,000. No approval from headquarters is required and no justifications need to be submitted'.[93] For example, in 1965-6, £700,000 was divided between the authorities of South-West Division. Has an aggrieved local authority any means of appealing against the DRE's decision? Practically, no. 'Deputations are not often sent to the department by the local authorities. The answer they would receive is so predictable, and it is abundantly clear that since the department have a limited allocation of money from the Treasury very little more can be extracted for any single authority than its original allocation. . . . One local authority can succeed only at the expense of others.'[94] Appeal to parliament would be even less effective. But it does not follow that DREs behave irresponsibly. 'The reaction of local highway authorities to . . . decisions on road programmes and the allocation of money is normally temperate.'[95] This is because the ministry official takes his decisions in the face of a public, consisting of members of his own profession—chief officers of the local authorities in his division—some of whom are at least as well qualified as himself. But the problem of co-ordinating remains. That could be performed, not only more effectively, but also more responsibly, if control were delegated by parliament to elected regional authorities.

[91] Griffith, 195. [92] ibid., 170. [93] ibid., 196.
[94] ibid., 204-5. [95] ibid., 204.

But it would be naïve to ignore the fact that control of administration by regional authorities would be subject to many of the same limitations as parliamentary control. The remedy for this, and much else, is to develop a system of public law which would permit of appeals against administrative decisions on a much wider basis than is now the case. At present the appeal in many cases is to parliament —a feature of British government in which it has been customary to take pride. 'There is . . . one very real check which prevents delegation to civil servants from giving rise to bureaucracy. The responsibility of ministers to parliament means that every decision, even if it is taken far down in the official hierarchy, may be criticized in parliament. If a member considers that injustice has been done to an individual . . . he can ask a question in the House. . . . Let us take [an example] at random. On 16 January 1940, . . . the Minister of Health [was asked] about a pension for Mr C. F. Mott.'[96] The system may be criticized from several points of view. Does society want parliament to spend its time on such minutiae? Are there not more important uses to which it could be put? And does the system provide adequate safeguards to the individual? Is it right that he should be dependent on an M.P. to speak for him—given that they necessarily vary in intelligence, humanity and assiduity? In any case, does the individual get satisfaction? A civil servant's definition of a perfect parliamentary answer is worth bearing in mind here: 'One that is brief, appears to answer the question completely, if challenged can be proved to be accurate in every word, gives no opening for awkward "supplementaries", and discloses really nothing.'[97]

The Parliamentary Commissioner's investigation of the Sachsenhausen affair illustrates this point. An Anglo-German agreement of 1964 provided £1 million for the benefit of British nationals who were victims of Nazi persecution. The Foreign Office was given the task of distributing the money. Applications were finally closed on March 31, 1966, and final payments were made later that year. Four ex-prisoners of the concentration camp at Sachsenhausen had their applications turned down. The matter was raised in parliament, but the complainants received no satisfaction. The Foreign Secretary wrote: 'I cannot accept, on the basis of the evidence which has been assembled from various sources, including the officers' own state-

[96] Jennings (1950), 138.

[97] H. E. Dale, *The Higher Civil Service of Great Britain* (Oxford, 1941), 105.

ments, that they suffered treatment in any way comparable to that endured by the inmates of the main camp at Sachsenhausen or of any other concentration camp, about which I need hardly say we have abundant evidence.'[98] The M.P. to whom this letter was addressed then referred the matter to the Parliamentary Commissioner. He concluded, not only that the complainants' application had been unjustly rejected, but also criticized Foreign Office officials for their 'presentation of the case to Secretary of State'[99]—in other words, the brief from which he answered charges in parliament.

Those who praise the work of parliament—before or since the Parliamentary Commissioner—often sound like those who advocate fixing pipes outside buildings so that they will be readily accessible when they freeze. The fact that many people take their grievances to parliament does not show that it is the right place for them. 'The forum for political debate may often not be the appropriate place to argue a question of maladministration.'[100] It only shows how inadequate other means of dealing with them are. A parliamentary 'answer, even when it is followed by rectification of an administrative error, lacks the quality of a judgement in two respects. It lacks the enduring and formative quality of a judgement which enters into a system of jurisprudence, and it lacks the ability of a judgement to decree compensation. Very often the mere rectification of an error without compensation is today an inadequate remedy'.[101] The recommendations of the Parliamentary Commissioner go further in both respects. They will constitute a case-law from which it will eventually be possible to distil a jurisprudence. And they can secure compensation for aggrieved persons. But he is not a substitute for a system of administrative law, any more than previous forms of parliamentary control were.

From whence could such a system develop? Hitherto, attempts to deal with the problem have started at the wrong end. The Franks Committee and the Tribunals and Inquiries Act, 1958, for example, were both 'essentially concerned with trimming the mode of taking decisions to fit an inadequate system of law rather than being concerned with the law itself'.[102] There has been an obsession with technicalities which impede the administration without giving any corresponding satisfaction to the citizen. An undue preoccupation with procedural safeguards imposes delay on the administration. At the same time, there is a reluctance on the part of the public to give

[98] 3rd Report of the Parliamentary Commissioner for Administration (1967–8), 18.
[99] ibid., 17.   [100] Mitchell, 99.   [101] ibid.   [102] ibid., 108.

them up precisely because it is so hard to appeal effectively against decisions after they have been taken. From the time of Dicey, it has been customary to insist on the fact that 'with us every official, from the Prime Minister down to a constable or a collector of taxes is under the same responsibility for every act done without legal justification as any other citizen'.[103] The implication is that grievances arising out of acts done by officials *with legal justification* are no concern of the law, and can be remedied only by political means. In contemporary society, such a view is highly artificial. It ignores the myriad clashes of private right with public interest which arise throughout modern government—in planning, housing, and the construction of motorways, to take only three examples. The institutions of private law treat the parties as equals. But in questions such as these, there is a necessary and proper inequality between the parties. Public interest should prevail over private interest. Hence, public law must differ from private law. 'The mechanisms appropriate to striking a balance in the one condition will of necessity be inappropriate or inefficient in the other.'[104]

Is any help to be expected from the courts? First the common law, and then equity, evolved from the ratiocinations of medieval judges. Could their twentieth-century brethren emulate them? Unfortunately, they seem incapable of doing so. Generally speaking, the bench has been so obsessed with the perfection of parliamentary control of administration that it has drawn back from the task of fashioning appropriate methods of legal control. Three sentences from the majority opinions in *Liversidge v. Anderson* make the point. Lord Maugham stressed that the Secretary of State was 'a member of the government answerable to parliament' and that 'he would be answerable to parliament in carrying out his duties.' Lord Macmillan emphasized that the same dignitary was 'answerable to parliament for the conduct of his office'. Lord Wright agreed, adding that 'the safeguard of British liberty is in the good sense of the people and in the system of representative and responsible government'. The implication was that what is the business of parliament is not the business of the courts.

What is wanted is a genuine administrative jurisdiction, which could be most fittingly entrusted to the Privy Council. This was the body which had begun to operate in this field, and from which a native system of administrative law might have grown, but for the upheavals of the seventeenth century. 'If with us the conciliar courts could have been quieter and duller their history might have

[103] Dicey (1893), 183.　　　　　　　　　　　　[104] Mitchell, 102.

been longer.'[105] The Privy Council already contains many people well suited to be members of an Administrative Committee, and the Judicial Committee provides a precedent for such a body. The tribunal's initial staff could be formed partly by transfer from existing ministries, and partly by recruitment from outside—from other branches of administration and from the universities, plus a few lawyers. Thereafter, recruitment could follow the pattern of other central departments. There should be arrangements for interchange between the Administrative Committee's staff and the staff of the other departments, in order to keep the former in touch with active administration. The aim would be to make the administration responsible for remedying grievances against itself, and for elaborating in public the standards to which civil servants should conform. And if this seems to be making the civil servant judge in his own cause, it should be remembered that other professions—for example, medicine and the law are regulated in a similar way and not without success.

The terms of reference of such an Administrative Committee should be broad but simple. It would probably be possible to avoid legislation. This would be desirable, because it would permit the Committee's powers to develop under their own momentum, without recourse to parliament for further powers. Probably it would be enough to give the Committee power to annul any administrative act, or to compensate any person aggrieved by an administrative act but without a remedy at law. Such wide powers would attract a host of cases and raise a great many problems. What is 'an administrative act'? Under what circumstances can a citizen interpret the administor's silence as a rejection of his claim? Or should silence be taken to mean acceptance of a claim? What limit of time could be allowed for appeals? (Clearly the administration would be hamstrung if the possibility of appeal remained open indefinitely.) When is annulment a possible remedy and when is compensation more appropriate? What would be the limits of jurisdiction? Could an appeal against the minister's grant of money to a local authority be used as a means of extending the Committee's jurisdiction to local government? It is not possible to answer such questions in advance. But neither is it desirable. The proper way would be to answer them as and when they arose in the context of cases. The elaboration of such a jurisprudence could have all the excitement of the great days of the common law in the latter part of the twelfth century. A body set up under the Privy Council would have the

[105] ibid., 105.

313

prestige necessary to command the co-operation of departments in the discovery of documents, etc., and to ensure that its rulings were carried out.

REPRESENTATIVE BUREAUCRACY

The extension and refinement of parliamentary control, the creation of new bodies, such as regional councils, capable of taking responsibility off central government, the development of public law, would all be valuable means of retaining the accountability of administrators to society. But at bottom, a sense of administrative responsibility is not a question of institutions at all. 'There is . . . almost universal misunderstanding of the conditions of bureaucratic responsibility. . . . It has long been assumed and widely published that ministerial responsibility and parliamentary criticism are the only means by which the British people are preserved from a bureaucratic despotism; and the assumption has persisted despite the accumulation of evidence to show that these devices are clearly inadequate to assure responsible administration.'[106] In reality, 'the essence of responsibility is psychological rather than mechanical. It is to be sought in an identity of aim and point of view, in a common background of social prejudice, which leads the agent to act as though he were the principal. In the first instance, it is a matter of sentiment and understanding, rather than of institutional forms. . . . If the essence of responsibility is psychological, the degree to which all democratic institutions are representative is a matter of prime significance. No group can safely be entrusted with power who do not themselves mirror the dominant forces in society; for they will then act in an irresponsible manner or will be liable to corruption at the hands of the dominant groups'.[107] The conditions most favourable to a sense of responsibility in administrators occur 'when ministers and civil servants share the same backgrounds and hold similar social views —when, in other words, the bureaucracy is representative'.[108]

In the past the fear was often expressed that if Labour came to power, its leaders would be so far out of harmony with the civil service elite that the old balance would break down. 'The civil service as now constituted would be much less representative of a state in which Labour wielded power than it has been of a state in which that prerogative belonged to the upper middle classes.'[109] For good or bad, this analysis overlooked the changes which had occurred in the character of the Labour leadership itself since the early days of the

[106] Kingsley, 266.   [107] ibid., 282.   [108] ibid., 273.   [109] ibid., 279.

314

party. When Labour did come to power—as distinct from office—in 1945, no great difficulties appear to have arisen. Lord Morrison has recorded that 'the belief among some of the public and even some Members of Parliament that civil servants do not work in harmony with ministers I have hardly ever found to be justified'.[110] The reason why had been pointed out some years earlier. 'Higher civil servants [and] Members of Parliament (at least, those who predominantly lead the fortunes of the older political parties, *and who have a large share in directing the Labour party*) . . . come from not greatly different social classes, they have much the same kind of education, and their vague mental pictures of the public welfare, their common master, are sufficiently alike to induce and maintain smooth co-operation.'[111] The working class may not have made notable inroads into the higher civil service. But the middle-class *weltanschauung* had thoroughly penetrated the higher ranks of the Labour Party.

Whatever its faults, the British civil service has been outstanding in its sense of responsibility to society. Failure to keep this fact constantly in view is the great blind-spot of the Fulton Committee. (Admittedly, its terms of reference did not encourage it to do so.) Compared with this fact, the kind of defects so often alleged are of a secondary order. In any case, they are often defects shared with other British institutions. If there is an excessive proportion of Oxbridge graduates in the Administrative Class, so is there in the House of Commons. The electorate ought to be blamed for making the wrong choice just as much as the Civil Service Commissioners. If too few higher civil servants have scientific and technological backgrounds, the same criticism can be made of industrial managers. If the key positions in all departments could be transferred overnight to Fulton-type technocrats the results would not necessarily be Utopia. Instead, government might break down because administrators and politicians would no longer be able to understand one another. Undoubtedly, changes in recruitment and training are needed. Indeed, important developments had begun well before the Fulton Committee was set up. But recommendations for change should be judged by this test: will they produce civil servants with at least as high a sense of responsibility as those of the past? In comparison, such issues as the proportion of statisticians to classicists are of trivial importance. Training matters, not because it leads to managerial prowess, but because it can be used to induce a habit of

[110] Lord Morrison, *Government and Parliament* (3 e., 1964), 344.
[111] Finer (1937), 17. (My italics.)

315

responsible behaviour. In the plain literal sense of the word—being ruled by people in offices—Britain already has a bureaucracy. For a century and a half, it has had a constitutional bureaucracy. The over-riding issue for all would-be reformers is, how can Britain retain that form of government?

LIST OF BOOKS AND ARTICLES CITED
MORE THAN ONCE

C. K. Allen, *Law and Orders*, (1945).

M. A. Anderson, 'Edmund Hammond, Permanent Under-Secretary for Foreign Affairs, 1854–1873' (Ph.D. thesis, London University, 1956).

E. Ashley, *Life of . . . Viscount Palmerston, 1846–1865*, 2 v. (1876).

W. Bagehot, *English Constitution* (2 e., 1872).

F. Balfour, *Life of George, 4th Earl of Aberdeen*, 2 v. (n.d.).

S. B. Baxter, *Development of the Treasury, 1660–1702* (1957).

H. C. F. Bell, *Lord Palmerston*, 2 v. (1936).

M. Beloff, 'Defining the Limits of Official Responsibility', *The Times*, September 11, 1967.

J. Bentham, *Economic Writings*, 3 v. (ed. Stark, 1952).

A. H. Birch, *Representative and Responsible Government* (1964).

L. Brown, *Board of Trade and the Free Trade Movement, 1830–1842* (Oxford, 1958).

Sir H. L. Bulwer, *Life of . . . Viscount Palmerston*, 3 v. (3 e., 1871–4).

W. L. Burn, *Age of Equipoise* (1964).

Sir C. Carr, *Delegated Legislation* (Cambridge, 1921).

Sir C. Carr, *Concerning English Administrative Law* (1941).

D. N. Chester, *Central and Local Government* (1951).

G. K. Clark, 'Statesmen in Disguise', *Historical Journal*, ii (1959).

A. V. Dicey, *Law of the Constitution* (4 e., 1893).

A. V. Dicey, *Lectures on the Relation between Law and Public Opinion during the Nineteenth Century* (2 e., 1914; reprinted in a paperback version, 1962).

K. L. Ellis, *Post Office in the Eighteenth Century* (1958).

H. Finer, *British Civil Service* (1937).

S. E. Finer, *Life and Times of Sir Edwin Chadwick* (1952).

A. S. Foord, *His Majesty's Opposition, 1714–1830* (Oxford, 1964).

Fulton Report on the Civil Service (v. 1, 1968), Cmnd. 3638.

Greville Memoirs, 1814–1860, 8 v. (ed. Strachey and Fulford, 1938).

Earl Grey, *Parliamentary Government* (1858).

J. A. G. Griffith, *Central Departments and Local Authorities* (1966).

E. Halévy, *Growth of Philosophic Radicalism* (1928).

H. L. Hall, *Colonial Office* (1937).

R. S. E. Hinde, *British Penal System, 1773–1950* (1951).

Sir W. Holdsworth, *History of English Law*, 16 v. (1903–66).

CONSTITUTIONAL BUREAUCRACY

E. E. Hoon, *Organization of the English Customs System, 1696–1786* (New York, 1938).

C. Hughes, *British Statute Book* (1957).

E. Hughes, *Studies in Administration and Finance, 1558–1825* (Manchester, 1934).

E. Hughes, 'Sir James Stephen and the Anonymity of the Civil Servant', *Public Administration*, xxxvi (1958).

Sir C. Ilbert, *Legislative Methods and Forms* (Oxford, 1901).

Sir C. Ilbert, *Mechanics of Law Making* (New York, 1914).

Sir W. I. Jennings, *Law and the Constitution* (1933).

Sir W. I. Jennings, *British Constitution* (Cambridge, 3 e., 1950).

N. Johnson, *Parliament and Administration* (1966).

K. Jones, *Lunacy, Law and Conscience, 1744–1845* (1955).

N. S. Jucker (ed.), *Jenkinson Papers, 1760–1766* (1949).

Sir D. L. Keir, *Constitutional History of Modern Britain, 1485–1951* (5 e., 1953).

Sir G. Kekewich, *Education Department and After* (1920).

R. K. Kelsall, *Higher Civil Servants in Great Britain* (1955).

J. D. Kingsley, *Representative Bureaucracy* (Yellow Springs, Ohio, 1944).

R. Lambert, *Sir John Simon, 1816–1904, and English Social Administration* (1963).

A. Lang, *Life etc. of . . . Sir Stafford Northcote*, 2 v. (1890).

J. Leese, *Personalities and Powers in English Education* (Leeds 1950).

Letters of Queen Victoria . . . 1837–1861, 3 v. (ed. Benson and Esher, 1907).

R. A. Lewis, *Edwin Chadwick and the Public Health Movement, 1832–1854* (1952).

N. McCord, *Anti-Corn Law League* (1958).

O. MacDonagh, 'Nineteenth-century Revolution in Government: a Reappraisal', *Historical Journal*, i (1958).

O. MacDonagh, *Pattern of Government Growth* (1961).

R. M. MacLeod, 'Alkali Acts Administration, 1863–84: the emergence of the civil scientist', *Victorian Studies*, ix (1965).

F. W. Maitland, *Constitutional History of England* (Cambridge, 1908).

A. P. Martin, *Life and Letters of the Rt. Hon. Robert Lowe, Viscount Sherbrooke*, 2 v. (1893).

G. Marshall and G. C. Moodie, *Some Problems of the Constitution* (3 e., 1964).

J. D. B. Mitchell, 'Causes and Effects of the Absence of a System of Public Law in the United Kingdom', *Public Law* (1965).

318

BIBLIOGRAPHY

Sir L. Namier, *England in the Age of the American Revolution* (1930).
Sir L. Namier, *Personalities and Powers* (1955).
Sir L. Namier, *Structure of Politics at the Accession of George III* (2 e., 1957).
M. Nicholson, *The System: the misgovernment of Modern Britain* (1967).
R. Pares, *George III and the Politicians* (Oxford, 1953).
C. S. Parker (ed.), *Sir Robert Peel from his Private Papers*, 3 v. (2 e., 1899).
C. S. Parker, *Life and Letters of Sir James Graham, 1792–1861*, 2 v. (1907).
H. Parris, 'Nineteenth-century Revolution in Government: a Reappraisal Reappraised', *Historical Journal*, iii (1960).
H. Parris, 'Home Office and the Provincial Police, 1856–1870', *Public Law* (1961).
H. Parris, ' "On the Best Mode of Constituting Public Offices": an unpublished document by Sir Henry Taylor', *Political Studies*, ix (1961).
H. Parris, *Government and the Railways in Nineteenth-century Britain* (1965).
W. Plowden, 'Failure of Piecemeal Reform', *New Society*, July 18, 1968.
H. Preston-Thomas, *Work and Play of a Government Inspector* (1909)
R. S. Rait (ed.), *Memorials of A. V. Dicey* (1929).
Lord Robbins, *Theory of Economic Policy in English Classical Political Economy* (1952).
D. Roberts, *Victorian Origins of the British Welfare State* (New Haven, 1960).
W. A. Robson (ed.), *British Civil Servant* (1937).
Lord Salter, *Slave of the Lamp* (1967).
B. B. Schaffer, 'Consideration of the use of non-ministerial organization in ... central government ... 1832–1919' (Ph.D. thesis, London University, 1956).
A. Shonfield, *Modern Capitalism* (1965).
C. H. Sisson, *Spirit of British Administration* (1959).
Adam Smith, *Wealth of Nations*, 2 v. (ed. Cannan, 1950).
Sir H. Taylor, *The Statesman* (1836).
M. W. Thomas, *Early Factory Legislation* (Leigh-on-Sea, 1948).
Lord Thring, *Practical Legislation* (new ed., 1902).
A. Todd, *On Parliamentary Government in England*, 2 v. (1867–9).
A. Todd, *On Parliamentary Government in England*, 2 v. (2 e., 1887–9).

319

G. M. Trevelyan, *England under Queen Anne*, 3 v. (1930–4).

W. R. Ward, *English Land Tax in the Eighteenth Century* (1953).

W. R. Ward, 'Some Eighteenth-century Civil Servants', *English Historical Review*, lxx (1955).

S. and B. Webb, *English Prisons under Local Government* (1922).

Sir C. Webster, 'Lord Palmerston at Work, 1830–1841', *Politica*, i (1934–5).

Sir A. West, *Recollections*, 2 v. (1899).

F. M. G. Willson, 'Ministries and Boards: some aspects of administrative development since 1832', *Public Administration*, xxxiii (1955).

E. Yates, *Recollections and Experiences*, 2 v. (Leipzig, 1885).

D. M. Young, *Colonial Office in the Early Nineteenth Century* (1961).

INDEX

INDEX

Tilley, Sir John, 141
Tomlins, Sir Thomas, 172–4, 176
Treasury, 26, 32, 34, 39, 41, 45–7,
  50–2, 55, 58–9, 65, 67, 70, 72–3, 76,
  82, 84, 91, 95, 113, 116, 129, 132–3,
  135, 139–40, 143, 153, 172–4, 176–7,
  192, 211, 247–57, 283, 285, 289,
  296, 309
Trevelyan, Sir Charles, 55, 86–7, 91,
  94–5, 139, 149, 250–1, 254
Trollope, Anthony, 149–50, 251

U.S.A., 29, 32–3, 158

Waddington, Horatio, 139, 145, 185–
  186, 232
Walpole, Sir Robert, 26, 28
Walpole, Spencer, 62, 169–70
War Office: see Defence
West Indies, 116, 156
West, Sir Algernon, 151
Wood, Sir Charles, 86, 89, 170, 175,
  206, 208–9, 253–4

324